Understanding TCP/IP

A clear and comprehensive guide to TCP/IP protocols

Libor Dostálek

Alena Kabelová

BIRMINGHAM - MUMBAI

Understanding TCP/IP

A clear and comprehensive guide to TCP/IP protocols

First published: April 2006

Production Reference: 1130406

Published by Packt Publishing Ltd.
32 Lincoln Road
Olton
Birmingham, B27 6PA, UK.

ISBN 1-904811-71-X

www.packtpub.com

Cover Design by www.visionwt.com

This is an authorized and updated translation from the Czech language.

Credits

Authors
Libor Dostálek
Alena Kabelová

Contributing Authors
Marta Vohnoutová
Luděk Rašek
Michal Hojsík

Technical Editors
Abhishek Shirodkar
Darshan Parekh

Development Editor
Louay Fatoohi

Editorial Manager
Dipali Chittar

Indexer
Abhishek Shirodkar

Proofreader
Chris Smith

Production Coordinator
Manjiri Nadkarni

Illustrator
Shantanu Zagade

Cover Designer
Helen Wood

About the Authors

Libor Dostálek was born in 1957 in Prague, Czech Republic. He graduated in mathematics at the Charles University in Prague. For the last 20 years he has been involved in ICT architecture and security. His experiences as the IT architect and the hostmaster of one of the first European Internet Service Providers have been used while writing this publication.

Later he became an IT architect of one of the first home banking applications fully based on the PKI architecture, and also an IT architect of one of the first GSM banking applications (mobile banking). As a head consultant, he designed the architecture of several European public certification service providers (certification authorities) and also many e-commerce and e-banking applications.

The public knows him either as an author of many publications about TCP/IP and security or as a teacher. He has taught at various schools as well as held various commercial courses. At present, he lectures on Cryptology protocols at the Charles University in Prague.

He is currently an employee of the Siemens.

Alena Kabelová was born in 1964 in Budweis, Czech Republic. She graduated in ICT at the Economical University in Prague. She worked together with Libor Dostálek as a hostmaster. She is mostly involved in software development and teaching. At present, she works as a senior project manager at the PVT and focuses mainly on electronic banking.

Her experiences as the hostmaster of an important European ISP are applied in this publication.

Acknowledgements

This book has a long history. In every new edition, there were new chapters and sections added by different co-authors. We extend our special thanks to our following co-authors:

- Luděk Rašek wrote Chapter 17 (Lightweight Directory Access Protocol).

- Marta Vohnoutová wrote section 4.7 (Wireless Local Area Network).

- Michal Hojsík wrote section 7.4.2 (Link State Protocols).

The English edition was really a tough one. The original book was split into two volumes: *Understanding TCP/IP* (ISBN: 1-904811-71-X) and *DNS in Action* (ISBN: 1-904811-78-7). The book has been rewritten and the content list is not the same as the original book. The person who urged us to rewrite the book was the book's editor from Packt Publishing, Abhishek Shirodkar. Thanks to Abhishek, the English edition of this has turned out to be really good.

Table of Contents

Preface

You are probably wondering whether to refer to this book to understand more about TCP/IP or to read some other good books describing similar topics and containing the word TCP/IP in their titles. Let us explain to you what moved us to write another publication about the TCP/IP protocols on which the Internet is based.

Publications about the Internet are usually of two types:

- Publications involved with concrete operating systems (Microsoft Windows, UNIX, CISCO, etc.). The goal of such publications is to train readers in a particular TCP/IP implementation, while describing the main TCP/IP principles is only their secondary goal.

- Publications written for the academic environment. Even if their main goal is to describe the basic TCP/IP principles, they could be too tedious for many readers.

So we faced the task of creating a basic TCP/IP guide, independent from any concrete environment (for example, Microsoft Windows, UNIX, CISCO, etc.), emphasizing presentation of the text in a clear and apt form to readers so that they understand the main coherences. To explain the basic principles and coherences in the best way, we have used a lot of illustrations. These illustrations were not created by chance. We drew and constantly refined them according to the requirements from our countless TCP/IP courses. First we chalked them on a blackboard, next we drew them on a white blackboard, and finally we drew them in Microsoft Visio. It has been twenty years since we started teaching TCP/IP.

If you say to yourself that you will not pay for this book and will study TCP/IP directly from the Internet RFC standards, you have unknowingly found the next goal of this publication. Exploring the huge number of RFC standards takes a lot of time, and moreover their study is very difficult for a beginner. (The idea of someone reading international standards as a novel in his or her bed before sleep is funny.) So another goal of this publication is to equip readers with such knowledge that they would be able to study RFC by themselves after reading this book.

We, the authors, wish you good luck and hope that you get a lot of useful information by reading this publication.

What This Book Covers

Chapter 1 contains a general introduction to computer networks. The ISO OSI model is mentioned and compared with the TCP/IP protocol family.

Chapter 2 acquaints the reader with the basics of network sniffing. Network sniffing is demonstrated with the help of two tools: MS Network Monitor and Ethereal. We use network sniffing as our basic means to clarify principles of particular protocols.

Chapter 3 deals with the physical layer. Concretely, it deals with serial lines, modems, ISDN, and LAN.

Chapter 4 deals with a link layer. It describes the SLIP, CSLIP, PPP, FrameRelay, Ethernet, WiFi (IEEE 802.11), and FWA protocols.

Chapter 5 describes the Internet Protocol (IP) including ICMP, IGMP, ARP, and RARP protocols.

Chapter 6 clarifies the meaning of an IP address and a network mask. It also emphasizes the historical process by which the meaning of the term IP network has developed.

Chapter 7 describes the term 'routing', which is, without any doubt, the most complicated area of IP networks. This chapter explains the principles on which particular types of routing protocols are based. However, a detailed description of individual routing protocols is beyond the scope of this publication.

Chapter 8 deals with the new IP generation—the Internet Protocol version 6.

Chapter 9 turns to the TCP protocol.

Chapter 10 describes the little brother of the TCP protocol—the UDP protocol.

Chapter 11 discusses the Domain Name System (DNS), which translates names into IP addresses and vice versa.

Chapter 12 describes the Telnet protocol. It is rarely used today, but because it is often a base of application protocols, we will use it to explain the principles of these application protocols (excluding the LDAP protocol).

Chapter 13 addresses the File Transfer protocol (FTP).

Chapter 14 describes probably the most popular protocol, HTTP.

Chapter 15 deals with electronic mail. It describes the following protocols: SMTP, ESMTP, POP3, IMAP4, and MIME; and even mailing lists are mentioned here.

Chapter 16 describes discussions forums (the NNTP protocol).

Chapter 17 deals with the Lightweight Directory Access Protocol (LDAP).

Appendix A contains the basic principles of working with CISCO routers for beginners.

What You Need for This Book

This publication is created to help beginners who are already familiar with computers to discover the secrets of TCP/IP. It will be useful for students, advanced users, computer and network administrators, computer managers, and security managers. Professionals who want to discover secrets of Internet technology can also appreciate it. It will be also useful as a textbook of TCP/IP lectures.

This publication contains a lot of examples. Please do not blame us if we take the side of some particular operating system; we have put here examples from both Windows and UNIX, and sometimes even CISCO. We have added a supplement containing the basics of the CISCO system because a basic knowledge of the operating system of CISCO routers is essential not only for network administrators, but also for the general readers.

This book explains the TCP/IP concepts to users, independently of the hardware and software they use. Readers can effectively work with TCP/IP even in a *not-so-powerful* personal computer.

Conventions

In this book, you will find a number of styles of text that distinguish between different kinds of information. Here are some examples of these styles, and an explanation of their meaning.

There are three styles for code. Code words in text are shown as follows: "You can set it explicitly for the ping and traceroute commands."

A block of code will be set as follows:

```
C: HEAD / HTTP/1.1;;
C: Host: www.iana.org
C:
S: HTTP/1.1 200 OK
S: Date: Tue, 20 Dec 2005 21:17:06 GMT
S: Server: Apache/1.3.27 (Unix)  (Red-Hat/Linux)
S: Last-Modified: Thu, 04 Nov 2004 19:34:30 GMT
S: ETag: "1acad9-153a-418a8446"
S: Accept-Ranges: bytes
S: Content-Length: 5434
S: Connection: close
S: Content-Type: text/html
```

When we wish to draw your attention to a particular part of a code block, the relevant lines or items will be made bold:

```
+ FRAME: Base frame properties
  + ETHERNET: ETYPE = 0x0800 : Protocol = IP: DOD Internet Protocol
  IP: ID = 0x673D; Proto = ICMP; Len: 84
      IP: Version = 4 (0x4)
      IP: Header Length = 44 (0x2C)
    + IP: Service Type = 0 (0x0)
      IP: Total Length = 84 (0x54)
      IP: Identification = 26429 (0x673D)
    + IP: Flags Summary = 0 (0x0)
      IP: Fragment Offset = 0 (0x0) bytes
      IP: Time to Live = 32 (0x20)
```

New terms and **important words** are introduced in a bold-type font. Words that you see on the screen, in menus or dialog boxes for example, appear in our text like this: "clicking the Next button moves you to the next screen".

> Warnings or important notes appear in a box like this.

Reader Feedback

Feedback from our readers is always welcome. Let us know what you think about this book, what you liked or may have disliked. Reader feedback is important for us to develop titles that you really get the most out of.

To send us general feedback, simply drop an email to feedback@packtpub.com, making sure to mention the book title in the subject of your message.

If there is a book that you need and would like to see us publish, please send us a note in the SUGGEST A TITLE form on www.packtpub.com or email suggest@packtpub.com.

If there is a topic that you have expertise in and you are interested in either writing or contributing to a book, see our author guide on www.packtpub.com/authors.

Customer Support

Now that you are the proud owner of a Packt book, we have a number of things to help you to get the most from your purchase.

Errata

Although we have taken every care to ensure the accuracy of our contents, mistakes do happen. If you find a mistake in one of our books—maybe a mistake in text or code—we would be grateful if you would report this to us. By doing this you can save other readers from frustration, and help to improve subsequent versions of this book. If you find any errata, report them by visiting http://www.packtpub.com/support, selecting your book, clicking on the Submit Errata link, and entering the details of your errata. Once your errata have been verified, your submission will be accepted and the errata added to the list of existing errata. The existing errata can be viewed by selecting your title from http://www.packtpub.com/support.

Questions

You can contact us at questions@packtpub.com if you are having a problem with some aspect of the book, and we will do our best to address it.

1

Introduction to Network Protocols

Just as diplomats use diplomatic protocols in their meetings, computers use network protocols to communicate in computer networks. There are many network protocols in existence; TCP/IP is a family of network protocols that are used for the Internet.

A **network protocol** is a standard written down on a piece of paper (or, more precisely, with a text editor in a computer). The standards that are used for the Internet are called **Requests For Comment (RFC)**. RFCs are numbered from 1 onwards. There are more than 4,500 RFCs today. Many of them have become out of date, so only a handful of the first thousand RFCs are still used today.

The **International Standardization Office (ISO)** has standardized a system of network protocols called as **ISO OSI**. Another organization that issues communication standards is the **International Telecommunication Union (ITU)** located in Geneva. The ITU was formerly known as the CCITT and, being founded in 1865, is one of the oldest worldwide organizations (for comparison, the Red Cross was founded in 1863). Some standards are also issued by the **Institute of Electrical and Electronics Engineers (IEEE)**. RFC, standards released by **RIPE (Réseaux IP Européens)**, and **PKCS (Public Key Cryptography Standard)** are freely available on the Internet and are easy to get hold of. Other organizations (ISO, ITU, and so on) do not provide their standards free of charge—you have to pay for them. If that presents a problem, then you have to spend some time doing some library research.

First of all, let's have a look at why network communication is divided into several protocols. The answer is simple although this is a very complex problem that reaches across many different professions. Most books concerning network protocols explain the problem using a metaphor of two foreigners (or philosophers, doctors, and so on) trying to communicate with each other. Each of the two can only communicate in his or her respective language. In order for them to be able to communicate with each other, they need a translator as shown in the following figure:

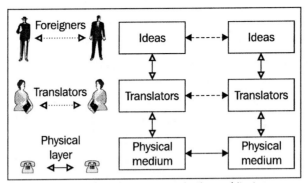

Figure 1.1: Three-layer communication architecture

The two foreigners exchange ideas, i.e., they communicate. But they only do so virtually. In reality, they are both handing over information to their interpreters, who then transmit this information by sending vibrations through the surrounding air with their vocal cords. Or if the parties are far away from each other, the interpreters communicate over the phone; thus the information is physically transmitted over phone lines. We can therefore talk about virtual communication in the horizontal direction (philosophical communication, the shared language between interpreters, and electronic signals transmitted via phone lines) and real communication in the vertical direction (foreigner-to-interpreter and interpreter-to-phone). We can thus distinguish three levels of communication:

1. Between two foreigners
2. Between interpreters
3. Physical transmission of information using media (phone lines, sound waves, etc.)

Communication between the two foreigners and between the two interpreters is only virtual. In fact, the only real communication happens between the foreigner and his or her interpreter.

Even more layers are used in computer networks. The number of layers depends on which system of network protocols you choose to use. The system of network protocols is sometimes referred to as the *network model*. You most commonly work with a system that uses the Internet, which is also referred to as the TCP/IP family. In addition to TCP/IP, we will also come across the ISO OSI model that was standardized by the ISO.

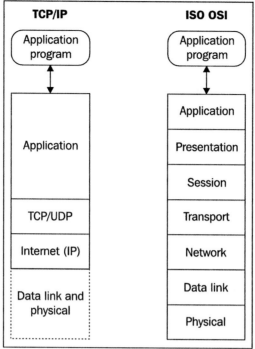

Figure 1.2: Comparison of TCP/IP and ISO OSI network models

The TCP/IP family uses four layers while ISO OSI uses seven layers as shown in the figure above. The TCP/IP and ISO OSI systems differ from each other significantly, although they are very similar on the network and transport layers.

Except for some exceptions like SLIP or PPP, the TCP/IP family does not deal with the link and physical layers. Therefore, even on the Internet, we use the link and physical protocols of the ISO OSI model.

1.1 ISO OSI

Communication between two computers is shown in the following figure:

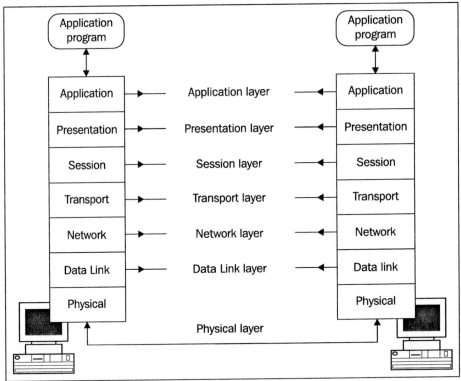

Figure 1.3: Seven-layer architecture of ISO OSI

1.1.1 Physical Layer

The physical layer is responsible for activating the physical circuit between the **Data Terminal Equipment (DTE)** and **Data Circuit-terminating Equipment (DCE)**, communicating through it, and then deactivating it. Additionally, the physical layer is also responsible for the communication between DCEs (see Figure 1.3a). A computer or router can represent the DTE. The DCE, on the other hand, is usually represented by a modem or a multiplexer.

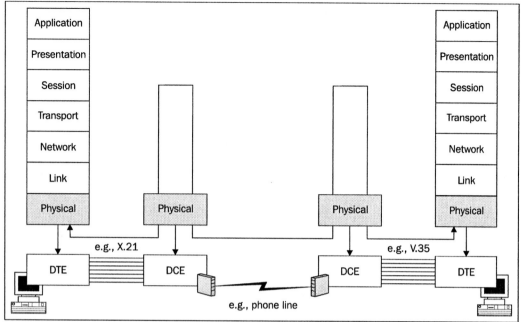

Figure 1.3a: DTE and DCE

To put it differently, the physical layer describes the electric or optical signals used for communicating between two computers. Physical circuits are created on the physical layer. Other appliances such as modems modulating a signal for a phone line are often put in the physical circuits created between two computers.

Physical layer protocols specify the following:

- Electrical signals (for example, +1V)
- Connector shapes (for example, V.35)
- Media type (twisted pair, coaxial cable, optical fiber, etc.)
- Modulation (for example, FM, PM, etc.)
- Coding (for example, RZ, NRZ, etc.)
- Synchronization (synchronous and asynchronous communication, time source, and so on)

1.1.2 Data Link Layer

As for serial links, the link layer provides data exchange between neighboring computers as well as data exchange between computers within a local network.

For the link layer, the basic unit of data transfer is the data link packet frame (see Figure 1.4). A data frame is composed of a header, payload, and trailer.

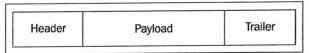

| Header | Payload | Trailer |

Figure 1.4: Data link packet or frame

A frame carries the destination link address, source link address, and other control information in the header. The trailer usually contains the checksum of the transported data. By using the checksum, we can find out whether the payload has been damaged during transfer. The network-layer packet is usually included in the payload.

In Figure 1.3a, the link layer does not engage in a conversation between DTE and DCE (the link layer *does not see* the DCE). It is engaged, however, in the frame exchange between DTEs. (It relies on the physical layer to handle the DCE issue.)

The following figure illustrates that different protocols can be used for each end of the connection on the physical layer. In our case, one of the ends uses the X.21 protocol while the other end uses the V.35 protocol. This rule is valid not only for serial links, but also for local networks. In local networks, you are more likely to encounter more complicated setups in which a switch that converts the link frames of one link protocol into link frames of a second one (for example, Ethernet into FDDI) is inserted between the two ends of the connection. This obviously results in different protocols being used on the physical layer.

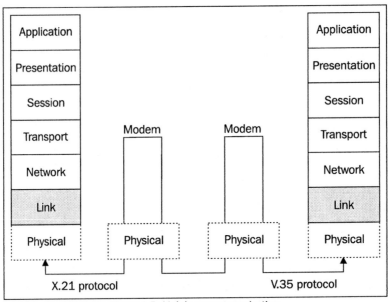

Figure 1.5: Link layer communication

A serial port or an Ethernet card can serve as a link interface. A link interface has a link address that is unique within a particular **Local Area Network (LAN)**.

1.1.3 Network Layer

The network layer ensures the data transfer between two remote computers within a particular **Wide Area Network (WAN)**. The basic unit of transfer is a datagram that is wrapped (encapsulated) in a frame. The datagram is also composed of a header and data field. Trailers are not very common in network protocols.

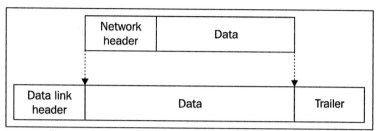

Figure 1.6: Network packet and its insertion in the link frame

As shown in the figure above, the datagram header, together with data (network-layer payload), creates the payload or data field of the frame.

There is usually at least one router on WANs between two computers. The connection between two neighboring routers on the link layer is always direct. The router unpacks the datagram from a frame, only to wrap it again into a different frame (or, more generally, in a frame of different link protocol) before sending it to a different line. The network layer does not see the appliances on the physical and link layers (modems, repeaters, switches, etc.).

The network layer does not care about what kind of link protocols are used on route between the source and the destination.

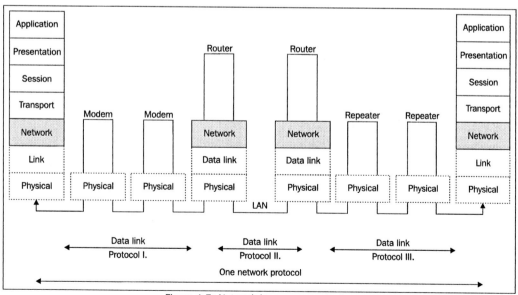

Figure 1.7: Network layer communication

A serial port or an Ethernet card can be used as a network interface. A network interface has a one or more unique address within a particular WAN.

1.1.4 Transport Layer

A network layer facilitates the connection between two remote computers. As far as the transport layer is concerned, it acts as if there were no modems, repeaters, bridges, or routers along the way. The transport layer relies completely on the services of lower layers. It also expects that the connection between two computers has been established, and it can therefore fully dedicate its efforts to the cooperation between two distant computers. Generally, the transport layer is responsible for communication between two applications running on different computers.

There can be several transport connections between two computers at any given time (for example, one for a virtual terminal and another for email). On the network layer, the transport packets are directed based on the address of the computer (or its network interface). On the transport layer, individual applications are addressed. Applications use unique addresses within one computer, so the transport address is usually composed of both the network and transport addresses.

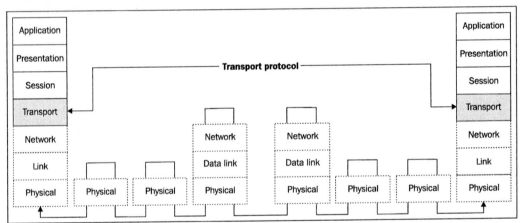

Figure 1.8: Transport layer connection

In this case, the basic transmission unit is the segment that is composed of a header and payload. The transport packet is transmitted within the payload of the network packet.

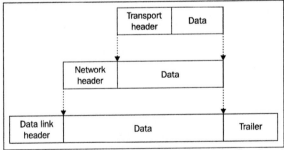

Figure 1.9: Inserting transport packets into network packets that are then inserted into link frames

1.1.5 Session Layer

The session layer facilitates exchange of data between two applications. In other words, it serves as a checkpoint and is involved in synchronizing transactions, correctly closing files, and so on. Sharing a network disk is a good example of a session. The disk can be shared for a certain period of time, but the disk is not used for the entire time. When we need to work with a file on the network disk, a connection is established on the transport layer from the time when the file is opened to when it is closed. The session, however, exists on the session layer for the entire time the disk is being shared.

The basic unit is a session layer PDU (Protocol Data Unit), which is inserted in a segment. Other books often illustrate this with a figure of a session-layer PDU, composed of the session header and payload, being inserted in the segment. Starting with the session layer, however, this does not necessarily have to be the case. The session layer information can be transmitted inside the payload. This situation is even more noticeable if, for example, the presentation layer encrypts the data, and thus changes the whole content of the session-layer PDU.

1.1.6 Presentation Layer

The presentation layer is responsible for representing and securing data. The representation can differ on different computers. For example, it deals with the problem of whether the highest bit is in the byte on the right or on the left. By securing, we mean encrypting, ensuring data integrity, digital signing, and so forth.

1.1.7 Application Layer

The application layer defines the format in which the data should be received from or handed over to the applications. For example, the OSI Virtual Terminal protocol describes how data should be formatted as well as the dialogue used between the two ends of the connection.

Application	X.400, FTAM, CMIP
Presentation	X.226, X.216, ASN.1
Session	X.225, X.215
Transport	TP 0-4, TP noncontinuous
Network	X.25, X.75, ISDN
Data Link	HDLC, LAPB, ISDN
Physical	V.24, V.35, X.21, ISDN

Figure 1.10: Examples of network protocols from the ISO OSI protocols family

1.2 TCP/IP

With a few exceptions, the TCP/IP family does not deal with the physical or link layers. In practice, Internet protocols often use protocols that adhere to the ISO OSI standards for the physical and link layers.

What is the correlation between the ISO OSI protocols and TCP/IP? Each group of protocols has its definition of its own layers as well as the protocols used on these layers. Generally speaking, ISO OSI protocols and TCP/IP are incompatible. In practice, ISO OSI-compliant communication appliances need to be used for transferring IP datagrams, or on the other hand, services based on ISO OSI need to be provided via the Internet.

1.2.1 Internet Protocol

Internet Protocol (IP) basically corresponds to the network layer. IP is used for transmitting IP datagrams between remote computers. Each IP datagram header contains the destination address, which is the complete routing information used for delivering the IP datagram to its destination. Therefore, the network can only transmit each datagram individually. IP datagrams of one session can be transmitted through different paths and can thus be received by the destination in a different order than they were sent.

Each network interface on the large Internet network has one or more IP address that is unique worldwide. (One network interface can have several IP addresses, but one IP address cannot be used by many network interfaces.) The Internet is composed of individual networks that are interconnected via routers. Routers are also referred to as gateways in old literature.

1.2.2 TCP and UDP

TCP and UDP correspond to the transportation layer. TCP transports data using TCP segments that are addressed to individual applications. UDP transports data using UDP datagrams.

TCP and UDP arrange a connection between applications that run on remote computers. TCP and UDP can also facilitate communication between processes running on the same computer, but this is not very interesting for our purposes.

The difference between TCP and UDP is that TCP is a connection-oriented service—the destination confirms the data received. If some data (TCP segments) gets lost, the destination requests a retransmission of the lost data. UDP transports data using datagrams (the delivery is not guaranteed). In other words, the source party sends the datagram without worrying about whether it has been received. UDP is connectionless-oriented service.

The port is used as the address. To understand the difference between an IP address and port number, think of it as a mailing address. The IP address corresponds to the address of a house, while the port tells you the name of the person that should receive the letter.

TCP is described in Chapter 9 and UDP in Chapter 10.

1.2.3 Application Protocols

Application protocols correspond to several ISO OSI layers. The session, presentation, and application ISO OSI layers are reduced to one TCP/IP application layer.

The absence of a presentation layer is made up for by introducing specialized presentation-application protocols such as SSL and S/MINE that specialize in securing data or the Virtual Terminal and ASN.1 protocols that are designed for presenting data. The Virtual Terminal protocol (not to be confused with the ISO OSI protocol of the same name) specifies the network data presentation for character-oriented network protocols (Telnet, FTP, SMTP, and, partly, HTTP). Similarly, ASN.1 is often used for binary-oriented network transport. ASN.1 (including BER or DER encoding) was initially used by SNMP, but today it is also used by S/MINE.

There are many different application protocols. For practical purposes, they can be divided into two groups:

- User protocols utilized by user applications (HTTP, SMTP, Telnet, FTP, IMAP, PIP3, and so on).

- Service protocols, i.e., the protocols that ordinary Internet users rarely encounter. These protocols make sure the Internet functions correctly. For example, these could be routing protocols that are used for mutual communication by routers to correctly set their routing tables. Another example is SNMP usage in network administration.

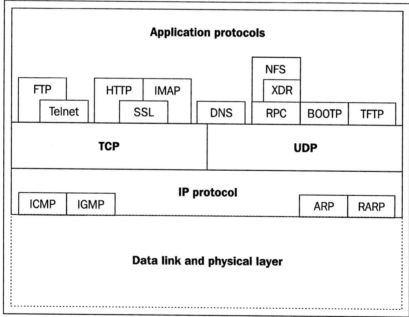

Figure 1.11: Some protocols of the TCP/IP family

1.3 Methods of Information Transmission

There are many different network protocols and several protocols can be available even on a single layer. Especially with lower-layer protocols, we distinguish between the types of transmission that they facilitate, whether they provide connection-oriented or connection-less services, if the protocol uses virtual circuits, and so on. We also distinguish between synchronous, packet, and asynchronous transmission.

1.3.1 Synchronous Transmission

Synchronous transmission is needed when it is necessary to provide a stable (guaranteed) bandwidth, for example, in audio and video. If the source does not use the provided bandwidth it remains unused. Synchronous transmission uses frames that are of fixed length and are transmitted at constant speeds.

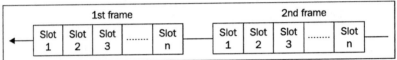

Figure 1.12: Frames divided into slots in synchronous transmission

In synchronous transmission, the guaranteed bandwidth is established by dividing the transmitted frames into slots (see Figure 1.12). One or more slots in any transmitted frame are reserved for a particular connection. Let's say that each frame has slot 1 reserved for our connection. Since the frames follow each other steadily in a network, our application has a guaranteed bandwidth consisting of the number of slot 1s that can be transmitted through the network in one second.

The concept becomes even clearer if we draw several frames under each other, creating a 'super-frame' (see Figure 1.13). The slots located directly under each other belong to the same connection.

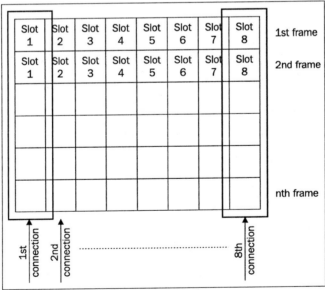

Figure 1.13: Super-frame

Synchronous transmission is used to connect your company switchboard to the phone company exchange. In this case, we use an E1(or T1 in United States) link containing 32 slots of 64 Kbps each. A slot can be used for making a phone call. Therefore, in theory, 32 calls are guaranteed at the same time (although some slots are probably used for servicing).

The Internet does not use synchronous transmission, i.e., in general, does not guarantee bandwidth. Quality audio or video transmission on the Internet is usually achieved by over-dimensioning the transmission lines. Recently, there has been a steady increase in requests for audio and video transmission via the Internet, so more and more often we come across systems that guarantee bandwidth even on the Internet with the help of Quality of Service (QoS). In order for us to reach the expected results, however, all appliances on route from the source to the destination must support these services. Today, we are more likely to get involved with only those areas on the Internet that guarantee bandwidth such as within a particular Internet provider.

1.3.2 Packet Transmission

(From now onwards we will use the term **packet** to refer to 'packet', 'datagram', 'segment', 'protocol data unit'.) Packet transmission is especially valuable for transferring data. Packets usually carry data of variable size.

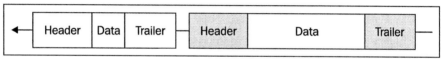

Figure 1.14: Packet data transmission

One packet always carries data of one particular application (of one connection). It is not possible to guarantee bandwidth, because the packets are of various lengths. On the other hand, we can use the bandwidth more effectively because if one application does not transmit data, then other applications can use the bandwidth instead.

1.3.3 Asynchronous Transmission

Asynchronous transmission is used in the ATM protocol. This transmission type combines features of packet transmission with features of synchronous transmission.

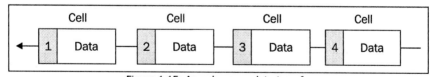

Figure 1.15: Asynchronous data transfer

Similarly to synchronous transmission, in asynchronous transmission, the data are transmitted in packets that are rather small, but are all of the same size; these packets are called **cells**. Similarly to packet transmission, data for one application (one connection) is transmitted in one cell. All cells have the same length; so if we guarantee that the nth cell will be available for a certain application (a particular connection), the bandwidth will be guaranteed by this as well. Additionally, it doesn't really matter if the application does not send the cell since a different application's cell might be sent instead.

1.4 Virtual Circuit

Some network protocols create virtual circuits in networks. A virtual circuit is conducted through the network and all packets of a particular connection go via the circuit. If the circuit gets interrupted anywhere, then the connection is interrupted, a new circuit is established, and data transmission continues.

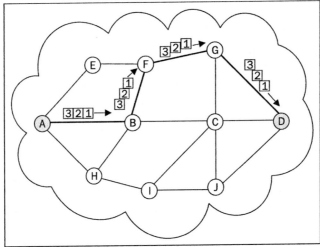

Figure 1.16: Virtual circuit

In the figure above, a virtual circuit between nodes A and D is established via nodes B, F, and G. All packets must go through this circuit.

Datagrams can be transmitted via the virtual circuit in two ways:

- The circuit does not guarantee the datagram's delivery to its destination. (If network congestion occurs, the circuit can even throw the datagram away.) An example is the Frame Relay protocol.

- The virtual circuit can establish a connection and guarantee the data delivery, i.e., the data packets transmitted are numbered and the destination confirms their reception. If any data gets lost, a request to resend the data is made. For example, this mechanism is used in the X.25 protocol.

The advantage of virtual circuits is that they are first established (using signalization) and then the data is inserted only into the established circuit. Each packet does not have to carry the globally unique address of the destination (complete routing information) in its header. It only needs the circuit ID.

The virtual mechanism is not used on the Internet, which was primarily aimed for use by the U.S. Department of Defense, since the destruction of a node in the virtual circuit would result in the transmission being interrupted—a fact that the authors of TCP/IP did not like. For this reason, IP does not use virtual circuits. Each IP datagram carries a destination IP address (complete routing information) and is therefore transported independently. If a node is destroyed, only the IP datagrams currently being transmitted through that particular node are destroyed. The remaining datagrams are routed via different nodes.

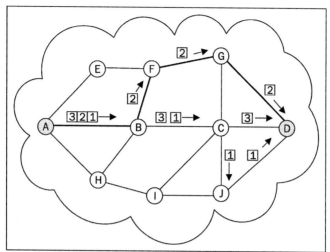

Figure 1.17: IP does not use virtual circuits.

As the figure above shows, IP datagrams 1, 2, and 3 start from the node A to node B, but from this point, datagrams 1 and 3 are routed through a different path than datagram 2. The destination (node D) is then reached by each of them via a different path. Generally, IP datagrams may reach their destination in a different order than the order in which they were sent. So our IP datagrams could be received in the following order: 2, 1, and then 3.

In the Internet hierarchy, TCP—a higher-layer protocol that establishes a connection and guarantees the delivery of data—is used above the connectionless IP. If some of the data packets are lost, their retransmission is requested. If the data packets were lost due to the destruction of a node along the way and there is another routing possible within the network, then the transmission is automatically repeated using the other path.

Virtual circuits are divided into the following groups:

- Permanent (**Permanent Virtual Circuit (PVC)**), i.e., circuits permanently built by the network administrator.

- Switched (**Switched Virtual Circuit (SVC)**), i.e., virtual circuits that are created dynamically as the need arises. An SVC is created with the help of signalizing protocols that can be used for communicating between the user and the network itself. The network signalizes to the user various events that can be used for network monitoring and administration. SVC communication consists of two steps: creating the virtual circuit and using it for communication.

PVC corresponds to leased lines and SVC corresponds to the dial-up lines of a phone network.

> Protocols using virtual circuits are called **Connection-Oriented Network Services (CONS)** and protocols transporting their packets without using virtual circuits are called **Connection-Less Network Services (CLNS)**.

2

Network Monitoring Tools

Network monitoring tools can be used to monitor data transfers on your network. Monitoring is a process of capturing link frames in the network and storing these frames in memory. Monitoring also includes viewing the contents of the individual captured frames.

Network monitoring tools are mostly used by network administrators to look for network configuration errors or monitor network workload. These tools are also an indispensable resource for programmers who develop network applications. To give you an example, let's say you have written a client/server application. You start the application and nothing happens—the client does not even connect to the server. At this point, you cannot be sure whether the problem lies with the client or the server. By capturing frames, however, you can establish that the client sent a data frame, but the server did not react and the fault is therefore likely on the server's side. Or you might notice that the data sent by the client is different from what you expected.

We will mainly use the two programs, Network Monitor and Ethereal, to demonstrate different network protocols. Both programs have a similar graphical user interface. A wide selection of similar programs is available in the market. The UNIX operating system offers the `tcpdump` command. As opposed to the programs mentioned above, `tcpdump` does not have a graphical user interface and is designed to be used mainly for scripts.

In addition to these tools, network monitoring hardware is also available. What are the advantages of hardware network monitors? These tools are particularly important for technical staff. Software monitors only display frames that are undamaged. It may be that a station has a damaged network interface card, which produces faulty frames. Software monitors have a difficult time recognizing these damaged stations. Moreover, Fiber Distributed Data Interface (FDDI) service frames are not displayed by software monitors.

The bigger problems with using network monitoring tools are in the area of security. The argument used against them is that they can be easily used to capture the password of network users that work with Telnet, FTP, and web browsers (in the case of the HTTP protocol).

The authors of this book, on the contrary, consider it useful to demonstrate password capturing. Even more than initial security problems, these demonstrations serve to convince companies to change their authorization method from the dangerous username/password system.

2.1 Packet Drivers

In order to keep track of incoming and outgoing packets, we have to insert a component between the network interface and the rest of the operating system. This component is able to track the passing packets or perhaps hand them over to other programs to be protocolled or displayed. This component is often called a **packet driver** or **packet filter**. In MS Windows NT (Windows 2000, XP etc.), the packet driver is called the Network Monitor Agent. The program that protocols or displays the packets captured by the packet driver, is the Network Monitor for Windows or the tcpdump command for UNIX.

The network interface cards of systems connected to the LAN listen to the traffic on the LAN, i.e., they read individual passing link frames. Link frames of protocols for local networks usually start with the destination link address, so if the station finds that the incoming frame is not addressed to itself, then it usually ignores the rest of the frame. In practice this means that the packet driver can only accept frames that are addressed to the station where the packet driver is running (and also the frames that this station sends onto the network). If this is not enough and you want to track all the traffic in your LAN segment, then you have to switch the network interface card into promiscuous mode. In promiscuous mode, the network card reads all the frames and we can track all the traffic in your LAN segment. You can switch the network interface card into promiscuous mode using the Network Monitor program, which is a part of the SMS Server.

If the network interface card is not in promiscuous mode, you can see the frames sent out by your station and the ones that are addressed to it. These not only include frames that have one of your station's addresses, but also all broadcasts. You will also see all multicasts that your station accepts. This is a somewhat complex problem that is discussed in detail in Section 5.7. Another problem is keeping track of traffic on a switched Ethernet. If you want to track communication in LAN segments other than the one your PC connects to, you must keep in mind that the frames are usually not repeated in the segment where your PC is located. This can be solved by using a switch diagnostic output or by poisoning the ARP cache.

These days, ordinary repeaters are not used very frequently; almost everything is done with switches. So if you want to keep track of traffic on a station or a server, you need to get hold of an old repeater with at least three interfaces. One interface will be connected to a switch distribution, i.e., the repeater will be plugged into the interface into which the station was originally plugged, the second interface will be connected to the station we want to watch, and the third interface will be connected to a notebook with the relevant packet driver.

If you want to use Network Monitor, you must add the Network Monitor Agent to your network configuration.

In UNIX-type operating systems, the packet driver is usually added to the operating system kernel. For example, you add PACKETFILTER options into the configuration file of a kernel for UNIX True64. Then you create a new kernel. By using the pfconfig command, you can switch individual interfaces into promiscuous mode. You can use the pfstat command to examine the configuration of a particular interface.

The WinPcap packet driver is another interesting component (see http://netgroup-serv.polito.it/). It is a packet driver that is compatible with Windows 95 and higher, and it also acts as a UNIX packet driver. Ethereal is one of the several programs that uses this packet driver and thereby works on both Windows and UNIX.

2.2 MS Network Monitor

MS Network Monitor is supplied with certain Microsoft products (such as SMS Server). Installing the program on Windows NT must be done very carefully and exactly according to the instructions in the guide. In the middle of the installation process, you will usually be asked to install Network Monitor Agent. If you do not follow the instructions exactly, the program will not function and will need to be reinstalled.

Starting with Windows 2000 and later, Network Monitor is supplied as a part of the server (Network Monitor Tools). On the other hand, Windows 2000 and XP restricts the use of the program. Therefore, we more often find Ethereal used in PCs.

The Network Monitor handles frame display well. Not only can it separate the header from the actual data, but it can also dissect individual items in the network protocol headers.

2.2.1 Frame Capturing

When you start Network Monitor, the window shown in Figure 2.1 pops up. Inside this window should be the Capture window. If this inner window does not open, then the Network Monitor or the Network Monitor Agent is not installed properly and needs to be reinstalled.

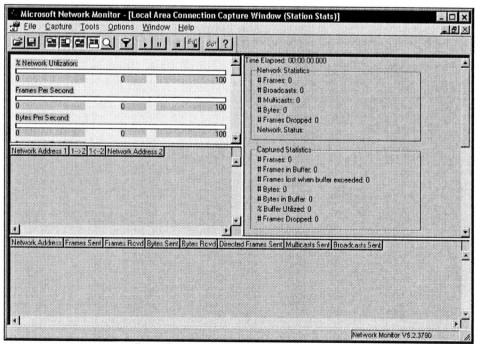

Figure 2.1: Initial MS Network Monitor screen

First of all, you have to choose the appropriate network interface to use for frame capturing. This is done by choosing Capture | Networks. There's also another interesting detail that we have to pay attention to. After looking at the following figure, in the left window we will choose the interface we want to sniff:

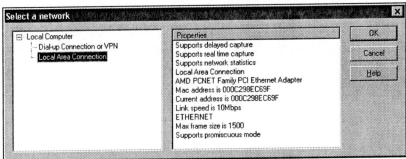

Figure 2.2: Selecting the network interface used for frame capturing

The issue here is the Windows 2000 architecture. It has an NDIS layer located above the network interface cards that ensures a standard communication between the operating system and network interface cards, although this only applies to LAN cards.

An NDISWAN driver (Ndiswan.sys) inserted between the serial lines ports, changes the communication format of the serial port into a format that adheres to the Ethernet protocol (in other words, into a form commonly processed by the NDIS layer). This has two practical results:

1. If you want to capture frames on a serial line, then you have to choose an interface with Dial-up Connection that is set to TRUE.

2. After you have captured the frames on the serial line, they have (for example, when establishing a connection through the PPP protocol) special link addresses inside the Ethernet frame:

   o For the frame being sent, both the sender and receiver fields contain the SEND string.
   o For the frame being received, both fields will contain RECV.

> It is important to not confuse this with the 'PPP over Ethernet' protocol that is supported by Microsoft Windows XP.

Now, we can start capturing frames by clicking Start capture (see Figure 2.3) or by choosing Capture | Start or pressing *F10*. Once the capturing has started, the window shown in Figure 2.3 appears.

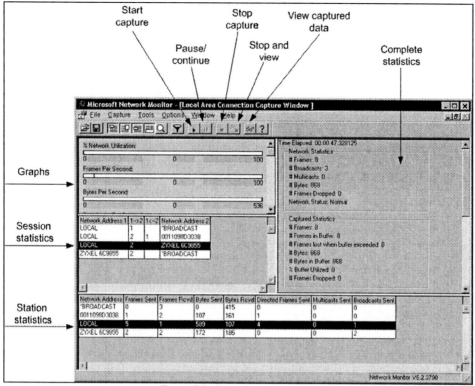

Figure 2.3: Capturing data frames

The window for capturing data frames consists of several smaller windows. The window on the top left contains graphs that describe:

- % Network Utilization, i.e., rate of the utilization of all network resources that are available for current capturing

- Frames Per Second, i.e., the number of frames that the network transfers each second

- Bytes Per Second, i.e., the number of bytes transported each second

- Broadcast Per Second, i.e., the number of broadcasts per second

- Multicast Per Second, i.e., the number of multicasts per second

The complete statistics window is on the top-right. The time that has elapsed from the beginning of capturing is shown on the first line. Each particular area of information has its own graph:

- Network Statistics shows the total number of frames that have gone through the LAN segment; it also shows how many of them were broadcast, etc.

- Captured Statistics gives statistics for only those frames that have been captured. This can be different from the information under Network Statistics because you can define a capturing filter that sets rules for which frames are accepted and saved. You set capturing filters using the Capture | Filter option or pressing *F8*.

- Per Second Statistics shows the average statistical values per second.
- Network Card Statistics shows the network interface card's average connection speed.

The session statistics window gives you statistical data for individual sessions. A session is an interval during which two stations exchange data. There is one line for each pair of stations. The numeric value shows the number of frames sent from one station to the other (or vice versa).

Network Monitor displays session statistics for the first 100 unique network sessions that it detects. To reset statistics and view information about the next 100 detected unique network sessions, click Capture | Clear Statistics.

In addition to capturing frames, you can also choose Capture | Activation to prepare an action that can be automatically activated, like when a certain part of the buffer memory is exhausted. One interesting option is to activate whenever a frame containing a specified string in a particular position appears. The activation can also be triggered when a program starts up or when a file opens.

2.2.2 Viewing Captured Frames

When you click Stop and View to switch to the mode for viewing captured frames, the following window with the captured frames appears:

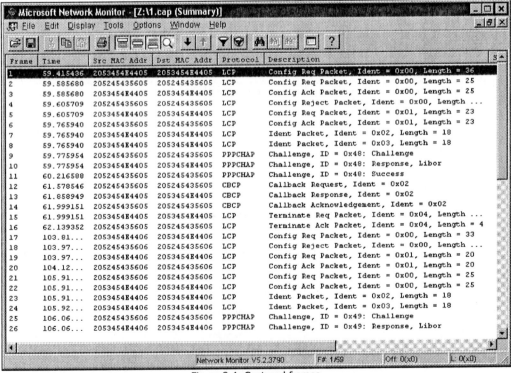

Figure 2.4: Captured frames

You can see your chosen frame in the captured frame display. To view detailed information of any frame, click it in the window as shown in the following figure:

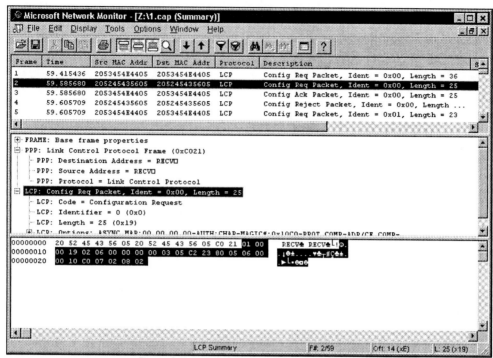

Figure 2.5: Detailed display of the second frame

Detailed information appears in three frames of windows. The top window displays the captured frames, the middle window shows the details of the selected captured frame, and the bottom window shows the captured frame in hexadecimals and characters (dump format).

The middle window is the one we're most interested in. Figure 2.5 shows the link header followed by a network packet header. Anything from the transport header to the application layer can be displayed here. Even at the application layer, detailed information for many packets is provided as well.

Some header entries have a + sign in front of them. This tells you that detailed information can be obtained by clicking the + sign. We will therefore discuss the individual headers of all protocols described in this book.

The dissected frames can also be printed by selecting File | Print. The frame in Figure 2.5 is as follows:

```
+ Frame: Base frame properties
PPP: Unknown Frame (0x0)
    PPP: Destination Address =  RECV_
    PPP: Source Address =  RECV_
    PPP: Protocol = Link Control Protocol
LCP: Config Req Packet, Ident = 0x00, Length = 25
    LCP: Code = Configuration Request
```

```
        LCP: Identifier = 0 (0x0)
        LCP: Length = 25 (0x19)
    LCP: Options: ASYNC.MAP:00 00 00 00-AUTH:CHAP-MAGIC#:0x10C0-PROT.COMP-
    ADR/CF.COMP-
    + LCP: ASYNC.MAP:00 00 00 00
    + LCP: AUTH:CHAP
    + LCP: MAGIC#:0x10C0
    + LCP: PROT.COMP
    + LCP: ADR/CF.COMP

    00000:  20 52 45 43 56 05 20 52 45 43 56 05 C0 21 01 00    RECV. RECV.À!..
    00010:  00 19 02 06 00 00 00 00 03 05 C2 23 80 05 06 00    ..........Â#□...
    00020:  00 10 C0 07 02 08 02                               ..À....
```

(The Network Monitor version used in Windows 2000 Server has a drawback in that the statement is in UNICODE. This would not be an issue if there were two bytes containing a hexadecimal FF or FE at the beginning, which would signal to Windows that it is a UNICODE file. After adding these characters to the beginning by using the WinVi editor, the statement resulted in the form shown above.)

2.2.3 Filters for Displaying Captured Frames

The most common problem when using network monitor programs is finding the required frame often from huge numbers of frames. You can use filters to make the task easier. There are two kinds of filters:

- Frame capturing filters that are activated in Network Monitor before capturing starts (Capture | Filter or *F8*).
- Filters for displaying captured frames that are activated upon viewing frames. These filters let you display only selected captured frames (Display | Filter or *F8*).

Filters consist of logical conditions that are linked by the AND, OR, and NOT logical operators. A condition might involve:

- An address (for example, IP address in the case of IP protocol)
- A protocol, i.e., only frames with specified protocols will be shown (IP, HTTP, etc.)
- The value of a specific protocol's item, for example, the TCP port of the sender is 1345

2.3 Ethereal

Ethereal is an alternative to Network Monitor and can be used with Windows 2000 Professional or Windows XP. You can download the program at http://www.ethereal.com/. In addition to the graphical Ethereal program, the distribution also contains other utilities such as a command-line version called Tethereal.

For starters, we have to install the packet driver. As mentioned earlier, if you are going to run Ethereal on Windows, use the WinPcap packet driver, which can be found at http://netgroup-serv.polito.it/.

After you have successfully installed the packet driver, you can install and configure Ethereal. When you run the program, you are presented with the window shown in Figure 2.6, which is similar to the Network Monitor window shown in Figure 2.5. Choose Capture | Start to open a window where you can enter parameters for frame capturing. For example, by clicking Interface you can choose the network interface used to capture frames. Click OK to begin capturing. After the capturing has finished, you can view the individual captured frames in the same way as you would in Network Monitor.

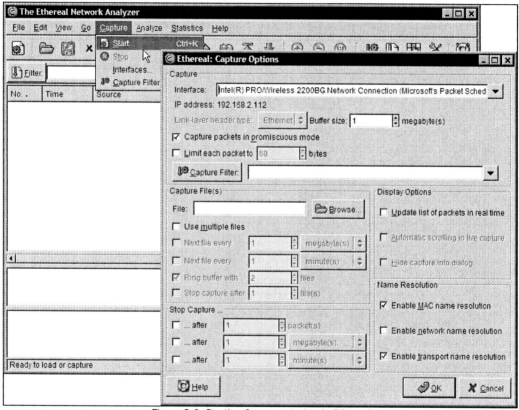

Figure 2.6: Starting frame capturing in Ethereal

Ethereal can also open files with stored frames generated by various other programs, including Network Monitor.

Ethereal contains a range of interesting tools like the Follow TCP Stream command, which is available in the Tools menu. By choosing this command, the contents of a particular TCP connection can be displayed in ASCII characters or in hexadecimals.

Figure 2.7 shows an example of a TCP connection. This connection was produced by using an FTP program to connect to the ftp.ripe.net server. One packet from this connection was found and then Tools | Follow TCP Stream was clicked to get the following figure:

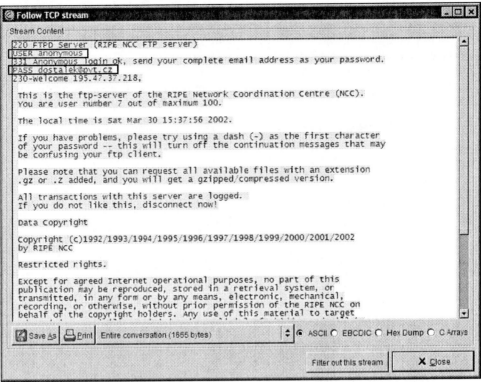

Figure 2.7: TCP connection statements in Ethereal

The boxes in the figure above outline the user name anonymous and password dostalek@pvt.cz. If you had connected to a non-anonymous server, your *real* password would have been disclosed in this way.

2.4 Homework

You should now be ready to experiment with Network Monitor or Ethereal. It is recommended that you try to capture your own password as the first exercise. (The authors strongly discourage you from trying to capture somebody else's password—after all, this would not be possible without switching your network card into promiscuous mode or using switched Ethernet.) Try these two exercises:

1. **Telnet protocol**: You do not even need an account on a server. Choose whatever server you like that works with Telnet. Start up Network Monitor and, using Telnet, try to establish a connection and choose your username and password. The server will refuse the connection, but stop Network Monitor and use the frame search to find the username and password that you entered. You should be patient, since the terminal first tries to set the terminal characteristics using the <IAC> command of the Telnet application protocol. You should just skip this dialogue. In Ethereal, this process is simpler since the only thing you have to do is to choose Tools | Follow TCP Stream.

2. **HTTP protocol**: Find some HTTP server with basic authentication with username and password and sniff the communication of this server. The name and password form a part of each user's query. But since the HTTP header lines cannot contain any characters that are not a part of ASCII, the username and password are separated by a colon and the whole thing is coded in Base64 format. Decoding needs to be done either manually or using a suitable program. (This does not work with HTTPS protocol as passwords cannot be captured there, because the connection is encrypted.)

The header contains the following information:

`Authorization: Base64 (username:password)`

Or for firewall authorization:

`Proxy-Authorization: Base64 (username:password)`

Where `Base64()` means that the Base64 argument is coded in seven-bit form.

If you do not feel like decoding Base64 by hand on a piece of paper, you can use programs such as the OpenSSL program with the `enc -a -d` parameters.

Specialized programs designed specifically for password capturing can also be found on the Internet.

3

Physical Layer

Protocols of the physical layer are for the vast majority of users They are completely hidden protocols that describe signals on the connectors (commonly referred to as plugs) on the back part of the computer, to which a cable connecting the computer with the network is attached. Users tend to shift the responsibility to technical staff, whom they consider people "who take care of wires, by measuring something with a voltmeter." The situation today is completely different. A technician more or less administers software that controls all the mysterious boxes in locked rooms. This idea does not actually refer to the physical layer only, but encompasses the link layer as well. The users usually get involved only in the IP protocol (or network protocols), since in this protocol, they either *see* or *do not see* servers or neighbors. In contrast, the physical and link layers only provide communication with some kind of a box halfway down to the server, the existence of which is usually not known to regular users.

Generally, we distinguish between two types of network: a **Local Area Network (LAN)** and a **Wide Area Network (WAN)**. Regarding the physical layer, for one group of protocols are LAN protocols, while another group are WAN. However, the currently popular ATM protocol eliminates the differences between LAN and WAN, and it not only uses new protocols, but is also able to use the current WAN lines, including their protocols (for example, T1 lines in America or E1 lines in Europe). In addition, the ATM emulates protocols for the LAN protocol as well.

LAN

The LAN is used by several stations to communicate mostly on a shared medium. Within one LAN, the same link protocol is used (for example, Ethernet). Today, however, the term LAN also covers the so-called extended LANs that are composed of individual LANs. The extended LANs are created by connecting individual LANs via switches. Switches often have interfaces for various types of link protocols and are able to convert frames of one link protocol into frames of a different link protocol. An individual LAN composed of just two items, with one of them being the switch, is increasingly common.

As for the physical layer, we will be interested in just the individual LAN since the extended LANs are viewed only as a complex of several individual LANs. LANs commonly use broadcasts.

Routers are used to connect a LAN to a WAN. A router is a box that transfers an IP datagram from one network interface to another one, while each interface may be a part of a different LAN or may be an interface for the WAN.

The transfer rate on today's LANs ranges from 10 Mbps to 10 Gbps.

WAN

Wide Area Networks cover a wide variety of situations, ranging from connecting a home PC to the Internet via a serial asynchronous line at rates in Kbps to intercontinental lines via underwater cables or satellite connection in tens of Gbps.

PAN

A Personal Area Network is used to exchange data between appliances (such as telephones, cell phones, and Personal Digital Assistants) within the range of a person; typically within the range of 10 meters. The most often used protocols for PAN networks are Bluetooth and WiFi (IEEE 802.11).

MAN

A Metropolitan Area Network is used to exchange data within some municipality or a group of them. MAN can use various protocols, but probably the most typical is using cable television cabling.

3.1 Serial Line

A PC has connectors for the COM1 and COM2 serial interfaces usually on the back. COM1 is commonly used for a mouse; hence after the serial line has been connected to our PC, only COM2 is left. The serial interface is usually used for connecting the modem.

Serial PC outputs use signals specified by the ITU-T V.24 standard (corresponding to the US standard—RS-232). It is an interface for serial asynchronous arrhythmic data transport. It is usually used for rates up to 64 Kbps although, you are most likely to connect your modem at home using 115,200 bps, and surprisingly, it is going to work well.

3.1.1 Serial and Parallel Data Transport

Serial transmission means that there is only one pair of wires (or one wire and a shared ground for asymmetric interfaces) for transporting information from the sender to the receiver. Therefore, the individual bits of every single character are transported following each other, i.e., serially.

Parallel transmission uses eight wires (or multiples of eight) for transporting a group of bits. In other words, all bits of the character being transported can be transported at the same time, i.e., in parallel. Parallel transmission is used especially in (internal) computer buses and also for communicating with a parallel printer. There are also modems using a parallel interface.

3.1.2 Symmetrical and Asymmetrical Signals

There are at least two signals used with serial interfaces: data reception and data transmission. If two wires carry each signal, then it is a symmetrical or differential signal. Symmetrical signals for data transfer are used, for example, by the V.35 and X.21 interfaces.

If each individual signal is carried via one wire and a shared ground, then this is an asymmetrical signal. Asymmetrical signals are used, for example, by the V.24 interface. The V.35 interface uses asymmetrical controlling signals, but uses symmetrical signals for data.

3.1.3 Synchronous and Asynchronous Transport

If you try to communicate information to someone (for example, by a phone), you have to speak at an appropriate rate so the other person understands what you say. If you speak, say, ten times faster than normal, then the person is very unlikely to understand. The person listening has to *synchronize* with the person speaking.

For the purpose of synchronization, we recognize the following transport types:

- **Synchronous**: Information is transported bit by bit. The time elapsed from the moment of transporting one bit to the next bit being transmitted is always equal. (Do not confuse this with synchronous transmission described in Section 1.3.1 in Chapter 1.)

- **Asynchronous**: The time elapsed from the moment of transporting one bit to the next bit being transported varies. A subset of asynchronous data transport is called **arrhythmic** data transport. In the case of arrhythmic data transport, characters are transported in an asynchronous way, while particular bits in the scope of a character are transported in a synchronous way. If an asynchronous transport is mentioned, it mostly means an asynchronous arrhythmic transport.

When using asynchronous arrhythmic transport, the character being sent is wrapped in an envelope formed by a start bit, parity bits, and stop bits as shown in the following figure:

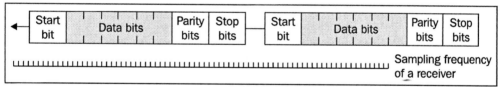

Figure 3.1: Asynchronous arrhythmic character transport

A receiver generates a sampling frequency at the next higher frequency level than the maximum possible frequency for transporting one bit. The computer uses this frequency to test the incoming signal samples. If the sample corresponds with a certain probability to the start bit, it supposes that it has detected a character being transported. It keeps on sampling and considers everything in front of the stop bits as the bits of the transported character. The data bits of the transported character are located between the start bit and stop bits and, additionally, there can be a parity bit providing a simple checksum of the transported character.

Asynchronous transmission has the advantage of the receiver being able to adjust itself with a lot of tolerance to the transmitter frequency. On the other hand, the envelope usually contains one start bit, one parity bit, and one, one and half, or two stop bits. That can result in the envelope causing a 50% transport overhead (a character that is being transported usually contains 5 to 8 bits).

In the case of synchronous transport, the overhead is low. In the past, Binary Synchronous Communication (BSC) data transmission protocol (when data were transported in blocks in a synchronous manner) was used. The beginning of the block was formed by one or more synchronizing characters that corresponded to the start bit. The receiver would synchronize using these synchronizing characters. The block was then transported synchronously.

Today, however, a completely different principle prevails. Besides the transported data, a synchronizing signal (clock) is transported via wires as well. In Figure 3.2, there are four appliances participating in communication (two modems and two computers).

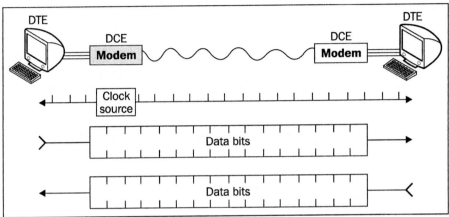

Figure 3.2: Synchronous transport

Similar to a philharmonic orchestra having one conductor, only one of these four appliances can be the time source. It is usually one of the modems (originator). Other appliances adjust the pace of their circuits according to this conductor. Since all of the appliances are synchronized, they can communicate directly, without the need for sampling. If one of the computers served as the time source, then we would set the modem of the time-generating computer as the originator for communication between modems. The modem would also be set for using an external time source (from the computer).

3.1.4 V.24, V.35, and X.21 Protocols

At the physical level, the V.35, X.21, and the PC-friendly V.24 (RS-232) protocols are usually used for serial interfaces. There are, of course, other protocols as well, although these are not that common. The user usually encounters these interfaces at the modem-computer (or router) interface.

The V.24 interface is popular with PC users due to the fact that almost all PCs are equipped with at least COM1 port built in accordance with the V.24 protocol. The V.24 interface is usually not recommended for rates above 64 Kbps. Therefore, we should consider using the V.35 or X.21 interfaces in these cases, but these interfaces are not present in most PCs.

All of the three protocols use a different connector type so it is quite difficult to get the interconnecting cables mixed up.

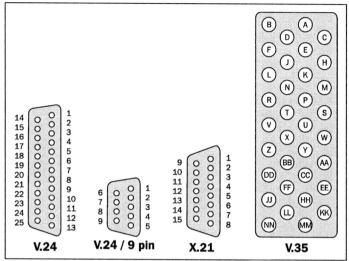

Figure 3.3: Connectors used for V.24, X.21, and V.35 interfaces

Regarding the V.35 and X.21 interfaces, the data transmission always happens via wire pairs, with the signal value being set between wires of a given pair (symmetrically). Signals with a shared ground (asymmetrical) are used only for signaling data flow control. Symmetrical signals enable the use of higher frequencies.

It is possible to directly connect two computers by using the V.24, V.35, or X.21 interfaces, but only for distances not exceeding several meters. Longer distances require the use of modems.

Table 3.1 is a list explaining the meaning of individual signals on the V.24, X.21, and V.35 interfaces. For the sake of simplicity, we have adjusted the terms so they would correspond to communication of computers with modems. We describe the modem cable interconnecting the computer and modem. In Table 3.1, the 'From' column describes the signal source, which is either computer (C) or modem (M). The 'Signal Type' column describes whether it is a symmetric signal (between A and B) or an asymmetric one (between A and the shared signal ground).

	Signal Description	From	Abbreviation EIA	Abbreviation ITU	V.24 25 Pin	V.24 9 Pin	X.21 15 Pin A	X.21 15 Pin B	V.35 Signal Type	V.35 34 Pin A	V.35 34 Pin B
Ground	Frame Ground (screen or chassis)		FG	101	1		1			A	
	Signal Ground		SG	102	7	5	8			B	
Data	Transmitted Data	C	TxD	103	2	3	2	9	both	P	S
	Received Data	M	RxD	104	3	2	4	11	both	R	T
Signal Control	Ready To Send [DTE → DCE]	C	RTS	105	4	7	3	10	asymmetrical	C	
	Clear To Send [DCE → DTE]	M	CTS	106	5	8			asymmetrical	D	
	Data Set Ready [DCE → DTE]	M	DSR	107	6	6			asymmetrical	E	
	Data Terminal Ready [DTE → DCE]	C	DTR	108/2	20	4			asymmetrical	H	
	Data Carrier Detected (Tone from a modem) [DCE → DTE]	M	DCD	109	8	1	5	12	asymmetrical	F	
	Ring Indicator (ringing tone detected)	M	RI	125	22	9			asymmetrical	J	
Clock	Transmit Signal Element Timing (DTE Source)	C	TTC	113	24				symetrical	U	W
	Transmitter Signal Element Timing (DCE Source)	M	TC	114	15		6	13	symetrical	Y	AA
	Receiver Signal Element Timing (DCE Source)	M	RC	115	17				symetrical	V	X
Test	Remote Loopback	C	RLB	140	21						
	Local Loopback/Quality Detector	C	LLB	141	18						
	Test Mode	M	TM	142	25						

Table: 3.1: V.24, X.21, and V.35 signals

The dialog between the computer and modem is schematically described in the following figure:

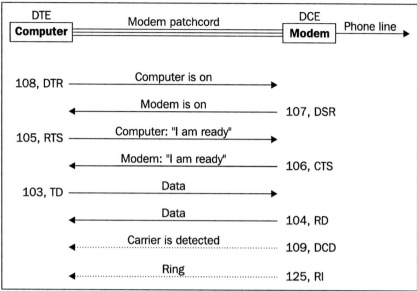

Figure 3.4: Scheme of the dialogue between the computer and modem

The DTR and DSR signals inform their counterparts that the appliance is on. In reality, though these signals are sometimes not used (the outlets are not connected or, on the contrary, the DTR and DSR outlets are connected directly in the connector). If the DTR and DSR are not connected, then both ends of the connection have to be ready (configured) for this situation so they do not wait endlessly for the other party's signal.

The RTS and CTS signals are important for data flow control. If the buffer memory of the modem is full, it unsets the CTS signal, signaling to its counterpart to delay data transmission. After the buffer memory has been emptied, the modem again resets the CTS signal and the computer can continue sending data. On the other hand, if the computer is currently unable to process the data received, it interrupts the RTS signal.

We have the option to completely leave out the RTS and CTS signals (for example, no relevant outlets are connected with the cable). Then we need to configure both ends so they are aware of this fact. In this case, data signals (always in opposite directions) can be used for data flow control. If the reception needs to be delayed, the XOFF character is sent by the receiving party to the transmitting party. The XON character renews the transmission. The XON/XOFF protocol also needs to be set up on both ends and can be used only for an asynchronous connection transporting characters.

Data signals (both the TD and RD) can, at the beginning, transmit data only between the computer and modem, such as the AT commands for dialing. Only after a connection between the modems has been established, can the TD and RD signals also be used for data transmission between computers.

Data flow control using the RTS and CTS signals is effective especially in the case of the V.24 interface. The V.35 and X.21 interfaces are aimed for higher rates, and we can use them to connect to, for example, a Frame Relay network provider. In such cases, several sub-interfaces (logical interface) go through one interface (physical interface), and in a Frame Relay, each sub-interface corresponds to one DLCI (Data Link Connection Identifier), i.e., one virtual circuit. Should one virtual circuit get overloaded by data, it is impossible to stop the data flow using the RTS or CTS signals since such an interruption would also involve an interruption of all sub-interfaces, irrespective of the number (one is enough) of such *overloaded* sub-interfaces.

3.1.5 Null Modem

If you want to connect two computers placed next to each other by using the V.24, X.21, or V.35 interfaces (both sides must use the same protocol), then the connecting cable must be connected in a special way. The problem, however, is that the signals transmitted by one party on a corresponding pin must be received by the destination party by the receiving pin (the transmission must be crossed with the reception). Such an interconnecting cable is called a **null modem**.

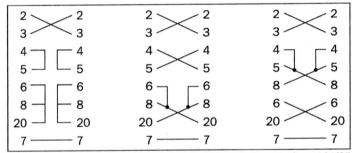

Figure 3.5: Some variants of null modem connections for the interface V.24/25 pin

In the case of synchronous transport, one party has to be the time source. If either party is unable to generate the clock, then just the cable is not sufficient for a null modem, but there has to be another intermediate box between the computers that are clock source (see Figure 3.2).

3.2 Modems

The telephone network is often used for long-distance connections. The telephone is used for audio communication. If we want to use phone lines for computer communication, then the data information has to be modulated at the source party and demodulated at the destination party. The communication happens both ways, so both parties need a **modulator/demodulator**, i.e., a **modem**.

A modem is an appliance that connects to a PC or a router using a modem cable (i.e., in the case of a PC, by the V.24 interface on the COM port). The second outlet of the modem is used to connect to the phone line. The modem might be built into the computer or in the form of a PCMCIA card inserted into a notebook or laptop. In such cases, there is no need for a modem cable. Today general users are recommend to use modems with USB ports. USB modems are connected to a USB port on the computer's side.

We can build the line between modems ourselves (for example, between two buildings). In such cases, it is usually a leased line. If we want to use a phone operator, then we have basically two possibilities:

- A dial-up connection
- A leased line

3.2.1 Dial-Up Connection

Everybody has used a dial-up connection for phone calls. Firstly, by dialing a phone number, a virtual circuit is created that can be used for making phone calls or for transferring data.

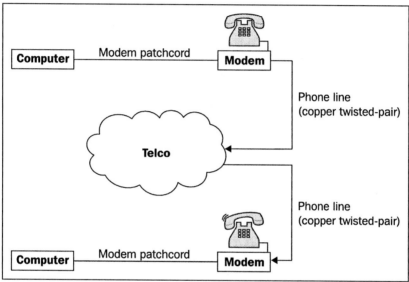

Figure 3.6: Dial-up connection

The existing phone line is usually used by connecting the modem to the user's phone jack. The phone is then connected to the second modem outlet. The user commands the modem via his or her PC to disconnect the phone and use the line for computer communication. After data communication is over, the phone is reconnected and it is possible to use it again for making phone calls.

3.2.2 Leased Lines

The second possibility is the leased line. If we prefer not to dial phone numbers all the time, nor worry about having the line busy by being online, we can lease a line for computer communication, i.e., technicians will establish a permanent circuit—a leased line.

There are no doubts about its advantages. We do not have to dial all the time, the connection is permanent, and last, but not least, we are charged a set rate. Companies will tend to use leased lines since not only it is more convenient, but the transmission rate is significantly higher as well.

To achieve a high transmission rate in leased lines, sometimes we use two circuits (quadruple wire) instead of one circuit (double wire). One of the circuits is then dedicated for transmission, the other for reception, so both circuits have to be crossed. The circuit originating in the first of the two modems as transmission must be connected to the other modem as reception. This is called a full-duplex connection.

3.2.3 Automatic Modem

There is a problem with a dial-up connection. Who is going to dial the number? Formerly, *non-automatic* modems were used with dial-up connections as well as with leased lines. That resulted in the user having to dial the phone number manually using a phone and then switch the modem into the data transmission mode (VOICE/DATA switch).

Automatic modems are able to accept commands from the computer once they are switched on, and can also be used for dialing the appropriate number. After establishing the connection, the modems themselves mutually agree on the highest transmission rate and switch into the data mode automatically.

AT commands, introduced in early 1980s by the Hayes Company, are used today for communication between the modem and the PC controlling it. AT commands are aimed at controlling the modem on asynchronous interfaces. Each AT command is composed of characters.

AT commands are also used for setting the modem for synchronous transmission if the V.24 interface is used. The procedure is as follows:

- The modem connects to the COM port.
- Start HyperTerminal or a similar program and then set up this program for asynchronous communication with the modem.
- Set up the modem by using AT-commands. The final command switches the modem to synchronous mode. The modem seems to *freeze* (because it already wants to communicate in synchronous mode), but the PC still communicates in asynchronous mode.

The set up modem then can be consequently connected to, for example, a router where it will work in synchronous mode. Using buttons, the modem switches back to the default setting (asynchronous transmission is usually the default setting).

3.2.3.1 AT Commands

AT commands are simple orders, used to control the computer modem. For example, the ATH command means that the computer sends to the modem (or more specifically, to the COM port) an ATH string. The modem then interprets the ATH string as a command.

Initially, the computer communicates with the local modem using the AT commands. Once the connection between modems has been established, the local modem informs of its establishment by sending the CONNECT command to the local computer and, subsequently, switches to data mode. From this moment, the computers are able to communicate directly with each other, i.e., the computers communicate as if there were no modems (or as if they were connected via a null modem). If the computer wants to switch the modem back to command mode in order to send AT commands, it sends the +++ string in the form of data.

If you work using Windows XP, start the HyperTerminal application. Create an arbitrary connection with the number and name that you choose. Click Properties in the File menu and click the Configure button and then the Advanced tab. Check Bring up terminal window before dialing. Confirm the choice and click Call in the taskbar button. The Terminal window before dialing window will pop up. There, you can practice the AT commands described in the following paragraphs.

The PC sends an AT command AT to the modem ("*Modem, are you ready to work*"?). If the modem is ready to work, it answers, "*OK*" (You can try entering AT characters into the Terminal window before dialing window).

Now, the PC is ready to send the modem the dial command in the form of ATDtn (for example, ATDP1234560), where the t is the type of dialing (p for pulse dialing and t for tone dialing) and the n is the destination party's telephone number. The destination modem answers the call and both modems agree on the highest possible transfer rate. The source modem informs the PC by sending the CONNECT command, which may use the agreed transfer rate as a parameter. Then both modems switch to data mode, i.e., both computers start communicating as if there were no modems. The mechanism is described in Table 3.2, without including the error messages and the AT commands for setting up the destination modem.

	Local Computer		Local Modem (dialing)	Phone Circuit	Remote Modem (answering)		Remote Computer
Signalization	105, RTS	→				←	105, RTS
		←	106, CTS		106, CTS	→	
AT commands	AT	→		Inactive			
		←	OK				
	ATDph. no.	→					
Dialing				Circuit establishing (agreement on a common highest possible speed)	Answering		
Signalization		←	109, DCD	Established	109, DCD	→	
AT commands		←	CONNECT				
Data transfer				Data transfer			

Table 3.2: AT command communication

Today, modems not capable of dialing numbers are used only for synchronous leased lines where no dialing is needed.

3.2.4 Synchronous Transmission

We've already mentioned that transmission can be either synchronous or asynchronous. Synchronous modems are used for synchronous transmission and asynchronous modems are used for asynchronous transmission. Today's modems are usually capable of both modes of transmission.

Note that PCs support, as a standard, only asynchronous transmission. Therefore, a modem that is set as synchronous needs to be set to asynchronous mode before using the PC, otherwise it seems to malfunction. The situation is different for modems inserted into computers in the form of a PCMCIA card or a modem card, and for USB modems. This is because these modems do not use the standard COM ports and, consequently, we can theoretically use synchronous transmission as well.

When configuring synchronous modems, we should not forget to set one modem as the timing source (originator). If the originator is the computer, then we set the modem of the time-generating computer as the originator. This modem also needs to be configured so as to be capable of using an external time source.

Modems having rates up to 64 Kbps can usually work both in synchronous and in asynchronous mode. Modems having rates that exceed 64 Kbps are usually synchronous.

There are also modems supporting auto-synchronous mode. They communicate with the computer in asynchronous mode, store the data in memory, and then send the data in synchronous mode. The Internet uses these modems only rarely; they are mostly found in public data networks based on the X.25 (or X.32) protocol.

3.2.5 Baseband, Voice Band, and ADSL

When transmitting phone-quality voice, we need to transmit in the band from 0.3 to 3.4 kHz.

Telephone wires (the subscriber loop) usually lead from your home jack to the patch panel of the local phone exchange. The local exchange connects the phone circuit using other exchanges all the way to the exchange of the destination party. Since this often encompasses long distances, the signal needs to be strengthened by repeater stations from time to time (see Figure 3.7). The repeater station strengthens the signal only in the band from 0.3 to 3.4 kHz. If the phone connection leads through repeater stations, then modems have to translate the data-carrying signal into the appropriate band. This creates the Voice Band.

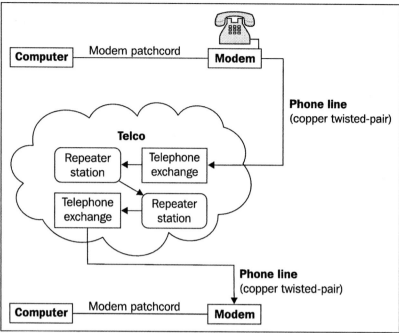

Figure 3.7: Telephone circuit goes through repeater stations and telephone exchanges

The Voice Band is used today for transmitting data at rates up to 56 Kbps. However, the transmission band of a twisted-pair, connecting an end user's plug and a patch panel of a local phone exchange, is much broader.

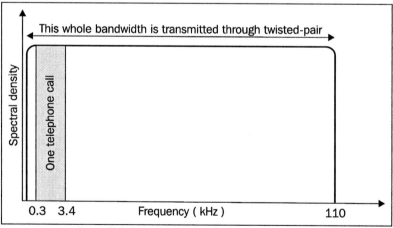

Figure 3.8: Transmission band of twisted-pair wiring

The situation is different for transmission that does not use repeater stations (for example, when we set up the lines ourselves between two buildings) or if both ends of the connection are transmitting to the same exchange as shown in the following figure (there are no repeater stations used):

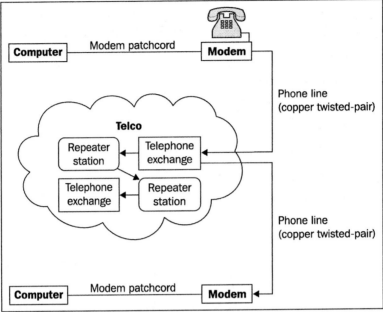

Figure 3.9: Baseband modems using a direct metallic connection

In such cases, the wires can be connected directly to each other providing a significantly broader baseband. In practice, of course, we will not connect wires together; instead, we will use the existing local telephone lines to connect to a high transmission rate data network.

Modems working in the baseband provide for much higher transmission rates. Sometimes these modems are referred to as **Baseband Modems**.

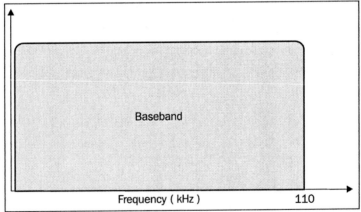

Figure 3.10: Baseband

Modems working in the baseband are usually *not automatic*, because they are used on leased lines and use synchronous transmission.

Till now, we have presumed that the transmission rate is the same in both directions. But from the point of view of an end user, the situation seems to be a bit different. An end user would prefer to have a higher downstream rate (from Internet to a user) than upstream rate (the opposite direction). Users mostly download data from the Internet and send data less often to the Internet (maybe with the exception of MS Word attachments in emails). A technology having a different transmission rate for each direction is called **asymmetric**. Later, we will discuss asymmetrical technologies in connection with the V.90 protocol. Now, we will also describe ADSL—one of technologies using a baseband (see Table 3.3).

The **Asymmetric Digital Subscriber Line** (ADSL) technology is suitable for end users having a subscriber loop realized with the help of a twisted-pair at their disposal. The transmission band of a twisted-pair is divided as follows:

- A lower frequency range for an analog.

- A phone circuit.

- An upper frequency range for a baseband. This is an asymmetrical technology having a higher transmission bandwidth from an Internet provider to an end user.

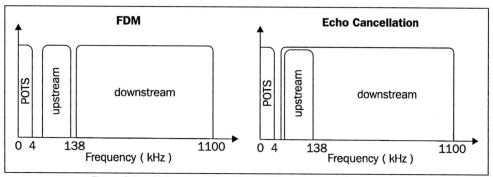

Figure 3.11: ADSL uses either FDM or EC transmission band system

ADSL leaves the band from 0 to 4 kHz for phone circuits (POTS). The ADSL data is transmitted within the band from 4 kHz upwards. We distinguish two methods of signal transmission (see Figure 3.11):

- **Frequency Division Multiplexing (FDM)**: The main principle is based on separating the frequency bands of upstream and downstream transmission.

- **Echo cancellation**: The two directions of data transmission use overlapping frequency bands. The main advantage is that both channels use the lowest possible frequency, which means less noise and reaching longer distances.

If we use the ADSL technology in a subscriber loop on the end user side, this subscriber loop ends in an appliance called **splitter**, which splits frequencies below 4 kHz for an analog/digital phone circuit and frequencies above 4 kHz for data transfer:

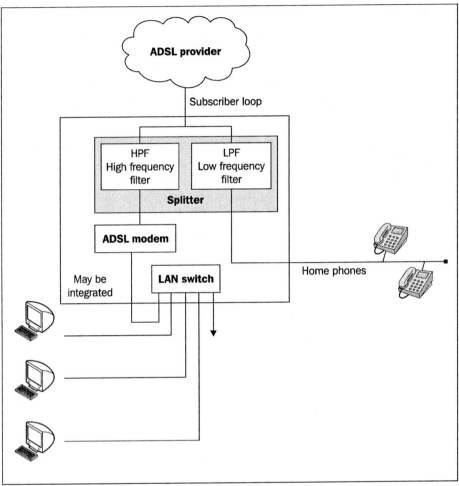

Figure 3.12: Splitter

The following table shows the transmission rates supported by the modem:

	Protocol	Transfer Capacity			Usage
		Symmetrical	Asymmetrical		
			Upstream	Downstream	
Analog Transfer	V.32	9.6 Kbps			Connection from home
	V.32bis	14.4 Kbps			
	V.34	28.8 Kbps			
	V.34+	33.6 Kbps			
	V.90		33.6 Kbps	56 Kbps	

	Protocol	Transfer Capacity			Usage
		Symmetrical	Asymmetrical		
			Upstream	Downstream	
xDSL	Digital Subscriber Line (DSL)	160 Kbps			Data communication
	High data-rate Digital Subscriber Line (HDSL)	1.544 Mbps to 42.048 Mbps			T1/E1 circuits, remote connection of local networks (LANs)
	Symmetric Digital Subscriber Line (SDSL)	1.544 Mbps to 2.048 Mbps			Like HDSL
	Asymmetric Digital Subscriber Line (ADSL)		16 to 640 Kbps	1.5 to 9 Mbps	Internet access, Video-on-Demand, LAN access, interactive multimedia applications
	Very high data-rate Digital Subscriber Line (VDSL)		1.5 to 2.3 Mbps	13 to 52 Mbps	This is the future

Table 3.3: Transmission rates

3.2.6 Transmission Rate

Modems send/receive data from two sides: the computer and the phone line. Both transmission rates, however, do not have to be the same. Problems occur only if data piles up in the modem for a while. Therefore today's modems are equipped with buffer memory.

When we speak of the modem transmission rate, we refer to the transmission rate of the phone wires. The transmission rate is given by the recommendations of the ITU that are supported by the modem. The most up-to-date recommendations for voice band circuits are shown in Table 3.3. (Transmission rates on leased lines with the transmission in the baseband or on digital circuits are different).

3.2.6.1 The V.90 Recommendation

The V.90 recommendation is not aimed at being used by the modem under all circumstances. It is not suitable for connecting from home to office equipped by an analog phone. On the contrary, the V.90 recommendation is very suitable for connecting a PC to an Internet Service Provider, if the latter is connected to the phone company via a digital line.

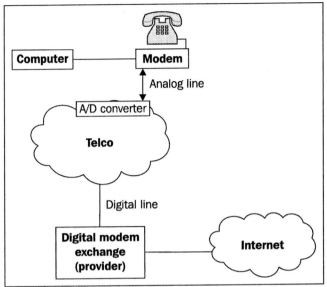

Figure 3.13: V.90 recommendation

Today, phone exchanges are fully digital. The signal carried via the analog line from a user to the phone company is digitized by the A/D converter (once it reaches the phone company) and subsequently processed as data. If the signal went to the user of a classic analog phone, then it would need reconverting by the A/D converter once it reached the destination user.

Internet providers are usually directly connected to the phone company via a high volume digital circuit. If that is the case, then the signal conversion at the provider's side is not needed. In the opposite direction, however, things get more interesting. The provider digitally hands over the data to the phone company and that data is converted to analog on the user's side. What is so interesting about it? There is loss of information when converting the signal from analog to digital, but not in reverse. So the line can function at higher rates (up to 56 Kbps) in the direction from the phone company to the user.

3.2.7 Data Compression

If the modem managed to compress the data before transmitting and the destination modem were capable of decompressing the data, then more data would be transferred at the same transmission rate. Compression is only possible with asynchronous transmission of characters. Microcom has developed the MNP 5 protocol for data compression. The ITU has issued the V.42bis recommendation for data compression.

If we compress the data, it is transferred at rates exceeding 100 Kbps even on lines with a transfer rate of 28.8 Kbps.

Why do we use a higher transmission rate on the computer-modem interface than on the line between two modems? The answer is simple. It is important, especially, when modems use data compression to communicate with each other. The maximum supported rate of the COM port is 115,200 bps, which allows maximum compression of 4:1 at the rate of 28.8 Kbps. Some data types (for example, video) can be compressed up to 40:1 in some cases.

3.2.8 Error Detection

The idea is that data is transmitted between modems in data blocks, i.e., frames. The source modem calculates the checksum from the data block and adds it to the transmitted data. The destination modem again calculates the checksum from the transmitted data (without the added checksum) and compares it with the one previously calculated by the first modem. If the results are the same, the modem hands over the data to the destination computer. Should they differ, it is considered an error in transmission, and the modem requests that the data be sent one more time.

Originally, the most widely used protocols were introduced by Microcom under the name of MNP 2 to 4. Subsequently, the protocols were also specified by the ITU in the V.42 recommendation.

The V.42 protocol also describes the two-phase process of establishing a connection. In the first *detection* phase, the modems mutually investigate their capacity by exchanging predefined characters. In the second *confirmation* phase, the modems mutually exchange information about the maximum capacity of data blocks as well as the number of blocks transmitted, followed by a request for confirmation of data block reception.

3.3 Digital Circuits

Until now, we have discussed only analog circuits. Gradually, however, analog distribution is being replaced by digital distribution. Initially, this process was confined only to the phone companies. Today, even users can take advantage of digital circuits, i.e., ISDNs.

3.3.1 ISDN

Telecom companies offer the following two types of ISDN connections:

- **Basic Rate:** This type of connection consists of one line (a twisted-pair) containing two B data channels, each with a capacity of 64 Kbps and one signalization D channel with a capacity of 16 Kbps.
- **Primary Rate**: This type of connection consists of the following:
    - In North America: 23 B data channels, each having a capacity of 64 Kbps, and 1 D signalization channel with a capacity of 64 Kbps.
    - In Europe: 30 B data channels, each having a capacity of 64 Kbps and 1 D signalization channel with a capacity of 64 Kbps.

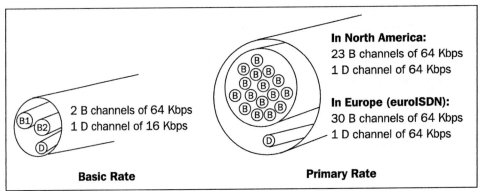

Figure 3.14: Basic Rate and Primary Rate

The D channel is used in ISDN for signaling, i.e., for establishing a virtual circuit (dialing). If the B channels are busy because of phone calls, then the D channel can signal another incoming call. The current call can be put on hold, while answering the new incoming call. It can also be used to indicate caller ID.

3.3.1.1 Basic Rate

Basic Rate uses the current subscriber loops via copper twisted-pairs. Therefore, the current metallic distribution network for analog telephones can also be used for the Basic Rate distribution. ISDN is described by the V.110 protocol. The twisted-pair coming from the phone company creates a U interface as illustrated in the following figure:

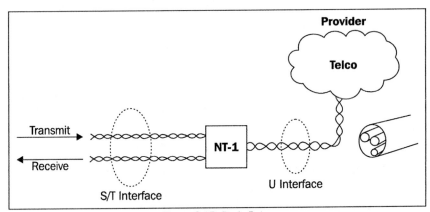

Figure 3.15: Basic Rate

The U interface is an interface between the phone company and the NT-1 appliance (box) that is usually supplied and installed by the phone network provider. The NT-1 appliance has two twin-leads of the S/T interface. The S/T functions as a bus bar to which individual digital appliances connect.

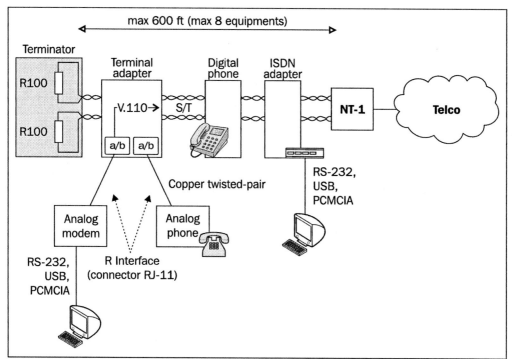

Figure 3.16: Connecting appliances to the S/T interface

Figure 3.16 shows that the individual appliances connect to the S/T interface as to a bus bar. Since the Basic Rate has two B data channels, two appliances can communicate at the same time (for example, one digital phone and one modem or two digital phones).

Although we have just two B data channels, we can connect more than just two digital appliances to the S/T interface (but only two can communicate at any given time). Let's say we have five digital phones, with each of them possibly having a different phone number. For the user, it gives the impression that they have five phone lines, however, in reality, they can use just two phones at the same time.

A terminal adapter can connect to the S/T interface, thus enabling it to connect to the commonly used analog modems, faxes, and telephones.

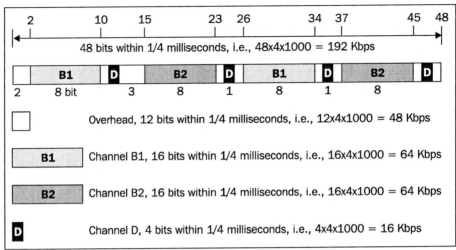

Fig. 3.17: Basic Rate divided into individual slots

It is also important to say a few things about *digital modems*. Many people seem to dislike this expression because a modem is an appliance that modulates/demodulates digital signal into an analog one. The digital modem does not do anything like that. It just converts one type of digital interface (for example, V.24 on PC) to the S/T interface (the RJ45 connector).

ISDN uses synchronous data transfer (as described in Section 3.1.3). Basic Rate uses a transmission rate of 192 Kbps, which is divided into slots for individual channels, as shown in Figure 3.17.

3.3.1.2 Higher Layer Protocols and Signalization

B channels can be used for phone calls, in which case, each slot of the relevant B channel contains one sample of the call (sound signal). But we are more interested in data transmission.

When transmitting data, LAPB protocol frames are inserted in the B channels and LABD protocol frames are inserted in the D channel. (There are also other protocols used by ISDN, such as LABF, I.465, V.120, etc.) Both the LAPB and LAPD protocols are derived (see Figure 3.18) from the HDLC protocol (see Section 4.3).

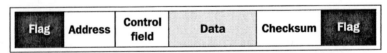

Figure 3.18: The Schema of the LAPB and LAPD link protocol frames

Network packets are inserted into LAPB protocol frames. The packets of the network layer may belong to, for example, the X.25 protocol. More important to us, however, is that IP datagrams may be inserted into the LAPB protocol frames.

So far, we have looked at a situation where the B channel used for transmitting data or a call. The question of creating (dialing) the virtual circuit, one of the functions of signalization that uses the D channel, is yet to be answered.

We recognize two levels of signalization. In DSS1 signalization, a user requires the creation of a circuit and other services. On the provider's part, DSS1 signalization is wrapped into the SS7 signalization (used also for the signalization of classic analog calls) and then transferred to the called party. An incoming call is signaled at the destination again by DSS1 signalization.

DSS1 signalization is specified by ITU recommendations Q.931 and Q.932. Q.931 provides basic services such as creating circuits and is considered a network protocol within the ISO OSI network model. The Q.932 protocol provides other services such as putting a call on hold and, within the ISO OSI network model, the protocol coverage ranges from the transport to application layer.

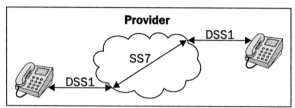

Figure 3.19: DSS1 and SS7 signalization

Messages are sent in the DSS1 signalization. Table 3.4 shows some basic types of messages.

DSS1 Signalization	POTS Analogy
Setup	Circuit making
Call Proceeding	Dialing
Alerting	Ringing
Connect	Pick up
Disconnect/Release	Hang up

Table 3.4: Messages

The following figure illustrates the DSS1 in the ISO OSI model:

From transport to application layer Q.932
Network layer Q.931
Data link layer LAPD
Physical layer S/T and U Interface

Figure 3.20: DSS1 in the ISO OSI model

3.3.2 E and T Lines

We spoke about the E1 line in Chapter 1. The E1 line is the lowest parameter in the hierarchy of transmission paths specified in ITU recommendations G.702 and G.703. There are also hierarchies of transmission paths for the U.S. (T lines), and Japan as well as transatlantic connections.

Line	Transmission rate	Maximum distance
DS1 (T1)	1.544 Mbps	6 km
E1	2.048 Mbps	5.2 km
DS2 (T2)	6.312 Mbps	4 km
E2	8.448 Mbps	3 km
¼ STS-1	12.960 Mbps	1.5 km
½ STS-1	25.920 Mbps	1 km
STS-1	51.840 Mbps	0.3 km
E3	34.368 Mbps	
E4	239.264 Mbps	

Table 3.5: Line transmission rates

A line with a transmission rate of 64 Kbps forms the basis. The E1 line contains 32 basic lines. The T1 line contains 25 such basic lines. The E2 line contains 4x E1. The E3 line contains 16 x E1 (or 4 x E2) etc.

Although the E1 line contains 32 basic lines, we can still use only 30. Slot number 0 and 16 are used for *servicing* particular frames. These two slots also contain the super-frame checksum (see Figure 3.17).

You can rent either one slot (64 Kbps) or more. The maximum bandwidth for an E1 line is 30 x 64 = 1,920 Kbps. If we rent the whole 1,920 Kbps, then this is known as an **undivided E1**.

E1 can be connected by two twisted-pairs (120 Ω), coaxial cable (75 Ω), or optical cable.

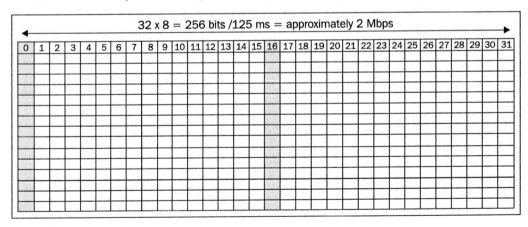

Figure 3.21: E1 super-frame divided into 32 slots of 64 Kbps each

More often, however, you would rent only n x 64 Kbps. Then the E1 line itself is invisible and in practice finishes at the provider, where it connects to a multiplexer. Users connect using a metallic connection, and it is also possible to use modems with base band transmission that are commonly available for the rate of Mbps (i.e., they are capable of containing the whole E1 line). The user connects a baseband modem with a V.35, V.24, or X.21 connector.

3.4 LAN

Local networks are used for connecting computers over short distances (from hundreds of feet to several miles). In local networks, the choice of the physical layer depends on the choice of the link protocol, especially when considering three types of link protocols: Ethernet, Fast Ethernet, and Gigabyte Ethernet. The FDDI, Token Ring, and Arcnet protocols are not used widely.

3.4.1 Structured Cables

Structured cables are a comprehensive solution to the low-voltage wiring in buildings. It involves, especially, phone and LAN wiring. The original idea of joining these cables with the fire and security signalization has been dropped, since the two will require different security measures.

LAN sockets, phone jacks, and other outlets are distributed in individual rooms within buildings. These connect to a patch panel placed in the building (see Figure 3.18). As for optical wiring, optical fibers connect to an optical distribution box.

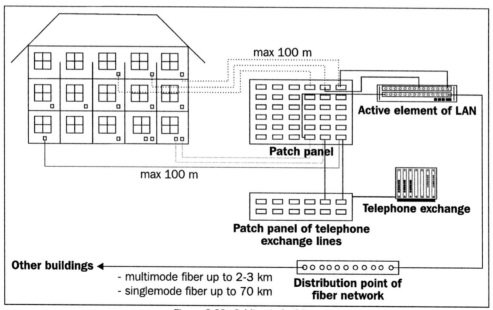

Figure 3.22: Cabling in buildings

The patch panel and optical distribution box are usually enclosed together in a rack-mount, along with active LAN elements or even the phone exchange. The interconnection between active LAN elements and the patch panel is provided by patch leads.

The wiring leading from sockets to the patch panel is quite expensive since very often this also involves building adjustments. Therefore, we should try to do our best in setting the wiring so that it will not need any additional adjustments. One of the key elements of the philosophy of new network protocols is using, as much as possible, the existing cabling. Quality cabling originally created for Ethernet 10Base-T also served the needs of 100Base-TX.

Let's have a look at the following examples of cabling standards (according to EIA/TIA):

- Category 5 (no longer in use) where the supplier guaranteed bandwidth up to 100 MHz, regardless of the protocol used (Ethernet, Token Ring, CDDI, etc.).
- Category 5E also uses bandwidths up to 100 MHz, although it needs new ways of measuring parameters that might be sometimes stricter.
- Category 6 with a bandwidth of up to 250 MHz.
- Category 7 with bandwidths up to 600 MHz is proposed. At the time of writing this book, connector types have not been approved yet, the measuring method has not been specified, and so on.

There used also to be Categories 3 and 4. Cabling built according to these standards needs redoing.

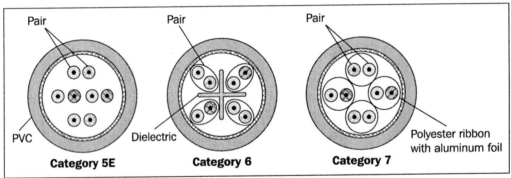

Figure 3.23: Cross section of interconnecting cables

3.4.1.1 Copper Distribution

Copper cabling is composed of twisted-pairs. Rooms are equipped with jacks for the RJ45 connector:

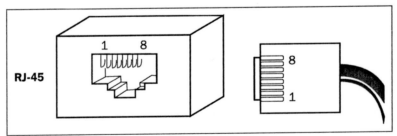

Figure 3.24: The RJ-45 connector

The RJ-45 connector (sugar cube) contains 8 outlets for 4 pairs. Most often, they are connected according to the EIA/TIA 568B standard (see Figure 3.25). This connection enables the use of pair 1, for example, as telephone (analog) and pairs 2 and 3 as, for example, Ethernet (pair 4 remains unused in this case).

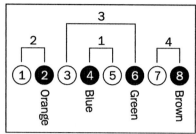

Figure 3.25: EIA 568B—interconnecting individual pairs

3.4.1.2 Optical Fibers

Optical fibers are composed of two glass layers, each with a different refractive index. One type of glass is used as the nucleus of the fiber and a different type is used as the wrapper. An optical beam is transmitted through the nucleus and it bounces within the interface (mirror) formed by the two different types of glass:

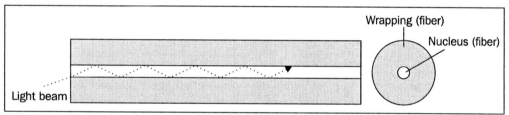

Figure 3.26: Optical fiber

Glass has only little optical resistance for just three light wavelengths: 850 nm, 1,300 nm, and 1,500 nm; therefore, one of these wavelengths is used to excite the beam.

The optical fiber is always a simplex connection, i.e., there is a transmitter on one side and a receiver on the other. Fiber pairs are required for duplex connections (which is usually the case), i.e., one fiber in each direction.

Although, the fiber usually has a diameter of 125 µm, the nucleus can be of two different diameters:

- 50 µm (or 62.5 µm): This is called **multi mod fiber**. Multi mod fibers are excited by using an LED, although nowadays, lasers are used for gigabyte Ethernets.

- 9 µm: This is called single mod fiber. Single mod fibers have a nucleus so narrow that the beam advances in the parallel direction, i.e., it does not bounce from the glass interface. This fiber is excited only by using a laser. Single mod fibers are used for long distance communication.

Figure 3.27 shows the means of protecting optical fibers. Optical fibers are wrapped in a primary protection that provides the fiber with elasticity. The fiber is very vulnerable without it. Secondary protection only increases the level of protection. The secondary protection layer is sometimes removed, for example, from optical interconnecting cables.

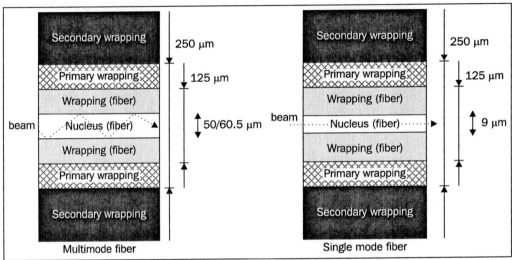

Figure 3.27: Multi- and single-mod fiber

Working with optical cables that have their secondary protection layer removed is quite complicated in a usual office environment. In this area, optical fiber with tight secondary protection (with the diameter of 900 μm or 0.9 mm) is quite popular. This type of protection integrates the primary and secondary protection. These cables are somewhat more expensive, which makes them a poor choice for long distance cabling, although optical connectors can connect directly to them.

If cables with primary protection are used, then we also need to use prefabricated optical connectors fixed onto a piece of optical fiber, known as **pigtails**. Pigtails are then welded onto the fiber.

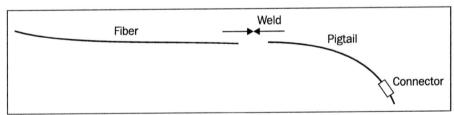

Figure 3.28: Pigtail

Welding two optical cables (i.e., also welding a pigtail) is a whole science. Just imagine the fact that we have to weld a fiber consisting of two kinds of glass (wrapping and nucleus), which would simply melt and clog the cable if we used the usual method of welding.

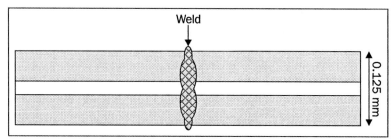

Figure 3.29: Faulty welding of optical fiber preventing the beam from advancing

The fibers need to be welded in a way that does not create any obstacles to the beam. A quality weld can only be achieved by using a very expensive appliance.

In many cases, trying to avoid welding is much more effective. Instead, we should use fibers with tight secondary protection, fixing optical connectors onto the fibers and, subsequently, interconnecting these fibers via optical connectors.

Optical fibers, including primary and secondary protection (or tight protection) are usually stored in optical cables. Fiber bunches in optical cables are wrapped in Kevlar and all this is encapsulated in the external layers of the cable. External layers depend on where the cable is placed (floor, buildings, underwater, etc.).

Cutting the cable constitutes another problem. If it breaks in your hand, its end gets frazzled; therefore, special tools are used for cutting it. Even then we still need to reface both cut ends as well as check them using a microscope in order to find out whether all the cracks have been removed by refacing.

The following figure shows an optical fiber with tight secondary protection and an optical connector attached to it:

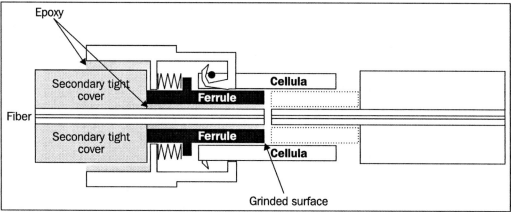

Figure 3.30: The principle of optical connector

The protection has been removed from the end of the fiber. A ceramic ring (ferrule) has been put into place where the removed protection layer used to be. The end part with ferrule was refaced and checked under the microscope. Two fibers with their ends adjusted in this way were inserted into a cavity facing each other in order to prevent them from shifting. In the cavity, the nucleus of one of the fibers touches the nucleus of the other one and the light beam can move freely form one fiber into the other.

3.4.2 Ethernet (10 Mbps)

Ethernet uses four types of interfaces: AUI, BNC, TP, or an optical connector.

3.4.2.1 AUI

AUI (also referred to as 10BASE-5) is an interface (the CANNON 15 connector) onto which the cable connects the computer with a transceiver. A transceiver is an appliance that originally transmitted/received signals over the thick coaxial cable of the LAN. There are also transceivers with thin coaxial cable (the AUI/BNC reduction) as well as transceivers for twisted-pairs (the AUI/TP reduction). This means that the AUI interface is universal, since it contains the power source for any possible reductions. On the other hand, the TP/BNC reduction needs to be created by using an independent repeater with its own power source, which makes it a bit expensive.

3.4.2.2 BNC

BNC (also referred to as 10BASE-2) is an interface used for connections via thin coaxial cable. The coaxial cable is interrupted in the point of connection. The BNC connector is attached to both connecting ends using special tongs. Both BNC connectors connect to a BNC T-connector that connects to the computer.

3.4.2.3 Twisted-Pair

Twisted-pair (also referred to as TP or 10BASE-T) is connected via the RJ-45 connector (a "sugar cube"). The twisted-pair is usually led together with the telephone network to the central patch panel.

For Ethernet, two pairs are used in the RJ 45 connector—one pair for transmitting and the other pair for receiving. If the Ethernet segment is shared only by two stations that are directly interconnected via a patch cord, then the pairs must be crossed (i.e., the transmission is crossed with the reception).

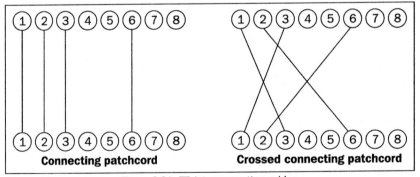

Figure 3.31: TP interconnecting cables

TP uses two pairs in the RJ45 connector, as shown in Figure 3.32. Note that outlets 4 and 5 remain free, so it is possible to use them for connecting a telephone (an analog one).

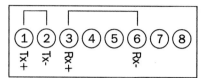

Figure 3.32: Connecting the outlets for 10BASE-T or 10BASE-TX

A segment composed of only two stations is a very interesting one. The network interfaces located in such a segment switch into the full duplex mode, completely separating the transmission from the reception. No collisions can occur in such segments (the transmission connects directly to the reception and no third parties can get involved), therefore, we can achieve rates approaching the theoretical maximum (10 Mb/s for Ethernet, 100 Mb/s for Fast Ethernet) independently in each direction. Switched Ethernet is based on this principle. Due to the collision-free traffic in this segment, the maximum length of the segment can reach up to 45 miles.

Optical Fiber

Ethernet on optical fibers is also referred to as 10BASE-F. As a rule, a pair of optical fibers is used—one in each direction of communication.

3.4.3 Fast Ethernet (100 Mbps)

Fast Ethernet connects via twisted-pair (100BASE-TX) or an optical connector (100BASE-FX). The only difference when compared with the usual Ethernet is just the quality of wires. The current distribution system is of at least grade 5 quality, so the introduction of fast Ethernet is not a problem.

3.4.4 Gigabyte Ethernet (1 Gbps)

Gigabyte Ethernet is standardized for optical appliances and for twisted-pairs (four pairs). When using twisted-pairs, whether category 5E or 6 cabling has been used is of great importance. For the 5E category, duplex distribution on all four pairs is used. As for category 6, full duplex transmission is used, i.e., two pairs are reserved for reception and the other two for transmission.

When using duplex transmission (5E category), all four pairs need to transmit as well as receive. As a result, the circuits tend to be more complicated, expensive, and prone to errors. This raises the question whether we are better off changing the cable as opposed to buying expensive interfaces. Anyway, it is a reason for preferring cabling in category 6.

Single mode fibers should comply with the 100BASE-LX standard. They are excited by a laser of frequency 1,300 nm with a maximum segment length of 1.2 miles. (Single mode fibers in fully duplex segments are up to 25 miles.) The same standard is applicable to multimode fibers up to 450 yards.

The 1000BASE-SX standard is used only for multimode fibers. This standard is excited by a laser of 850 nm and works for distances up to 25 yards.

4

Link Layer

There are many link protocols. In this chapter, we'll take a closer look at **Serial Line Internet Protocol (SLIP)**, **Compressed SLIP (CSLIP)**, **High-level Data Link Control (HDLC)**, **Point-to-Point Protocol (PPP)**, **Frame Relay**, and **Ethernet**.

4.1 Serial Line Internet Protocol

Serial Line Internet Protocol places IP packets directly into the serial line. In order to control the line, escape sequences are placed between data (analogous to communication between a computer and a printer).

SLIP protocol is specified by the standard RFC 1055. SLIP is a very simple protocol, which is used to transfer packets of the network layer.

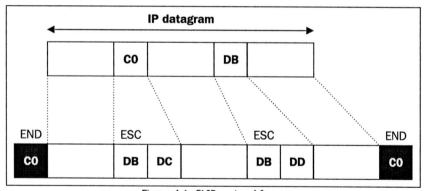

Figure 4.1: SLIP protocol frame

Each protocol frame begins and ends with a flag. In the case of SLIP protocol, the flag is known as END ($C0_{16}$). Most implementations of SLIP place an END flag at the beginning as well. If the byte $C0_{16}$ appears in the transferred data, it is substituted with a SLIP escape sequence couplet—$DB_{16}DC_{16}$ (not the ASCII Esc-sequence $1B_{16}$)—and if the byte DB_{16} appears it is substituted with the couplet $DB_{16}DD_{16}$.

SLIP protocol is very simple, but there are a few negative aspects to it as shown in the following bullet list:

- SLIP protocol does not ensure error detection during transfer. That's why it is recommended to use error detection on at least the modem level—for example, according to the V.42 recommendation—otherwise error detection would not be ensured at all. (The IP protocol has a checksum only on headers and the checksum in UDP is not obligatory.) That's why it's dangerous to place DNS servers and NFS servers, which don't have the checksum turned on in a UDP datagram, behind lines using SLIP.

- The SLIP frame does not carry any transfer protocol information concerning the network layer. That's why it's possible to transfer only one network protocol at any given time. This means it's not possible to mix, for example, IP packets with IPX packets on the same line. There is a problem with ARP as well. When we have a PC behind a line using SLIP, we won't get the effect *'as if the PC were on the LAN'* using an ARP proxy.

- It's not possible for both ends to, for example, inform each other about their IP address or other configuration parameters.

- It's not possible to use SLIP on synchronous lines.

Thanks to its ease of use, SLIP has an advantage as well. As it provides almost no services, it transfers a minimum of service information, so it's often favored on less error-free and slower serial lines.

4.2 Compressed SLIP

The variant of SLIP with compression is called **Compressed SLIP (CSLIP)**. CSLIP, specified by RFC 1144, reduces 40 bytes of headers from the TCP and IP protocols (20 from TCP and 20 from IP) to anything between 3 and 16 bytes. It is the TCP header and the IP header that are compressed, not the data!

It's possible to use the same TCP and IP header compression with the PPP protocol. In contrast to CSLIP (where both ends of the connection have to be configured for the header compression in advance), when using PPP, one end of the connection offers the possibility of compressing the header to the opposite end of the connection—if both ends agree, they will then use compression.

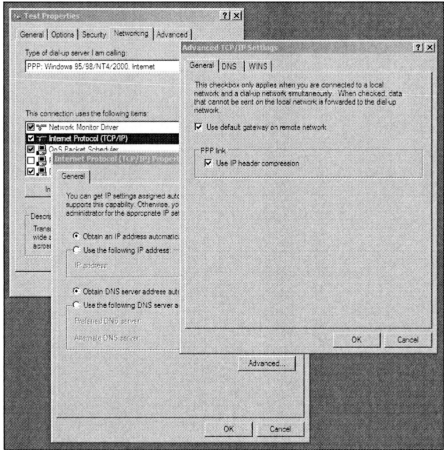

Figure 4.2: IP and TCP header compression can be set when configuring PPP protocol in Windows XP

Even though we are talking about the compression of the header, it's not actually the same compression that we are used to, for example, with the ZIP program. This is not a question of data compression.

The idea is that the author of the TCP/IP header compression (Van Jacobson) had thought about the TCP and IP headers (see Figure 4.3) and found out that a lot of data in the header doesn't change or changes just a little during a TCP connection. So it was possible to transfer just the changed items in the TCP and IP headers or even their increment (delta). Actually, only the following items are changed: IP datagram identification, the sequence number of sent bytes, the sequence number of received bytes, some attributes, window size, TCP header checksum, and the urgent pointer. Changes in other items are rare. The whole header items, the IP datagram length, and the header checksum, are unnecessary.

0		8		16	24		31
IP version 4 bits	Header length	Service class 8 bits			Total IP packet length 16 bits		
Identifier of IP packet 16 bits				Flags	Fragment offset 13 bits		
Time to Live (TTL) 8 bits		Next level protocol (protocol) 8 bits			Header checksum (*checksum*) 16 bits		
Source IP address 32 bits							
Destination IP address 32 bits							
Source port 16 bits					Destination port 16 bits		
Sequence number of sent byte (*sequence number*) 32 bits							
Sequence number of received byte (*acknowledgement number*) 32 bits							
Trailer length 4 bits	Reserved for future use 6 bits	U R G	A C K	P S H	R S T	S Y N	F I N	Window size
TCP checksum 16 bits					Urgent pointer 16 bits		

Figure 4.3: IP and TCP headers

The header compression (as described in RFC 1144) will compress the header only in the TCP protocol and when only the items listed earlier are changing. In other instances (for example, ICMP packets, UDP datagrams, or IP-datagram fragments, or when some of the RST, SYN, FIN flags are set, or when the ACK flag is not set, etc.), compression will not occur and the uncompressed frame is transferred by the line.

When the sender wishes to transfer a TCP packet, the packet is passed through the component labeled Compressor on the sender side in the following figure:

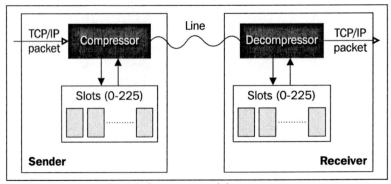

Fig. 4.4: Compressor and decompressor

The compressor then either compresses the packet or sends it unchanged. There is a decompressor on the recipient side, which reconstructs the compressed packet into the original one.

The compressor compresses individual data flows (individual connections). For each data flow a slot is kept, in which there is all the information from the TCP and IP headers necessary for both compression and decompression, i.e., reconstruction, of both headers.

Now let's consider the situation when the sender's packet has arrived at the compressor. The compressor first examines whether the packet can be compressed or not. If the packet cannot be compressed (for example, it is an ICMP packet, UDP datagram, or IP-datagram fragment, or when any of the RST, SYN, FIN attributes are set, or when the ACK attribute is not set, and so on), compression will not be done, and the uncompressed frame is transferred by the line. If the packet can be compressed, the compressor starts searching its slots for a TCP + IP header for the data flow to which the packet belongs.

Two situations may occur:

- The appropriate TCP + IP header is found in none of the slots. The packet is therefore the first compressible packet of a new connection (the very first packet of a new TCP connection has the attribute SYN set and therefore cannot be compressed). In that case, the compressor inserts the TCP and IP headers into the first free slot it finds. If there is no free slot available, the compressor uses the slot that has not been used for the longest time. The compressor does not compress the packet, but only changes the value 6 (for TCP protocol) in the 'higher-layer protocol' field to the number of the slot used.

- The compressor finds the TCP + IP headers corresponding to the preceding packet for this connection in slot number N. The compressor has found that this packet corresponds to connection N. In that case, the compressor compresses the packet.

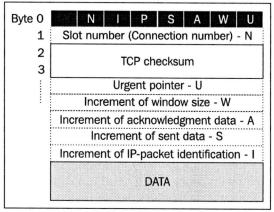

Figure 4.5: Compressed header

The structure of a compressed packet is shown in the figure above (optional items are dotted). The TCP and IP headers of the packet have been compressed. The compression does not pertain to the data part of the packet.

A compressed header contains a **mask** in the first byte. This is because the individual bits of the mask specify which items of the original packet's header have changed. That is why the whole items or their increments must be transferred as part of the compressed header. If a flag is set, then the compressed header includes that particular item; if it is not set, then the corresponding item is not included into the compressed header.

The TCP header checksum is always transferred.

The individual bits of the mask are as follows (see Figure 4.5):

- N stands for the slot number. The slot number is optional; the assumption is that where it is not stated, it is identical with the slot number of the preceding compressed packet transferred by the line. The length of the slot number is 1 byte (i.e., its value is in the 0-255 interval). This is because the slot number is transferred between the compressor and the decompressor in the higher-layer protocol field, whose length is just 1 byte.

  This is why a maximum of 255 connections can be compressed on a line at the same time. This makes compression suitable for lines connecting PCs to the Internet rather than for connecting backbone routers.

- U stands for urgent pointer. It signals that the urgent data pointer field of the packet has been filled in.

- W stands for increment of window size. The compressed header does not transfer the value of the whole window, but just its increment. Where the increment is negative or exceeds 64,000 (i.e., surpasses 2 bytes), the packet is not compressed. The same is the case with the A, S, and I bits.

- A stands for increment of acknowledged data.

- S stands for increment of sent data.

- I stands for increment of IP packet identification.

- P stands for the PUSH flag. This attribute differs from the rest by not having any corresponding item in the compressed header. If the flag is set, the PUSH flag in the TCP segment header of the original packet is also set.

The compressed header's form depends on its length, which may be one of the following types:

- Compressed headers do not transfer null values of items. For example, when the increment of sent data is unchanged, i.e., if the increment has a null value, then the increment of the sent data item is not included in the compressed header.

- If the value of the compressed header item is between 1 and 255, then it is transmitted in one byte.

- If the value of the compressed header item is greater then 255 and less than 65,536, then it is transmitted in three bytes where the first byte is 00. (The fact that the zero is not transferred is used to signal that three bytes were spent on the item.) For example, the maximum value possible (65,535) is stored in hexadecimal notation in three bytes as 00 FF FF.

Although the TCP connection is fully duplex, TCP and IP header compression is entirely independent in either direction, i.e., it is treated as if there were two independent simplex connections. Strictly speaking, it is the data flow rather than the fully duplex TCP connection that is being compressed.

Should a compressed header have the A, W, and U flags set simultaneously, the packet does not have a normal compressed header. This case is an exception reserved for Telnet, rlogin, and some other protocols. With these protocols, compressed headers consist of the mask with the A, W, and U flags set and the checksum, i.e., the compressed header has 3 bytes only. In this case, when a key of a terminal is pushed, only 4 bytes instead of 41 bytes are transferred (3 bytes of the compressed header plus 1 byte of data). For details, please refer to RFC 1144.

IP header compression has already been improved to such an extent that even protocols other than TCP protocol (for example, UDP or IP version 6) can be compressed. This new specification is dealt with in detail in RFC 2507 to RFC 2509.

4.3 High-Level Data Link Control Protocol

High-level Data Link Control (HDLC) protocol provides error detection and data stream control. HDLC is governed by the following standards: ISO 3309, ISO 4335, ISO 7776, ISO 7809, ISO 8471, and ISO 8885.

HDLC was derived from the SDLC protocol created by IBM. SDLC was used for synchronous transfer. Today, SDLC is mostly understood as a subset of HDLC, even though not all of the options of the SDLC protocol were included in HDLC.

Later, the HDLC standard was extended for asynchronous transfer as well. The asynchronous variant of HDLC is usually used by the PPP protocol that is described in Section 4.4. From now on in this chapter, we will assume synchronized, bit-oriented transfer on a physical layer.

HDLC is a very extensive standard with a large number of options (many of them are optional or even mutually exclusive). Single producers usually utilize only a part of this standard and create a lot of details according to their own requirements. That's why implementations of HDLC by, for example, Digital and from CISCO (or other companies) aren't compatible with each other. That's why most of the companies today are distributing programs not only for their own HDLC implementation, but also for the implementations of their most important competitors as well. So you could hear about CISCO HDLC, DEC HDLC, and so on.

A device attached to a data link that handles data link protocol functions is called a **station**. The data link connecting stations can be either balanced or unbalanced. An unbalanced link connects two or more stations. One of the stations is designated a primary station while all the others are secondary ones. In the case of unbalanced data links, the primary station sends commands and the secondary stations send replies. A balanced data link connects only two stations, either of which can start the transmission at any time.

HDLC protocol uses the following modes:

- **Asynchronous Balanced Mode (ABM)** is used to connect two stations with a fully duplex connection. This means that both stations can transmit at the same time, without making the line busy. Currently, this is the most commonly used mode.

- **Normal Response Mode (NRM)** is used to support unbalanced data links to connect two or more stations using half-duplex connection (switching duplex between transmission and reception). A common transfer medium is used for the reception

  and transmission of data—you can either transmit or receive at any one time. One of the stations is a primary station and the others are secondary. A secondary station cannot initiate transmission without receiving permission from the primary station first. The primary station uses **polling** do determine which secondary stations wish to transmit and assign permission to a single station to transmit at a given time. Only the primary station can transmit without permission. Other stations can transmit only when they have been given permission from the primary station. The Poll/Final (P/F) bit in the control field of an HDLC frame sets the permission. This mode is used rarely on the Internet. We won't take a closer look at it—it's listed here mainly as a means of explaining the meaning of a P/F bit.

- In **Asynchronous Response Mode (ARM)**, each station performs the function of both a primary and a secondary station. ARM is very rare at present.

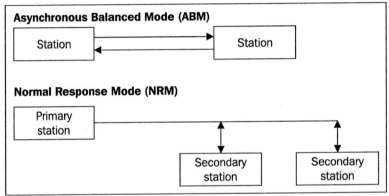

Figure 4.6: ABM and NTM

The HDLC frame format is shown in the following figure:

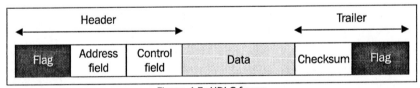

Figure 4.7: HDLC frame

4.3.1 Flag

The flag delimits an HDLC frame, which means that each HDLC frame begins and ends with a flag. In the communication line, sequences of flags might appear. When two flags arrive, one after another, they define an empty frame—which is not processed.

A flag consists of 8 bits: 0111 1110. Six 1s in a row indicate a flag. You can easily argue that a transferred character could have more than six consecutive 1s. But a bit-oriented synchronous version of HDLC uses a trick. On input, whenever data contains five 1s in row, a 0 is automatically added after these 1s. Logically, on the output, when there is a zero after five 1s, this 0 is omitted. If there's a 1 and not 0 after these 1s, it's the flag. This technique is called **bit stuffing**.

This technique is possible only in bit-oriented transfer when a stream of bits is transferred; in character-oriented transfer, this technique is not possible because the number of bits must be divisible by the length of the character (usually 7 or 8 bits). Adding an extra bit would disobey this rule.

4.3.2 Address Field

The address field is 8 bits long. It stands for the address of the station to which the frame is supposed to be delivered. It's evident that this field has its usage in NRM mode (or SDLC protocol) when often more than two stations are communicating. But it's highly desired; that's why it appears in all of the HDLC mutations. For the purpose of completeness, let's say that PPP uses, for example, a 1111 1111 value, which is broadcast. An address field in this sense (within HDLC) doesn't have anything in common with an IP address. It's a link address.

4.3.3 Control Field

The control field is the most complicated field. The control field is 1 or 2 bytes in length. The two lowest bits of the control field differentiate three types of HDLC frames:

- **Information frames** or **I-frames** (in which the lowest bit is 0) are primarily used for data transfer. But they can carry control information in their control field as well (for example, positive confirmation of a received frame).

- **Unnumbered frames** or **U-frames** (in which the two lowest bits are 11) are used not only to transfer data, but also for many control functions as well (for example, beginning an initializing dialogue, line control, and diagnostics).

- **Supervisor frames** or **S-frames** (in which the two lowest bits are 10) are used to control the data stream (for example, sending a request, confirming an I-frame, and so on). S-frames are used together with I-frames after the link is initialized. S-frames usually don't contain any data fields.

The control field within U-frames has 8 bits. Within I- and S-frames, it can have either 8 or 16 bits. In the following figures, the 16-bit control field is used, which is enhanced mode.

ABM and **NRM** modes usually use an 8-bit control field. Enhanced modes with 16-bit control fields are usually called **ABME** or **NRME**.

What is omitted in an 8-bit control field? Only 3 bits for numbering N(S) and N(R) are used, which means that frames are not numbered modulo 128, but just modulo 8.

4.3.3.1 I-Frame

The N(S) and N(R) fields in an I-frame are used for numbering the frames. They're numbered from 0 to 127 (the highest possible number with 7 bits). After reaching 127, the counting starts from 0 again. N(S) defines the number of a *sent* frame. The N(R) field, on the contrary, is used for *received* frame confirmation. Since the communication is duplex (two-way), correctly received frames are confirmed in the opposite direction.

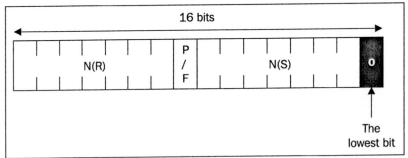

Figure 4.8: I-frame

When sending data in the opposite direction is not necessary, an S-frame is used for received data confirmation (using the RR command). If the received frame is found to be incorrect after checking the checksum, an S-frame is used to ask for a repeat of the transfer (using the REJ command)—a negative confirmation. This S-frame will repeat the number of the last correctly received frame within its N(R) field.

It's possible to confirm frames one by one. But that prolongs the response time because you have to wait for every frame to confirm. That's why frames are usually confirmed with the help of a window.

When, for example, the window equals three (see Figure 4.9), then after three packets are sent, the sender waits for the confirmation of the first one. After confirming the first one a fourth one is sent, after confirming the second one a fifth one is sent, and so on. It's necessary to keep the whole window of unconfirmed frames in the buffer memory of the sender, in case repetition of a damaged or lost frame is requested.

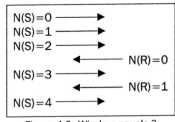

Figure 4.9: Window equals 3

The P/F bit is important for the NRM mode of HDLC. A primary station in NRM mode allows a secondary station to transmit data by setting this bit on P (Poll). The secondary station lets this bit remain set during transmission, to signal that the station wants to continue the transmission. With the last transmitted frame, the bit is set on F (Final).

4.3.3.2 S-Frame

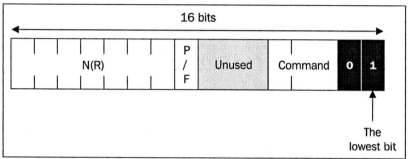

Figure 4.10: S-frame

An S-frame can confirm a correctly received frame in the Command field. It can carry the following commands or responses:

- **RR** (Receiver Ready) informs the other side that the receiver is ready to accept I-frames, or it's used like a signal that the line is free again (if it was busy before). It can also be used to confirm the number of the last correctly received frame (as was mentioned in the I-frame description).

- **RNR** (Receiver Not Ready) informs the other side about a temporary inability to receiving I-frames and confirms the frames received until now at the same time.

- **REJ** (Reject) informs the other side that a damaged frame has been received. It is used either as a command or as an answer requesting repetition of the transmission.

4.3.3.3 U-Frame

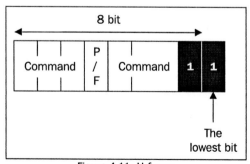

Figure 4.11: U-frame

U-frames can carry both data and commands/responses:

- **SABM** (Set Asynchronous Balanced Mode) sets the line to ABM mode with an 8-bit control field.
- **SABME** (Set Asynchronous Balanced Mode Extended) sets the line to ABM mode with a 16-bit control field; it's the version of HDLC that we described earlier.
- **SNRM** (Set Normal Response Mode) sets the line to NRM with an 8-bit control field.
- **SNRME** (Set Normal Response Mode Extended) sets the line to NRM mode with a 16-bit control field.
- **UA** (Unnumbered Acknowledgement) is used for SABM, SABME, SNRM, SNRME, and DISC confirmation.
- **DISC** (Disconnect) when used within dial-up lines is a hang-up request. Within leased lines it enables you to cancel the operating mode (the actual set up).
- **DM** (Disconnect Mode) is used for positive DISC confirmation.
- **FRMR** (Frame Reject) is used to indicate an incoming damaged frame, when it's not possible to correct by retransmission. After receiving FRMR, you begin again with setting up the line mode, that is with one of the following commands: SABM, SABME, SNRM, and SNRME. The beginning of the data part of the packet contains 2-3 byte fields with the error code (for example, error in the control field of a frame, error in the information field, frame capacity exceeded, error in the received frame sequence, and so on).
- **XID** (Exchange Station Identification) commands and responses are used for the beginning initialization sequence, when the stations agree on checksum length, transferred higher-layer protocol, and so on.
- **UI** (Unnumbered Information) is used for unnumbered data frame transmission. These frames can contain transferred protocol specification at the beginning of a data field, so it's possible to mix different protocols (such as IP and IPX) within one line.

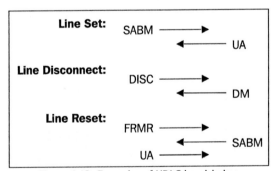

Figure 4.12: Examples of HDLC handshakes

4.3.4 Data Field and a Transferred Protocol Type

The data field (officially called **information field**) contains either transferred data or control information. A data field may be omitted. Most implementations of HDLC require the data field to be some multiple of 8 bits.

The HDLC-frame header doesn't enable the option of higher-layer protocol specification. This means that it doesn't enable, for example, mixing IP frames with IPX. And the choice of protocol happens in the beginning initialization dialogue. These restricts apply to numbered frames; it's possible to put the protocol specification at the beginning of a data field with unnumbered frames.

4.3.5 Checksum

The **Frame Check Sequence (FCS)** also called **checksum** is calculated from the transferred data, the address, and control field, and is usually 32 or 16 bits long. The recipient also calculates a checksum from an incoming frame and compares it to the checksum from the frame it received. If they are the same, it can assume that the incoming frame has been transferred correctly. If not, in the case of numbered frames, it can ask for transfer repetition. The definition of which checksum is going to be used is part of the initial dialog between the stations during the connection initialization (with the help of the XID command).

4.3.6 HDLC Protocol Summary

HDLC is an advanced link protocol, which enables the following:

- Checking for damaged frames with the help of a checksum.

- Requesting frame transfer repetition after receiving a damaged numbered frame (unnumbered damaged frames are discarded).

- Mixing different network protocols within one line with the help of unnumbered frames; but in this case retransmission isn't possible.

In HDLC protocol the line can be in the following states:

- Down (no communication)

- Setup (only U-frames can be used)

- Up (the state of data transmission having regular conditions, only I- and S-frames are transferred—U-frames are not used for data transmission)

- Disconnecting (only U-frames are transferred)

4.4 Point-To-Point Protocol

Almost every Internet user will sooner or later come across PPP. It's precisely the protocol that gives you trouble when you want to connect your PC to the Internet through a dial-up line or ADSL line. PPP most often uses frames similar to those of HDLC protocol. However, it doesn't use all the possibilities that HDLC offers by far. But perhaps it introduces even more new features.

The basic features of PPP are as follows:

- On the physical level, it is able to use an interface in accordance with the recommendations V.24, V.35, and so on. It doesn't require any control signals (RTS, CTS, DCD, DTR, etc.). However, control signals can be used to enhance its efficiency.

- It can use both asynchronous and synchronous (bit or character) data transmission.
- For asynchronous transmission, it uses 1 start bit, 8 data bits, and 1 stop bit (no parity).
- It requires fully duplex (two-way) point-to-point leased or dial-up lines.
- As a rule, it uses 16 or 32 bits for a checksum to detect whether the frame was damaged during transmission.
- The aim of PPP is to allow the transfer of several network protocols at the same time through one line (to mix protocols). It doesn't use I-frames, only U-frames. Therefore, it cannot number the frames nor repeat them if it detects damaged ones.
- At the beginning of the data field, it places an 8-bit or 16-bit identification of the transmitted network protocol.

PPP is specified by RFC 1661. The form of a PPP frame, encapsulated in a way similar to HDLC, is specified by RFC 1662. Figure 4.13 shows a PPP frame structure. The Protocol field specifies the transmitted protocol.

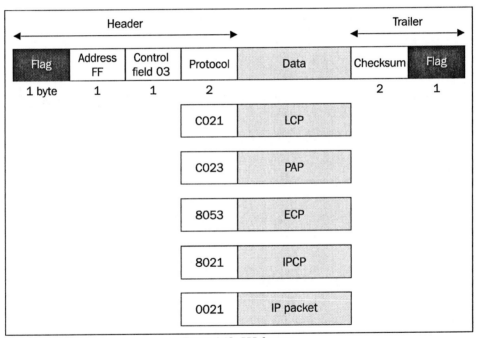

Figure 4.13: PPP frames

In addition to the encapsulation of a PPP frame similar to HDLC, other methods of PPP encapsulation are also specified. For an example of Frame Relay encapsulation or Ethernet encapsulation, see RFC 2516.

However, let's go back to HDLC encapsulation. A PPP frame contains a value of FF_{16} (broadcast) in the Address Field and always contains the value of 03_{16} in the Control Field (U-frame with the P/F bit set to 0). If only frames with this Address and Control Field are in the line, then both ends of the line can use **Address-and-Control-Field-Compression** option. If this option is used, both fields are simply left out during the transmission.

Let's describe the flag. Flags are at the beginning and the end of each PPP frame. The flags contain binary 0111 1110, i.e., $7E_{16}$. But what if the 7E character must be transmitted within the data? In binary synchronous lines, we have described the technique of **bit stuffing** (see Section 4.3.1).

In asynchronous connections (also in character synchronous lines) escape sequences will be used (as in the SLIP protocol). The 7E character will be replaced by a 7D 5E couplet and the 7D character will be replaced by a 7D 5D couplet.

Implicitly, the 7D escape sequence also introduces all ASCII control characters (characters from the ASCII table with a decimal code smaller than 32). Moreover, 32_{10} (i.e., 20_{16}) is added to the value of these characters. For example, $7E23_{16}$ is transmitted instead of character 03. As a result, even the terminal driver cannot damage the transmitted characters by wrongly interpreting them as, for example, BELL, BAKSPACE, and so on. Maybe you were surprised by the word 'implicitly' at the beginning of this paragraph. However, using the **Async-Control-Character-Map (ACCM)** option, both stations can agree on the table of characters that will be introduced by an escape sequence.

In binary synchronous lines, escape sequences are not used. However, this is not always the case. Escape sequences can be found also in binary synchronous links. Why? If there is a need to convert a transmission from asynchronous to bit synchronous (and vice versa), escape sequences pass from asynchronous to synchronous transmission as characters. When answering, the synchronous side must add escape sequences to synchronous data, so that it is possible to communicate with the counterpart after the conversion. Therefore, synchronous stations can use the ACCM option as well. Such a conversion is used, for example, when a synchronous line is connected to a PC and an autosynchronous modem is used. It means that asynchronous communication comes out of the PC and in the autosynchronous modem, where it is converted into synchronous communication.

Five types of service protocols that are a part of PPP are as follows:

- LCP, which establishes a connection.
- Protocols responsible for authentication (PAP, CHAP, EAP, and so on).
- Protocols for call-back.
- Other protocols: protocols for data encoding, protocols for data compression, Multilink Protocol, Bandwidth Allocation Protocol, and so on.
- The NCP protocol group. Each network protocol that uses the PPP link protocol has its own standard for NCP. The protocol number of the protocol is always a part of this standard, and it is used in the Protocol field for the particular NCP protocol (the number always begins with the digit 8) and for data frames (the number begins with the digit 0). Among others, there are the following NCP protocols:

- o IPCP (protocol number 8021_{16}) is a variant of NCP for IP version 4. IPCP is specified by RFC 1332. Data frames use the value 0021_{16} in the Protocol field.
- o IPV6CP (protocol number 8057_{16}) is a variant of NCP for IP version 6 (RFC 2023). Data frames transmitted by IP version 6 use protocol number 0057_{16}.
- o SNACP (protocol number $804D_{16}$), i.e., NCP for IBM SNA (RFC 2043). Data frames use protocol number $004D_{16}$.
- o DNCP (protocol number 8027_{16}), i.e., NCP for DECnet Phase IV (RFC 1762). Data frames use protocol number 0027_{16}.
- o IPXCP (protocol number $802B_{16}$), i.e., NCP protocol for IPX (RFC 1552). Data frames use protocol number $002B_{16}$.
- o OSINLCP (protocol number 8023_{16}), i.e., NCP for OSI protocols, for example, protocols ES-IS, IS-IS, etc. (RFC 1377). Data frames use protocol number 0023_{16}.

4.4.1 Dialing a Phone Line

Before we begin to describe the individual protocols of the PPP family, let's have a look at the actual dialing of a line. Practical problems often appear even before the actual PPP connection is established.

In Windows there are, for example, options that allow you to open the terminal window. The terminal window can be opened at two specific moments:

- Before the modem starts dialing. At this moment, the user can type commands into the terminal window to control the modem (for example, the AT command). The user can specify a dialed phone number manually (for example, ATDT123456789 in the case of phone number 123456789) and monitor how the modem works.
- After the phone circuit is established, i.e., the modems on both sides are switched into data mode.

If the phone circuit is established, the users can find themselves in either of the two situations:

- The other side waits for only PPP communication (in the terminal window only gibberish is shown, i.e., frames with a Configure-Request command in binary form). This situation happens, for example, when establishing communication with Windows servers. The only reasonable thing to do in such a situation is to close the terminal window and to continue communication by PPP.
- The other side awaits the terminal dialog. This situation is common, for example, in UNIX servers or CISCO boxes. The user is asked to enter username and password. Again, two situations can happen:
  - o The user enters a username that can work interactively in the given system, then a command line of the given operating system appears and the user can work as he or she is used to on this system. The user can also activate PPP by the ppp command (gibberish appears again); close the terminal window, and leave the line for the computer to communicate by PPP.

   o   The user cannot work interactively in the given operating system. After entering the correct password, PPP is automatically activated. The only thing to do for the user after his or her authentication is to close the terminal window and continue communication by PPP.

In both cases the user had been authenticated; however, with a terminal dialogue, not PPP.

After establishing the phone circuit, the terminal window can be set according to the settings of a particular dial-up connection. In HyperTerminal, open the Properties window of a particular dial-up connection and then choose the Connect To tab. Afterwards, press the Configure... button. In the Advanced tab, check Bring up terminal window after dialing.

4.4.2 Link Control Protocol

Link Control Protocol (LCP) is used before the question of which network protocol will run through the line is even considered. LCP (unlike NCP protocols) is a common protocol for all network protocols. The function of LCP is to establish a connection, terminate a connection, negotiate an authentication algorithm, and so on. The line gradually undergoes the following phases: establishing a connection, authentication, network protocol, and disconnection as shown in the following figure:

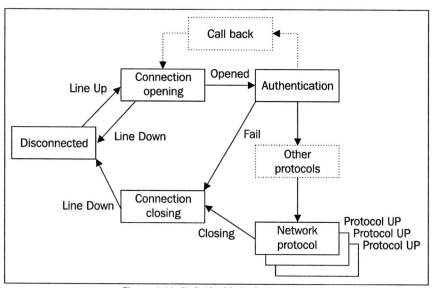

Figure 4.14: Individual link phases in PPP

Link Disconnection is always the starting and ending point of your session. If any external event happens (for example, the modems lose their connection or the network administrator issues a command to terminate the connection), the line switches to this phase.

This disconnection phase leads to an **Connection opening** phase. The connection is opened through an exchange of configuration packets. No data packets (i.e., network protocol packets, for example, IP) are transmitted during this phase. If a data packet appears during this phase, it is discarded. The aim of this phase is to establish connectivity between both ends of the line.

Authentication is the phase during which the client proves its identity. The word *client* is used on purpose. You might be asking yourself, "*Who's the client here?*" The client is the side (station) that is asked to prove its identity. After proving that station's identity, the stations can then exchange their roles, and the other side can be asked to prove its identity. In practice, only one side usually proves its identity (for example, a PC user against an Internet provider).

Authentication is not compulsory and can be skipped. During the process of authentication, again, no data (i.e., network protocol) packets can be transmitted.

Authentication only transmits the data that is used as the actual proof of identity. This means that LCP doesn't describe any authentication algorithm; it only transmits data, which is then used by the authentication protocols. **Password Authentication Protocol (PAP)**, **Challenge-Handshake Authentication Protocol (CHAP)**, and similar protocols are used as authentication protocols. Additionally, as a rule, terminal authentication is also possible.

After the authentication phase, both ends (peers) can agree to do a call back using the call-back protocol. After this the connection is established again and another authentication phase is possible.

If a connection is established (line is up), further protocols can be activated. Mostly, however, they are activated immediately after the authentication phase. By using these protocols, both ends can agree on things like transmission encoding, data compression, spreading of bandwidth over several phone lines (Multilink Protocol), dynamic bandwidth allocation to several phone lines if needed (**Bandwidth Allocation Protocol (BAP)**), and so on.

The phase described in Figure 4.14 as **Network protocol** can contain in itself a whole range of steps. At this point, the individual NCP protocols take over. Each network protocol that wants to use the line must set the line to an open state for this particular protocol with the help of its own NCP. Data packets of a network protocol for which the line is not open will be discarded.

For example, if both IP packets (version 4) and IS-IS protocol packets are to be transmitted by the line, the line must be opened twice during this phase: once using IPCP protocol and a second time using OSINLCP. Data of a particular network protocol can start being transmitted only after the line is open for this particular network protocol. The line can be open for several network protocols at the same time.

Connection termination is the last phase. During this phase all packets, except for LCP packets, are discarded. Connection termination is also signaled to the physical layer. The physical layer can react, for example, by hanging up the dial-up line.

The LCP frame format is shown in Figure 4.15. It is important to emphasize that all of the PPP family's control protocols will have similar frames that consist of the Code Identification (ID), Length, and Option fields (for example, command parameters).

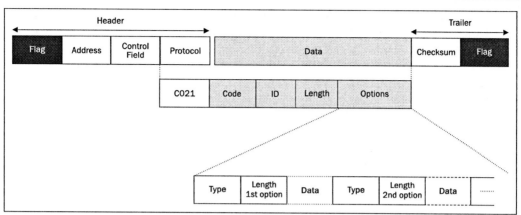

Figure 4.15: LCP Frame Format

The 8-bit Code field specifies the type of command (or reply) of LCP:

Code	Code Name	Description
1	Configure-Request	Configuration packet carrying requests to change implicit line parameters.
2	Configure-Ack	Configuration packet with positive confirmation of requests to change implicit line parameters, i.e., all the requested changes to parameters are identified and accepted.
3	Configure-Nak	Configuration packet with the response that the opposite side did identify all options, but didn't accept all of them. The ones that were not accepted are specified in this packet and their alternative values are proposed.
4	Configure-Reject	Configuration packet that refuses all requests. This can also be a result of an invalid option code, for example, the request was not identified.
5	Terminate-Request	Request for connection termination.
6	Terminate-Ack	Confirmation of the request for connection termination.
7	Code-Reject	Request refused due to an unknown code. It can also occur when the opposite station uses a different protocol version.
8	Protocol-Reject	The opposite side does not support the given protocol.
9	Echo-Request	Test loop support on the link level.
10	Echo-Reply	Compulsory response to Echo-Request.
11	Discard-Request	Discards the packet. This is used to test the line load, i.e., the sender generates an artificial line load using these packets.
12	Identification	This is an extended option containing a 4-byte *magic number* and a text of a variable length. The meaning of the magic number is similar to the Magic-Number option. The text can contain, for example, the type of hardware, the version of software, and so on.

Table 4.1: Code names

The 8-bit **ID** field is the request identification. The sender generates the request identification into this field and the receiver copies it into its response. This field is used to couple a response to the given request.

The 16-bit **Length** field contains a number that states the sum of the lengths of the following fields: code, ID, length, and options.

The **Options** field contains individual requests (or responses) to change implicit line parameters. This field consists of one or more options. Individual options are placed in a sequence, as shown in Figure 4.15. The Type and Length fields are both 8 bits long.

The following table presents some of the options:

Type	Option Name	Description
1	Maximum-Receive-Unit	Using this option, the stations can agree on a frame length (MTU) longer than 1,500 bytes (all stations are obliged to transmit frames of at least 1,500 bytes). The Data field of the option then specifies the length of the frame.
2	ACCM (ASYNC.MAP)	Four bytes of the Data field, i.e., 32 bits, are used to specify which control characters (the first 32 characters of ASCII table) are replaced by an escape sequence ($7D_{16}$) and the value of the actual character increased by 32 (20_{16}). If, for example, the 5th bit in the 32-bit string is set to 1, then $7D25_{16}$ will be transmitted instead of the character 05_{16}. If there is no risk of misinterpretation, then, as a rule, both sides agree on an ACCM that consists of zeros only.
3	Authentication-Protocol	Request for authentication by a specific authentication protocol. For example, for PAP the Data field of this option contains hexadecimal C023, for CHAP it contains C223, for EAP it is C227, and so on. When dealing with CHAP, this option, in addition to protocol ID (C223), also carries a one-way function identifier: 05_{16} for MD5 algorithm, 80_{16} in the case of the MS CHAP protocol in version 1 (which uses MD4 algorithm), 81_{16} in the case of MS CHAP protocol version 2.
5	Magic-Number	This contains a random 4-byte *magic number* that serves to detect the feedback (loop) in the line. If the recipient receives a Configure-Request with the magic number filled in, it finds out whether by chance the previous Configure-Request had the same magic number. If so, it is probably a case of feedback. In this case, it generates a different magic number for its response. If it is not a case of feedback, it copies the original magic number into its response. Some PPP implementations repeat the first frame in the line until they receive the first response. By presenting the same magic number, they signal that it is a case of frame repetition.
7	Protocol-Field-Compression	Compression of leading zeros in the protocol number. The PPP frame contains a 2-byte field that specifies the type of protocol (e.g., 0021_{16} for IP-datagrams). At the beginning of communication, it must always be a 2-byte field. After the confirmation of Protocol-Field-Compression, a 1-byte field is used, i.e., the first byte is left out if it contains 0.
8	Address-and-Control- Field-Compression	In PPP frames, the Address field always contains the value FF and the control field always contains the value 03. After the Address-and-Control-Field-Compression is confirmed, the sender leaves out this field and the recipient automatically fills it back in.

Code	Option Name	Description
13	Call-Back	Request for call back. After the confirmation of this request, the authentication phase should be carried out and the LCP dialog should lead to hanging up the line, after which the second end of the line establishes a connection. The data field of this option includes the phone number type (phone address type). As a rule, it contains the value 06, i.e., it will be negotiated by CBCP (see RFC 1700).
17	Multilink-MRRU	Confirmation of this option signals that the system has MP protocol implemented. The data field of this option contains the maximum packet size that the system is able to rebuild (see Section 4.4.5).
18	SSNH	Request to shorten the MP header from 4 to 2 bytes (see Section 4.4.5).
19	Multilink-Endpoint Discriminator	Explicit identification of the computer as the end of the connection for MP (see Section 4.4.5).
23	Line-Discriminator for BAP	Explicit identification of the line within one computer (see Section 4.4.5).

Table 4.2: Option names

To understand better the function of individual fields, see the list of frames shown below that details the Configure-Request command by which the Windows server specifies its connection requests. (A standard configuration for the dial-up connection was used, and the PAP authentication protocol was used, which, for security reasons, Windows server is quite reluctant to use. But it wouldn't have been possible to capture the password if a different authentication protocol was used.)

```
+ Frame: Base frame properties
  PPP: Unknown Frame (0x0)
    PPP: Destination Address = SEND_
    PPP: Source Address = SEND_
    PPP: Protocol = Line Control Protocol
  LCP: Config Req Packet, Ident = 0x00, Length = 44
    LCP: Code = Configuration Request
    LCP: Identifier = 0 (0x0)
    LCP: Length = 44 (0x2C)
    LCP: Options:
      LCP: ASYNC.MAP:00 00 00 00
        LCP: Option Type = Async-Control-Character-Map
        LCP: Option Length = 6 (0x6)
        LCP: Async Control Character Map = 00 00 00 00
      LCP: AUTH:PAP
        LCP: Option Type = Authentication-Protocol
        LCP: Option Length = 4 (0x4)
        LCP: Authentication Protocol = Password Authentication Protocol
        LCP: Option Data: Number of data bytes remaining = 0 (0x0000)
      LCP: MAGIC#:0x6147A40
        LCP: Option Type = Magic-Number
        LCP: Option Length = 6 (0x6)
        LCP: Magic Number = 102005312 (0x6147A40)
      LCP: PROT.COMP
        LCP: Option Type = Protocol-Field-Compression
        LCP: Option Length = 2 (0x2)
      LCP: ADR/CF.COMP
        LCP: Option Type = Address-and-Control-Field-Compression
        LCP: Option Length = 2 (0x2)
      LCP: CALL.BACK:Unkn
        LCP: Option Type = Callback
        LCP: Option Length = 3 (0x3)
```

```
         LCP: CallBack = 0x06
      LCP: MRRU
         LCP: Option Type = Multiline-MRRU
         LCP: Option Length = 4 (0x4)
         LCP: Multiline MRRU = 1614 (0x64E)
      LCP: Option Summary = N/A
         LCP: Option Type = Multiline-Endpoint-Discriminator
         LCP: Option Length = 9 (0x9)
      LCP: Option Summary = N/A
         LCP: Option Type = Line Discriminator for BACP
            LCP: Option Length = 4 (0x4)
```

The above list contains the PPP frame that Windows server *recalculated* in the Ethernet frame format. This frame can be recognized by the **SEND** Ethernet address, by which the Network monitoring program says that it is dealing with a transmitted frame (see Section 2.2.1). The PPP frame consists of the following:

- Code (Configuration Request=1)
- Identifier (=0)
- Length (44 bytes)
- Options. Here is a list of available options:
    - **ASYNC.MAP** (Async–Control–Character–Map): This option specifies which of the first 32 characters of the ASCII table are to be introduced by an escape sequence. Since, in our case, the data field of this option contains only zeros, no characters will be introduced, i.e., it is a line that is not used, for example, as a terminal line; therefore there is no risk of control character misinterpretation.
    - **AUTH.PAP**: Request authentication by PAP.
    - **MAGIC:** This option contains the magic number.
    - **PROT.COMP**: Request Protocol-Field-Compression (i.e., a request omitting the leading zeros in protocol numbers).
    - **ADR/CF.COM:** Request Address-and-Control-Field-Compression (i.e., requesting that these fields be omitted).
    - **CALL.BACK**: Proposes that the call-back protocol be activated.
    - **Multilink MRRU:** Is MP supported? How big a packet is it possible to rebuild?
    - **Option Summary (Multiline-Endpoint-Discriminator)**: An explicit identification of the connection (of the computer) in MP. The value of the identifier is not shown in this listing; however, it is in a hexadecimal listing.
    - **Option Summary (Line-Discriminator for BACP)**: An explicit identification of the line within the computer.

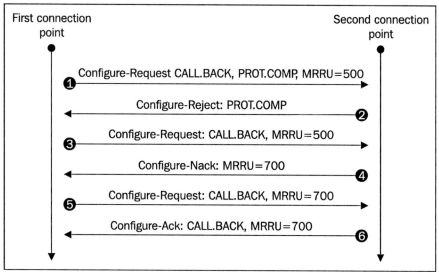

Figure 4.16: A fictional example of an LCP dialog

The above figure shows an example of an LCP handshake that is described as follows:

1. The first side sends its connection requests by a `Configure-Request` command.

2. The second side doesn't know the PROT.COMP option, which it communicates via a `Configure-Reject` command with the PROT.COMP option.

3. The first side therefore sends a command that it thinks the other side should understand.

4. The second side understands it, but prefers the MRRU=700 option, which it communicates via a `Configure-Nack` command with the MRRU=700 option.

5. The first side sends a command with options that it thinks will be acceptable for the second side.

6. The second side confirms everything by the `Configure-Ack` command.

4.4.3 Authentication

Identity can be proven in two ways within PPP (the third possibility is, of course, to leave out authentication):

- By terminal dialogue. This possibility was described in Section 4.4.1.
- By the authentication protocols of PPP family, namely:
  - **Password Authentication Protocol (PAP)**. This protocol is similar to authentication by terminal dialog, i.e., the users also prove their identity with their username and password, but they enter both values into the PAP protocol (RFC 1334) and not directly into the terminal line.
  - **Challenge Handshake Authentication Protocol (CHAP)**. This protocol is specified by RFC 1994 and is regarded as superior to PAP. Both ends of the connection share a secret. The station that initiates

the authentication generates a random string to use as a *challenge*, which it sends to the other side. The second side concatenates this string to the shared secret and, from the result, calculates the checksum by using a one-way algorithm (for example, MD5). The result, which is a one-time access password, is sent back. So, the one-time access password is sent back to the station that initiated the process of authentication. This station, however, knowing both the shared secret and the challenge, is also able to calculate the one-time access password. Therefore, it compares both passwords and, if they are identical, confirms the successful result of the authentication to the other side.

o **MS CHAP** version 1 and 2.

o **EAP** (see Section 4.4.3.3).

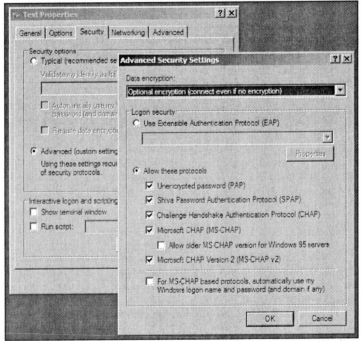

Figure 4.17: Configuration of authentication protocols and encryption in Windows XP

In the figure above, the server side is set in accordance with the particular server in the Routing and Remote Access program (PPP card).

4.4.3.1 Password Authentication Protocol

PAP is a simple protocol. The communication, as a rule, consists of two packets. An authentication packet is submitted by an Authenticate-Request command, and the other end either confirms the authentication with an Authenticate-Ack command or refuses it with an Authenticate-Nak command.

Code	Code Name	Description
1	Authenticate-Request	The packet that begins communication via PAP. It carries an option with code 1, which contains the name and the password.
2	Authenticate-Ack	Authentication confirmed.
3	Authenticate-Nak	Authentication failed.

Table 4.3: PAP commands

An example of a Network monitoring program listing is as follows:

```
+ Frame: Base frame properties
+ PPP: Unknown Frame (0x0)
  PPPPAP: Authenticate Request
  PPPPAP: Code = Authenticate Request
  PPPPAP: ID = 5 (0x5)
  PPPPAP: Length = 27 (0x1B)
  PPPPAP: Side ID Length = 13 (0xD)
  PPPPAP: Side ID = Administrator
  PPPPAP: Password Length = 5 (0x5)
      PPPPAP: Password
```

4.4.3.2 Challenge Handshake Authentication Protocols

The advantage of CHAP is that both ends share the same secret. Therefore, it is easy to carry out authentication from both ends. But sharing the secret is also a disadvantage of CHAP because it is impossible to prevent misuse of the secret by the other side (unlike in the case of authentication by a password, where the other side has access only to a password, which is invalidated by a one-way function).

CHAP communicates in three steps. In the first step, a request containing a random string is sent to the side to be authenticated with the Challenge command. The side to be authenticated then runs both the shared secret and the challenge (random string) through a one-way function (for example, the MD5 algorithm). The result is entered into a Response and sent back. The first side's reaction is then either a confirmation of the authentication (Success) or a refusal (Failure).

Code	Code Name	Description
1	Challenge	Carries the Challenge option
2	Response	Carries the Response option
3	Success	Positive confirmation of authentication
4	Failure	Authentication failed

The disadvantage of CHAP is that both ends must have the shared secret at their disposal in an open format. In many operating systems, however, this is not a common feature. In most operating systems, the user specifies a password, but this password is not saved in an open format in the operating system's user database. The operating system invalidates the password with a one-way function and only the result of this operation is saved in the user database. Within the user authentication process, the user passes his or her password to the system. The system applies the above mentioned one-way function to the password and only the result of this operation is compared with the data in the user database.

Microsoft has introduced a modified version of CHAP, specified as MS CHAP version 1 (RFC 2433). In Windows operating systems, passwords to which the MD4 one-way function has been applied are kept. The user's password, invalidated by the MD4 algorithm, then represents a shared secret. The client's software then applies the MD4 algorithm again to both the shared secret and the random challenge.

The basic advantage of MS CHAP version 1 is its backward compatibility with LAN Manager systems. However, double-sided authentication is not possible and, in particular, there is a problem with the encryption of transmitted data. We will learn more about this in Section 4.4.5 that deals with other protocols, especially encryption protocols. It is important to realize that encryption keys are, as a rule, derived from data that was exchanged during the authentication phase. MS CHAP version 1 allows these keys to be derived from the shared secret only, which means that when a user is using the same password, he or she is also using the same encryption keys. These drawbacks have been resolved by MS CHAP version 2 (RFC 2759) which, however, doesn't have backward compatibility with LAN Manager systems.

We should bear in mind that the selection of the specific CHAP version to be used (CHAP, MS CHAP version 1, MS CHAP version 2, etc.) is already negotiated during the connection establishment phase by LCP. With CHAP-type protocols, the `Authentication-Protocol` option specifies two values. The first value specifies that it is a CHAP-type authentication protocol, and the second value specifies the particular authentication protocol.

4.4.3.3 Extensible Authentication Protocol

Even though, in terms of frame format, EAP is very similar to CHAP, it is based on an entirely different philosophy. While in PAP, CHAP, or MS CHAP, the authentication protocol is negotiated by LCP during the connection establishment, in EAP, the only thing that is negotiated during this phase is the fact that EAP will be used. EAP is specified by RFC 2284.

The fact that both ends agree to use EAP doesn't mean that a specific authentication algorithm will be used—that is negotiated later by EAP itself. EAP therefore allows the use of an arbitrary authentication mechanism; it is sufficient to implement this mechanism on both sides of the connection. If EAP is used, the authentication phase has two steps: negotiation of the specific authentication algorithm (which we call the **authentication scheme**) and then the actual authentication. It is thus possible to implement authentication schemes that use various authentication calculators to generate one-time passwords; you can use TLS (RFC 2716) authentication and so on. At any rate, the EAP-MD5 scheme, which is a variant of CHAP, should be implemented as follows:

1. The side that verifies the identity of the other side sends an `EAP-Request` message in which it asks the other side to prove its identity.

2. If the side to be authenticated agrees with this authentication, it signals its agreement in the EAP-Response.

3. The side that verifies the identity of the other side sends an `EAP-Request` message (`Challenge`).

4. The side to be authenticated adds the shared secret (password) to the challenge and applies the MD5 one-way function to it. The result is entered into the `EAP-Response`.

5. The side that verifies the identity of the other side confirms the authentication with an EAP-Success message or refuses the authentication with an EAP-Failure message.

One very interesting aspect of authentication is an authentication scheme that uses the TLS protocol, namely EAP-TLS. This scheme utilizes server authentication (based on the server certificate) and user authentication (based on the user's personal certificate).

Windows 2000 (2003 or XP, as the case may be) supports the use of smart cards that bear a private key, which complements the public key from the certificate. In terms of security, using smart cards and the EAP-TLS scheme together provides numerous possibilities for providing access to Intranet servers through phone line connections. In practice, this looks as follows: the user start his or her laptop, but is not logged into the system, puts a smart card into the card-reader of the laptop, and enters his or her PIN. Using PPP, the system establishes a dial-up connection with the server. Authentication against the server is done via EAP-TLS. If the authentication is successful, the user's laptop is logged into the system and the connection with the server is established. The user can use the same smart card to log into an intranet computer via a LAN, but this has nothing to do with PPP.

Another advantage of the EAP-TLS scheme is that on both ends of the connection, a *master secret* is created, from where it is possible to 'chip off' encryption keys, shared secrets ensuring the integrity of transmitted data, and so on. The disadvantage of the EAP-TLS scheme is that the user's certificates must also be kept in the user database (i.e., it requires a PKI infrastructure). This specifically means that on Windows 2000/2003, Active Directory must be available. Therefore, the EAP-TLS scheme should be used in sophisticated solutions that are backed by well-designed projects.

A well-designed project can give employees who are on business trips or at home secure log-in access to an internal network through a phone line, which could be even safer than using VPN.

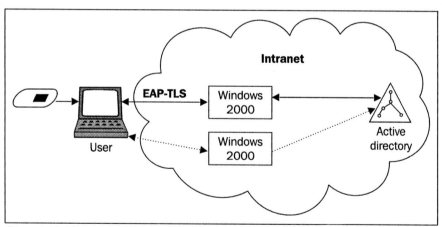

Figure 4.18: The user is authenticated using a chip card and EAP-TLS in Windows 2000/2003

4.4.3.4 Radius Protocol

The problem with authentication is that a client usually does not want to log into the same access server, but rather into various access servers. A classic example is connection to an Internet provider that has its **points of presence (POP)** in various cities. In this case, the authentication information would have to be kept in each access server. The idea here is to centralize the authentication information. There is one main server (or several back-up servers) in the network, which keeps authentication information for each user. In addition to authentication information, configuration information can also be kept (for example, the user's IP address, access filters, etc.).

The Internet provider's access server acts as a client for this type of server(s) and asks for the following specific service: to verify the authentication end user's response, or to provide an IP-address that is to be given to the user by IPCP protocol, and so on. The RADIUS protocol is currently widely used as the protocol between the access server and the server with authentication and configuration information. RADIUS is an application protocol.

In addition to RADIUS, there is also the **RADIUS Accounting Protocol**. With this protocol, Access Servers can pass among themselves information about users' logins and logouts. The RADIUS Accounting Server collects this information, which can later be used for various purposes such as charging Internet users. On Windows 2000/2003, Radius is a part of **Internet Authentication Service (IAS)**.

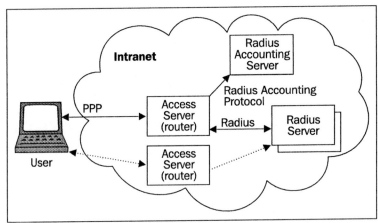

Figure 4.19: Radius and Radius Accounting protocols

4.4.4 Call-Back Control Protocol

The **Call-Back Control Protocol (CBCP)** serves to negotiate a call-back with dial-up lines. Basically, there are two possible call-back situations:

- The client establishes connection with the server and passes to the server the phone number it should call back. The server calls back without checking the number. In terms of security, this possibility doesn't provide anything new, except that the client doesn't have to pay for the call. A better scenario would be for the server to check in the database of users whether the number specified by the client is acceptable.

- The client establishes a connection with the server and doesn't pass the server a phone number. The server then finds the number in the database of users (don't forget that call-back negotiation is carried out only after the client is authenticated so that the server knows who is on the other side).

It must be emphasized that a call-back in which the server checks the phone number it is calling back has very strong potential in the area of security. In security jargon, this is called double-locking.

A potential hacker would not only have to break the authentication protocol, (which, in the case of EAP-TLS with a private key on a smart card, is very difficult), but would also have to break the telephone exchange security system in order to create a dial-up circuit leading to himself or herself instead of to the client. CBCP packets have the same format as LCP packets (the only difference is that the protocol number is C029 instead of C021). CBCP uses the following commands: CB-Request (code 1), CB-Response (code 2), and CB-Ack (code 3).

CBCP uses following options:

Code	Code Name	Description
1	No Call-Back	Without call-back or call-back to the phone number specified by the client.
2	Call-Back to user-specified number	Call-back to the phone number specified by the client.
3	Call-Back to administrator-defined number	Call-back to the phone number chosen from a database of users.
4	Call-Back to any number from a list of numbers	Server calls back to one phone number from the phone number list.

Table 4.4: CBCP options

When a client submits a phone number, the dialog is as follows:

1. The server sends a CB-Request with the No Call-Back option.
2. The client replies with a CB-Response command and the call-back to the user-specified number option that contains three pieces of data:
   o Time delay in the phone call.
   o The phone number type (for example, 01 for classical analog networks (PSTN) or ISDN networks).
   o The phone number.
3. The server confirms the result by CB-Ack command.

It can also be possible for the client to refuse to submit a phone number and for the established connection to carry on without a call-back.

When the server uses a phone number listed in the database of users, the dialog is as follows:

1. The server sends a CB-Request with the Call-Back to administrator-defined number option.
2. The client replies with a CB-Response command and the call-back to administrator-defined number option.
3. The server confirms the result with the CB-Ack command.

4.4.5 Other Protocols

4.4.5.1 Multilink Protocol

MP is specified by RFC 1990 and specifies how to use several physical lines between two computers at the same time. The result is that several lines create one virtual bundle—a thick wire.

Another important aspect for this protocol is that the individual lines that form the bundle can be physically based on various technologies (dial-up lines, leased lines, X.25, etc.). A classic example is a connection of both B channels in ISDN (Basic Rate).

The following figure shows an example of one-way communication:

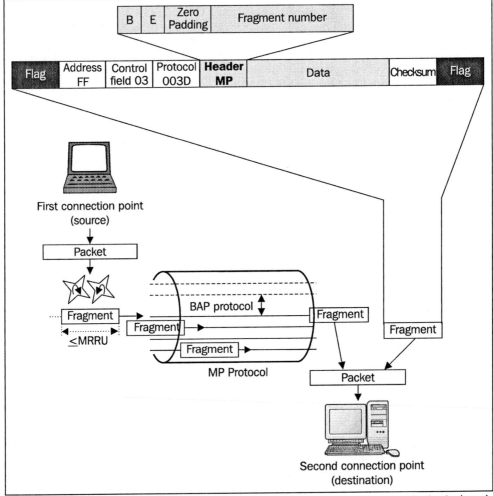

Figure 4.20: MP and BAP (this is a two-way connection, although only one-way communication is shown)

It is assumed in the figure opposite that the individual lines have already established a connection by LCP and with the help of the same protocol negotiated MP support. To achieve this, both sides have to mutually confirm the MRRU support option that includes the maximum packet size that both sides are able to assemble (1,500 bytes minimum). Both ends exchange their explicit identifications via the `Multiline-Endpoint-Discriminator` option.

This identification allows PPP to recognize that certain lines lead to the same computer (the other end of these lines has sent the same identification) and can therefore be put into the same bundle. The end of the line identification consists of the following two parts:

- The class it specifies as the address type (2=IP address, 3=Ethernet address, 5=phone number).

- The actual address. Windows uses Ethernet addresses. So, for example, if the phone connection lines are active, and you execute the `ipconfig` command with the `/all` switch, you will see that the system has created Ethernet addresses for the serial lines.

Once the bundle has been formed, it can carry packets. As shown in Figure 4.20, the sender takes a PPP packet consisting of the protocol number and data and inserts it into the bundle. But what if the bundle consists of several lines?

The process that the sender carries out is called **fragmentation** (not to be confused with IP fragmentation).

Packets can be (but don't need to be) cut into smaller pieces (fragments). Fragments are then inserted into individual lines. Fragments have a completely normal PPP frame format (as shown in Figure 4.13), but they use $003D_{16}$ as the protocol number. The MP header introduces the data field. The receiver reconstructs the original PPP packets (consisting of the protocol number and data) from the fragments.

The MP header contains the fragment number and the flags B and E. The header serves the following two purposes:

- Allows the reconstruction of original packets from the fragments.

- Makes sure that the packets are reconstructed in the same order as they were inserted into the virtual bundle. You have to remember that this is not on the network layer, so PPP knows nothing about IP properties, and IP doesn't take care of keeping the correct frame order. Moreover, certain protocols might not like changes in the frame order.

Numbers in the MP header serve to preserve the order of the fragments (the numbers are strictly incremental). The B (begin) and E flags (end) signal that the fragment carries the beginning (or the end) of the packet. If a fragment has the B and E bytes set up, it is a fragment carrying the whole (uncut) packet. The MP header is 4 bytes long, and the fragment number is 24 bits long and has a 6-bit padding containing zeros.

Using the **Short Sequence Number Header (SSNH)** option, it is possible to negotiate a 2-byte header. In this case, the padding is only 2-bits long and the remaining 12 bits carry the fragment number. The above mentioned options are LCP options with codes 17 to 19 (i.e., these options are negotiated during the 'establishing connection' phase).

4.4.5.2 Bandwidth Allocation Protocol and Bandwidth Allocation Control Protocol

These protocols are specified by RFC 2125, and they allow you to dynamically add or subtract individual lines from a line bundle (see Section 4.4.5.1). If BAP and BACP are implemented, then each line that establishes a connection must, during the connection establishment phase, specify its identification (within the computer) by the Line-Discriminator for BAP, which is an LCP option. Thus we have the following two different identifications negotiated by LCP during this phase:

- Multiline-Endpoint-Discriminator, which identifies the entire computer. This identifier uses MP.
- Line-Discriminator for BAP, which identifies a specific line within the bundle. Each side of the connection uses independent IDs.

After this point, the BACP is activated. It is a simple control protocol with a simple function. If both ends of the lines make a request to add or subtract a line from the bundle at the same time, then the BACP kicks in to solve the situation and it does this basically by throwing dice. The side with a smaller number wins and its requests will have priority. If both sides cast the same number, the throw is simply repeated.

To put in a slightly more technical way, BACP is a protocol whose packets have a similar format to LCP packets (protocol number $C02B_{16}$), so it uses the Configure-Request, Configure-Ack (when different numbers are cast), Configure-Nack (when the same numbers are cast), or Configure-Reject commands. These commands contain only one option, **Favored-Peer**, which carries a random 4-byte nonzero number. The side that is *favored* is the side that generates the smaller number. And they don't throw a die with six sides, but with 2^{32} sides.

The goal of BAP is to add and subtract lines. BAP uses the following commands:

Code	Command Name	Description
1	Call-Request	"I'd like to establish a connection through another line." (Before a side starts to add a line it has to be confirmed by the other side.)
2	Call-Response	Add-line request confirmed.
3	CallBack-Request	"I'd like to add a line, but you will have to dial it up. Do you agree?"
4	CallBack-Response	Add-line by a call-back request is confirmed.
5	Line-Drop-Query-Request	"I'd like to drop a line."
6	Line-Drop-Query-Response	Drop-line request is confirmed.
7	Call-Status-Indication	After the confirmation of the add-line request, the Call-Status-Indication option notifies whether it was successful or not.
8	Call-Status-Response	Response to Call-Status-Indication.

Table 4.5: BAP commands

Note that all these responses are of the 'request confirmation' type (i.e., the response doesn't say if the confirmation is positive or negative). We can get to know this even from the data segment of the response. This segment starts with 1 byte (8 bits), which contains the error code:

- 00000000—Request-Ack
- 00000001—Request-Nack
- 00000010—Request-Reject
- 00000011—Request-Full-Nak (the requested action is refused when, for example, the maximum or the minimum number of lines in the bundle has been reached)

The following options can be appended with the commands:

Code	Option Name	Description
1	Line-Type	Speed and type of line. The types are, for example, 0=ISDN, 1=X.25, 2=analog, and so on.
2	Phone-Delta	Contains information needed to dial the phone number (for example, the phone number itself).
3	No-Phone-Number-Needed	Information needed to dial the phone number is not transmitted. (For security reasons, you may not want to transmit the number.) It is saved in the configuration and due to security reasons, we do not want it to be transmitted.
4	Reason	The reason for adding or dropping a line (a text string).
5	Link-Discriminator	This is used when a line is taken away. It contains the identification of the line being removed (see the Line-Discriminator for BAP LCP option).
6	Call-Status	Information on the add-line status and on the action that follows a failed dial-up connection. Status codes are according to Q.931 (0 indicates a successful connection) and the actions can be 0=dialing won't be repeated and 1=dialing will be repeated.

Table 4.6: BAP options

4.4.5.3 Compression Control Protocol

CCP (specified in RFC 1962) serves to negotiate the data compression algorithm. PPP frames, carrying CCP packets, use protocol number $80FD_{16}$ and again their format is derived from LCP. If the connection is implemented by more than one line (MP) and it is a case of individual compression in a particular line, then protocol number $80FB_{16}$ is used.

It's enough to look at Figure 4.20 and realize that either a packet or a fragment can be compressed. Compression can take place either above the gear wheels (compression of the whole packet) or beneath them (fragment compression). If the compression takes place beneath the gear wheels, then, theoretically, it is possible to carry out compression only in certain lines and not in all of them (for example, if they use compression on the physical layer with the V.42bis protocol).

Data frames carrying compressed packets then use protocol number $00FD_{16}$ (or $00FB_{16}$), i.e., a compressed datagram. If compression fails (for example, the compressed packet would be bigger than the original one), an uncompressed packet is sent. The protocol number tells the receiver whether to carry out decompression or not.

CCP generally serves to negotiate the compression algorithm. The commands it uses are similar to LCP commands and they are: `Configure-Request`, `Configure-Ack`, `Configure-Nak`, `Configure-Reject`, `Terminate-Request`, `Terminate-Ack`, and `Code-Reject` with codes 1 to 7. There are two special commands in CCP:

- `Reset-Request` (code=14): It is recommended that compressed data is periodically compared with a checksum. If the receiver finds out that the compression failed, i.e., the checksum failed, then by means of the `Reset-Request` command, it requests that the sender initiates (resets) all its compression counters, dictionaries, etc. In other words, it starts compression from the beginning.

- `Reset-Ack` (code=15): When the sender resets all its counters and dictionaries, it informs the receiver about it by means of the `Reset-Ack` command. The receiver also has to carry out a reset to be able to decompress incoming data correctly.

Options serve to negotiate a particular algorithm. If this negotiation fails, it doesn't matter, because communication still goes on without compression. Option codes then correspond to individual algorithms. For example, Stac LZS has code 17, MPPC has code 18, and so on.

A particular negotiated compression algorithm is specified by the following standards:

- RFC 1967: PPP LZS-DCP Compression Protocol.
- RFC 1974: PPP Stac LZS Compression Protocol.
- RFC 2118: Microsoft Point-To-Point Compression (MPPC) Protocol.

When data is compressed, its encryption can be carried out. To do it the in the reverse order is not very efficient, because encrypted data (gibberish) cannot be compressed very much.

4.4.5.4 Encryption Control Protocol

ECP (specified in RFC 1968) serves to negotiate an encryption algorithm. This protocol *doesn't* serve to exchange encryption keys. Its syntax is similar to CCP syntax, including `Reset-Request` and `Reset-Ack` commands. The principal difference shows itself when both ends cannot agree on a particular algorithm. This could be a problem depending on both sides; the configuration and communication may be terminated in such a case. For example, in Figure 4.17, it is decided a connection should be made even if encryption is not available.

There are standards that specify agreements on particular algorithms, for example, RFC 3078. It specifies that **Microsoft Point-To-Point Encryption (MPPE)** Protocol uses RC4 encryption. A part of MPPE is also an agreement on the length of the encryption key (40, 56, or 128 bytes).

4.4.5.5 Setting Encryption Keys

If we have agreed on the encryption algorithm, the only things we need to keep happy are the encryption keys. PPP derives encryption keys from the information that both sides exchanged during the authentication phase. We have to realize that for authentication by, for example, one of the CHAP protocols, both sides have to share a secret. The shared secret is essentially like a symmetrical encryption key. However, when the shared secret is used directly as a symmetrical encryption key, it could make the secret's disclosure quite easy. Therefore, the shared secret is *ground* by one-way functions and, as a spice, a random string challenge is also added to the *grinder*.

RFC 3079 derives keys for use with Microsoft Point-to-Point Encryption (MPPE) and specifies the derivation of encryption keys in the case of authentication by MS CHAP version 1 and MS CHAP version 2 protocols.

RFC 3079 also specifies the derivation of encryption keys in the case of authentication by EAP-TLS. If we use EAP-TLS authentication, we already have the so-called *master secret* created on both sides, from which we 'chip off' individual encryption keys (different ones for each direction of communication). After that, we can start to secure the communication in the way TLS protocol does. If the system is used in a well thought out way, EAP-TLS represents a rather high level of security. Without much experience, however, it can cause trouble.

4.4.6 Internet Protocol Control Protocol

After a connection between both ends has been established, authentication has been carried out, and the possible use of several lines as well as the compression and encryption have been agreed upon, individual network protocols enter into operation. Each network protocol must negotiate the opening of communication by its own control protocol.

IPCP is an NCP protocol for IP version 4 (see RFC 1332), i.e., IPCP is the control protocol for IP. The IPCP frame format is similar to the LCP frame format, but its protocol number is 8021_{16} (see Figure 4.13).

Code	Command Name	Description
1	Configure-Request	Configuration packet carrying requests for the change of implicit parameters.
2	Configure-Ack	Configuration packet with positive confirmation of the requests for the change of implicit line parameters. For example, all the requested changes of parameters are accepted.
3	Configure-Nak	Configuration packet with the response that the opposite side doesn't accept all the requests for the change of line parameters. The ones that are not accepted are specified in this packet. The rest of the requests made are accepted (i.e., requests not specified in the Configure-Nak packet are accepted).
4	Configure-Reject	Configuration packet refusing all requests. It can also be a consequence of an invalid request code.
5	Terminate-Request	Request for connection termination (termination of IP transmission).
6	Terminate-Ack	Confirmation of the request for connection termination.
7	Code-Reject	Request refused due to an unknown code. It can also be caused by the fact that the opposite station uses a different version of the protocol.

Table 4.7: IPCP commands

IPCP uses the following options:

Type	Option Name	Description
2	IP-Compression-Protocol	Compression of an IP header. The data field of this option contains the numberical identification of the compression protocol, for example, $002D_{16}$ for 'classical' compression according to RFC 1144, described in CSLIP part. For Van Jacobson compression, perfected in RFC 2507 to 2509, the data field contains 0061_{16}. Compression parameters follow the compression protocol number. For classical Van Jacobson compression, it carries two 1-byte parameters: Max Slot ID (the highest slot number will be from zero up to this number) and Comp Slot ID (if it's set to 0, the slot number cannot be left out even in a succession of compressed packets from the same data flow). Packets compressed according to RFC 2507 have, according to RFC 2507, the following parameters: TCP_SPACE, NON_TCP_SPACE, and so on.
3	IP-Address	Passing an IP address to the other side. This allows you to dynamically assign IP addresses. If a site wants to use a different IP address, it responds with a Configure-Nak packet, where this address is specified.
129	Primary-DNS-Address	Primary name server specification. The data field contains a 4-byte IP address of the primary name server.
130	Primary-NBNS-server-address	Primary WINS server.
131	Secondary-DNS-Address	Secondary name server.
132	Secondary-NBNS-server-address	Secondary WINS server.

Table 4.8: IPCP options

In PPP, protocol identification uses the following values for IP:

- 0021_{16} for the IP without any Van Jacobson's compression
- $002d_{16}$ for the Van Jacobson compressed TCP/IP
- $002f_{16}$ for the Van Jacobson uncompressed TCP/IP

In the case of compression, the situation is more complicated because not all packets have a compressed header. It is therefore necessary to differentiate between the transmitted packets, distinguishing the ones with a compressed TCP/IP header and the ones with an uncompressed one (for example, the first packets in the flow).

Therefore in a PPP frame, the header (in the Protocol field) of an uncompressed packet has the identification $002F_{16}$ (Protocol field in the IP-header is replaced by a slot number) and packets with a compressed IP-header have the identification $002D_{16}$.

Here is an example of a PPP protocol frame carrying the Configure-Request command of IPCP caught by a Network monitor program during communication between Windows XP and Windows server:

```
Frame: Base frame properties
+ PPP: Unknown Frame (0x0)
   IPCP: Configuration Request, Ident = 0x05
```

```
IPCP: Code = Configuration Request
IPCP: Identifier = 5 (0x5)
IPCP: Length = 16 (0x10)
IPCP: Option: Compression Prot. = 0x002D (Van Jacobson Compr. TCP/IP)
   IPCP: Option Type = Compression Protocol
   IPCP: Option Length = 6 (0x6)
   IPCP: Compression Protocol = Van Jacobson Compressed TCP/IP
   IPCP: Max Slot ID = 15 (0xF)
   IPCP: Comp Slot ID = Slot Identifier may be compressed
IPCP: Option: Address = 10.1.1.1
   IPCP: Option Type = Address
   IPCP: Option Length = 6 (0x6)
      IPCP: Source Address = 10.1.1.1
```

Please notice that classical Van Jacobson compression (RFC 1144) with Max Slot ID and Comp Slot Id parameters is requested.

4.5 Frame Relay

Frame Relay is a link-layer protocol used for large networks. It is specified in the following standards: I.122, I.441, and ANSI TI.606 and mostly in the standards of the **Frame Relay Forum (FRF)** group. See http://www.mfaforum.org.

Frame relay is usually used in permanent virtual circuits (dial-up lines are theoretically possible as well, but haven't seen them in reality yet). A permanent virtual circuit is similar to a leased line. A user would rent virtual circuits in his or her particular locality from a Frame Relay provider.

A Frame Relay is a datagram-oriented and connectionless service; so unnumbered frames are transferred by it. The provider doesn't guarantee the frame delivery. Each frame contains a checksum, so it is possible to check that the packet wasn't changed during the transfer. A damaged packet is discarded.

The primary parameter of a virtual circuit is the amount of data that can be transferred by the user to the virtual circuit within the time interval **Tc**. This quantity will be known as the **bandwidth interval**, and we will also use the abbreviation **Bc** for it. A rate Bc/Tc is used more often and is known as **Committed Information Rate (CIR)**. CIR tells us how much data a user can transfer to a Frame Relay network within a certain time unit. CIR is an abstraction because it is not possible to transfer the exact amount of data in one second that the averaged CIR says. That is because data are transferred to the network in whole frames and not just in parts. We are talking about a theoretical average.

A user makes an agreement with the provider on CIR for a particular bandwidth (for example, 64 Kbps) according to the user's needs. The user can also go over the agreed level during rush hour. Of course, everything is for a certain fee, so the user may make an agreement on another speed as well. It is called **Excess Burst Rate (BE)**. BE indicates how many bytes a user can go over the Bc in a Tc time interval.

Frame Relay is designed for speeds from 56 Kbps to 2 Mbps. But it is still effective even when reaching speeds of 100 Mbps. So when you rent a leased line from a public telephone network provider to interconnect, for example, four localities, you'll need four leased lines. You'll have three modems in each locality and three connected interfaces on the router. The following figure shows us the large site of a hypothetical company, which is situated in Berlin, Munich, Dortmund, and Cologne.

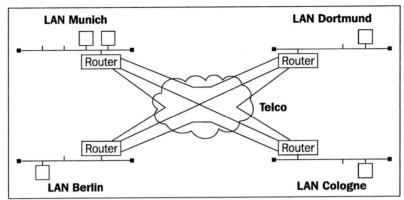

Figure 4.21: WAN based on leased lines

A Frame Relay provider, in contrast, runs its own data network as shown below:

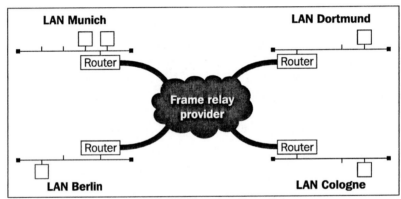

Figure 4.22: WAN based on Frame Relay

A user (customer) is connected to this network in particular localities usually with one line with a higher capacity. That user trusts data frames to the Frame Relay network provider and expects them to be delivered to the user's other localities. The provider's network is constructed from Frame Relay switches that transfer trusted frames between each other. The user actually doesn't care through which switches his or her frame is traveling; he or she probably doesn't even care if there's a Frame Relay protocol inside the provider's network.

It's enough to have one interface on a router in each locality and one line on the closest access point of a Frame Relay provider to connect all the desired localities.

Virtual circuits will be established between particular localities as shown in the following figure:

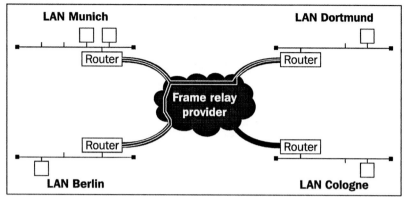

Figure 4.23: Virtual circuits

In this figure, we can see that virtual circuits have been established between Munich and Dortmund, Munich and Berlin, and Berlin and Dortmund. A network with the same topology as a network where the particular localities are connected with leased lines is created. But instead of leased lines, we have virtual circuits.

The physical line that is connecting, for example, the Berlin locality with a Frame Relay network serves two virtual circuits at the same time. The Frame Relay provider has created a large private network according to the customer's desire with the help of virtual circuits. But the Frame Relay provider has many customers and can create a private WAN for every one of them. The classical case of connecting a customer to the Frame Relay network is not that the actual computer would connect to the Frame Relay network. A router is connected to the Frame Relay and single computers are connected with the router in the locality by a local network.

Between the router of the user and the closest Frame Relay switch, there's a user-network interface defined (see Figure 4.24). The customer trusts his or her frames to the provider on this interface. A Frame Relay's characteristics that we're talking about are bound by this interface. The customer doesn't care what's inside. It's similar to data networks based on the X.25 protocol. X.25 is just an interface between the provider and the user.

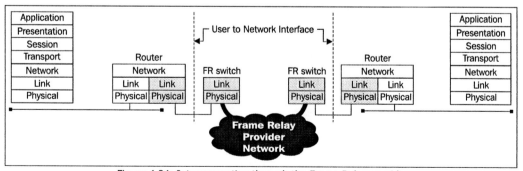

Figure 4.24: Interconnection through the Frame Relay provider

In the physical layer within Frame Relay networks, V.35 and X.21 interfaces are used. Circuits with synchronous transfer are used (clocks are generated by the Frame Relay network).

The frame has a lot of lines to go through on its way through the circuit from the source to the end. There's a line between the user and provider (user-network interface). Further, it has the particular lines from one Frame Relay switch to another on its way and at the end there is a user-network interface again. Every virtual circuit is identified with a **Data Link Connection Identifier (DLCI)**. DLCI is a part of Frame Relay header. If there are, for example, two virtual circuits going from one location to other locations, then particular locations differ by DLCI in the header frame.

A Frame Relay protocol header usually has 10 bits for DLCI; so DLCI values ranges from 0 to 1023. Adding DLCI usually follows these rules:

DLCI	Rules
0	LMI
1-15	Reserved
16-991	Virtual circuits
992-1007	Two-layer management
1008-1022	Reserved
1023	Virtual circuits management

Table 4.9: DLCI values

In Figure 4.25, a frame changes its DLCI gradually on its way from Berlin to Dortmund. The user in Berlin gives the frame with DLCI=22 to the Frame Relay provider. A switch, in its configuration table, has to change the DLCI to 32 and transfer the incoming frame from interface 1 to interface 2 (Dortmund locality of our customer through switch 2). Switch 2 is configured to change the DLCI from 32 to 62 (Dortmund locality of our customer through switch 3). Switch 3 is configured to change the DLCI from 62 to 92 and gives the frame to the end user.

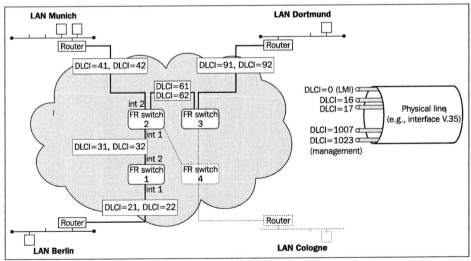

Figure 4.25: DLCI

From a customer's point of view, the situation is much easier. When customers want to send a frame from Berlin to Dortmund, they just fill the DLCI frame header with 22 and can be sure that they will receive it in Dortmund with DLCI=92. In addition, when a frame is sent with DLCI=21 from Berlin, then it is received in Munich with DLCI=41. Contrariwise, when a DLCI=41 frame is sent from Munich, it is received in Berlin with DLCI=21.

DLCI might be used within a Frame Relay network because of the following:

- It is unique in the context of the whole network of a Frame Relay provider.
- It is unique in the context of one Frame Relay switch.
- It is unique in the context of one Frame Relay switch interface.

4.5.1 A Frame Relay Protocol Frame

A Frame Relay protocol frame, unlike an HDLC frame, doesn't have an independent address and control field. It has the common field of the header, which contains the DLCI and other control information. A header is 2 to 4 bytes long. Usually, we see headers of 2 bytes in length (that is 10 bits for DLCI).

A header can have 2, 3, or 4 bytes. Each byte of the header contains an **EA** bit, which indicates whether the following byte is still part of the header or if it is a part of the transmitted data. If EA=0, the following byte is part of the header; if EA=1, this byte is the last byte of the header.

The DLCI field is the identification of a virtual circuit. The DLCI can be unique only within a concrete network interface, within one Frame Relay switch, or within the whole network. We usually meet DLCIs that are unique within a concrete network interface.

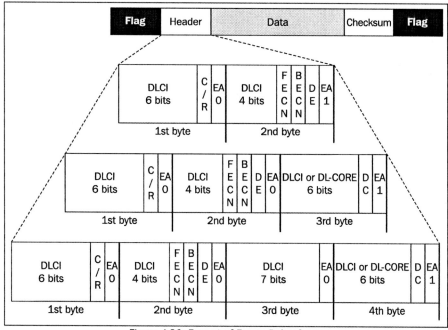

Figure 4.26: Format of Frame Relay frame

Bit **C/R** defines if it's a command (C) or response (R). Within a header 3 or 4 bytes long, we have a **DC** bit as well, which when set to 0, specifies that the last six bits are part of the DLCI. If it's set to 1, then the last six bits carry DL-CORE.

By setting **Discard Eligibility (DE)**, you signal that the frame may be discarded (a frame set like that has less importance). For example, when sending frames above the average line capacity (CIR), you can set the DE bit to 1. Then if the network is not able to transmit all the frames, it throws away first the frames with DE set to 1.

We still have **Backward Explicit Congestion Notification (BECN)** and **Forward Explicit Congestion Notification (FECN)** bits to look at.

Even though setting these bits is not obligatory, we'll take a closer look at them. We can solve the problem of congestion of the virtual circuit with their help. When sending data by a virtual circuit from one end to the other, it doesn't matter when some packets get lost (for example, on the TCP layer, the transmission will be repeated). The problem is with the congestion of the virtual circuit, which means there is some bottleneck along the way that is not able to send the frames with the desired speed. At such a point, frames are stored in buffers until the memory is full and other frames have to be discarded. We call this situation **line congestion**.

Loss of frames means that the higher layers have to request retransmission of the higher layer packets. Or it can even cause the loss of connection, so that the connection has to be re-established. In both cases, it means higher amount of transmitted data and bigger overhead.

When the line is overloaded, every other (even small) traffic increase is congesting the line even more and the line has less throughput. On the TCP protocol layer, the communication has to be renewed repeatedly until the connection is closed. The user is angry and he or she thinks that there is a network breakdown. The solution is in the response time prolongation on the virtual circuit. This means that the virtual circuit will be acting as if it has smaller throughput on the output. So the virtual circuit is getting the user's frames with less speed, but it tries to deliver those frames. The user thinks that the link slows down, but it at least doesn't seem to be not working.

In the case of congestion of the virtual circuit, the network signals to the sender by turning the BECN bit on and to the receiver by turning on the FECN bit (by sender and receiver, I mean the user's router on the user-network interface, see Figure 4.27).

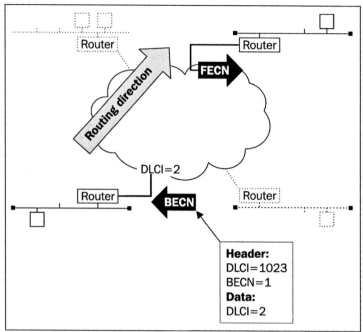

Figure 4.27: Frame Relay Congestion Notification

If the network is overloaded, the BECN and FECN bits are set. The network knows about the overload if it has prepared to throw away frames or it has already begun to do this. The network can also predict the congestion by finding out that some line is close to overloading when controlling the queue of gathered frames on the Frame Relay network points.

Setting the BECN and FECN bits is not pursued through the usual data links (data DLCI). A service DLCI=1023 is reserved for such a signal, whose frames are sent to the user on the user-network interface by the Frame Relay network. In the data part, such a service frame has a structure derived from the XID command frame of the HDLC protocol (U-frames of the XID commandof the HDLC protocol are used for commands and responses that carry configuration information). In our case, the XID command carries the DLCI number of the congested virtual circuit. Figure 4.27 shows us the situation when the disturbed virtual circuit has DLCI=2 on the sender side.

The problem is that the user's access router will get, via a BECN bit, information that the virtual circuit is congested. But is it possible for the router to lower the line load? It has to be intelligent enough to signal the load to the higher layer.

In the case of the Internet, IP is used as the higher layer (in Figure 4.28, it's the highest layer of the router).

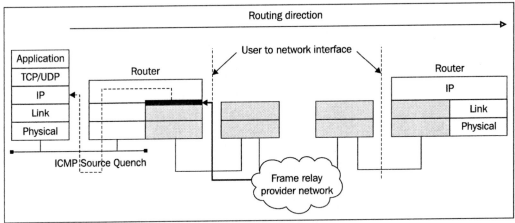

Figure 4.28: BECN signalization

The router has to contain support for this on the border of the Frame Relay and IP protocols. Support for link congestion treatment can lie in several mechanisms. IP has its own mechanism for the treatment of congested lines with the help of the ICMP protocol. A router that is forced to throw away an IP packet due to congestion, informs the sender of the IP packet by an ICMP datagram **Source Quench**.

After receiving the Source Quence ICMP, the receiver lowers the TCP connection speed. (Let's note that Source Quench is not used with the UDP protocol.)

The router checks the proportion of received frames with the BECN bit set at regular intervals on each virtual circuit. If the proportion is large, it begins to generate a Source Quench response in ICMP protocol for the incoming packets on the actual virtual circuit.

There are other options as well. For example, the access router doesn't process the BECN frames at all. Then on the TCP/IP protocol layer, TCP segments can be lost. The connection might seem to be not working.

Another option is that the user's access router can work not only with the third layer (IP protocol), but with the fourth layer as well (TCP protocol). Thus, the router could correct the window length directly in the TCP segments header or could artificially hold up the responses from the other side. The source would think that the line has a longer response to the destination, so it would lower the rate of sending TCP packets. But interventions into the TCP on the router are considered to be indelicate.

4.5.2 IP Through Frame Relay

If we look at Figure 4.29 with the Frame Relay protocol frame, we will not find a field that carries identification of a higher layer protocol. With the help from such a field, we could easily and effectively put packets of different network protocol into a link frame (in our case, into the Frame Relay frame). This problem is solved by RFC 2427 (Multi-protocol over Frame relay). A frame according to RFC 2427 is shown in the following figure:

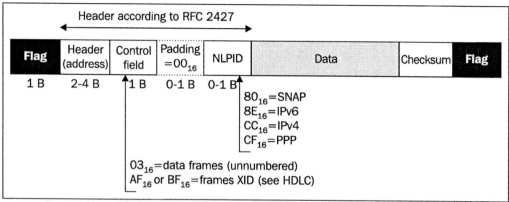

Figure 4.29: RFC 2427 Frame Relay frame format (see Figure 4.26 for header field 'Header')

This frame has the following added to it:

- A Control field derived from an HDLC control field, because Frame Relay uses unnumbered frames. The control field has, in the case of a data frame, value=3.

- Padding that contains binary zeros to ensure the even length of the whole header according to RFC 2427. So it's used when the Header (address) field has 3 bytes.

- A **Network Layer Protocol ID (NLPID)** field containing the higher-layer protocol. Unfortunately, it has only one byte. Therefore we cannot count on all protocols of a higher layer having their own number. For this reason, **Sub-Network Access Protocol (SNAP)** headers are added carrying higher-layer protocol identification; SNAP has 80_{16} as it's own NLPID identification (see Figure 4.30).

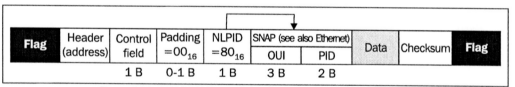

Figure 4.30: RFC 2427 Frame Relay frame format with SNAP header

A SNAP header contains an OUI field which identifies the organization that assigns higher-layer protocol numbers for the **Protocol Identifier (PID)** field. For example, an OUI containing zeros carries in the PID field any the same numbers that the Ethernet II protocol uses (for example, 0800_{16} for IP and so on). Because a SNAP header is 3 bytes long, the padding field is used only in the case that the Header (address) field is 2 bytes long. We can theoretically use three forms of Frame Relay frames for the IP protocol:

- A standard form of a frame according to the Figure 4.26, which contains neither the control field nor the NLPID field. The IP datagram is added directly into the data part.

- A frame according to RFC 2427 (without SNAP) when the NLPID field has a value CC_{16} (IPv4 protocol)

- A frame according to RFC 2427 with a SNAP header when the NLPID field has a value 80_{16}. The OUI field only contains zeros and the PID field has a value of 800_{16}.

There's another option possible. Within this option, we put PPP protocol into the Frame Relay frames (PPP in Frame Relay) and then into PPP we put IP. This alternative is specified in RFC 1973. It's derived from RFC 2427 (without SNAP), where the NLPID field has a value CF_{16}. It's an option for the PPP protocol that doesn't use HDLC encapsulation, but Frame Relay encapsulation.

4.5.3 Local Management Interface

We can use a Frame Relay network in a way where we mechanically put frames into a virtual circuit, take them out on the other side, and do not care about anything else. But a Frame Relay network is mostly able to give other information as well, such as various statistics, accounting information, information about any concrete interface that may have been connected, disconnected, configured, and so on. This communication works on the **Local Management Interface (LMI)** protocol.

For such information, the DLCI service with number zero is used, where the user exchanges with Frame Relay frames (carrying LMI), frames with appropriate information. During router configuration, we write in the type of the LMI protocol implementation.

4.5.4 Frame Relay Configuration on CISCO Routers

It's necessary to understand that a Frame Relay provider will probably place a synchronous baseband modem on our site (a modem that works in the base band), which we connect with, for example, a V.35 cable. So all the virtual circuits (all DLCIs) will be connected to one serial interface (they will be physically in one cable). Let's say they will be connected to the interface 'Serial 1'.

Each data DLCI will create a sub-interface and it will be marked in CISCO configuration with the suffix .1, .2, and so on (for example, Serial 1.1). We don't explicitly configure the DLCI service even if we activate, for example, LMI by a special command.

Frame Relay protocol can use standard encapsulation as shown in Figure 4.26 (frame-relay encapsulation) or encapsulation according to RFC 2427 (frame-relay IETF encapsulation).

Example (DLCI=112):

```
Interface Serial 1
 no ip address
 encapsulation frame-relay IETF
 frame-relay lmi-type cisco
!
interface Serial 1.1 point-to-point
 ip address naka
 no ip directed-broadcast
  frame-relay interface-dlci 112
```

4.5.5 Frame Relay Protocol

The customer usually agrees with the Frame Relay provider on the following:

- The localities that will be connected with the virtual circuit.
- The Committed Information Rate (CIR) and Excess Burst Rate (BE).

- The BECN and FECN bits setting. The user has to think about how to use them if the user's routers are able to use these bits.

- The line that connects the user and the provider (connection such as leased line, fiber optic, radio relay, etc.). Usually the Frame Relay provider provides the lines to connect its network with the user as well. It's very important to know which physical interface (V.35, X.21, and so on) will be used, so you would know which connection cable you're supposed to buy for your router.

A frequent question is: What is the difference between Frame Relay and a public X.25 network? Frame Relay is just a link-layer protocol (X.25 is a network layer protocol), so Frame Relay users usually don't have some unique worldwide address. The second difference is that Frame Relay is a datagram service, so the frame delivery is not guaranteed. X.25 stores data that couldn't be processed into its buffer and transmits it gradually. A common characteristic is that both protocols create virtual circuits.

4.6 Local Area Networks

Local Area Networks with transmission rates ranging between 10 Mbps and 10 Gbps belong among medium-speed networks. The aim of the LAN is to interconnect computers (and other communication appliances such as routers) within one or several buildings in a campus so they can mutually communicate. When using optical cables, the LAN can cover several miles.

Many different LAN systems have been developed over the last few years, although, just two of them have become more widespread: Ethernet and, to a lesser extent, the FDDI. (You can also come across the Token Ring system by IBM, but this usually applies only to users that are fully equipped with IBM appliances.)

In order to connect a computer to the LAN, we have to insert the appropriate network card first. The LAN link protocols are partially executed directly in the network card.

The LAN comprises of the following parts:

- Cabling belongs to the physical layer.

- Network cards are inserted into computers and other devices. This is part of both the physical and the link layer since part of the software for dealing with the link layer is executed directly within the network cards.

- Link protocol (including link frames and their handshake).

Several LAN systems have been created independently from each other. Ethernet II is still used. Some years ago, the **Institute of Electrical and Electronics Engineers (IEEE)** came up with a project. The aim of this project was to unify existing initiatives and work out standards for particular LAN types (for example, Ethernet, Arcnet, Token Ring, and so on). These standards described the **Media Access Control (MAC)** layer for each type. The IEEE 802.3 standard was created for Ethernet, IEEE 802.4 for Token Bus, IEEE 802.5 for Token Ring, and so on.

A joint standard, IEEE 802.2, was created for the **Logical Link Control (LLC)** layer of all systems.

In other words, the LAN link layer has been divided into two sub-layers. The bottom MAC layer—partially overlapping the physical layer—deals with access to the communication medium. The top LLC layer enables you to initiate, administer, and terminate logical connections between individual LAN stations.

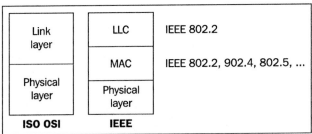

Figure 4.31: IEEE 802 architecture

ISO has taken over the IEEE standards. So ISO 8802-2 originates in the IEEE 802.2 standard, ISO 8802-3 in the IEEE 802.3 standard, and so on.

4.6.1 Ethernet

The Ethernet protocol was originally developed by DEC, Intel, and Xerox. Its 10 MHz version is known as Ethernet II. As stated above, the IEEE later normalized the Ethernet protocol as the 802.3 standard. This standard was taken over by ISO and published as ISO 8802-3. The frame format according to the Ethernet II standard slightly differs from the ISO 8802-3 standard. Gradually, the IEEE 802.3u standard for 100 MHz Ethernet (Fast Ethernet) and the IEEE 802.3z standard for 1 GHz (Gigabyte Ethernet) were created.

Originally 10BASE5 thick coaxial cable was used for Ethernet distribution. A coaxial cable, which could be only up to 500 meters in length, constituted one local network segment. The thick Ethernet segment (as it was often referred to) mostly consisted of one piece of coaxial cable. Transceivers would connect to the coaxial cable, connecting to the AUI ports of Ethernet cards added to computers. The DB15 connector would be usually used for the AUI port.

10BASE5 means that it is a network using the transmission frequency of 10 MHz (that, for Ethernet, also equals the theoretical transmission rate of the network).

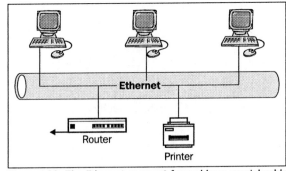

Figure 4.32: The Ethernet segment formed by a coaxial cable

The massive expansion of Ethernet came with the use of thin coaxial cable. The thin coaxial cable is interrupted at each station with a BNC connector welded or pressed by using special tongs onto both ends of the interruption. A BNC-T connector is inserted between two BNC connectors. The third BNC connector outlet is fixed directly onto the BNC connector of the Ethernet network card in the computer. There are also transceivers for thin Ethernet; the BNC-T connector then connects onto the thin Ethernet transceiver, and the cable leading from the transceiver connects onto the AUI port of the computer.

Thin Ethernet, known as 10BASE2, can form a segment of a maximum length of 185 meters. If the same auxilliary network cards are used in the segment, then with some types of these cards, it is possible to extend the segment to 300-400 meters.

The LAN segment length is maximum at 500 (or 185–300) meters. A LAN can be extended by using several segments that are interconnected by repeaters. A repeater is a box with two or more network interfaces that are mutually interconnected. If a data frame appears at one of the interfaces, it is automatically repeated to all others. A repeater may have both AUI and BNC ports, so some segments might use thin Ethernet while others use thick Ethernet.

A pair of optical cables may be used between two repeaters; this type is sometimes referred to as 10BASE-F. The length of the optical interconnection of two repeaters may reach 1 km.

The repeater might also use ports for twisted-pairs. However, the situation for twisted-pairs somewhat differs. A twisted-pair (to be more precise, two pairs of wires) is an connection between the repeater and the computer. This is more like the transceiver-AUI-connector interface (although, it does not have a power supply).

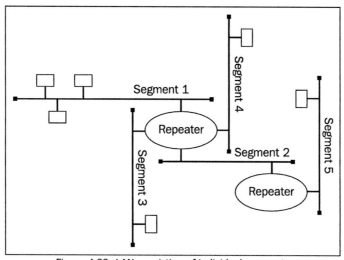

Figure 4.33: LAN consisting of individual segments

The repeater (as opposed to the coaxial cable) is the core of a network consisting of twisted-pairs. The twisted-pairs come out of the repeater in a star formation, connecting particular computers. A repeater for twisted-pairs is referred to as a **Hub** (hub was used for the active element of star-shaped networks).

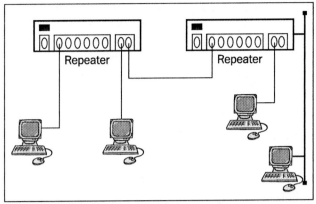

Figure 4.34: HUB (repeater)

The connection between the repeater and the computer is formed by two twisted-pairs (four wires). It is a duplex connection with one pair for each channel. From the viewpoint of the computer, one pair is used for transmission, the other one for reception. Hubs used for twisted-pairs can be mutually interconnected. Note that what is transmission to one is reception to the other, so the pairs must be mutually crossed in the patch cord (similarly to null modems). Most often, hubs are supplied with a switch fixed to one of the ports causing the pairs to cross. So a *normal* patch cord can be used, connecting it to the port with a switch that is set to the relevant position.

Ethernet using twisted-pairs is referred to as 10BASE-T. There are also a ten times faster version of Ethernet referred to as 100BASE-TX and Gigabyte Ethernet referred to as 1000BASE-CX.

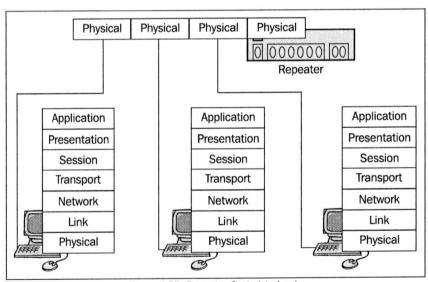

Figure 4.35: Repeater for twisted-pair

(Repeaters cannot be used for combining 10BASE-T, 100BASE-TX, and 1000BASE-CX. A switch must be used to interconnect them.) The length of the twisted-pair between a repeater and a station can normally be up to 100 meters.

From the network model point of view, the repeater (hub) functions on the physical layer. Communication over a LAN using repeaters between computers is transparent, i.e., the computers on the LAN communicate to each other without knowing about the repeaters existence.

A bridge also interconnects individual LAN segments, though unlike a repeater it does not repeat mechanically all the frames that appear at one of its ports. A **bridge** is a specialized computer that works with a bridging table. The table contains a list of all the link addresses (MAC addresses) of all of the LAN's network interfaces.

In the bridging table, each address has information behind which the network interface of the bridge is located. If the data frame appears on some network interface of the bridge, the bridge looks at the destination address in the data frame and (using the bridging table) finds out behind which interface the address is located. It then only repeats the frame onto the interface where the destination address is located. If it is the same interface, the frame is not repeated at all. Logically, broadcasts are repeated into all interfaces.

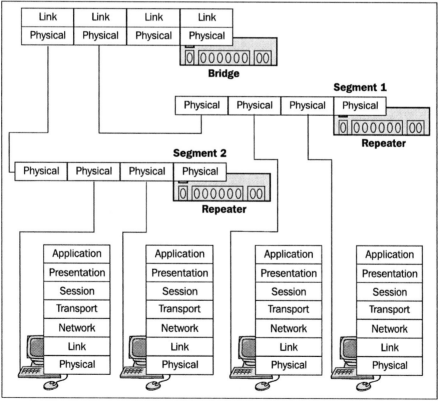

Figure 4.36: Bridge

The possible size of the bridging table, i.e., how much memory is allotted to it, is an important bridge parameter. The most important of all, however, is how to fill this table with correct data. One of the possible answers is that the network administrator inserts the data manually. This might sound ridiculous, but it is a suitable solution for high-security networks. In this case, the LAN administrator sets exactly who can communicate with whom. At present, the bridges are supplemented with another table that is a reversed version of the bridging table listing who is *not* allowed to communicate with whom.

How can data be filled into the table automatically? The algorithm is very simple. The bridge works similarly to a repeater when it is turned on, i.e., it repeats everything onto all interfaces. However, it checks the source address of all incoming frames. The bridge knows what the source interface is, so the source address as well as the relevant interface can be inserted into the bridging table as a new entry.

It is possible to have several bridges in one LAN. The frame handover between individual interfaces of the bridges may not be as fast as with repeaters (the response time can be longer). In some cases, it can be useful to interconnect two bridges by, for example, a serial line with modems or a laser connection.

The repeater is the core of LAN segments. Individual segments are interconnected via bridges. Computers that communicate with each other more intensely, such as computers within one department, share a common segment. It is advantageous to connect, for example, the router to the Internet or central servers to separate ports of the bridge. The bridge is used to separate the traffic between particular segments.

Another solution is to use a bridge with a high number of ports while not using repeaters for individual network segments. This solution is sometimes referred to as **switched Ethernet**. The core of switched Ethernet is the intelligent bridge that starts to process another frame immediately after it has recognized to which interface it should repeat the previous frame. Such a bridge has already been referred to as a **switch**.

Switches are powerful bridges that can repeat frames not only between individual Ethernet segments, but also between, for example, Ethernet and Fast Ethernet, Ethernet and FDDI, and so on. The switch has to not only change the frame format from, say, Ethernet to FDDI, but it also has to cope with different transmission rates. When transferring data, problems occur between fast segments (FDDI) and, for example, Ethernet, since FDDI can deliver data at a rate that Ethernet cannot handle. Frames must be stored in the buffer memory of the switch.

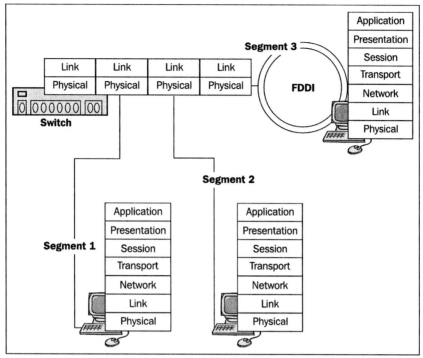

Figure 4.37: Switch

The CSMA/CD protocol is used for exchanging data between stations on Ethernet. Within this protocol all LAN stations are equal. If any of the stations needs to transmit, it listens on the LAN to find out whether any other station is transmitting. If the medium is not used (i.e., no other station is transmitting), the station can start transmitting. However, two stations might have decided to transmit at the same moment. So besides transmitting data, the station keeps listening to check whether another one has started transmitting at the same time. Should another station start transmitting, a collision occurs. For other stations to be capable of detecting such a collision, the two stations cannot cease the transmission immediately, but keep transmitting characters of no importance for a while, then they both stop transmitting at a randomly chosen moment.

The denser the traffic on Ethernet, the higher the probability of collisions. A reasonable workload for the network is approximately 20%. So for an Ethernet of 10 MHz frequency, the throughput of the network is calculated for approximately 2 Mbps, i.e., 256 Kbps.

If we have a segment with only two stations, a collision might also occur on the coaxial cable. The situation is different if the segment containing two stations is linked by a twisted-pair that has separate pairs for transmitting and receiving. Network cards then switch into the full duplex mode in which both stations can transmit and receive data at the same time. This is referred to as a **collision-free segment**. In these segments, speeds close to the theoretical maximum may be achieved. If the LAN core is not the repeater, but a switch with individual stations being connected via a collision-free segment, this is referred to as switched Ethernet. The collision-free segment consists of a computer on one side and the switch interface on the other.

The structure of the Ethernet protocol frame depends on the standard used. The structure within the Ethernet II protocol is shown in the following figure:

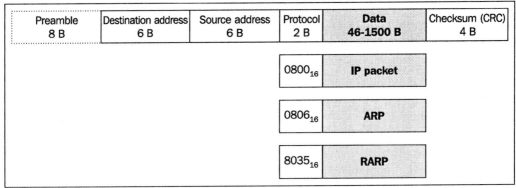

Figure 4.38: Ethernet II frame format

Ethernet II begins with a synchronizing preamble (part of the physical layer) where all stations receiving frames synchronize. The frame is finished by a checksum that reveals if any damage has been done to the frame. Additionally, it contains 6-byte link addresses of both the source and the destination. A field specifying the higher-layer (i.e., the network-layer) protocol and the transferred data themselves (protocol specification: IP version 4, ARP, and RARP) are clearly shown in Figure 4.38. The data field must be at least 46 bytes long, and if a lower amount of data must be transmitted, the rest is filled with useless padding.

The physical addresses have 6 bytes. The first three bytes specify the network card producer and the remaining bytes specify the particular card of that particular producer, so the addresses are unique worldwide. This applies only to **global addresses**. They are stored in the permanent memory of the network card. Upon initialization of the card by the driver, the card can be commanded not to use that particular address, but a different one. Therefore, it is possible to use your own local managed system of link addresses, for example, within one company. This mechanism was used, for example, by the DECnet phase IV protocol.

The network card can use a globally dedicated address or a locally managed address. Besides these dedicated addresses there are also broadcasts and multicasts. The broadcast (with an address composed of 48 1s) is aimed at all LAN stations. The multicast (with the lowest bit of the first byte set to 1) is aimed at only some LAN stations, i.e., the ones that accept the included address.

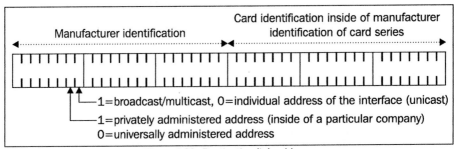

Figure 4.39: Destination link address

Bits zero and one of the first byte in a link address have a specific meanings that are as follows (see Figure 4.39):

- Bit zero specifies if it is a dedicated address (unicast address) or broadcast/multicast address.

- Bit one specifies if it is a globally managed address or a locally managed address.

As an example, let's have a look at an Ethernet II protocol frame statement from an MS Network Monitor:

```
+ FRAME: Base frame properties
  ETHERNET: ETYPE = 0x0800 : Protocol = IP:  DOD Internet Protocol
    ETHERNET: Destination address : 00000C31D211
        ETHERNET: .......0 = Individual address
        ETHERNET: ......0. = Universally administered address
    ETHERNET: Source address : 0010A4F18B3E
        ETHERNET: .......0 = No routing information present
        ETHERNET: ......0. = Universally administered address
    ETHERNET: Frame Length : 74 (0x004A)
    ETHERNET: Ethernet Type : 0x0800 (IP:  DOD Internet Protocol)
    ETHERNET: Ethernet Data: Number of data bytes remaining = 60 (0x003C)
+ IP: ID = 0xAB06; Proto = ICMP; Len: 60
+ ICMP: Echo,     From 195.47.37.200 To    194.149.105.18
```

For the ISO 8802-3 protocol, the situation is more complicated. The ISO 8802-3 protocol data frame only differs in one field in comparison with Ethernet II as shown in the following figure:

Preamble 8 B	Destination address 6 B	Source address 6 B	Length 2 B	Data 46-1500 B	Checksum (CRC) 4 B

Figure 4.40: IEEE 802.3 protocol frame (ISO 8802-3)

The data field (see Figure 4.41) can contain not only data, but also the ISO 8802-2 protocol packet, the header of which can by extended by two more fields that form SNAP. In other words, the stations are able to communicate to each other with the help of the following:

- Raw frames of the ISO 8802-3 protocol (without ISO 8802-2 and SNAP).

- ISO 8802-3 protocol frames that encapsulate ISO 8802-2 without SNAP, colloquially referred to as Ethernet ISO 8802-2.

- The ISO 8802-3 protocol frames that encapsulate ISO 8802-3 with SNAP, colloquially referred to as Ethernet SNAP.

The length field expresses the length of the data transferred. The two Ethernet standards differ in this field. During operations, it is impossible to get the frame types mixed up, since the data length is up to 1,500 B and the protocol specifications of the Ethernet II standard are expressed by numbers higher than 1,500.

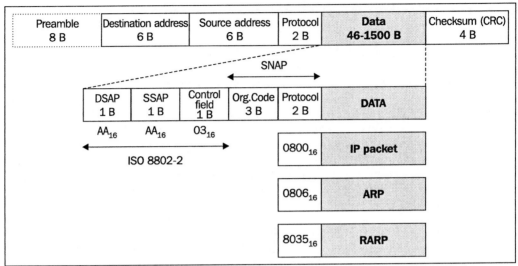

Figure 4.41: ISO 8802-2 and SNAP

We will now see an example of an Ethernet SNAP frame statement:

```
+ FRAME: Base frame properties
  ETHERNET: 802.3 Length = 60
      ETHERNET: Destination address : 010081000100
          ETHERNET: ......1 = Group address
          ETHERNET: ......0. = Universally administered address
      ETHERNET: Source address : 0000810C3D50
          ETHERNET: ......0 = No routing information present
          ETHERNET: ......0. = Universally administered address
      ETHERNET: Frame Length : 60 (0x003C)
      ETHERNET: Data Length : 0x0013 (19)
      ETHERNET: Ethernet Data: Number of data bytes remaining = 46 (0x002E)
  LLC: UI DSAP=0xAA SSAP=0xAA C
      LLC: DSAP = 0xAA : INDIVIDUAL : Sub-Network Access Protocol (SNAP)
      LLC: SSAP = 0xAA: COMMAND : Sub-Network Access Protocol (SNAP)
      LLC: Frame Category: Unnumbered Frame
      LLC: Command = UI
      LLC: LLC Data: Number of data bytes remaining = 43 (0x002B)
  SNAP: ETYPE = 0x01A2
      SNAP: Snap Organization code = 00 00 81
      SNAP: Snap etype : 0x01A2
          SNAP: Snap Data: Number of data bytes remaining = 38 (0x0026)
```

The chosen frame does not carry an IP-datagram as you might have expected. As for the Internet, each station must support the Ethernet II protocol. Only the stations that somehow agree on using Ethernet ISO 8800-3 can actually use it. That is the reason for the Ethernet II protocol being by far the most widespread.

Let's get back to the field description. The **Destination Server Access Point (DSAP)** and **Source Service Access Point (SSAP)** specify the source and destination applications sending/receiving the particular frame. For example, the IP-protocol uses DSAP=SSAP=AA$_{16}$ and NetBIOS uses DSAP=SSAP=F0$_{16}$. When using the ISO 8802-2 protocol, it is possible to deliver data all the way to the particular applications running on the station. There are even network protocols that use this kind of address identification (do not use the network layer) for LAN communication. While the use of such protocols is effective (one layer faster), they are non-routable, i.e., they are aimed at being used only by a LAN, not the WAN. The NetBEUI protocol is an example of such an exotic protocol.

The control field is completely analogous to the control field of the HDLC protocol. Again, the stations can use U-, I-, and S-frames to communicate. The frames can be numbered; so if they get lost or if an error occurs, retransmission can be requested and so on. As for the IP protocol, only U-frames are used and the P/F bit is set to zero, i.e., the control field has a value of 03_{16} (similar to the PPP protocol).

The **Sub-Network Access Protocol (SNAP)** header is used for specifying the higher layer protocol, which is similar to the protocol field in Ethernet II. It consists of two fields. The 3-byte **Organization code** field specifies the organization that administers the assignment of numbers for higher-layer protocols that are carried in the Protocol field. Even the $00\text{-}00\text{-}00_{16}$ organization code has the same higher layer protocol specifications as the Ethernet II protocol. In short, what was missed in the ISO 8802-3 protocol in comparison with the Ethernet II protocol (the protocol field) is clumsily taken care of by the SNAP header.

4.7 Wireless Local Area Network

Currently, the use of WLAN is rising. There are several reasons for this:

- Mobility—the user is not limited by the cable and socket.
- Fast and easy setup.
- Lower overall cost of building the network (no need to build expensive cable distribution infrastructure).
- Extendibility by choosing a suitable antenna and setting its polarization appropriately. In this way both the capacity and territory covered can be extended.
- Roaming is an important WLAN feature. If roaming is set, mobile stations can freely move within an area covered by the signal of access points if these access points are interconnected, for example, by the backbone network. Mobile stations log onto the access point providing the best signal-noise ratio (SNR). Should this ratio decrease below the limit set or should the signal disappear completely, the mobile station switches into the promiscuous mode or looks for another access point with the best signal-noise ratio. Roaming does not disturb the network communication of particular applications in any way.

Usually, a WLAN is found:

- Outdoor environment:
  - In places where it is impossible to use appliances attached by cables and sockets such as hospitals or production halls.
  - In combination with infrastructural cabling with desktops being connected in the classical way with infrastructural cabling and laptops being connected wirelessly.
  - In temporary networks such as exhibition grounds, college dormitories, etc.

- Indoor environment:
  - Internet and intranet networks.

WLANs use radio transmission in the 2.4 GHz or 5 GHz band as the transmission medium. No broadcasting license is usually needed. Therefore, in this case no authority coordinates the assignment of licenses; so you can end up interfering with other WLANs (such as those of Internet providers). If we do not set up the network properly, we can even interfere with our own network. Other interference sources can be appliances using the same band such as microwaves, Bluetooth, personal wireless networks, etc.

The IEEE 802.11 standard specifies WLAN. WLAN use a **Media Access Control (MAC) Protocol** referred to as **Carrier Sense Multiple Access/Collision Avoidance (CSMA/CA)**. It was derived from the CSMA/CD (collision detection) that we know from Ethernet. As opposed to Ethernet, however, wireless transmitters do not detect airborne collisions; therefore, the confirmation system is used for their detection. The CSMA/CA protocol is also used for association and re-association of the end station with the access point.

The signal can advance in one of the following ways in the WLAN:

- **Direct Sequence Spread Spectrum (DSSS)**: This is the transmission of radio waves in the band from 2.4 to 2.4835 GHz using DSSS. The transmitter changes the data (bit) flow into the flow of symbols with each symbol representing a group of one or more bits. Using a modulation technique such as the **Quadrature Phase Shift Keying (QPSK)**, the transmitter modulates or multiplies each symbol by a pseudo-random interference sequence. This operation artificially increases the bandwidth used in connection to the sequence length. The DSS divides the band into 14 channels of 22 MHz each, partially overlapping. There are just three non-overlapping channels in the band.

- **Frequency Hopping Spread Spectrum (FHSS)**: The transmission of radio waves of 2.4 to 2. 4835 GHz using FHSS transmits one or more data packets via one frequency (the band is divided into 75 sub-channels, each of 1 MHz) then hops onto a different frequency. The method of hopping between individual frequencies is not random, but uses a repeating order that is known to both the transmitter and receiver. In order to minimize the possibility of simultaneously using one sub-channel, it is possible to set various conversations using different keys.

- **Diffused Infrared (DFIR)**: Local infrared data communication is limited to one office or another undivided space. This is due to the fact that infrared rays do not go through solid matter, but bounce off.

There have been and there still are many different attempts to extend the IEEE 802.11 standard in order to improve the functionality of the WLAN. This includes 802.11b, known as **Wireless Fidelity (WI-FI)**, which enables reaching a theoretical rate of 11 Mbps in the 2.4 GHz band. This is provided by **Complementary Code Keying (CCK)**. The transmission rate changes dynamically based on the signal and noise levels. The 11 Mbps rate already includes **overhead** so the usable rate is approximately 40% lower with a strong correlation to many factors such as the number of end stations, the transport protocol used, the length of the files transported, and so on.

4.7.1 Typical WLAN Configuration

4.7.1.1 Peer-To-Peer Networks

This is also called the **ad-hoc mode**. Wireless stations communicate directly with each other. No access point is needed nor any configuration. This method is suitable for a maximum of 8 to 10 computers.

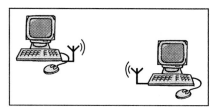

Figure 4.42: Peer-to-peer WLAN

4.7.1.2 Access Point

The WLAN access point is stationary and forms a base radio station and data bridge. The access point is usually connected to the network via, for example, an Ethernet.

Security features such as encryption or filtration of link or IP addresses can also be set in the access point. The number of end stations that can be connected to one access point is 15-38.

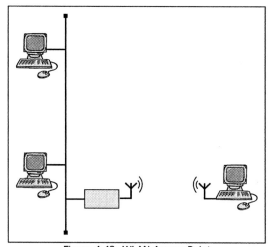

Figure 4.43: WLAN Access Point

123

4.7.1.3 Roaming (Several Access Points)

If roaming is enabled, the end stations can move freely with individual access points handing them over between each other.

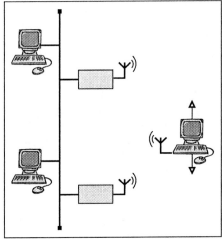

Figure 4.44: Roaming WLAN

4.7.1.4 Backbone Point-to-Point Connection

This is the interconnection of two networks via access points in the point-to-point configuration. This connection is typical for an outdoor solution using a supplementary beam antenna.

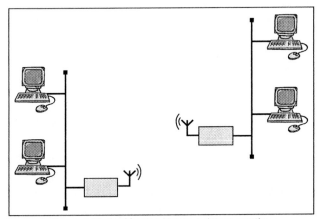

Figure 4.45: Backbone point-to-point connection

4.7.2 Antennas

WLANs are used not only indoors as an alternative to a classical 'wired' Ethernet, but they are being also used more and more outdoors. In such cases, lighting arresters and supplementary antennas are used. By combining powerful transmitters and good antenna gains, it is possible to communicate over significant distances. These appliances usually work in the half-duplex mode, but they can be modified into a full-duplex connection by using two parallel pairs of antennas, one for the transmission and the other for the reception. An antenna with high gain located at the destination point will also help us solve the problem of radiated power fall-off with distance.

The antennas are used with horizontal, vertical, or circular polarization. The vertical or horizontal polarizations are set by turning the antenna; however, circular polarization requires a different antenna type such as a spiral antenna. Parabolas of various diameters are used for the point-to-point connection while for the point-to-multipoint communication, Yagi antennas, i.e., horizontal multidirectional antennas or sector antennas are used.

When building antennas outdoors, it is necessary to respect and verify physical rules governing radio communication such as the Fresnel zone, which sets the maximum height of objects located between antennas.

4.7.3 Security of WLAN

Until recently, WLANs were using several not-very-secure features of wireless network protection. Let's have a look now at some security features used by WLANs.

4.7.3.1 Service Set ID

The SSID is a reference to the access point, which can be set as needed (also called **network name**). It is possible to set the access point so it transmits the network ID at regular intervals thus enabling the user to choose the appropriate network based on the revealed SSID. This is not very secure since the SSID is revealed to potential hackers as well. Another possibility is the manual configuration of the SSID at the end stations.

4.7.3.2 Wired Equivalent Privacy

The WEP protocol is a facultative part of the IEEE 802.11b standard, which provides authentication of stations and transmission encryption. However, many WLANs do not use it. It is switched off implicitly, although it is vital for data security and network management, and for these reasons, it should be switched on. The WEP protocol uses symmetrical encryption.

For the authentication of end stations, all stations use an identical 40-bit long shared secret that will be used by the end stations together with their link addresses for access point authentication. It is a one-sided authentication of the end stations (appliances), not user authentication.

For **data encryption**, a 64-bit key is used (although, some producers offer a 128-bit key) consisting of the user key and a changeable initialization vector of 24 bits. The initialization vector changes with every packet. The RC4 algorithm is used as the encryption algorithm.

The security of the WEP protocol is questionable since captured data can be easily used for decrypting the cipher using commonly accessible programs such as WEPcrack or AirSnort. Due to holes in the system of security keys, AirSnort is capable of breaking the cipher within seconds after one day of passive sniffing.

Oftentimes, WLANs are used at a point-to-multipoint Internet user connection. In such cases, users using the same access point for connection must realize that by sharing the same Ethernet segment they are also sharing the same key. We recommend that our users use other means of protecting their data from their neighbors such as IPsec or security measures at the application level (SSL/TLS, S/MINE, SSH, etc.).

4.7.3.3 IEEE 802.1X

WLAN security was questionable. The IEEE 802.1X standard is becoming increasingly common for security measures. It involves user authentication, encryption, and secure distribution of keys. Figure 4.46 shows a typical way of using this security system (used, for example, by Lucent for the WLAN in the Orinoco network.). Again, EAP-TLS is used here (see Section 4.4.3.3).

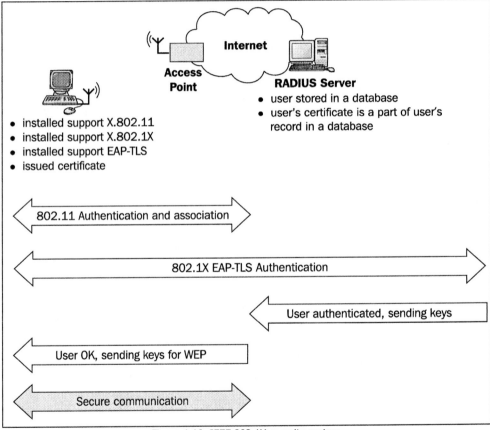

Figure 4.46: IEEE 802.1X security system

4.8 Fixed Wireless Access

Fixed Wireless Access networks (also called **Wireless Local Loop**) is a wireless technology enabling broadband connection such as point-to-multipoint. The FWA is an alternative solution to the 'last mile', giving telecommunication service providers an option to access end users directly. The main feature of this technology is the high throughput of the band enabling attainment of high-rate data transport and voice communication, as well as provision of other telecommunication services.

This is a cellular system based on a large number of mutually overlapping cells that work similarly to the GSM networks with the end terminals being stationary (they can be located, for example, on the customer's building) in direct visibility with the base station.

The base station is composed of shared managing hardware and an antenna system that provides signal transmission for a 360° radius of 7-9 km. The signal transmission can be divided into sectors ranging between 15° to 90°. By using frequency planning, it is possible to increase the overall capacity of the base station and use the frequency spectrum optimally.

One base station with one or more sectors composes the basic construction unit of the FWA. By mutually interconnecting the individual base stations, a network covering extensive areas is created. A managing and operational center is a part of the network where the network operations are checked and monitored as well as the quality of the services provided.

An end terminal is used to connect the customer. It consists of a compact antenna system and an inner unit with a telecommunication interface that is used to connect the customer's network.

The FWA is formed by a broadband network in the bands of either 26 GHz or 3.5 GHz giving the operators and Internet providers the option to offer quality services such as:

- Fast Internet access (up to 8 Mbps)
- Virtual Private Networks (VPN)
- High-rate transport of extensive data volumes
- Voice services based on the EuroISDN30 principle
- Conference services
- Multimedia services

The configuration as well as the modular nature of end terminals at the user's premises also enables one to combine these services.

4.8.1 The Differences Between FWA and WLAN

These technologies are aimed at different targets. Thus FWA in contrast to WLAN:

- Does not have mobile stations and does not support roaming.
- Has assigned licensed frequency bands. Interferences from other networks does not occur. It is usually possible to guarantee the client a certain bandwidth. But the FWA provider pays a fee for the frequency assigned.

- The transfer rates and the capacity of both base and end stations are significantly higher while the distant range is smaller.
- The FWA is aimed at voice transport; the end stations can be equipped with various interfaces for connecting a router. They do not usually provide an Ethernet interface.
- The price of the end and base stations differs from WLAN appliances by up to two orders of magnitude.

4.8.2 The Main Benefits of FWA

The main advantages are as follows:

- Guaranteed bandwidth
- High degree of reliability of transmission (99.995%) comparable to optical cables
- Flexibility and high capacity
- Effective use of the frequency spectrum width

5
Internet Protocol

Some link protocols are designed for data transportation within a local network, while other link protocols transport data between neighboring routers in a wide network. Unlike link protocols, IP protocol transports data between any two arbitrary computers within the Internet, i.e., through many LANs.

Usually, the data is transported (routed) from the sender to the recipient through many routers. A number of routers can appear between the sender and the recipient. Each router resolves routing to the next router (next hop) independently. The data is thereby transferred from one router to another. A hop means the next junction (a router or a destination machine) to which the data is being transferred.

The IP is a protocol that enables the connection of individual (often local) networks into a worldwide Internet. The Internet also got its name from Internet Protocol. The acronym Internet Protocol means InterNet Protocol, i.e., a protocol connecting particular networks. Later it became an established custom to write Internet instead of InterNet and that is how the term Internet originated.

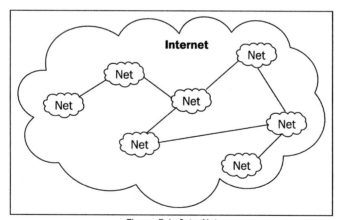

Figure 5.1: InterNet

The IP consists of several individual protocols that are as follows:

- The actual IP.
- **Internet Control Message Protocol (ICMP)** that serves specifically to signal abnormal states.
- **Internet Group Management Protocol (IGMP)** that serves for local transportation of multicasts.
- **Address Resolution Protocol (ARP)** and **Reverse Address Resolution Protocol (RARP)** that are often seen as independent protocols because their packets are not encapsulated in IP datagrams.

Whereas in the link protocol, each network interface has its physical (i.e., link) address, which for LANs consists of 6 bytes, in the IP protocol, each network interface has at least one IP address, which for IP version 4 is 4 bytes and for IP version 6 is 16 bytes.

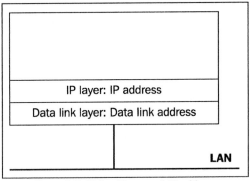

Figure 5.2: Link address and IP address

The basic element used to build a **Wide Area Network (WAN)** is a router with which individual LANs are connected into a wide network. For a router, you can use a normal computer with several network interfaces and a normal operating system or a specialized box into which you usually do not connect a monitor or keyboard. The word *router* thus has two meanings. The first general meaning of the word is a computer (classic computer or specialized box) that serves to transfer data packets between two network interfaces. The second more practical meaning of router is a specialized box that works as a router.

The ability to transfer data packets between the network interfaces of a router is called **forwarding**. While this function is required for routers, for computers with a classic operating system (UNIX, Windows, etc.), we have to solve the question of how to make the operating system kernel prohibit forwarding.

The basic question is "*Why are two protocols needed? Why is one link protocol not enough?*" A link protocol only serves for transporting data within a LAN (i.e., for transporting to the nearest router, which *unpacks* the data from the link framework and *repacks* the data into a different link frame). A different link protocol may be used at each interface of a router. Do not be fooled when a router uses the same link protocol on its different interfaces, for example, Ethernet. Even in this case, repacking is happening—we just have to keep in mind that an Ethernet frame uses different physical addresses before unpacking than it does after reassembling.

A particularly strong argument in the debate as to whether two protocols are necessary is the characteristics of protocols that only use a link layer for transporting data. For example, certain communication participants only have link (6 byte) addresses such as the NetBEUI (Microsoft) or LAT (Digital) protocols. These protocols are simple and usually faster at creating and processing packets. However, because it is only possible to address a recipient within the LAN, it is not possible to send data to a recipient behind a router, i.e., in a WAN. That is why these protocols are marked as non-routable. They are usable only within a local network, not outside it.

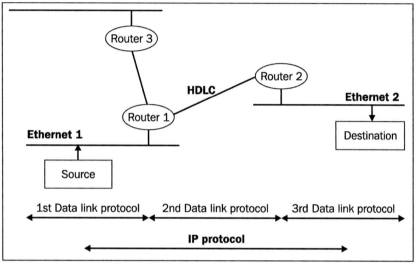

Figure 5.3: Link protocols and IP protocol

Figure 5.3 shows that, unlike IP, which transports data between two remote computers on a WAN, the link protocol only transports data frames to the next router. While each router throws away the envelope in which the data is wrapped on a link layer and creates a new one, an IP datagram (IP packet) is not changed by the router. The router must not change the IP datagram content. The only exception is the **Time To Live** (TTL) entry in the IP datagram header. Each router is obliged to diminish the entry by a minimum of 1. When the entry reaches 0, the IP datagram is thrown away. Using this mechanism, the Internet tries to prevent endless wandering of packets through the Internet. There are also other exceptions (like fragmentation, source routing, and so on), which we will talk about later.

While for link protocols, the basic unit of transferred data is called a **link frame**, in the IP the basic unit of transferred data is called an **IP datagram**.

Let's look at the situation illustrated in Figure 5.4 in which a sender from the local **Ethernet 1** network sends an IP datagram to a recipient on the **Ethernet 2** network. To make things simpler in Figure 5.4, we marked the IP addresses of the sender and recipient with the words **From** and **To**, as if the datagram were an email. We also marked the link addresses in the same way. For example, in the figure the sender has HW1 as a link address.

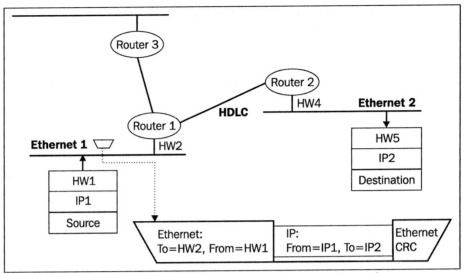

Figure 5.4: Sender sending IP datagram encapsulated into Ethernet frame

The sender wants to send an IP datagram to the recipient with the IP address IP2. It creates an IP datagram, but to insert it into a local network, the sender must insert it into a link frame (in our case, Ethernet). It's good to note the analogy that the IP datagram was embarked on an 'Ethernet 1 ship'. However, the data can only travel through the link protocol to router 1, which unpacks the IP datagram from the Ethernet frame and looks at the recipient's IP address. Depending on the recipient's IP address, it decides to which of its routers the IP datagram should be sent, i.e., on which link protocol the IP datagram should be embarked.

However, making this decision is not easy. The router decides based on its routing table (which we discuss in detail in Chapter 7). Let us suppose that the router has decided on the HDLC line.

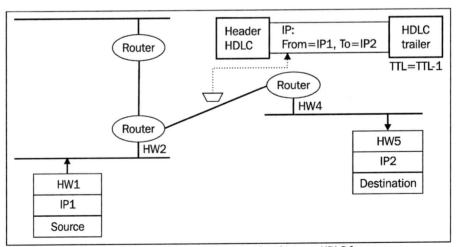

Figure 5.5: The IP datagram is encapsulated into an HDLC frame

The router lowers the value of the TTL entry by a minimum number of 1 and inserts our IP datagram into a different link protocol, which in our case is the HDLC protocol (see Figure 5.5). If we compare the HDLC protocol to a container transport, then our IP datagram was reloaded from the Ethernet 1 ship into an HDLC company container.

Our IP datagram is transported via the HDLC protocol to the next router, which again unpacks the IP datagram from the HDLC envelope, lowers the value of the TTL entry, and, after wrapping it in an Ethernet envelope, inserts it into the destination LAN.

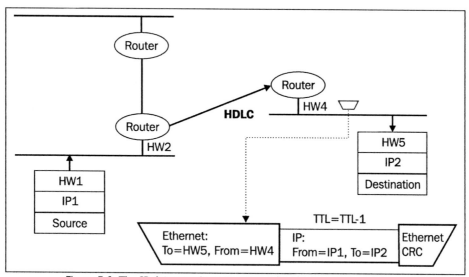

Figure 5.6: The IP datagram is again encapsulated into an Ethernet frame

The same link protocol is purposely chosen (Ethernet) for both LANs to illustrate that the link frames of these two LANs are totally different. In the sender's LAN, the Ethernet frame has the sender's HW1 address and the recipient's HW2 address—whereas in the recipient's LAN, an Ethernet frame is also used, but the sender's address is HW4 and the recipient's address is HW5.

5.1 IP Datagram

In explaining the TCP/IP protocol family, it is common to draw everything in a table that has a line of 4 bytes, i.e., bits 0 to 31. We too will often refer to this description.

An IP datagram consists of a header and transmitted data. A header usually has 20 bytes. However, a header can also contain optional entries that can make it longer.

The structure of an IP datagram is shown in the following figure:

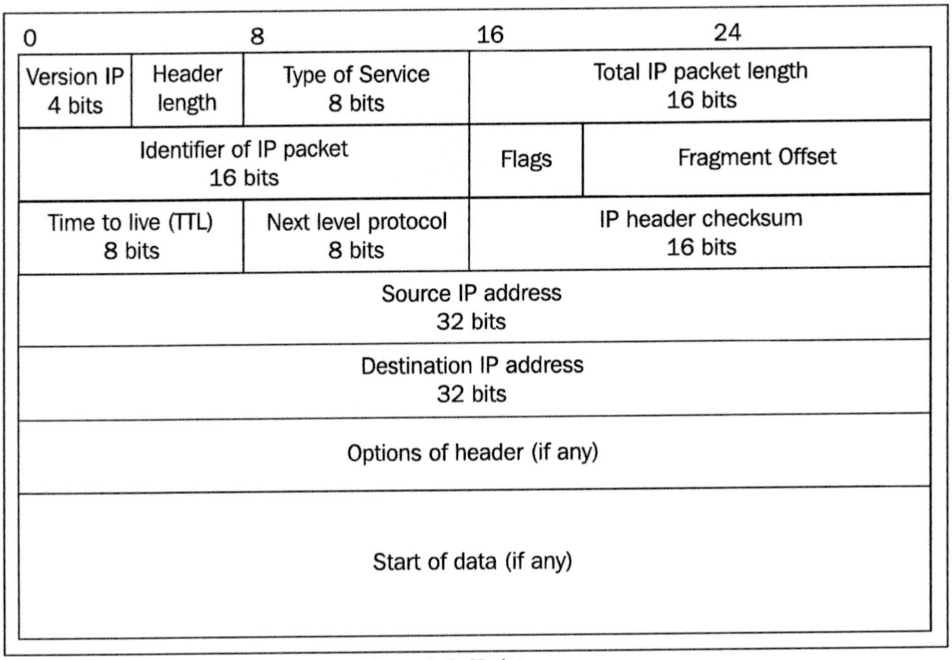

0		8	16	24
Version IP 4 bits	Header length	Type of Service 8 bits	Total IP packet length 16 bits	
Identifier of IP packet 16 bits			Flags	Fragment Offset
Time to live (TTL) 8 bits		Next level protocol 8 bits	IP header checksum 16 bits	
Source IP address 32 bits				
Destination IP address 32 bits				
Options of header (if any)				
Start of data (if any)				

Figure 5.7: IP datagram

Before we start to describe particular header entries, we will capture an IP datagram using MS Network Monitor. This way we will immediately be able to see whether what we are describing is really being transmitted through the network. Now we can begin to look at the meaning of individual entries in the IP datagram header.

```
+ FRAME: Base frame properties
+ ETHERNET: ETYPE = 0x0800 : Protocol = IP: DOD Internet Protocol
    IP: ID = 0x5814; Proto = ICMP; Len: 60
    IP: Version = 4 (0x4)
    IP: Header Length = 20 (0x14)
        IP: Service Type = 0 (0x0)
        IP: Precedence = Routine
        IP: ...0.... = Normal Delay
        IP: ....0... = Normal Throughput
        IP: .....0.. = Normal Reliability
    IP: Total Length = 60 (0x3C)
    IP: Identification = 22548 (0x5814)
    IP: Flags Summary = 0 (0x0)
        IP: .......0 = Last fragment in datagram
        IP: ......0. = May fragment datagram if necessary
    IP: Fragment Offset = 0 (0x0) bytes
    IP: Time to Live = 32 (0x20)
        Protocol = ICMP - Internet Control Message
    IP: Checksum = 0xEBF0
    IP: Source Address = 194.149.104.198
    IP: Destination Address = 194.149.104.203
    IP: Data: Number of data bytes remaining = 40 (0x0028)
+ ICMP: Echo, From 194.149.104.198 To 194.149.104.203
```

Version IP is the first entry in the IP datagram header. This 4-bit (half-byte) entry consists of an IP protocol version. In this chapter, we talk about version 4 of the IP protocol, which is why in this case this entry has a value of 4.

Header Length contains the header length of the IP datagram. In the case of the captured IP datagram shown below, the header length is 20. However, you can see from the MS Network Monitor hexadecimal printout, the header length has a value of 5 (not 20). The explanation is simple. The length is not expressed in bytes, but in 4-byte units, and 5 x 4 equals 20. Thus, even when using optional entries, the header length must be a multiple of four. If the header is not a multiple of four bytes, it will be padded to a multiple of four using a meaningless value.

The maximum length of an IP datagram header is limited by the fact that the entry header length only has 4 bits available ($1111_2 = F_{16} = 15_{10}$). The maximum IP datagram header length is 60_{10} bytes (=15 x 4). Since mandatory entries have 20 B, there is a maximum of 40 B remaining for optional entries.

Type of Service (TOS) is an entry that for a long time did not have a practical use. The TOS entry is used to specify the IP datagram's transmission quality. The original meaning of the particular bits of this entry is illustrated in the following figure:

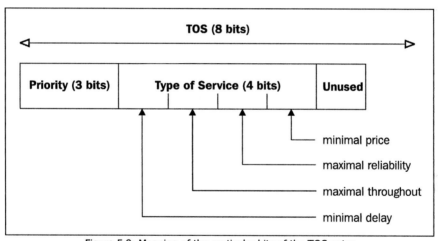

Figure 5.8: Meaning of the particular bits of the TOS entry

However, RFC 2474 defines the entry in a new way. It does not even call it TOS anymore; the entry is now called **Differentiated Services (DS)**. The importance of this entry increased with the requirement to guarantee bandwidth even in networks based on TCP/IP protocols and hence it was introduced. These requirements were brought on especially by applications requiring sound and video transmission.

It is necessary to provide a corresponding bandwidth on all lines leading between the sender and the recipient for applications that have to guarantee a certain transmission bandwidth. For this purpose, a **Resource ReSerVation Protocol (RSVP)** specified by RFC 2205 is used. If any machine on this route does not support the RSVP protocol, the building of the guaranteed path is threatened. We can use the following command in Windows XP to test whether it is possible to build the route to a fictional address, `http://www.company.com`: `pathping -R www.company.com`

Total IP packet length contains the total length of the IP datagram in bytes. Because this entry only has two bytes, the maximum IP datagram length is 65,535 bytes.

Identifier of IP packet contains the IP datagram identification that is inserted into the IP datagram by the sender's operating system. This entry, together with the **Flags** and **Fragment Offset** entries, is used by the datagram fragmentation mechanism.

If the DF bit is set to 1, fragmentation is forbidden (see Figure 5.9). Setting it to 0, on the other hand, means that fragmentation is possible. If the MF bit is set to 1, it specifies that this is not the last fragment.

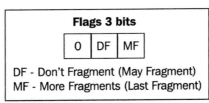

Figure 5.9: Flags

Time To Live (IP datagram lifespan) prevents endless wandering of an IP datagram through the Internet. Each router is obliged to diminish the positive TTL entry by a minimum of 1. When it reaches 0, the IP datagram is thrown away. The sender of the IP datagram is informed about this via the ICMP protocol.

How do we set the value of the TTL entry? You can set it explicitly for the `ping` and `traceroute` commands. If, however, the program developer does not set it explicitly, we are generally dealing with an operating system kernel parameter. In Windows XP, you can change the default TTL with the `HKEY_LOCAL_MACHINE\SYSTEM\CurrentControlSet\Srvices\Tcpip\Parameters\ DefaultTTL` register key. We have to add it to the register (it is of type `REG_DWORD`).

Next level protocol contains the identification number of the higher-layer protocol that is encapsulated in the IP datagram. In practice, we would rarely come across a case in which the IP protocol is communicated with directly. A higher-layer protocol (TCP or UDP) or one of the ICMP or IGMP service protocols is always used. The ICMP and IGMP protocols are formally part of the IP protocol. However, they act as higher-layer protocols, i.e., there is an IP protocol header in the transported packet followed by the ICMP or IGMP protocol header.

The numbers of higher layer protocols are given to the protocols' authors by the IANA organization. The assigned numbers can be found at `http://www.iana.org./numbers.html`. As a point of interest, the numbers of some of the protocols described in this publication are listed in the following table:

Number of Higher Layer Protocol	Protocol
1	ICMP
2	IGMP
6	TCP
$17_{10}=11_{16}$	UDP

Table 5.1: Protocol numbers

A higher-layer protocol is not the only thing that can be encapsulated in the IP protocol. For example, we can also encapsulate protocols that are not supported by the Internet and for some reason need to be transported over the Internet such as Novell's IPX protocol (IPX over IP). Even an actual IP datagram can be encapsulated over the IP protocol. At first sight, encapsulation of IP over IP can seem like a waste of time. However, if we want to transmit data between two parts of a private network over the Internet with an address 10.0.0.0/8 range, then this type of encapsulation becomes necessary. Moreover, it is also possible to secure intra-IP datagrams with encoding and a simple **Virtual Private Network (VPN)** can thus be created.

Number of Higher Layer Protocol (Decimal)	Protocol
4	IP over IP
97	Ethernet within IP
111	IPX in IP

Table 5.2: Encapsulated protocol number (decimal)

If we need to transport IP protocol version 6 datagrams over a network that only supports IP protocol version 4, then again we have no choice but to encapsulate IPv6 over IPv4. Table 5.2 lists the numbers of some encapsulated protocols.

IP header checksum contains the checksum, but only from the IP datagram header and not from the entire datagram. Its use is therefore limited. More detailed information on the calculation of a checksum can be found in RFC 1071 and RFC 1141.

The problem with a checksum is that when a router changes any entry in the IP datagram header (for example, it has to change TTL), it also has to change the checksum value, which requires a certain overhead in the router.

Source IP address and Destination IP address contain a 4-byte IP source address and a 4-byte IP datagram destination address.

5.2. Internet Control Message Protocol

ICMP is a service protocol that is part of IP. It is used to signal abnormal events in networks built on the IP protocol. ICMP wraps its packets into an IP datagram, i.e., if we capture transported datagrams, we can later find a link header then an IP header followed by the header of the ICMP packet.

It is possible to signal various states with ICMP; however, the reality is that any specific implementation of TCP/IP can only support a certain number of these signals and, above all, many ICMP signals may be discarded by routers for security reasons.

An ICMP packet header is always 8-bytes long (see Figure 5.10). The first four bytes always have the same meaning, and the contents of the remaining four depend on the ICMP packet type.

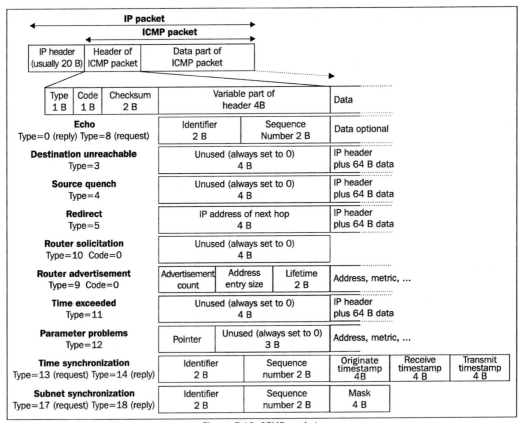

Figure 5.10: ICMP packet

The first four bytes of the header always contain the message type, message code, and a 16-bit checksum. The message format depends on the value of the type field. The type field is a rough division of ICMP packets. The field code then specifies a particular problem (soft division) that is being signaled by ICMP.

Individual types and codes are listed in the following table:

Type	Code	Description	What does it signal?	Who processes it?
0	0	**Echo**	Reply to User Application	User Application
3		**Destination unreachable**	Error	User Application
	0	*Network unreachable*		
	1	*Host unreachable*		
	2	*Protocol unreachable*		
	3	*Port unreachable*		
	4	*Fragmentation needed, but fragment bit not set*		
	5	*Source route failed*		
	6	*Destination network unknown*		
	7	*Destination host unknown*		
	9	*Destination network administratively prohibited*		
	10	*Destination host administratively prohibited*		
	11	*Network unreachable for TOS*		
	12	*Host unreachable for TOS*		
	13	*Communication administratively prohibited by filtering*		
4	0	**Source quench**	Error	OS kernel for TCP Thrown Away for UDP
5		**Redirect**	Error	OS kernel
	0	*Redirect for network*		
	1	*Redirect for host*		
	2	*Redirect for TOS and network*		
	3	*Redirect for TOS and host*		
8	0	**Echo request**	User Application Request	OS kernel
9	0	**Router advertisement**	User Application Reply	User process
10	0	**Router solicitation**	User Application Request	User process
11		**Time exceeded**	Error	User process
	0	*TTL equals 0 during transit*		
	1	*Fragment Reassembly Time Exceeded*		

Type	Code	Description	What does it signal?	Who processes it?
12		**Parameter problem**	Error	User process
	0	*Pointer indicates the error*		
	1	*Missing a Required Option*		
	2	*Bad Length*		
13	0	**Timestamp request**	User Application Request	User process
14	0	**Timestamp reply**	User Application Reply	OS kernel
17	0	**Address mask request**	User Application Request	User process
18	0	**Address mask reply**	User Application Reply	OS kernel

Table 5.3: List of ICMP messages

Now let's look at some specific message types.

5.2.1 Echo

This is a simple ICMP tool that we can use to test the accessibility of particular nodes in the Internet. The applicant sends an 'Echo request' ICMP packet and the destination node is obliged to reply with an ICMP 'Echo' packet.

All operating systems supporting the TCP/IP protocol contain the ping program, which the user can use to send an echo request to the destination junction. The ping program then displays the reply.

The purpose of the identification field in an ICMP packet header lies in pairing the request with the reply (so that we can find out to which request belongs a particular reply).

For example, in Windows XP, we would like to find out if the system on IP address 194.149.105.18 is *alive* (the word 'alive' is important because some systems reply "alive"):

```
D:\ >ping 194.149.105.18

Pinging 194.149.105.18 with 32 bytes of data:

Reply from 194.149.105.18: bytes=32 time<10ms TTL=63
Reply from 194.149.105.18: bytes=32 time<10ms TTL=63
Reply from 194.149.105.18: bytes=32 time<10ms TTL=63
Reply from 194.149.105.18: bytes=32 time<10ms TTL=63
```

This system has sent the echo application four times. The reply had a 32-byte long data part and it was received within 10 milliseconds. The TTL entry had a value of 63 in the reply.

5.2.2 Destination Unreachable

If the IP datagram cannot be transmitted further to the recipient, then it is thrown away, and the sender is informed with the ICMP 'Destination Unreachable' message. Some specific reasons are listed in Table 5.3.

5.2.3 Source Quench (Lower Sending Speed)

If some part of the network between the sender and the recipient is overloaded, then a router that is not able to further transmit all IP datagrams, signals 'Source Quench' to the sender. If the sender uses the TCP protocol, it lowers the speed by sending TCP segments. With the UDP protocol, Source Quench messages are ignored. We are already acquainted with this message from the FrameRelay protocol.

5.2.4 Redirect

With the help of this ICMP packet, dynamic changes are made in the routing table.

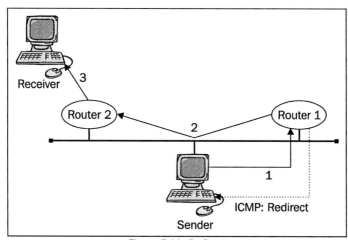

Figure 5.11: Redirect

In the figure above, Router 1 receives an IP datagram that needs to be forwarded to another address thorough the same network interface through which the IP datagram came. It forwards the IP datagram, but uses an ICMP redirect packet to instruct the sender to change its own routing table and not to ask for such strange services anymore.

This situation occurs mostly when we have several routers on the local network, but individual PCs on a LAN only have one default entry pointing to one of the routers after startup.

5.2.5 ICMP Router Discovery

This is a rather new feature—thanks to which do not have to manually configure any default entries in the routing table of LAN computers (usually client PCs). After startup, the computer sends an ICMP 'Router Solicitation' message and the routers on the LAN reply with an ICMP

'Router Advertisement' message packet that contains the address of the router, the length of the address, and IP address/preference pairs. The computer can automatically generate the default entry from the reply.

The higher the value of the preference, the more the IP address is preferred. The preference value 80000000_{16} signals that this address should be excluded from the routing table.

The routers reply back to the application for routing; however, at a random interval between 450 and 600 seconds, they should generate multicast for all systems on the LAN (224.0.0.1) or broadcast (255.255.255.255) into the local network with ICMP 'Router Advertisement' message packets.

The lifespan entry states the time for which the information is valid, i.e., for which the entry is to be kept in the PC's routing table.

5.2.6 Time Exceeded

This type includes two very different cases that are as follows:

- For Code=0, it signals that the TTL entry was lowered to 0 on the router, i.e., there is a suspicion that the IP datagram got lost on the Internet and it will therefore be eliminated.

- For Code=1, it signals that the recipient's computer is not able to complete the entire IP datagram from the fragments within the set time (time exceeded for IP datagram reassembly).

The ICMP **time exceeded** packet with code=0 is used by the `traceroute` (UNIX) or `tracert` (Microsoft) program.

The tracert program is simpler than traceroute. This program sends ICMP 'Echo request' packets from the source computer to the destination node. However, it sets the TTL entry to 1 in the first packet. The first router in the path throws the packet away and returns an ICMP 'Time exceeded' packet because it has to lower the TTL by at least 1, but in doing so it generates 0.

Thus in the IP datagram, the source computer receives an ICMP 'Time exceeded' packet from the first router in the path. It is possible to find out the address of the first router in the path from the sender's address entry in the IP header. The time interval between sending and receiving the packet is measured, and thus the program knows the packet's traveling time from the sender to the recipient and back. This repeats three times and all three times are displayed. At the end of the line, the name of the router and its IP address (in brackets) are also displayed. The name is taken from reverse resolution in DNS.

If the reply is not acquired within a time limit, an asterisk (*) is displayed instead of the time. Then everything is repeated with a TTL=2 value, and so on. The router terminates its operation when it receives an ICMP 'Echo' message from the destination node. The termination can also occur when a router does not know the way to the destination computer, and the source computer is sent an 'Destination unreachable' message.

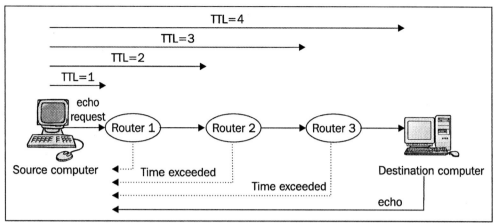

Figure 5.12: Tracert command

```
D:\> tracert kula.usp.ac.fj
    Tracing route to kula.usp.ac.fj [144.120.8.11]
    over a maximum of 30 hops:

     1    <10 ms     10 ms    <10 ms  cbuN002e00.pvt.net [194.149.104.193]
     2     10 ms     10 ms     10 ms  phucbu.pvt.net [194.149.96.13]
     3    601 ms    561 ms    641 ms  951.Hssi5-0.GW1.NYC2.ALTER.NET [157.130.0.117]
     4    591 ms    571 ms    571 ms  143.ATM2-0.XR1.EWR1.ALTER.NET [146.188.177.50]
     5    591 ms    581 ms    571 ms  193.ATM1-0-0.BR1.EWR1.ALTER.NET
     6    400 ms    381 ms    360 ms  sl-pen-11-h3.sprintlink.net [137.39.44.130]
     7    811 ms    591 ms    661 ms  sl-bb10-pen-0-1.sprintlink.net [144.232.5.5]
     8    500 ms    651 ms    731 ms  sl-bb22-stk-6-0.sprintlink.net [144.232.8.178]
     9    871 ms    831 ms    932 ms  sl-bb23-stk-8-0.sprintlink.net [144.232.4.110]
    10    691 ms    650 ms    611 ms  sl-bb10-sj-6-0.sprintlink.net [144.232.8.193]
    11    811 ms    771 ms    771 ms  sl-gw2-sj-0-0-155M.sprintlink.net
    12    641 ms    651 ms    641 ms  sl-cais-1.sprintlink.net [144.228.111.18]
    13    801 ms    811 ms    861 ms  hssi9-0-0.hk-T3.hkt.net [202.84.128.253]
    14    801 ms       *       811 ms  f5-0.yck06.hkt.net [205.252.130.201]
    15    821 ms    831 ms    822 ms  a6-0.tmh08.hkt.net [205.252.130.81]
    16   1402 ms   1342 ms   1362 ms  s4-3b.tmh08.hkt.net [205.252.128.158]
    17   1381 ms   1362 ms   1352 ms  202.84.251.6
    18   1362 ms   1362 ms   1352 ms  202.62.120.6
    19   1422 ms   1372 ms   1392 ms  202.62.125.134
    20   1412 ms   1382 ms   1412 ms  kula.usp.ac.fj [144.120.8.11]

    Trace complete.
```

The traceroute program operates on a similar principle. However, it does not send ICMP 'Echo request' packets, but instead, generates UDP datagrams (you can change the UDP port with the -p parameter). If a filter is applied on a router on route to the destination computer, you can choose a different UDP port number to find a 'hole' in the filter and find the route all the way to the destination computer. One useful example for this technique is port number 53 (-p 53), which is used by DNS.

```
$ /usr/sbin/traceroute -p 20000 libor.pvt.net
    traceroute to libor.pvt.net (194.149.104.198), 30 hops max, 40 byte packets
    1 cbuN003f00.pvt.net (194.149.105.17) 1 ms 1 ms 1 ms
    2 Libor.pvt.net (194.149.104.198) 1 ms 1 ms 1 ms
```

The destination computer usually replies with an ICMP 'Port unreachable' packet (type=3, code=3). In addition to the time or an asterisk, the traceroute program can also write out !H (unreachable destination), !N (unreachable network), !A (network administratively prohibited), or !S (explicit routing failed).

5.2.7 Subnet Address Mask Request

Using this ICMP packet, a diskless station can ask for a mask of its network once it has received its IP address via RARP protocol.

This mechanism is not very commonly used anymore. A station can acquire a mask of its network by using the BOOTP protocol, with which it can also acquire other information. However, even the BOOTP protocol is currently being replaced by the DHCP protocol, which is more complex and provides more information. The BOOTP and DHCP protocols are both application protocols.

5.2.8 Time Synchronization

Using this ICMP packet, a destination computer is asked for the time. The mechanism is illustrated in the following figure:

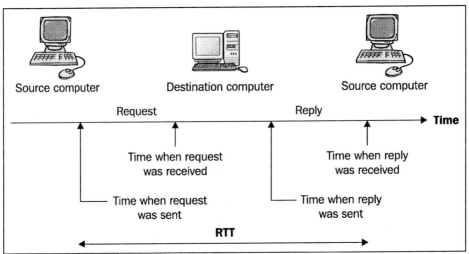

Figure 5.13: Time synchronization

The source computer enters the time of the request that was sent into the ICMP 'Timestamp request' packet.

The destination computer enters 'Timestamp reply' two times into its reply:

- The time when the request was received
- The time when the reply was sent

The source computer thus finds out the time the reply was received (which of course is not transmitted in any ICMP packet). By subtracting the time the request was sent from the time the reply was received, the traveling time from the source computer to the destination computer and back (**Round Trip Time (RTT)**) is deduced.

The time is stated in milliseconds from the previous midnight using the **Greenwich Mean Time (GMT)**. (Technically, we should write **Coordinated Universal Time (UTC)** instead of GMT. We use GMT out of habit.)

5.3 Fragmentation

IP datagrams are wrapped into link frames. The link protocols only enable data transmission within their frames up to a certain maximum limit. The maximum data size that can be inserted into one link frame is called **Maximum Transfer Unit (MTU)**.

Link Protocol	MTU
Ethernet II	1500
Ethernet 802.3 SNAP	1492
Frame Relay	1600
FDDI	4478

Table 5.4: MTUs of link protocols

It is obvious from looking at the previous table that most link protocols have MTU in ones of kilobytes. On lines connecting remote locations, we also sometimes encounter an MTU smaller than 1 KB. The total field length of an IP datagram, however, is 16 bits long; so theoretically, it is possible to create an IP datagram up to 64 KB long.

But what happens when an IP datagram on route from the sender to the recipient encounters a router (see Router 2 in Figure 5.14), from which the line leading in the direction of the recipient has an MTU less than the size of our IP datagram?

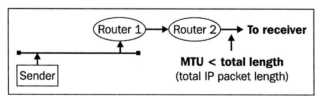

Figure 5.14: MTU between the router and the recipient

The router is not able to send the IP datagram. The router decides how to proceed based on the 'Fragmentation possible' flag (DF bit) in the header of the IP datagram (we will ignore the possibility that there is another line leading to the recipient, even if with a worse metric). The 'Fragmentation possible' flag can either be set or not. So there are two options:

- If fragmentation is possible, then fragmentation will be performed as described later in this chapter.
- If fragmentation is not possible, then the router throws the IP datagram away and informs the sender with an ICMP 'Fragmentation needed but fragment bit not set' signal.

If we use a flag to prohibit fragmentation, we can also find out what the smallest MTU between the sender and the recipient is, i.e., the maximum IP datagram size that does not need to be fragmented.

For example, we can do so using the ping command. Microsoft's implementation of the ping command lets you prohibit fragmentation with the help of the -f parameter and allows you to set the length of the IP datagram using the -l parameter.

```
c:\> ping -f -l 2000 recipient
```

This command either announces that the recipient is functional displays the RTT, or it will display an error message, so we can find out whether on route fragmentation was needed for a 2000 B long IP datagram. If fragmentation is needed, we can decrease the size of the sent IP datagram and watch whether or not fragmentation is needed this time. We can proceed doing this until we find the limit after which fragmentation is needed.

It would be much easier if the ICMP signal contained the MTU value that is valid for the line causing the problem. This option was originally not considered. However, the MTU field was later added to ICMP packets exactly for this purpose. This extension is rarely implemented.

The second two bytes from the header's unused four bytes were used in the ICMP packet. The ICMP packet structure is displayed in the following figure:

0	8	16	24
Type=3	Code=4	Checksum	
Unused (always set to 0)		MTU	
IP header + 8 B of data part of a dropped packet			

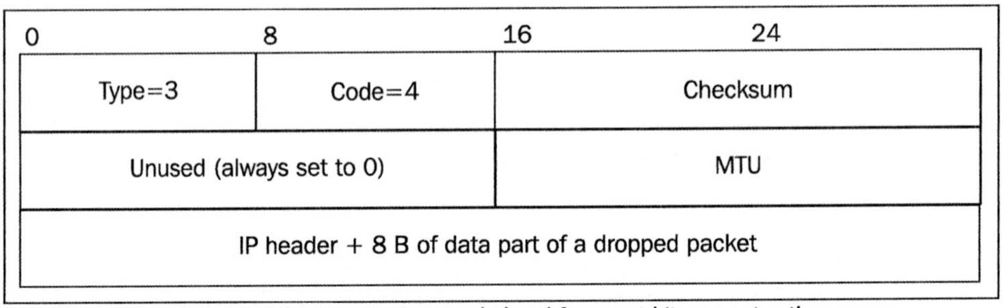

Figure 5.15: ICMP 'Fragmentation needed and fragment bit was not set' message

If the MTU field is 0, the router does not support this new extension.

Now let's go back to the situation where it is specified in the IP packet that fragmentation is possible. The router divides longer IP datagrams to fragments whose total length is smaller than or equal to the MTU of the following line as shown in the following figure:

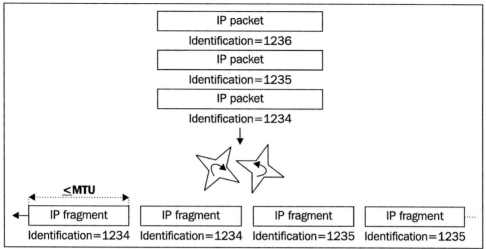

Figure 5.16: IP datagram shredding

The header of each IP datagram contains its identification, which is then inherited by its fragments. Because of this identification, the recipient can find out which fragments it should use to complete the datagram. No one except the recipient is eligible to complete the original datagram from the fragments—not even a router that has a line leading from it with a big enough MTU to accommodate the entire datagram. The reason is simple; the Internet does not guarantee that individual fragments will travel the same route (it does not even guarantee the order in which they will be received). So a router that tries to reassemble the datagram could jeopardize the connection because it would never acquire fragments that take a different route.

Identification of IP datagrams can be unambiguous only within the frame of one higher-layer protocol because the header of an IP datagram also contains the 'Protocol' field (meaning 'higher-layer protocol'). A global identification can be understood as the chaining of the 'identification' field and the 'protocol' field (plus, of course, the IP addresses of the sender and recipient). So theoretically, two IP datagrams with the same identification can be sent in a row. However, one carries a TCP packet and the other a UDP packet. Once again, this implementation is not very common.

Each fragment creates an independent IP datagram, which is needed to create a new IP header for each fragment during fragmentation. Some data items (such as the higher-layer protocol or the IP addresses of the sender and recipient) are acquired from the original IP datagram's header.

During fragmentation, the 'Fragment offset' field, which expresses how many bytes of the original IP datagram's data part were inserted into previous fragments, enters the equation. The 'Total length of IP datagram' field contains the length of the fragment, not the length of the original datagram. In order for the recipient to find out how long the original datagram is, the last fragment is labeled with a 'Last fragment' flag. The whole mechanism is illustrated in the following figure:

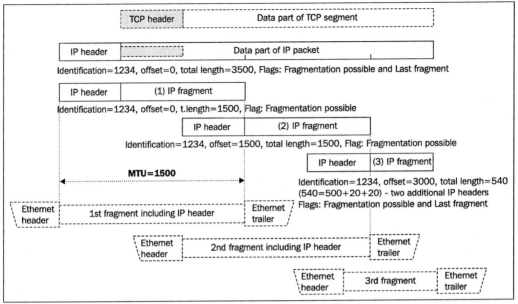

Figure 5.17: IP datagram fragmentation

The network does not distinguish differences between the transmission of a fragment and the transmission of the entire (non-fragmented) IP datagram. A non-fragmented datagram is a fragment with an offset of 0 and a 'Last fragment' flag. That's why the words 'IP datagram' and 'fragment' are often interchanged.

The fragmentation mechanism even permits the fragmentation of fragments, if the fragment gets to a router whose leaving line has an even smaller MTU.

It is important that each subsequent fragment entails loading at least 20 B of it header. As an interesting aside, Figure 5.17 shows a TCP packet inserted into an IP packet. So what is so interesting about it?

The interesting thing is that the TCP header is included only in the first IP fragment. So if the IP datagrams are being filtered on the router, based not only on information from the IP header, but also on information from the TCP header, it is only possible to filter the first fragment; the others are left out. After a certain interval, the recipient finds out that it is missing the first fragment from the IP datagram and signals this to the recipient with an ICMP 'Fragment reassembly time exceeded' message. So during TCP packet filtering, it is important to not forget to filter these ICMP packets in the opposite direction, if you do not want to provide an attacker with the information that we ourselves are protecting through filtering.

Fragmentation is considered a necessary evil; applications requiring extremely secure communication forbid fragmentation.

5.4 Optional Entries in the IP Header

Optional entries in the IP header are one of the more interesting facets of TCP/IP protocols. We will demonstrate how dangerous it can be to use optional entries, and why many Internet providers throw away IP datagrams that contain them. However, from the pure TCP/IP protocol point of view, this practice is inexcusable (even if performed in good faith), and it can be compared to requiring everyone to carry crutches in case they break their leg.

If a recipient receives an IP datagram with any of these options, it should also use the option in its reply. Optional entries widen the IP header. Due to the IP header's maximum length of 60 B (out of which 20 B is mandatory), the optional entries are limited to 40 B. Currently there are several options for widening the IP header. They are as follows:

- Record route
- Timestamp
- Loose source routing
- Strict source routing
- IP Router Alert option
- Security options for Internet Protocol (RFC 1108), which is obsolete

Optional entries in an IP header follow the mandatory entries. Generally, optional entries have the format displayed in the following figure:

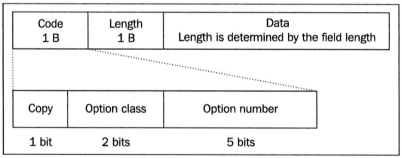

Figure 5.18: IP datagram header options

Where the Copy bit is set to 1, it specifies that this option should be copied into all fragments originating from this datagram. If the bit is set to 0, it is only copied into the header of the first fragment.

The two bits that make up the Option class field have the following values:

- Value 0 if the IP datagram is carrying regular data or data earmarked for network management
- Value 2 (=10_2) if the IP datagram serves to synchronize or measure the network

The Option number field then specifies a particular option. The following table lists the commonly used options:

Code	Hexadecimal Value	Decimal Value	Length	Option
0 00 00000	00	0	Does not exist	End of options list. This is used if the options do not end with the IP header. The length field and data will not be used.
0 00 00001	01	1	Does not exist	No operation. Header padding up to multiples of 4 bytes. The length field and data will not be used.
0 00 00111	07	7	Variable	Record route.
0 10 00100	44	68	Variable	Timestamp.
1 00 00011	83	131	Variable	Loose source routing.
1 00 01001	89	137	Variable	Strict source routing.
1 00 10100	94	148	4	IP Router Alert Option.

Table 5.5: Option number field options

5.4.1 Record Route

If the header contains the option field Code=7, then each router on route to an IP datagram's destination adds the IP address of its output interface into the IP header. Individual 4-byte fields in the header of the IP datagram for IP addresses are called **slots**. It is possible to insert up to 9 slots into the IP header for IP addresses.

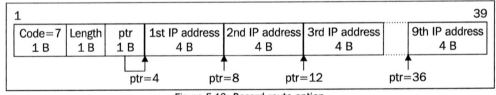

Figure 5.19: Record route option

The length field contains the total length of the widening, and the ptr (pointer) field shows the first free slot that is available for input (each subsequent router enters a new IP address and increases the ptr entry by 4).

A datagram, on route from the source to the destination, collects the router's outgoing IP addresses into its slots. If the destination machine supports this option too, then it uses this option in its reply after first copying all slots from the received datagram into the sent datagram.

So using the ping command with the 'record route' option, we can find out the list of outgoing addresses not only on the datagram's route from the source to the destination, but also on its way back.

With the Microsoft `ping` command, a 'record route' widening can be created with the `-r` parameter, followed by the number of created slots. For example:

```
D:\> ping -r 5 ns.pvt.net
```

This generates an ICMP packet with the 'record route' option for five IP address slots. Although the sender creates five slots, none of them are filled in. Therefore, the indicator for the first free ptr slot points to the first slot.

The IP header is widened by $3 + 5 * 4 = 23$ bytes as we can see from the captured IP datagram below:

```
+ FRAME: Base frame properties
  + ETHERNET: ETYPE = 0x0800 : Protocol = IP: DOD Internet Protocol
    IP: ID = 0x673D; Proto = ICMP; Len: 84
      IP: Version = 4 (0x4)
      IP: Header Length = 44 (0x2C)
    + IP: Service Type = 0 (0x0)
      IP: Total Length = 84 (0x54)
      IP: Identification = 26429 (0x673D)
    + IP: Flags Summary = 0 (0x0)
      IP: Fragment Offset = 0 (0x0) bytes
      IP: Time to Live = 32 (0x20)
      IP: Protocol = ICMP - Internet Control Message
      IP: Checksum = 0xCB51
      IP: Source Address = 194.149.104.198
      IP: Destination Address = 194.149.105.18
      IP: Option Fields = 7 (0x7)
        IP: Record Route Option = 7 (0x7)
          IP: Option Length = 23 (0x17)
          IP: Next Slot Pointer = 4 (0x4)
          IP: Route Traveled = 0 (0x0)
        IP: End of Options = 0 (0x0)
      IP: Data: Number of data bytes remaining = 40 (0x0028)
  + ICMP: Echo,      From 194.149.104.198 To    194.149.105.18
```

The user can see the reply on his or her screen:

```
Pinging ns.pvt.net [194.149.105.18] with 32 bytes of data:
Reply from 194.149.105.18: bytes=32 time<10ms TTL=63
    Route: 194.149.105.17 ->
           194.149.105.18 ->
           194.149.104.193
```

So on route from the sender to the recipient (194.149.105.18) and back, there is only one router, which on route to the recipient has the address 194.149.105.17 and on route to the sender has the address 194.149.104.193. (By 'sender', we mean the user who issued the `ping` command).

This reply originated from an ICMP 'Echo' packet. The following frame displays the captured reply with the slots filled in:

```
+ FRAME: Base frame properties
+ ETHERNET: ETYPE = 0x0800 : Protocol = IP: DOD Internet Protocol
  IP: ID = 0x2DD8; Proto = ICMP; Len: 84
    IP: Version = 4 (0x4)
    IP: Header Length = 44 (0x2C)
  + IP: Service Type = 0 (0x0)
    IP: Total Length = 84 (0x54)
    IP: Identification = 11736 (0x2DD8)
  + IP: Flags Summary = 0 (0x0)
    IP: Fragment Offset = 0 (0x0) bytes
    IP: Time to Live = 63 (0x3F)
    IP: Protocol = ICMP - Internet Control Message
```

```
          IP: Checksum = 0x3334
          IP: Source Address = 194.149.105.18
          IP: Destination Address = 194.149.104.198
          IP: Option Fields = 7 (0x7)
             IP: Record Route Option = 7 (0x7)
                IP: Option Length = 23 (0x17)
                IP: Next Slot Pointer = 16 (0x10)
                IP: Route Traveled = 194 (0xC2)
                   IP: Gateway = 194.149.105.17
                   IP: Gateway = 194.149.105.18
                   IP: Gateway = 194.149.104.193
             IP: End of Options = 0 (0x0)
          IP: Data: Number of data bytes remaining = 40 (0x0028)
        + ICMP: Echo Reply, To 194.149.104.198 From 194.149.105.18
```

5.4.2 Timestamp

This option is a variation on the record route option. Each router enters a timestamp into the IP header when the datagram passes through it. A in ICMP time synchronization, the time is registered in milliseconds from the last midnight (GMT).

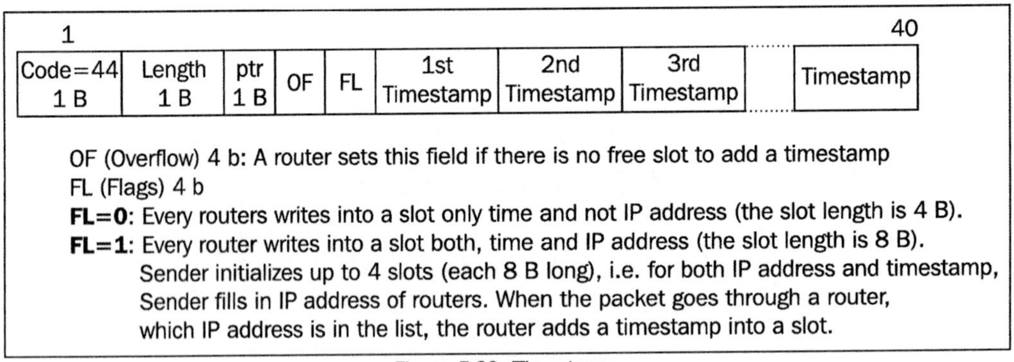

1									40
Code=44 1 B	Length 1 B	ptr 1 B	OF	FL	1st Timestamp	2nd Timestamp	3rd Timestamp	....	Timestamp

OF (Overflow) 4 b: A router sets this field if there is no free slot to add a timestamp
FL (Flags) 4 b
FL=0: Every routers writes into a slot only time and not IP address (the slot length is 4 B).
FL=1: Every router writes into a slot both, time and IP address (the slot length is 8 B).
    Sender initializes up to 4 slots (each 8 B long), i.e. for both IP address and timestamp,
    Sender fills in IP address of routers. When the packet goes through a router,
    which IP address is in the list, the router adds a timestamp into a slot.

Figure 5.20: Timestamp

The field code for this option has a value of $44_{16}=68_{10}$. Two 4-bit fields, OF and FL widen the format of this option.

The Microsoft ping command with the -s parameter generates an ICMP packet with the 'Timestamp' requirement. The number listed after the -s parameter states the number of allocated slots. If you have to use both the timestamp and an IP address, it is possible to allocate a maximum of four slots.

The ping -s 3 194.149.105.18 command generates the following IP datagram (shortened):

```
   ...
          IP: Option Fields = 68 (0x44)
          IP: Internet Timestamp Option = 68 (0x44)
             IP: Option Length = 28 (0x1C)
             IP: Time pointer = 5 (0x5)
             IP: ....0001 = Both time stamps and IP addresses
             IP: Missed stations = 0 (0x0)
             IP: Time Route = 0 (0x0)
                IP: Gateway = 0.0.0.0
                IP: Time Point = 0 (0x0)
                IP: Gateway = 0.0.0.0
```

```
IP: Time Point = 0 (0x0)
IP: Gateway = 0.0.0.0
IP: Time Point = 16792576 (0x1003C00)
IP: Data: Number of data bytes remaining = 40 (0x0028)
```
...

The user is then shown the IP addresses and timestamps. The milliseconds need to be transformed to hours, minutes, and seconds, and we must not forget daylight savings time.

```
Pinging 194.149.105.18 with 32 bytes of data:
Reply from 194.149.105.18: bytes=32 time<10ms TTL=63
      Timestamp: 194.149.105.17 :   52251609 ->
                 194.149.105.18 :   52531841 ->
                 194.149.104.193 : 52251610
```

Which was brought by the IP datagram (shortened):

...

```
IP: Option Fields = 68 (0x44)
IP: Internet Timestamp Option = 68 (0x44)
IP: Option Length = 28 (0x1C)
IP: Time pointer = 29 (0x1D)
IP: ....0001 = Both time stamps and IP addresses
IP: Missed stations = 0 (0x0)
IP: Time Route
    IP: Gateway = 194.149.105.17
    IP: Time Point = 52251609 (0x31D4BD9)
    IP: Gateway = 194.149.105.18
    IP: Time Point = 52531841 (0x3219281)
    IP: Gateway = 194.149.104.193
    IP: Time Point = 52251610 (0x31D4BDA)
IP: Data: Number of data bytes remaining = 40 (0x0028)
```
...

5.4.3 Source Routing

Source routing lets you explicitly set through which routers an IP datagram should be transmitted over the Internet. This is good news for hackers because it means that they can divert the transmission of IP datagrams as needed.

There are two types of source routing:

- **Loose source routing** (code=83_{16}) when an IP datagram is transmitted through named routers. However, not all routers through which the IP datagram is transmitted have to be named.

- **Strict source routing** (code=89_{16}) when a list of routers must contain all routers through which the IP datagram is routed. If the IP datagram is routed through a different router, the routing will fail.

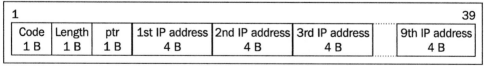

Figure 5.21: Source routing option

The source routing mechanism is quite complicated. Individual participating routers correct not only the ptr field, but also the recipient's address in the IP datagram.

Even if the sender addresses the destination directly from the application, the destination's address in the IP datagram always contains the next router (next hop) from the list of routers. The whole process is automatically secured by an IP layer that takes an IP address from the first slot on the sender's machine and replaces it with the original destination address. The contents of particular slots are moved to the left (the first slot was emptied after an address was entered into the destination address field). The original destination address is saved in the last (free) slot. The ptr (pointer) indicator points to a slot with an IP address one hop down the route.

The following routers proceed similarly. The entire process is illustrated in the following figure, where the asterisk represents the slot to which the ptr field points:

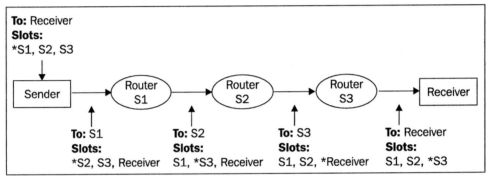

Figure 5.22: Source routing

The Microsoft `ping` command lets you specify source routing with the help of the `-j` parameter for loose source routing and the `-k` parameter for strict source routing. The parameter is followed by the list of IP addresses through which the routing should be performed.

Example:

```
D:\ >ping -j 195.47.1.1 10.1.1.1
Output:

...
        IP: Source Address = 194.149.104.198
        IP: Destination Address = 195.47.1.1
        IP: Option Fields = 131 (0x83)
            IP: Loose Source Routing Option = 131 (0x83)
                IP: Option Length = 7 (0x7)
                IP: Routing Pointer = 4 (0x4)
                IP: Route To Go
                    IP: Gateway = 10.1.1.1
            IP: End of Options = 0 (0x0)
        IP: Data: Number of data bytes remaining = 40 (0x0028)
    ...
```

When a user makes a mistake, he or she receives the following error message:

```
Pinging 172.17.101.1 with 32 bytes of data:
Reply from 194.149.104.193: Invalid source route specified.
```

This message results from the fact that source routing was prohibited on a particular router. Why is source routing prohibited? The reasons involve security. Source routing can be abused in two ways:

- It is possible to divert the transmission of IP datagrams through a different router, where the data will be sniffed or even changed with the help of source routing.

- It is possible to attack the inside of an intranet from the Internet with the help of source routing, even though the intranet uses addressing for private networks (for example, 10.0.0.0/8). These private networks are not directly addressable from the Internet; this is one of the protections offered by intranets. To gain access, you can use the firewall itself if it enables source routing (not very likely). An easier way is through a computer that for some reason has a direct connection to the Internet. For example, this could be the laptop of an employee, who connects to the Internet directly through a dial-up connection when out of the office. When in the office, the employee has a network card and works on the LAN. If the employee establishes connection on both sides, he or she allows IP forwarding in the operating system and thus supports source routing. The mechanism is illustrated in the following figure:

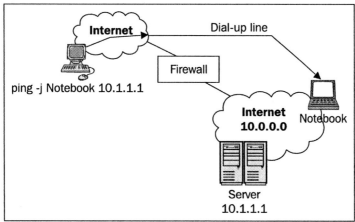

Figure 5.23: Source routing attack

5.4.4 IP Router Alert Option

An IP datagram is forwarded through the Internet via a series of routers. Under normal circumstances, the router does not care very much about the contents of the forwarded IP datagram, just as postal workers do not care about the contents of the letters they handle.

However, in addition to ordinary IP datagrams, some datagrams that are forwarded through the Internet are for routing protocols and are directed to routers. These IP datagrams have their destination address filled in (although it is the address of a router). The routers process these IP datagrams on their way to the destination (the destination router) just like any other IP datagram. However, the information carried in these IP datagrams can also be interesting to routers on the way (in other words, those routers to which the datagram is not directly addressed). Under normal circumstances, the routers on route do not even know that they were forwarding information that could be useful. At the same time, the sender does not know that there is a router on route to which it is directly sending such information.

An IP datagram header can carry a notification option for the router that alerts all the routers on the way that "*This IP datagram is not addressed to you directly, but it forwards information, which can also be interesting to you. If you know how, have a look at the information and use it.*"

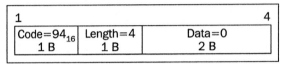

Figure 5.24: IP Router Alert Option

5.5 ARP and RARP Protocols

If I am a station on a local network and want to communicate with another station on the same network through an IP datagram, I address a 4-byte IP address to the station in the IP datagram. In performing the transmission, I know the source IP address (my address) and the destination IP address. I can therefore complete an IP datagram. But the problem is that this IP datagram must be wrapped in a link frame, for example, in an Ethernet frame. In order to create an Ethernet frame, I need the link (6 B) addresses of both the source and the destination. I am the source and I know my link address, but I do not know the destination link address. How do I find out what this address is? The answer is by using the **Address Resolution Protocol (ARP)**.

ARP lets you to get the link address of an opposite station when you know its IP address. The solution is simple and is shown in the following figure:

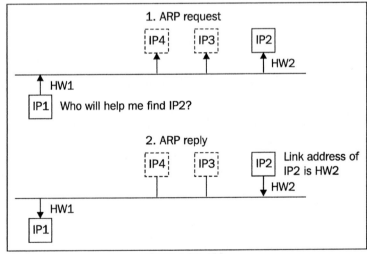

Figure 5.25: ARP

ARP sends a link broadcast to the LAN (link address FF:FF:FF:FF:FF:FF) with a request, "*I, a station with link address HW1 and IP address IP1, want to communicate with the station that has IP address IP2. Who can help me localize the link address of the station with IP address IP2?*". The IP2 station hears the message and replies. It states its link address (HW2) in its reply.

ARP packets (see Figure 5.26) are wrapped directly into the Ethernet, i.e., they are not preceded by an IP header. The ARP protocol is in fact independent of the IP protocol. That is why even other protocols that have nothing in common with the TCP/IP protocol family can use it.

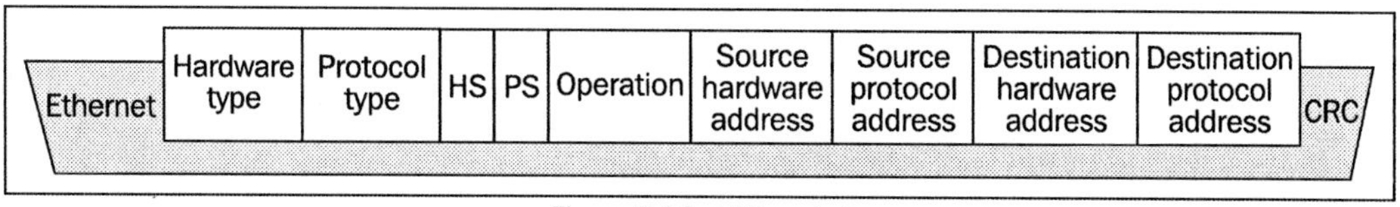

Figure 5.26: ARP packet

The **Hardware type** field specifies the link protocol used on the LAN. Number 1 is reserved for the link protocol of Ethernet II. The list of allocated numbers is published on http://www.iana.org.

The **Protocol type** specifies the network's protocol type. This uses the same numbers as are used for the protocol field in the Ethernet II protocol, i.e., the IP protocol is allocated the number 0800_{16}.

The **HS** field sets the length of a link address and the **PS** field sets the length of a network address. By default, HS=6 and PS=4.

The **Operation** field specifies which operation is running. The ARP request has a value of 1 and the ARP reply has a value of 2. This field is also defined for the reverse translation (RARP protocol), where the RARP request uses a value of 3 and the RARP reply has a value of 4.

This information is followed by the source link address, the source IP address, the destination link address (filled in with zeros in the request), and the destination IP address.

The request is sent with a link broadcast and has zeros in the destination link address field. The reply has all fields filled in and does not need to be sent by broadcast. We should point out that the destination and source will be interchanged in the reply. The following example makes this clear:

```
C:\ > ping 194.149.104.126
```

This command, which can send the first IP datagram (ICMP echo request packet), must use the routing table to find out whether the destination is on the LAN or behind a router. In other words, it must find the next hop. If the destination is behind a router, it looks for the link address of the router. If the destination is not behind a router, it looks directly for the link address of the destination (as in our case).

Now we already know that the destination IP address is 194.149.104.126 and is directly on the LAN. We now need to find out its link address. The source operating system will generate the following ARP request:

```
+ FRAME: Base frame properties
  ETHERNET: ETYPE = 0x0806 : Protocol = ARP:  Address Resolution Protocol
    + ETHERNET: Destination address : FFFFFFFFFFFF
    + ETHERNET: Source address : 0020AFFA2589
```

```
            ETHERNET: Frame Length : 42 (0x002A)
            ETHERNET: Ethernet Data: Number of data bytes remaining = 28 (0x001C)
      ARP_RARP: ARP: Request, Target IP: 194.149.104.126
            ARP_RARP: Hardware Address Space = 1 (0x1)
            ARP_RARP: Protocol Address Space = 2048 (0x800)
            ARP_RARP: Hardware Address Length = 6 (0x6)
            ARP_RARP: Protocol Address Length = 4 (0x4)
            ARP_RARP: Opcode = 1 (0x1)
            ARP_RARP: Sender's Hardware Address = 0020AFFA2589
            ARP_RARP: Sender's Protocol Address = 194.149.104.121
            ARP_RARP: Target's Hardware Address = 000000000000
            ARP_RARP: Target's Protocol Address = 194.149.104.126
```

The recipient immediately replies with the following packet:

```
   + FRAME: Base frame properties
     ETHERNET: ETYPE = 0x0806 : Protocol = ARP:  Address Resolution Protocol
       + ETHERNET: Destination address : 0020AFFA2589
       + ETHERNET: Source address : 00603E1D9001
         ETHERNET: Frame Length : 60 (0x003C)
         ETHERNET: Ethernet Type : 0x0806 (ARP:  Address Resolution Protocol)
         ETHERNET: Ethernet Data: Number of data bytes remaining = 46 (0x002E)
      ARP_RARP:
            ARP_RARP: Hardware Address Space = 1 (0x1)
            ARP_RARP: Protocol Address Space = 2048 (0x800)
            ARP_RARP: Hardware Address Length = 6 (0x6)
            ARP_RARP: Protocol Address Length = 4 (0x4)
            ARP_RARP: Opcode = 2 (0x2)
            ARP_RARP: Sender's Hardware Address = 00603E1D9001
            ARP_RARP: Sender's Protocol Address = 194.149.104.126
            ARP_RARP: Target's Hardware Address = 0020AFFA2589
            ARP_RARP: Target's Protocol Address = 194.149.104.121
            ARP_RARP: Frame Padding
```

From this packet, the system automatically adds an entry to its ARP cache, stating the link address that belongs to the listed IP address. In the next communication with computer 194.149.104.126, this entry is used and the ARP question is not generated again. The ARP cache content can be viewed with the following command:

```
D:\> arp -a
   Interface: 194.149.104.121
      Internet Address       Physical ADRESS      Type
      194.149.104.126        00-60-3e-1d-90-01    dynamic
      10.1.1.1               00-01-11-11-ff-08    static
```

There can be entries in the ARP cache that are acquired by ARP request. These entries are **dynamic**. We can also write entries in the ARP cache using the explicit `arp` command. These entries are **static**. It is also possible to erase entries from the ARP cache using the `arp` command.

The following is an example of static entry insertion:

```
D:\> arp -s 10.1.1.1 00-01-11-11-ff-08
```

The following example shows the deletion of the entry:

```
D:\> arp -d 10.1.1.1
```

How long do dynamic entries remain in the ARP cache? This interval is a parameter of the operating system kernel. Usually, the entries have a 2-minute lifespan, unless they are used for a second time. Each successive time they are used, their lifespan increases by another 2 minutes. However, this does not go on infinitely. It is usually possible to prolong the lifespan up to a maximum lifespan, which is usually 10 minutes. However, some systems also record negative replies into the ARP table, which usually have a 3-minute lifespan. Before a negative conclusion is performed, the ARP request is repeated after 5.5 seconds and again after another 24 seconds.

It is possible to change these constants in Windows 2000 or Windows XP by changing keys in the registry. The keys for controlling the ARP cache are placed in the HKEY_LOCAL_MACHINE\SYSTEM\ CurrentControlSet\Services\Tcpip\Parameters registry key. We can also add the following REG_DWORD keys into this registry key.

- ArpCacheLife containing the lifespan (in seconds) of an unused entry in the ARP cache.
- ArpCacheMinReferenceLife containing the maximum lifespan (in seconds) of an entry in the ARP cache.

Using the ARP protocol, it is possible to send a request with the IP addresses of the source and destination filled in and also with both link addresses filled in. You can think of this type of request as, "*Is there by any chance another station on the LAN that uses the same address as me?*". If a reply is received, the user is sent the following message: "Duplicate IP address sent from Ethernet address xx:xx:xx:xx:xx:xx." Of course, this indicates an error in the configuration of one of the stations using this address.

5.5.1 ARP Filtering

In fact, ARP filtering is not filtering, but it has a similar effect to filtering. This procedure is used when there are two firms (or two independent parts of one firm) on one LAN.

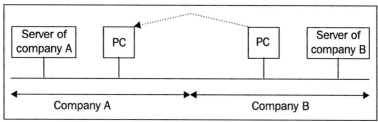
Figure 5.27: ARP filtering

The problem lies in preventing an employee from company B from accessing the company A server (in other words, preventing the company B employee from declaring his or her PC as the PC of a company A employee).

To solve this problem, we fill in the ARP cache on the company A server statically (manually). The server then always replies to the address of the company A employee's PC without using the ARP protocol and hackers are therefore out of luck.

Filtering is limited, however, because the company B employee can also forge a link address. This process is not trivial and is enough to discourage a novice hacker.

5.5.2 Proxy ARP

The ARP protocol only works within a LAN. There cannot be a router between the requesting and replying computers. The reason is simple: the destination address in the request is a broadcast, which is not forwarded by routers.

But what to do when you have two or more parts of a LAN separated by a router? The solution is a proxy ARP. Proxy ARP runs on a router.

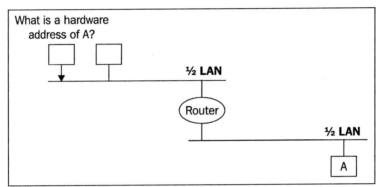

Figure 5.28: LAN separated by a router

The computer wants to use an ARP request to find out the link address for an IP address A that belongs to the second part of the LAN behind the router. The router cannot let this request go through, but if it is configured with proxy ARP, it will reply that its own link address corresponds to IP address A.

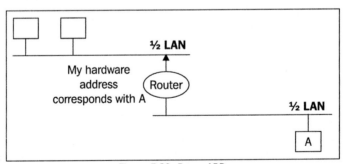

Figure 5.29: Proxy ARP

If the computer wants to send a link frame to A, it addresses the router, which then forwards the IP datagram to destination computer A.

5.5.3 Reverse ARP

While the ARP protocol serves to translate an IP address into a link address, **Reverse ARP (RARP)** serves to translate a link address into IP address. But why would you want to perform this type of translation?

The RARP protocol is used for diskless stations. Once it is turned on, a diskless station does not know anything other than its link address (which is stored in ROM on a network interface card by the producer). It needs to find out its IP address after startup. It therefore sends a broadcast onto the LAN with the following request: "*I have link address HW1. Who can tell me what my IP address is?*". Then there has to be an RARP server on the LAN, which will allocate the station its IP address and give the address to it in a reply. The RARP protocol uses the same packet format as the ARP protocol. Only the value of the **Operation** field is increased by two. Of course, the IP address of the applicant is not entered in the request.

In practice, the RARP protocol is seldom used any more as it was replaced by the more complex DHCP protocol.

5.6 Internet Group Management Protocol

Like ICMP, IGMP is a service protocol for IP. IGMP packets are wrapped into IP datagrams. It is used for forwarding multicasts. Currently, version 2 of the IGMP protocol is up to date with RFC 2236 norms.

The following figure shows the structure of an IGMP version 2 packet:

IP header	Type 1 B	MRT 1 B	Checksum 2 B	IP group address 4 B

Figure 5.30: IGMP v2 packet

The **Type** field acquires the values shown in the following table:

Value (hexadecimal)	Significance
11	IP Membership query ("*Are there any members on the LAN?*")
12	IGMPv1 Membership Report
16	IGMPv2 Membership Report
17	IGMPv2 Leave Group

Table 5.6: Type field values

The **MRT (Maximum Response Time)** field is only used in router requests and specifies (in tenths of a second) the time that members of the group have to repeat their requests for membership in the group. In all other cases, the MTR field has a value of 0.

The checksum is calculated in the same way as with the ICMP protocol. The **IP group address** field is zero for a general request, and in all other cases, specifies the particular IP address of a multicast.

The IP addresses of multicasts are in an interval of 224.0.0.0 up to 239.255.255.255. The interval 224.0.0.0 to 224.0.0.255 is earmarked for reserved purposes on the LAN (see Table 5.7). Because multicasts with these addresses are earmarked exclusively for LAN, they usually have a value of 1 set in the TTL entry.

IP address	Reserved for addressing
224.0.0.1	All systems within LAN
224.0.0.2	All routers within LAN
224.0.0.4	Distance Vector Multicast Routing Protocol (see RFC 1075)
224.0.0.5	OSPF All Routers (see RFC 1583)
224.0.0.6	OSPF Designated Routers (see RFC 1583)
224.0.0.9	RIP-2 etc

Table 5.7: IP addresses of multicast

All IGMP packets have TTL=1 set in the IP header. IGMP protocol version 2 packets use the (extension) IP header option 'IP Router Alert' option.

The core of the Internet is called **Multicast Backbone (Mbone)**, which is where multicast forwarding is ensured. Its complexity is obvious in Figure 5.31, in which the source of multicasts, for example, an internet radio station, forwards its data with the help of multicasts. If the multicasts were forwarded as avalanches without any control, the data could be gradually duplicated (flooding). For example, the same data could come to router C from router A and from router B.

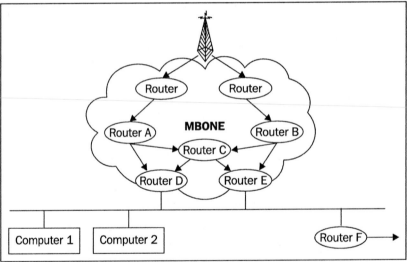

Figure 5.31: Multicasts flooding

The IGMP protocol solves multicast forwarding within a LAN.

Let's imagine that we are on a LAN and some routers accept multicasts from MBONE and decide whether to forward them to the LAN. In general, if no computer on the LAN needs the multicasts, it is useless to forward them—they would only increase the LAN workload.

So we have a situation where some routers on LAN can supply the LAN with multicasts, but do not do so, because multicasts are not required on the LAN.

For each IP address of a multicast on the LAN, a group of the multicast's members is defined. The routers keep a list of these groups. If any computer on the LAN is a member of a particular group, the routers will begin to forward the individual multicasts to the LAN.

When the last member leaves the group, the multicast forwarding on the LAN is terminated. Therefore the existence of the group means multicasts are forwarded. It is not important how many members the group has, but only that it has at least one member.

If an application that wants to listen to radio station 226.1.1.1 starts running on a computer, the computer sends out a request for membership in group 226.1.1.1 as shown in the following figure:

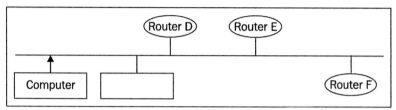

Figure 5.32: Computer on LAN sends out a request for membership in group

The request fields are as follows:

- **IP-header**:

    TTL=1

    IP-sender's address=Computer

    IP-recipient's address=224.0.0.2 (to all routers on LAN)

- **IGMP-packet**:

    Type=16_{16}

    MRT=0

    IP-multicast address=226.1.1.1

If no 226.1.1.1 multicasts have yet been spread on the LAN, then the forwarding begins.

If a computer accepts multicasts and is the last member of the group, it can stop the forwarding by sending a similar IGMP packet, but with the field type=17_{16}.

But let's look at what happens if the application is not properly terminated on the computer. The computer is simply taken out of the socket and does not have a chance to send a 'switch off packet'. Let's imagine that multicasts on the LAN are forwarded by router E (see Figure 5.35). For router E to find out whether it is still needed to spread our group, from time to time it has to send the IGMP membership query packet, "*Are there any members on the LAN?*" (i.e., the type field=11) to the LAN. This packet has two variations:

1. A general request that asks about all groups (the IP address field of the multicast is filled in with zeroes). Individual computers must repeat their request for membership in each group, one by one, within MTR (tenths of second). If they do not, it is assumed that they have left the group.

2. A request addressed for a particular group (the IP address field of the multicast is entered in an IGMP packet). All members of a particular group must repeat their request for membership within MTR (tenths of a second).

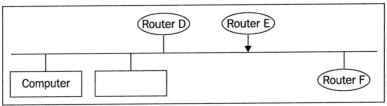

Figure 5.33: Router E says, "*Are there any members on the LAN?*"

The application fills the header fields in this way:

- **IP-header**:

    TTL=1

    IP-sender's address=Router E

    IP-recipient's address=224.0.0.1 (to all systems on LAN)

- **IGMP-packet**:

    Type=1116

    MRT>0 for version 2, =0 for version 1

    IP-address of a multicast=226.1.1.1 (addressed request), 0.0.0.0 (general request)

However, the question remains as to how particular routers will agree among themselves on the LAN, when there are more than one routers. The routers work in relation to the IGMP protocol in two modes:

- An Applicant that sends a membership request on the LAN.
- A Listener that is not active, but only listens to the operation and does not enter the game if there is an applicant on the LAN.

After being switched on, the router starts working as an Applicant. However, if it finds requests from a router with a higher IP address on the LAN, it switches itself to Listener mode.

5.7 Multicast and Link Protocol

So far we have been describing broadcast transmission, but the problem with LAN is identifying the link address of the recipient.

The ARP protocol specifies an unambiguous relationship between an unambiguous IP address (*unicast*) and the destination link address. This is possible when an unambiguous relationship exists between IP addresses and link addresses. This relationship is called **mapping** (mapping of IP addresses to link addresses).

The situation is different when a broadcast is sent to all LAN systems. For these purposes the link protocol uses a broadcast, which for the Ethernet, FDDI, and so on is ff:ff:ff:ff:ff:ff.

But how do we do this with multicasts that are addressed neither to one destination on the LAN nor to all systems on the LAN, but rather to several particular destinations?

First let's look at the problem. Under normal circumstances, the recipient processes only those frames that are broadcasts or addressed with the destination link address. (It is possible to switch a network card into promiscuous mode (in which it accepts everything), but this is not considered normal. Unfortunately, many WLAN and FDDI network interface cards cannot be switched into promiscuous mode).

Link protocols also enable multicasts. These are a type of link address in which the lowest bit of the link address's first byte is set to 1. For example, a broadcast is a special case of this multicast type. But how do you map the IP address of a multicast to a link multicast?

It is not as simple as it may seem at first sight. A 6-byte link address consists of three bytes specifying the network card's producer and three bytes of the card's serial number.

IANA (the highest Internet authority) registered itself as an imaginary producer of network cards and received the identification number 00:00:5e. It used the first half of these addresses for mapping IP multicasts to link multicasts (see Figure 5.34). Unfortunately, this half only has 23 bits, so the mapping cannot be unambiguous.

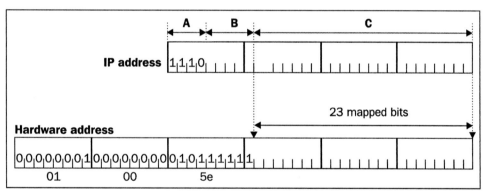

Figure 5.34: Mapping IP multicasts

The first byte of a link address must have the lowest bit set to 1 because it is a link multicast. So in fact, the prefix is not 00:00:5e, but 01:00:5e.

Part A of an IP address specifies a multicast, so it is always constant. Part B is not mapped.

So if two multicasts differ only in part B, then they are mapped to the same link address. For example, the IP addresses 224.0.1.1, 224.128.1.1, and 225.0.1.1 are always mapped to 01:00:5e:00:01:01.

The link layer of the computer accepts link frames that are as follows:

- Unicast addresses of this computer
- Broadcasts
- Multicasts whose list is forwarded to the link layer by higher layers

The list of accepted link multicasts contains the address 224.0.0.1 and all link multicasts originated due to unambiguous mapping. Surplus multicasts must be filtered out by the IP protocol. Some software programs switch the network interface card into promiscuous mode for the duration of all multicasts and leave everything up to the IP protocol. However, this uselessly increases the burden put on the operating system.

6

IP Address

In IP protocol version 4, an IP address has 4 bytes. An IP address uniquely addresses a network interface. Such a unique address is called a **unicast** IP address. If a system uses several network cards (several network interfaces) and all of them use IP protocol, then every network interface has its own IP address. It is similar to the address of a house; every house has only one address.

The other alternative is also possible. Several IP addresses may be assigned on one network interface. The first address is called a primary address while the others are called secondary addresses or aliases. Using secondary IP addresses is common with web servers; for example, the web servers of several different companies, each of which has its own homepage, can run on a single computer/server. The use of secondary IP addresses for web servers is, however, in practice considered as wasteful; so virtual web servers are used instead. In that case, many web servers share one IP address and server specification is accomplished on the application level in the HTTP protocol (via the *host* header).

As most computers use one network interface, it is common for the IP address of a network interface to be called the computer IP address.

An IP address has four bytes. It is written in a dotted notation—adjacent bytes of the 4-byte address are separated by a dot. The notations used are as follows:

- Binary notation, where all the individual bits of each byte are expressed as a binary number, for example, 10101010.01010101.11111111.11111000
- Decimal notation, where the four 8-digit binary numbers are converted to the decimal numerical notation, i.e., 170.85.255.248
- Hexadecimal notation, where each byte of the IP address is expressed as a hexadecimal number, i.e., AA.55.FF.F8

An IP address consists of two parts:

- A (local) network address
- A computer address in a (local) network

The problem is how to find out which part of an IP address is the network address and which part is the computer address. Even the term 'network' itself is slightly vague; its meaning has undergone some changes and terms such as subnetwork and super-network have come into use.

6.1 Network: First Period of History

This era lasted from the beginning of the Internet until 1993. In this era, the term 'net' was specified by RFC 796 standard (J. Postel, September 1, 1981). Those twelve years were marked by the idea that 4 bytes must be enough for an IP address.

An IP address was structured into a network address and a computer address within a network, as is shown in the following figure:

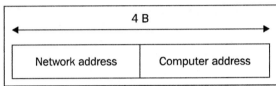

Figure 6.1: Structure of an IP address

It is the initial bits of the first byte of an IP address that determine how many bytes of the IP address make up the network address. There are five classes of IP address:

- **Class A**: The value of the highest bit of the first byte is 0. The remaining 7 bits of the first byte represent the network address and the rest (24 bits) are reserved for the computer address within the network. There are 126 networks within the A Class (0 and 127 are networks with a specific meaning). In each network there are 2^{24}-2 computer addresses (addresses consisting entirely of zeros or ones are addresses with a specific meaning).

- **Class B**: The value of the two highest bits of the first byte is 10_2. The remaining 6 bits of the first byte and the following second byte represent the network address. This allows us to have 2^{14} networks each consisting of 2^{16}-2 computers.

- **Class C**: The value of the three highest bits of the first byte is 110_2. The remaining 5 bits and the following two bytes represent the network address. This allows us to have 2^{21} networks each consisting of 128-2 computers.

- **Class D**: The value of the four highest bits of the first byte is 1110_2. The class D addresses are not divided into a network and a computer addresses, because they are multicast addresses themselves.

- **Class E**: The rest of the addresses are reserved for future use.

Class	1st byte of an IP address	2nd byte of an IP address	3rd byte of an IP address	4th byte of an IP address
A	0nnnnnnn $1\text{-}127_{10}$	computer address	computer address	computer address
B	10nnnnnn $128\text{-}191_{10}$	nnnnnnnn	computer address	computer address
C	110nnnnn $192\text{-}223_{10}$	nnnnnnnn	nnnnnnnn	computer address
E	1110mmmm $224\text{-}239_{10}$	mmmmmmmm	mmmmmmmm	mmmmmmmm
F	$>239_{10}$			

Table 6.1: IP address classes

The individual address classes are summed up in Table 6.1. Bits used for the network address are marked as n and bits used for the multicast address are marked as m.

It is clear from the table that the total of class A networks is 128–2=126 with 2^{8+8+8}=16 M addresses each. Similarly, there can be up to 14 K class B networks with 64 K addresses each. Finally, there can be up to 2M class C networks with 256 addresses each. Some addresses are reserved for special use.

6.1.1 Special-Use IP Addresses

The general form of an IP address is *network.computer*, where the network is represented by one byte for class A, two bytes for class B, and three bytes for a class C address.

If the network or computer address only consists of zeros (in binary notation) (00...0), it is understood as the address of 'this' computer/network. If there are only ones (11...1), it is understood as the address of 'all' computers/networks. A limited broadcast consists of only ones (255.255.255).

An overview of special-use IP addresses in binary notation is presented in Table 6.2:

Address type	Description
0.0.0.0	This computer in this network
00...0.computer	A computer in this network
network.00...0	An address of a particular network
network.11...1 (ones only in the computer address position)	A direct *broadcast* sent to the 'network' network—can be sent to a remote network
11...1 (ones only, in decimal notation: 255.255.255.255)	*Limited broadcast* (broadcast in local network only)—not routed further
127.whatever	A software loop (*loopback*)—never leaves the computer, usually 127.0.0.1

Table 6.2: Special-use IP address

Every network card (network interface) has at least one unique address (unicast); besides this, the whole system has a loopback address 127.0.0.1. The 127.0.0.1 address is not unique in the Internet, because it is the same for every computer (host).

For example, let us say, 192.168.6.0 network is a class C network. What is the identity of all the other computers in this network? The answer is simple: The IP address of a *broadcast* on this network is 192.168.6.255.

After executing the `ping 192.168.6.255` command, all the computers in this network that are switched on will respond by sending the ICMP Echo packet. The Microsoft implementation of the `ping` command unfortunately does not display all the answers, but most of the other implementations do. This enables us to see which computers are on.

Similarly, using the `ping` command (with TTL=1), it is possible to find out what computers in the LAN are dealing with what particular multicasts. One of multicast addresses is 224.0.0.1. It is a multicast for "All Systems on this Subnet" (see RFC 1112 or `http://www.iana.org/assignments/multicast-addresses`).

```
ping 224.0.0.1
```

Unfortunately Microsoft operating systems handle this command in a strange way by only telling us 'Is alive', but not telling us the IP address.

6.1.2 Network Mask

Network masks are used to help define the network address, which is part of the IP address, namely to specify which bits of the IP address represent the network address. A network mask is a four-byte number. The bits specifying the network address are ones while all the rest are zeros. How the network mask works can be illustrated with an the example using binary notation.

The length of the network address part of an IP address varies with different network classes. Class A uses the first byte. This means that the standard network mask for Class A addresses has ones only in the first byte and zeros only in the remaining three bytes (11111111.00000000. 00000000.00000000). In decimal notation it is 255.0.0.0 and FF.00.00.00 in hexadecimal notation. Similarly, the standard Class B network mask in decimal notation is 255.255.0.0 (FF.FF.00.00 in hexadecimal notation). And finally for Class C it is 255.255.255.0 (FF.FF.FF.00 in hexadecimal notation).

Network masks corresponding to classes A, B, and C are called standard network masks. Network masks help to work out the network address of a computer with a particular IP address. For example, 170.85.255.248 or 10101010.01010101.11111111.11111000 in binary notation.

The answer is simple. First, we look into the IP address class table to find out that the address is a Class B IP address. Provided we use the standard network mask, the Class B network mask is 11111111.11111111.00000000.00000000.

The network address can be determined by multiplying each bit in the IP address by the corresponding bit in the network mask:

```
10101010.01010101.11111111.11111000

x   11111111.11111111.00000000.00000000
    --------------------------------------------------
    10101010.01010101.00000000.00000000
```

Having converted the result to decimal notation, we find out that the computer is in network 170.85.0.0.

This method of network address identification may seem overcomplicated with standard network masks as the network mask may seem important for operating system developers, but unimportant for network administrators. We will be able to appreciate the significance of the network mask as soon as we proceed to the next period of history.

6.2 Network: Second Period of History

In 1993, the RFC 1517–1520 **Classless Inter-Domain Routing (CIDR)** specifications were released. These specifications are only seldom referred to nowadays, but had changed the understanding of the term 'network' in the context of the Internet. Networks started to be regarded in terms of network masks instead of network classes.

The computer address part of the IP address was divided into two parts, the subnetwork address and the computer address.

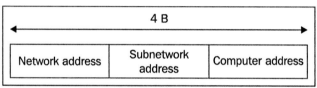

Figure 6.2: IP address structure

From the network address point of view, the network address and the subnetwork address form one unit. Briefly speaking, the IP address part with ones only in the network mask specifies the network. At this point, terminology becomes ambiguous. In some cases, the term network applies to an A, B, or C Class network while in other cases the term network refers to that part of the IP address for which there are ones in the corresponding network mask. If we forget the classes for a while and start using arbitrary masks, defining a network, for example, 192.168.0.0, will not suffice and the corresponding network mask has to be attached to specify the network. In terms of classes, the network will always have the 255.255.255.0 mask, for it is a Class C mask. The 255.255.255.0 mask for the 192.168.0.0 network is called the **standard network mask**.

Table 6.3 shows the division of a 192.168.0.0 network into subnetworks with various masks. (The standard mask is shown in bold.)

Mask	Number of ones in the mask	The network consists of an IP-address interval	Shortened network notation
255.248.0.0	13	192.168.0.0 to 192.175.255.255	192.168.0.0/13
255.252.0.0	14	192.168.0.0 to 192.171.255.255	192.168.0.0/14
255.254.0.0	15	192.168.0.0 to 192.169.255.255	192.168.0.0/15
255.255.0.0	16	192.168.0.0 to 192.168.255.255	192.168.0.0/16
255.255.248.0	21	192.168.0.0 to 192.168.7.255	192.168.0.0/21
255.255.252.0	22	192.168.0.0 to 192.168.3.255	192.168.0.0/22
255.255.254.0	23	192.168.0.0 to 192.168.1.255	192.168.0.0/23
255.255.255.0	**24**	**192.168.0.0 to 192.168.0.255**	**192.168.0.0/24**
255.255.255.128	25	192.168.0.0 to 192.168.0.127	192.168.0.0/25
255.255.255.192	26	192.168.0.0 to 192.168.0.63	192.168.0.0/26
255.255.255.224	27	192.168.0.0 to 192.168.0.31	192.168.0.0/27
255.255.255.240	28	192.168.0.0 to 192.168.0.15	192.168.0.0/28
255.255.255.248	29	192.168.0.0 to 192.168.0.7	192.168.0.0/29
255.255.255.252	30	192.168.0.0 to 192.168.0.3	192.168.0.0/30
255.255.255.254	*31*	*192.168.0.0 to 192.168.0.1**	*192.168.0.0/31*
255.255.255.255	32	The entire computer address (host address) 192.168.0.0	192.168.0.0/32

Table 6.3: Division of a 192.168.0.0 network into subnetworks

> * The network shown in italics is absurd as it would have two addresses only: one for the entire network and another for broadcast; hence no addresses are left for computers.

Addresses with masks of *fewer* ones than in the standard mask are called super-network addresses (see the upper part of the table) and addresses with masks of more ones than in the standard mask are called subnetwork addresses (see the lower part of the table).

Since the binary notation of a network mask is represented by a continuous series of ones from the left side, it is common to shorten "192.168.0.0 network with 255.255.255.252 mask" as 192.168.0.0/30, with number 30 defining the number of ones in the mask.

> I can hear the angry voices of readers questioning why the mask should consist of a *continuous* series of ones. Although this does not have to be so in theory, it is an unwritten rule, and a good one.

Let us take, for example, a 192.168.0.0 network with a 255.255.255.95 mask. 95 expressed in binary notation is 01011111, i.e., changes in positions x1x11111 are available, which as a result means that the network is 00000000 (0 in decimal notation) computer addresses are 00100000 (32 in binary notation) and 10000000 (128 in binary notation) and the broadcast is 10100000 (160 in binary notation). Inserting new subnetworks between these addresses is a problem that is hard to solve.

How do you feel now about administering such a network? The point is that most software does support such networks. The network mask does not differentiate between the network and subnetwork parts of an IP address.

6.2.1 Subnetworks

A subnetwork is a part of the Internet that corresponds to a company or a part of a company.

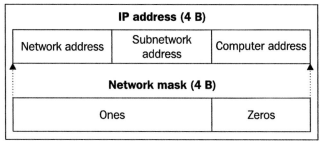

Figure 6.3: IP address and its network mask

Reserved addresses are used as well:

network.subnetwork.00...0	Address of the subnetwork as such
network.00...0.00...0	Network address
network.subnetwork.11...1	Subnetwork broadcast
network.11...1.11...1	This is a broadcast for all subnetworks of the entire network

Table 6.4: Special-use addresses

It is evident that a subnetwork with only zeros in the subnetwork part of the address presents a problem, as it is hard to differentiate between the network and subnetwork addresses. Another ambiguity arises when there are only ones in the subnetwork part of the address as it is unclear whether the multicast is for the entire subnetwork or all subnetworks. For these reasons, the use of these networks is avoided. Most software does not support these subnetworks at all while in other programs, special configurations must be set to support these subnetworks.

A broadcast sent to all subnetworks of a particular network is only a theoretical concept anyway. I have never come across a case of its use, probably due to the fact that the router lacks information on how the remote network is structured to subnetworks.

Subnetworks are used within companies for configuring individual local networks. Due to lack of IP addresses, most companies have been assigned C class subnetworks only. These are further divided into minor subnetworks.

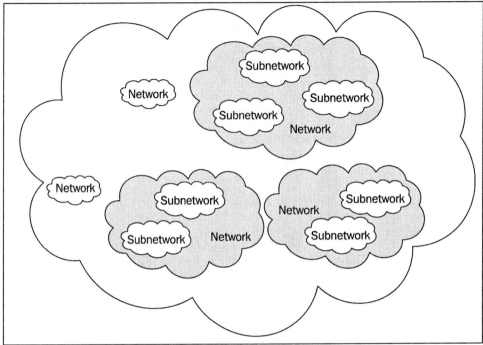

Figure 6.4: The Internet consists of networks that can be further divided to subnetworks

An example: I am trying to connect a company to the Internet. I have been assigned a C class address (e.g., 194.149.115.0 in decimal notation and 11000010.10010101.01110011.00000000 in binary notation). I was lucky to get a whole C class address.

The complicated structure of the company presents a problem. Its network consists of a variety of minor Local Area Networks (LAN) and serial lines connecting them. It is necessary to divide the network that has been assigned to the company into subnetworks. From outside, the company will appear as one network with a standard mask.

As the first three bytes of the assigned IP address are constant, only the last byte of the IP address will be quoted further in the text (the first three bytes remain constant, e.g., 194.149.115).

It is evident at first glance that to divide the subnetwork (instead of a standard network mask for a C class address, i.e. 255.255.255.0), a non-standard, but **constant network mask** 255.255.255.240 (11111111.11111111.11111111.11110000 in binary notation) can be used. Note that the first half of the last byte serves as the subnetwork address, which allows us to divide the assigned C class address into 16 subnetworks with 16 addresses each.

Subnetwork in binary notation (the last byte of the 194.149.115.0 IP address)	Network mask (in binary notation)	Subnetwork address (in decimal notation)	Network mask (in decimal notation)	Maximum number of computers within a particular subnetwork (without the subnetwork address and broadcast)
00000000 to 00001111	11110000	.0	.240	0 (non-unique subnetwork)
00010000 to 00011111		.16		14
00100000 to 00101111		.32		14
00110000 to 00111111		.48		14
01000000 to 01001111		.64		14
01010000 to 01011111		.80		14
01100000 to 01100000		.96		14
01110000 to 01111111		.112		14
10000000 to 10001111		.128		14
10010000 to 10011111		.144		14
10100000 to 10101111		.160		14
10110000 to 10111111		.176		14
11000000 to 11001111		.192		14
11010000 to 11011111		.208		14
11100000 to 11101111		.224		14
11110000 to 11111111		.240		0 (non-unique subnetwork)

Table 6.5: Subnetwork addresses

Each subnetwork consists of 16 addresses, 14 of which can be used since two addresses are reserved for special use. Zeros only mark the subnetwork address and ones only indicate the subnetwork broadcast. For example, the address 194.149.115.32 specifies the third subnetwork as such and the address 194.149.115.47 is a broadcast on this subnetwork (194.149.115.255 is a broadcast on the entire network 194.149.155.0). Addresses that can be assigned to network interfaces therefore ranges from 194.149.155.33 to 46 only.

Another problem is that it is not clear whether the address 194.149.155.255 is the broadcast on all subnetworks of this network or on the subnetwork 194.149.115.240 only. For this reason the last subnetwork is generally not used. A similar problem is the collision of network and subnetwork address 194.149.115.0. This is why the first subnetwork is generally not used either.

Dividing the assigned address into subnetworks consisting of the same number of addresses is usually not necessary in practice. For example, subnetworks of 14 addresses each is an unnecessary luxury for serial links while being insufficient for many LANs on the other hand. To divide a network into subnetworks of different lengths, a *variable subnetwork mask* can be used. See Table 6.6 for an example:

Subnetwork in binary notation (the last byte of the IP address)	Network mask (in binary notation)	Subnetwork address (in decimal notation)	Network mask (in decimal notation)	Maximum number of computers within a particular subnetwork (without the subnetwork address and broadcast)
00000000 to 00000011	11111100	.0	.252	0 (non-unique subnetwork)
00000100 to 00000111	11111100	.4/30	.252	2
00001000 to 00001111	11111000	.8/29	.248	6
00010000 to 00011111	11110000	.16/28	.240	14
00100000 to 00111111	11100000	.32/27	.224	30
01000000 to 01111111	11000000	.64/26	.192	62
10000000 to 10111111	11000000	.128/26	.192	62
11000000 to 11011111	11100000	.192/27	.224	30
11100000 to 11101111	11110000	.224/28	.240	14
11110000 to 11100011	11111000	.240/29	.248	6
11111000 to 11111011	11111100	.248/30	.252	2
11111100 to 11111111	11111100	.252/30	.252	0 (non-unique subnetwork)

Table 6.6: Subnetwork addresses

It is evident from the table above that the largest subnetwork can have up to 64 addresses; therefore, if we need a LAN of more than 62 network interfaces, it is reasonable to use a whole C class address.

Now we can show one more example. Work out the address of the network in which there is a computer whose IP address is 10.0.0.239 provided we use the network mask 255.255.255.240.

Let us convert the IP address and the mask to binary notation and multiply bit by bit:

00001010.00000000.00000000.11101111 ($10.0.0.239_{10}$)

x   11111111.11111111.11111111.11110000 ($255.255.255.240_{10}$)

\-

00001010.00000000.00000000.11100000 ($10.0.0.224_{10}$)

The address is on the network 10.0.0.224. But can this be a computer address? No. Why is that? Let us differentiate the network address from the computer address:

00001010.00000000.0000000.1110|1111
<————————network————————>|<comp.>

The form of the address is network.ones; this means it is not a computer address, but a broadcast of the network 10.0.0.224.

As with networks, a broadcast can be sent with the `ping` command:

`ping 10.0.0.240`

The command works if there is a computer in the subnetwork that is alive, and a UNIX implementation of the `ping` command shows us which of the subnetwork computers are on.

6.2.2 Super-Networks and Autonomous Systems

While subnetworks are used for LAN purposes, i.e., in configurations of individual network interfaces (network cards), super-networks are used for IP address aggregation. IP address aggregation is helpful for routing and administration in assigning IP addresses.

The Internet is a system of interconnected Internet providers (or similar organizations). An Internet provider provides a commercial or noncommercial Internet connection. Besides providers, the Internet comprises a few other organizations that are involved in the investigation and development of the Internet, and they, however, do not differ from providers in terms of networks.

Providers transfer IP datagrams either within their own network or between one another. Apart from providers who can transfer IP datagrams between one another, there are also transit providers by whom IP datagrams are transferred.

The Internet is not spoken of as being divided into providers, but into autonomous systems related to IP datagram routing. Each provider has one or several autonomous systems assigned. An autonomous system is represented by a two-byte number.

From routing point of view, the Internet is divided into **autonomous systems (AS)**. AS is a set of IP networks maintained by routers exchanging routing information via a common routing protocol.

Internet Service Providers (ISP) are administrators of autonomous systems usually. They apply for IP address intervals to assign themselves and their customers. A set of assigned IP intervals of the given ISP (including IP intervals of its customer) form AS.

Address intervals can be aggregated into one or more super-network addresses. The whole allocated address space of the given ISP can act as a single or few entries in the routing tables of a router of a remote AS. This saves the router's memory and makes administration easier.

Aggregation is simple. If, for example, a network address interval 62.177.64.0 to 62.177.127.0 has been assigned, it can be aggregated to the super-network address 62.177.64.0 with the network mask 255.255.192.0. The common notation of the address, however, is 62.177.64.0/18 (the mask 255.255.192.0 consists of 18 ones).

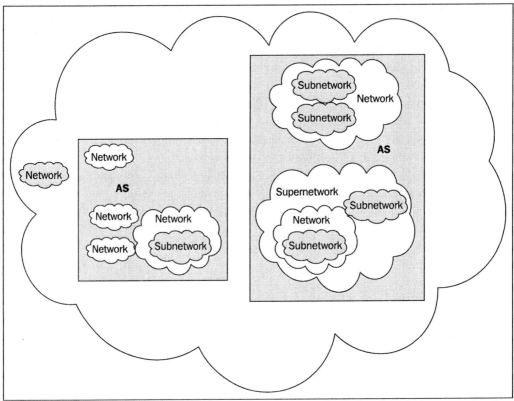

Figure 6.5: The Internet is divided into autonomous systems that can be further divided into super-networks. Super-networks are in turn divided into networks and are further divided into subnetworks.

Dividing a network into subnetworks involves a rise in the number of ones in the network mask, the opposite is the case with aggregation. Aggregated networks are called super-networks. From the viewpoint of an AS, a super-network appears as an integral whole. AS administrators regard networks as an integral whole. And subnetworks are seen as an integral whole by local network administrators.

When a company switches from one provider to another that belongs to a different autonomous system, a problem occurs. The company has to apply for new IP addresses with the new provider and have its networks renumbered. The computer's names (including the email address) can, nevertheless, be preserved.

Provider-independent addresses are used as well; they are assigned to companies connected to several providers simultaneously or companies connected to a LAN that creates a core of a **NIX (Neutral Internet eXchange)**, where IP datagrams are transferred collectively among individual providers.

Let us return to one of our previous hypothetical examples, where a company had been assigned the IP address interval 62.177.90.0/24. As the company is situated at several locations, the administrator assigned the Budweis subnetwork (Budweis is a town in the south of the Czech Republic), the IP address interval 62.177.90.176/28. At this location, there is a computer with IP address 62.177.90.190. The computer tries to communicate with a server in Fiji (to download a web page http://www.fijimuseum.org.fj/). The IP datagrams are transferred via the Internet to Fiji. Then the Fiji server tries to respond.

The address 62.177.90.190 belongs to the interval 62.0.0.0/8 assigned to RIPE (a Regional IP Registry in Europe and neighboring territories). As far as the Fiji server is concerned, the recipient is somewhere between Portugal, Svalbard and Kamchatka. The Fiji server theoretically does not need to work out to which autonomous system the address 62.177.90.190 belongs, provided that all transfers to Europe are sent through satellite or underwater cable. Theoretically, its routing table can have a single entry for Europe and neighboring territories (62.0.0.0 with the mask 254.0.0.0).

The geographical distance from Fiji to Europe is approximately the same whether the direction is to the west, east, south, or north, but the datagram is now sent to a router in the U.S. It is not that simple there. There are many lines from America to Europe, and it is necessary to work out in which direction the datagram should be transferred and by which line it should be sent. The router in the U.S. finds out that the address 62.177.90.190 belongs to the interval 60.177.64.0/18, which belongs to the autonomous system AS6706. The routing table of its routers must have one entry for each address interval assigned to the autonomous system AS6706. In this case it is 62.177.64.0 with the mask 255.255.192.0.

Important routers in the U.S. situated on the border of autonomous systems must have one entry for every IP address interval assigned to a provider anywhere on Earth. Such a router is said to have complete routing tables for the entire Internet. These routers with complete routing tables are needed as border routers of transit autonomous systems, i.e., autonomous systems through which datagrams are transferred to other autonomous systems. If our datagram has been received on the Western shore of the U.S., it will have to be transferred through American transit autonomous systems to the East coast where the underwater cables to Europe are located.

Exchanging IP datagrams between autonomous systems depends not only on technical factors, i.e., on the technically most advantageous route to the recipient, but also on the *routing policy* of individual autonomous systems. This, in familiar terms, means whether the other side pays for transit or not. Should there be any obstacles, the IP datagram can be transferred via a more complicated route or its routing can even be forbidden by the administration.

Our IP datagram has arrived from the U.S. via a border router of our autonomous system AS6706. The router has to analyze the address thoroughly, finding out that the IP address 62.177.90.190 belongs to the interval 62.177.90.0/24 assigned to our company.

In the routing tables of the autonomous system AS6706, there is the entry 62.177.90.0 with the mask 255.255.255.0.

The provider transfers the IP datagram to the border router of our company, which analyses the address 62.177.90.190 to figure out where the IP datagram is to be sent. The company's border router finds out that its routing table entry (the Budweis LAN) reads as 62.177.90.176 with the mask 255.255.255.240.

The IP datagram is transferred to a router in Budweis. The router works out that the network 62.177.90.176/28 is a network directly connected to its local interface. It finds out via the ARP protocol what the six-byte link address of the recipient is (if the address is not in its ARP cache) and sends the IP datagram to the recipient. The recipient discards the IP header and works out from the TCP header that the information is designed for a web browser, discards the TCP header, and the content in HTTP protocol is interpreted on a screen.

I have just tried it and found that the whole process between a server in Fiji and a client in Budweis (Europe) takes about 340 milliseconds. The example shows not only the speed and throughput of the routing links, but also the enormous capacity of the border routers that have to search the routing tables at an immense speed. For this reason, the border routers are often equipped with specialized co-processors designed to handle routing tables.

The numbers of autonomous systems are assigned by Regional Internet Registries. They are international agencies such as the RIPE agency in Europe, AfriNIC for African Countries, ARIN in North America, LACNIC in Latin America or APNIC in the Asian Pacific Region. These agencies keep information on assigned IP address intervals and assigned autonomous systems numbers in their databases.

On the ftp://ftp.ripe.net/tools/IRRToolSet FTP server, the **Information Sciences Institute (ISI)** offers the prtraceroute application that calls the traceroute command, while seeking information in the regional agencies' databases using the whois command from the traceroute command output. For example, as far as autonomous systems are concerned, a route to Fiji looks like the following:

```
$ prtraceroute www.fijimuseum.org.fj
    1 [AS6706] lo0.adsl-plus-jhc.adsl.vol.cz (212.20.125.148) 85 ms 14 ms 13 ms
    2 [AS6706] adsl-plus-1.adsl.ctc-ptp04.vol.cz (212.20.125.141) 99 ms 14 ms 15 ms
    3 [AS6706] ge3-42.c17.prg.vol.cz (195.122.209.37) 15 ms 15 ms 14 ms
    4 [AS6706] ge3-42.c17.prg.vol.cz (195.122.209.37) 14 ms 14 ms 16 ms
    5 [AS6706] ge5-1.tr3.prg.vol.cz (195.122.207.119) 16 ms 19 ms 15 ms
    6 [AS8447] AUX1-Czech-Online.highway.telekom.at (195.3.102.209) 26 ms 26 ms 25 ms
    7 [AS8447] IIX2-WARSSW02.highway.telekom.at (195.3.70.196) 29 ms 28 ms 27 ms
    8 [AS3356] 212.73.202.122 ms 20 ms 24 ms
    9 [AS3356] so-4-0-0.mp1.Vienna1.Level3.net (4.68.112.77) 22 ms 23 ms 22 ms
   10 [AS3356] ae-0-0.bbr2.NewYork1.Level3.net (64.159.1.42) 114 ms 121 ms 113 ms
   11 [AS3356] ae-11-51.car1.NewYork1.Level3.net (4.68.97.20) 114 ms 122 ms 114 ms
   12 [AS3356] mci-level3-oc48.NewYork1.Level3.net (4.68.111.30) 118 ms 118 ms 115 ms
   13 [AS701] 0.so-6-0-0.XL1.NYC4.ALTER.NET (152.63.21.78) 119 ms 118 ms 122 ms
   14 [AS701] 0.so-7-0-0.XL1.SAC1.ALTER.NET (152.63.53.249) 207 ms 206 ms 205 ms
   15 [AS701] POS6-0.IG3.SAC1.ALTER.NET (152.63.54.121) 241 ms 206 ms 207 ms
   16 [AS701] fintelfiji4-gw.customer.alter.net (157.130.214.186) 338 ms 335 ms 337 ms
   17 [AS9241] 202.170.33.15335 ms 336 ms 333 ms
   18 [AS9241] 202.137.176.253336 ms 332 ms 336 ms
   19 [AS9241] juniper1.is.com.fj (210.7.20.2) 338 ms 335 ms *
   20 [AS9241] www.fijimuseum.org.fj (202.62.120.2) 339 ms 337 ms 335 ms

Path taken:
AS6706 AS8447 AS3356 AS701 AS9241
```

The first column is the hop number, the second column is the autonomous system number (square bracket in decimal notation preceded by the AS string), the third column shows the router interface DNS name, the fourth one in parentheses is its IP address, followed by three round trip times.

The single line headed Path taken lists the route where a hop is defined, not as a router, but as an autonomous system.

The `prtraceroute` command is a great help to an autonomous system administrator because if a connection is lost, the autonomous system connected most recently can be found via the `prtraceroute` command. By entering string AS9241 into APNIC WHOIS Database Search in the web page `http://www.apnic.net` we obtain:

```
as-block:    AS9216 - AS10239
descr:       APNIC ASN block
remarks:     These AS numbers are further assigned by APNIC
remarks:     to APNIC members and end-users in the APNIC region
admin-c:     HM20-AP
tech-c:      HM20-AP
mnt-by:      APNIC-HM
mnt-lower:   APNIC-HM
changed:     hm-changed@apnic.net 20020926
changed:     hm-changed@apnic.net 20030205
changed:     hm-changed@apnic.net 20060103
source:      APNIC

aut-num:     AS9241
as-name:     FINTEL-FJ
descr:       Fiji International Telecomunications Ltd
country:     FJ
import:      from AS701
             action pref=5;
             accept ANY
import:      from AS7474
             action pref=15;
             accept ANY
export:      to AS701
             announce AS9241
export:      to AS7474
             announce AS9241
default:     to AS701
             action pref=5;
             networks ANY
default:     to AS7474
             action pref=15;
             networks ANY
remarks:     www.fintelfiji.com
admin-c:     IK136-AP
tech-c:      LN21-AP
mnt-by:      MAINT-FJ-LNAKACIA
changed:     lmnakacia@fintelfiji.com 20040316
source:      APNIC

person:      Ioane N Koroivuki
nic-hdl:     IK136-AP
e-mail:      inkoroivuki@fintelfiji.com
address:     FINTEL
address:     PO Box 59
address:     Suva
address:     Fiji
phone:       +679-3312933
fax-no:      +679-3300750
country:     FJ
changed:     lmnakacia@fintelfiji.com 20030128
mnt-by:      MAINT-FJ-FINTEL
source:      APNIC

person:      Laisiasa Nakacia
address:     C/- Fintel
address:     PO Box 59
address:     Suva, Fiji
country:     FJ
```

```
phone:      +679-312933
fax-no:     +679-300750
e-mail:     lmnakacia@fintelfiji.com
nic-hdl:    LN21-AP
mnt-by:     MAINT-NEW
changed:    lmnakacia@fintelfiji.com 20010310
source:     APNIC
```

The administrator can get in touch with an administrator of the autonomous system connected to most recently and ask him or her for help. With the help of the WHOIS database and searching on the Internet registries web pages, it is possible to find information about IP networks assignment and other interesting information.

6.3 IP Addresses in the Intranet and Special-Use IP Addresses

Using Internet technology inside corporate network is referred to as *intranet*.

IP addresses must be assigned uniquely worldwide. Just a few years ago, many companies had their networks built on the TCP/IP protocol and no one had ever dreamt of connecting them to the Internet. This is why they chose entirely arbitrary addresses for their networks. Nowadays, companies tend to connect their networks to the Internet through a firewall and some discover that their addresses are already used by someone else. They are forced to renumber their networks, which is a painstaking operation.

At first, companies using intranet addresses colliding with Internet ones mostly tried to find a fresh solution to avoid renumbering their intranet addresses. As a solution we mention **Network Address Translation** (**NAT**), but solutions of this kind have drawbacks of their own and these vain efforts are usually followed by renumbering the whole intranet anyway.

For interconnected corporate networks use IP addresses as specified in RFC 1918 and presented in Table 6.7.

Class A	10.0.0.0/8	10.0.0.0 to 10.255.255.255
Class B	172.16.0.0/12	172.16.0.0 to 172.31.255.255
Class C	192.168.0.0/16	192.168.0.0 to 192.168.255.255

Table 6.7: IP address specified in RFC 1918

The use of these addresses helps to increase security because they cannot be used in the Internet (they are used by hundreds of companies in their interconnected networks concurrently). Addresses in these ranges can be used without requesting them to be assigned.

A frequently asked question is how Internet providers ensure that these addresses are not used; do they filter them off? No filtering is needed since these addresses are simply not included in the routing tables and therefore cannot be routed to.

I also recommend going through RFC 3330 (*Special-Use IPv4 Addresses*). You will see that besides the intervals reserved for intranets that were mentioned, there are other intervals of IP addresses allocated for special use. I found the following ones especially interesting:

- 169.254.0.0/16: This is the **link-local** block. It is allocated for communication between hosts on a single link. These addresses are preferred by Microsoft. If a network interface is being auto configured by Windows and its IP address cannot be found (not even by DHCP protocol), then the network interface is assigned an IP address from this IP range.

- 192.0.2.0/24: This block is assigned as **TEST-NET** for use in documentation and example code. It is often used in conjunction with domain names example.com or example.net in vendor and protocol documentation. Addresses within this block should not appear on the public Internet.

- 198.18.0.0/15: This block has been allocated for use in benchmark tests of network interconnection devices (RFC 2544).

Intervals of autonomous system numbers are allocated in the same way as IP address intervals, i.e., the different Regional Internet Registries (RIPE, APNIC, ARIN, AfriNIC, and LACNIC) have been allocated intervals from which they allocate AS numbers to individual Internet providers.

Autonomous system numbers for private use on intranets are allocated too, namely, AS64512-65534 (see http://www.iana.org/assignments/as-numbers).

6.4 Unnumbered Interface

Let us consider serial links connecting LANs. For such a link, a subnetwork of at least four IP addresses is needed (a network address, a network broadcast, and two addresses for network interfaces on routers).

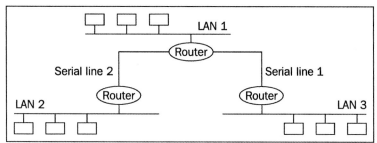

Figure 6.6: LAN connected via serial links

It is obvious from Figure 6.6 that besides the three IP address intervals for local networks, other addresses for serial link networks will be necessary. It is clear at first glance, that not using another network address for serial links would be very efficient.

Current routers are able to create an *unnumbered interface* on point-to-point links adjacent routers act as a single virtual router. Each physical router represents one half of this virtual router. The virtual router has two interfaces only—one per each LAN.

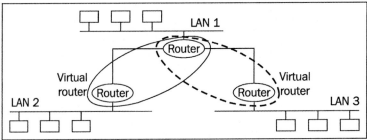

Figure 6.7: Unnumbered networks

There is no need then to waste IP addresses for serial links.

6.4.1 Dynamic Address Assignment

If a network has already been assigned an IP address interval, it is possible to start assigning addresses to network interfaces in the network. There are two ways of doing it:

- Static (permanent) IP address assignment
- Dynamic (at connection time) IP address assignment

Dynamic address assignment is dealt with by the DHCP application protocol usually. The DHCP protocol is based on older protocols such as ARP, RARP, and BOOTP. For further information, see RFC 2131.

In the DHCP protocol, a client requests to be assigned an IP address (or other services) by the DHCP server. The DHCP server can be represented by a process on a computer running UNIX, Windows, or any other operating system. Alternatively, the DHCP server can be represented by a part of a router, wireless access point, or switch.

While IP address assignment in a LAN is currently a DHCP protocol domain, the PPP protocol is usually used for IP address assignment to computers on a point-to-point lines.

The PPP protocol does not offer the same services as the DHCP protocol, but can assign an IP address to a station. Connecting a user to the Internet usually does not require anything else.

While the IP address assigned by PPP is usually assigned for the connection time (the involved router knows when the particular point-to-point connection starts and ends), an IP address assigned by the DHCP protocol is reserved for a longer time—the DHCP server does not know, for example, when a user takes his or her PC off the LAN.

6.5 Address Plan

Every company intending to be connected to the Internet must have an address plan first. It usually consists of two parts. The first is a schematic diagram of individual LAN to WAN connections, the other is a list of the individual LANs with estimated numbers of LAN interfaces. The address plan should include a reserve for potential expansion over the next two years. The reserve is usually double the present capacity. Then the address plan is sent to an Internet provider, implying a request for assigning a corresponding number of IP addresses.

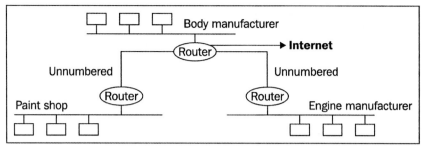

Figure 6.8: A fictitious company network

An example: We are supposed to connect to the Internet a company using three local networks: Car Body Works, Paint Shop, and Engine Plant (a Regional Internet Registry never accepts a general application for the three A, B, and C networks—the concrete request must always be specified).

There are 8 computers in the Car Body Works, and the number is expected to increase to 16; the nine computers in the Engine Plant are expected to become 18; and the 20 computers in the Paint Shop are expected to become 40.

The required number of IP addresses in the three networks is 128:

LAN	Present state	Next year	In 2 years	The closest possibility for LAN	Required
Car Body Works	8	10	16	32*	32
Paint Shop	9	15	18	32	32
Engine Plant	20	35	40	64	64

Table 6.7: Present and projected computer requirements. * 16 is not sufficient because the subnetwork and broadcast addresses are reserved; therefore the requirement is 32

It may seem strange to connect individual departments to the Internet. Nowadays, companies do not need more than 16 Internet IP addresses. They usually choose one of the firewall connections delineated in Figure 6.9.

A demilitarized zone is a LAN accessible from the Internet and therefore with official IP addresses. The privilege of a demilitarized zone is that it is the only network in the Internet, which can be at least partly accessed from within an intranet simultaneously.

No more than the following IP addresses are required:

- A four IP address network for a serial link to the Internet (the network can be unnumbered too).
- For the Internet side of the firewall.
- For a demilitarized zone network, where, for example, a corporate web server is situated.

6.6 Over 254 Interfaces in a LAN

Cases may occur when a local network includes say around 300 computers. In these instances, one C class network is not enough and therefore two C class networks are assigned. Using two separate C class networks creates the danger of incorrect configuration. The LAN must have a router for routing between them (or a proxy ARP must be used). Instead of communicating within the network directly with each other, the computers must use the router. But the real drawback is that the data is transferred twice, once from the sender to the router and for a second time from the router to the recipient, which is most cumbersome with 300 computers in the network.

A reasonable solution is to use a super-network consisting of two C class networks, i.e., a super-network with the mask /23, i.e., 255.255.128.0.

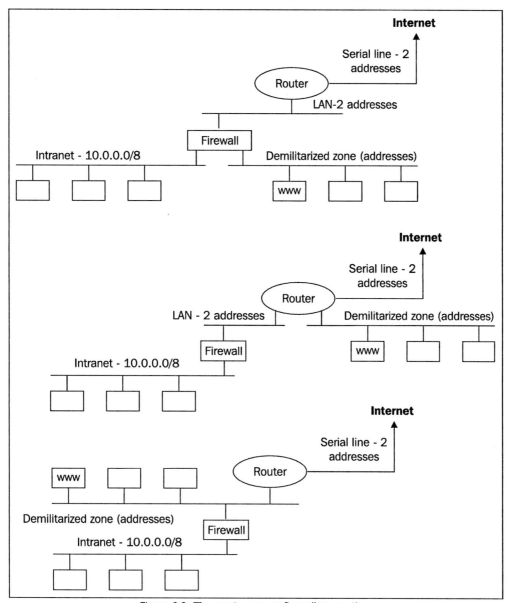

Figure 6.9: The most common firewall connections

7
Routing

IP routing and IP forwarding are two processes that are at the very foundation of the Internet. Every system with TCP/IP protocol installed has at least one network interface called **loopback**. Besides, it can have one or more network interface cards installed. Let us imagine we have received one link frame, carrying an IP datagram, through the first installed network interface card. Its processing, summarized in Figure 7.1, can be described in the following steps:

1. The IP datagram is extracted from the link frame. The sender's link address can be used to refresh the ARP cache.
2. The extracted IP datagram is inserted into an input queue and waits here for its processing.
3. Processing of the header options is the first step within the processing. First, the options 'Loose source routing' and 'Strict source routing' are processed. If the IP datagram belongs (according to the content of the source routing options) to another receiver, it is passed on for forwarding.
4. Next, we must know if the IP datagram belongs to this station, if not, it is also passed on for forwarding.
5. Now, we must know if the datagram is an ICMP datagram. If so, it is processed and the answer, if any, is passed on for routing back (step number 7).
6. At this point, all the duties of the IP layer are fulfilled, and the IP datagram is passed on to the higher TCP/UDP layers. They will extract either the TCP segment or the UDP datagram from IP datagram and process it.
7. All the outgoing IP datagrams and IP datagrams that should be forwarded are processed in the routing system first. The goal of routing is to find out to which network interface the IP datagram should be given for forwarding. To be able to make such a decision the routing system has routing tables at its disposal.
8. The routing system must know if the sent IP datagram is a broadcast addressed to this station; if so, then a copy must be also given to the loopback interface.
9. If the sent IP datagram is either a broadcast or a multicast, skip step 10.
10. Before the IP datagram is wrapped into a link frame, the station makes sure if the IP datagram is addressed to it, if so, it is passed on to the loopback interface.
11. If the IP datagram is either broadcast or multicast, direct mapping of the IP address to a link address is done. The IP datagram is put into a link frame and sent.
12. If it is a unicast, the IP datagram is wrapped into a link frame using the ARP protocol and sent.

Looking at Figure 7.1 in detail, you will find the answer to the question "*Why do I have to configure a loopback?*" Whenever an interface finds out that an IP datagram should be forwarded back to the input, it is instead forwarded to the program loop, which takes care of the operation.

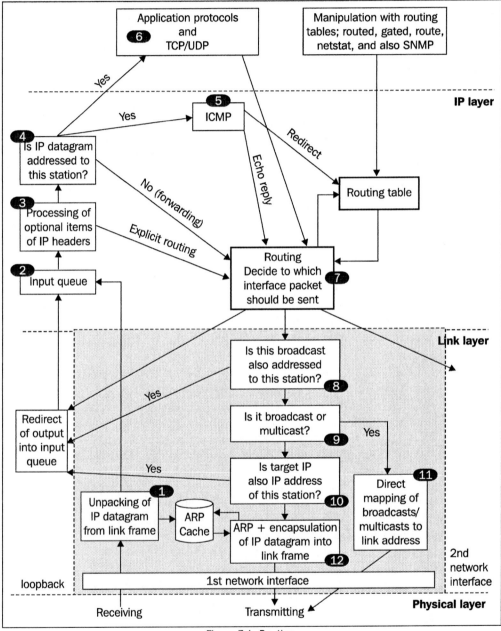

Figure 7.1: Routing

Among other things, Figure 7.1 shows that during the processing of input data, on some occasions, the operating system forwards the information automatically to the output (to the routing process), i.e., application programs do not interfere with the forwarding. These instances include:

- Source routing
- Forwarding
- Echo request
- Redirect

The kernel of the operating system always includes parameters enabling you to ban the automatic processing of IP datagrams. While the ban on source routing is very common, echo requests are banned only rarely.

7.1 Forwarding and Screening

Forwarding enables the use of a station (for example, computer) as a router. When a station finds out that an IP datagram is not addressed to it, it tries to forward it, i.e., send it in the same way as it sends its own IP datagrams.

Forwarding can be banned too, by configuring the kernel of the operating system. With older systems, such a ban required a recompilation of the kernel of the operating system. With current systems, the same can be done dynamically (for example, Windows 2000, Windows XP, or most UNIX systems). It may, however, be necessary to restart the system after such modification.

The situation with Windows 2000/XP is interesting. In Windows 2000/XP, forwarding is set by inserting the value 1 into the `IpEnableRouter` key, which is in the `HKEY_LOCAL_MACHINE\SYSTEM\CurrentControlSet\Services\Tcpip\Parameters` registry folder.

It is an interesting feature of many operating systems that they do not forward IP datagrams mechanically, but screen them, i.e., they do not forward all packets, but only some of them (the screened ones).

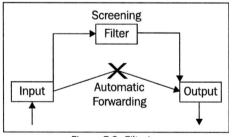

Figure 7.2: Filtering

The way screening most often works is that before an IP datagram is forwarded, the whole forwarding procedure is suspended and the decision to forward an IP datagram or not is left to a process (service) running in the background.

The forwarded IP datagram is handed over to a screening procedure that confirms or rejects the forwarding. The screening procedure makes a decision based on the information in:

1. The IP header, for example, if the addressee is or is not on the blacklist.
2. The TCP-header, for example, according to port numbers and/or an ACK or SYN flag are set.
3. The application protocol, used by some firewalls.

The implementation of the first two types of screening is common on routers. The third type of screening is a method used with firewalls working on the screening principle (as opposed to proxy firewalls).

7.2 Routing

The routing of IP datagrams is very similar to sorting letters at a post office. There is a sorting table with slots in it. Each slot has a mail pouch attached beneath. All slots are marked with the names of the respective towns with direct mail service from the town where the post office is situated.

Sorting is done by a post office clerk, who sorts letters one by one and checks the address of every letter. If the addressee is, say, in Vienna, the clerk drops the letter into the slot marked Vienna. If the addressee is in a village near Prague, the clerk drops the letter into the slot marked Prague (since there is no direct mail service to the village near Prague and the nearest point with direct mail service is Prague). When all the letters have been dealt with, the mail pouches are detached from the sorting table. A tag with the name of the town where the pouch is to be sent is attached to each of them and the mail pouches are sent.

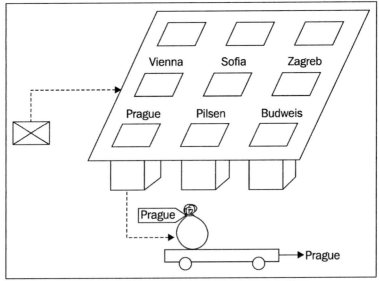

Figure 7.3: Manual sorting of letters in a post office

A router does not sort letters, but IP datagrams. The process is called **routing**. When a router receives an IP datagram, it must decide to which of its interfaces (slots on the sorting desk) it is to be fed and to which of its neighbors (*next hop)* it is to be sent.

To make the long story short, a router is a device that sorts and delivers IP datagrams among its interfaces. An IP datagram can be delivered to the same interface it came from, but since such cases are considered wasteful, the IP datagram sender is notified of the fact by means of a *redirect* ICMP packet.

The router in the following picture has received an IP datagram addressed to the destination 10.5.2.1 and has to decide whether the IP datagram is to be sent to Serial 1, Serial 2, or possibly to the Ethernet interface again.

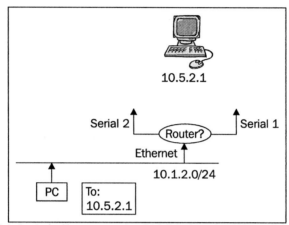

Figure 7.4: Router's dilemma over to which interface should it send the packet.

A router uses a routing table (a parallel to a sorting table in a post office) to make its decision. The routing table of the entire router is as follows:

Network	Mask	Next Hop	Network Interface	Metric
192.168.1.0	255.255.255.0	192.168.254.5	Serial 1	4
10.1.2.0	255.255.255.0	Local interface	Ethernet	0
10.5.1.0	255.255.255.0	10.10.10.2	Serial 2	3
10.5.0.0	255.255.0.0	10.5.5.5	Serial 1	2
...				
0.0.0.0	0.0.0.0	10.10.10.2	Serial 2	1

Table 7.1: Routing table

The first column of the routing table states the IP address of the destination network. To illustrate the situation, let us imagine that the routing table is arranged in descending order according to the first column. This allows us to apply the basic rule of routing easily, which is as follows: A more specific address of the destination network has priority over a less specific address.

A more specific address is understood as an address whose network mask includes more ones. If there are two or more pathways to the destination network in the routing table, the more specific one is used. If there are two pathways with the same level of specification, the pathway with the lowest metric (price) is used.

7.2.1 Processing

Provided that the lines of the routing table are arranged in descending order, the sorting table can be processed from the top to the bottom. A network mask is taken from every line and the IP address of the IP datagram's destination is multiplied with it bit by bit. The result is compared with the first column. If the result is not identical with the IP network address in the first column, the following line is processed. If the result is identical with the IP address in the first column, the next line is checked for another pathway to the destination address (then the metric would play a role).

Let us return to the example from Figure 7.4. The router is deciding to which of its network interfaces the IP datagram with the IP address 10.5.2.1 is to be sent. The router is processing its routing table:

1st line:

| 192.168.1.0 | 255.255.255.0 | 192.168.254.5 | Serial 1 | 4 |

By multiplying bit by bit the target address 10.5.2.1 with the mask 255.255.255.0, we obtain the result 10.5.2.0, which is not identical with the network IP address in the first column (the address is 192.168.1.0). Because no match was found the next line is processed.

2nd line:

| 10.1.2.0 | 255.255.255.0 | Local interface | Ethernet | 0 |

By multiplying bit by bit the target address 10.5.2.1 with the mask 255.255.255.0, we obtain the result 10.5.2.0, which is not identical with the network IP address in the first column (the address is 10.1.2.0). Because no match was found the next line is processed.

3rd line:

| 10.5.1.0 | 255.255.255.0 | 10.10.10.2 | Serial 2 | 3 |

By multiplying bit by bit the target address 10.5.2.1 with the mask 255.255.255.0, we obtain the result 10.5.2.0, which is not identical with the network IP address in the first column (the address is 10.5.1.0). Because no match was found the next line is processed.

4th line:

| 10.5.0.0 | 255.255.0.0 | 10.5.5.5 | Serial 1 | 2 |

By multiplying bit by bit the target address 10.5.2.1 with the mask 255.255.0.0 we obtain the result 10.5.0.0, which is identical with the network IP address in the first column (the address is 10.5.0.0). The IP datagram will, therefore, be sent to Serial 1 and delivered to a router with the IP address 10.5.5.5. If it was an Ethernet interface instead of a serial link, then the link address of a router with the IP address 10.5.5.5 would have to be found via ARP protocol.

The last line in the first column with the address 0.0.0.0 and the mask 0.0.0.0 is called the *default route.* All IP datagrams that satisfy no other row of the routing table are sent through the default route (note that this route suits every address: zero multiplied by zero is zero). An default route can be included in the routing table or not; the content of a routing table depends on its administrator. An default route is used, for example, by companies for routing to the Internet.

When driving, say, from Dover to London, the default route is to London, and only the need to leave the main road is marked at many crossroads. There is a sign showing the way to Canterbury or Brighton, but the sign for the direct route to London is often missing. The road leading to London is an implicit piece of information (i.e., the *default route* is to London) and there is no need to repeat it every time.

7.3 Handling Routing Tables

A routing table has to be filled up with individual entries. The static entries stay in the routing table until they are removed or the system is switched off. The dynamic entries fed into routing tables by application protocols have their lifespan monitored and are removed after its expiration.

The English commands often use the term *gateway* instead of *router*, especially, in older manuals. The term *gateway* in a routing table stands for the next router (next hop) in the trip.

7.3.1 List of Contents of a Routing Table in a Command Prompt

The netstat -r command lists the contents of a routing table.

7.3.1.1 Contents of a Routing Table in UNIX

UNIX is an operating system with considerable history. The older versions of UNIX operating systems did not list the network mask. The standard network mask was presupposed and this made the lists confusing when other masks were used.

The more recent versions of UNIX list network masks in decimal notation or simply put slash after IP address followed by the number of ones in the network mask. For example, Linux uses decimal notation:

```
$ netstat -rn
Kernel IP routing table
Destination     Gateway          Genmask         Flags   MSS Window   irtt Iface
160.217.208.0   0.0.0.0          255.255.255.0   U         0 0           0 eth0
192.168.0.0     160.217.208.1    255.255.0.0     UG        0 0           0 eth0
0.0.0.0         160.217.208.254  0.0.0.0         UG        0 0           0 eth0
```

In the above example, the Destination specifies destination network, the Gateway specifies next hop, and the Genmask specifies a network mask.

The most interesting is the Flags column. The significance of the flags is as follows:

- U (up). The route is up.
- G (gateway). The G flag indicates that the route to the target address leads through a router (gateway), i.e., the next hop is a router. The link layer will search for the link address of the particular router, not the target address (which is not available directly).
- H (host). The H flag indicates that the particular address is an interface address (a computer), not a network address, i.e., the mask is 255.255.255.255.
- D (dynamic). The entry is added based on the redirect ICMP announcement or by daemon.
- M (modified). The entry is modified based on the redirect announcement or by daemon.
- R (reinstate route for dynamic routing).
- A (installed by addrconf).
- ! (reject route).

The MSS column specifies TCP Maximum Segment Size (MSS) for connections over this route in bytes. The window column specifies TCP window size for connections over this route in bytes. The irtt column specifies the initial round trip time (IRTT) for TCP connections over this route in milliseconds. The Iface column specifies the interface's name.

7.3.2 Routing Table Listing in Windows 2000/XP/2003

The netstat -r command lists the contents of a routing table in ascending order, i.e., the routing table has to be processed from the bottom to the top.

Now, let's focus on the following listing of a routing table. The PC had an interface with the IP address 192.168.2.111. If you check the first column, however, IP datagrams addressed to 192.168.2.111 are to be sent to the interface 127.0.0.1. It is correct since it is the address of a local network interface of this PC.

The conclusion is that while interfaces in Unix systems have their names, for example, eth0, in Microsoft routing table's IP addresses are used instead.

```
C:\ > netstat -r
    Route Table
    ===========================================================================
    Active Routes:
    Network Destination        Netmask          Gateway        Interface  Metric
              0.0.0.0          0.0.0.0      192.168.2.1    192.168.2.111     30
            127.0.0.0        255.0.0.0        127.0.0.1        127.0.0.1      1
          192.168.2.0    255.255.255.0    192.168.2.111    192.168.2.111     30
        192.168.2.111  255.255.255.255        127.0.0.1        127.0.0.1     30
        192.168.2.255  255.255.255.255    192.168.2.111    192.168.2.111     30
            224.0.0.0        240.0.0.0    192.168.2.111    192.168.2.111     30
      255.255.255.255  255.255.255.255    192.168.2.111            10004      1
      255.255.255.255  255.255.255.255    192.168.2.111    192.168.2.111      1
    Default Gateway:       192.168.2.1
    ===========================================================================
    Persistent Routes:
      Network Address          Netmask  Gateway Address   Metric
         192.168.15.0    255.255.255.0    192.168.2.54        1
```

The network 224.0.0.0 with the mask 224.0.0.0 stands for all multicasts (including reserved IP addresses, i.e., the D and E class IP addresses).

In Windows 2000/2003 Server, the program Routing and Remote Access is available (it is a snap-in console module), which can be used to list the contents of a routing table and add/remove static entries. Besides this, the program can configure routing protocols in Windows 2000/2003.

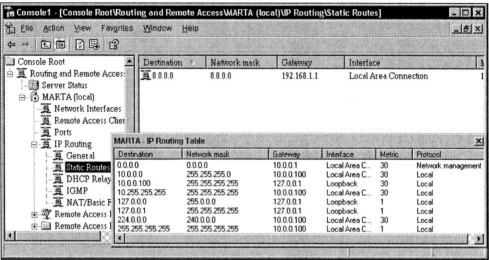

Figure 7.5: The contents of a routing table obtained using the Routing and remote access program

7.3.3 Contents of a Routing Table in Cisco Routers

The contents of CISCO routing tables can be listed by unprivileged users as well:

```
Router>sho ip route
    Codes: C - connected, S - static, I - IGRP, R - RIP, M - mobile, B - BGP
           D - EIGRP, EX - EIGRP external, O - OSPF, IA - OSPF inter area
           N1 - OSPF NSSA external type 1, N2 - OSPF NSSA external type 2
           E1 - OSPF external type 1, E2 - OSPF external type 2, E - EGP
           i - IS-IS, L1 - IS-IS level-1, L2 - IS-IS level-2, * - candidate
    default
           U - per-user static route, o - ODR

    Gateway of last resort is 195.47.37.192 to network 0.0.0.0

           195.47.37.0/27 is subnetted, 1 subnets
    C         195.47.37.192 is directly connected, Ethernet0
           10.0.0.0/24 is subnetted, 3 subnets
    S         10.4.6.0 [1/0] via 195.47.37.211
    S         10.4.4.0 [1/0] via 195.47.37.210
    S         10.4.5.0 [1/0] via 195.47.37.210
    S*    0.0.0.0/0 [1/0] via 195.47.37.192
```

The lower part of the list contains individual entries of the routing table. The list of entries is divided into sections corresponding to individual networks. For example, the header "10.0.0.0/24 is subnetted, 3 subnets" informs us that the network 10.0.0.0/24 is subnetted and there exists subsequent route for three subnetworks in the routing table.. Important information is conveyed by the first column in the list of the entries of the routing table. It shows the way the particular entry got into the routing table. The list in the example includes only two ways (a comprehensive list of codes are listed in the first part of the list):

- C for Connected: The entry got to the routing table from the configuration of the router's interface.
- S for Static: The entry was configured statically.

7.3.4 Routing Table Entry Addition and Removal

The routing table entries are set:

- During the configuration of a network interface, when defining the address and network mask of the interface. In UNIX, the ifconfig command is used.
- Statically (manually) using the route command.
- Dynamically from redirect ICMP announcements.
- Dynamically by routing protocols.

The routing table is filled statically using the route command. In Windows the route command is used with the following syntax:

```
ROUTE [-f/-p] [command [destination] [MASK netmask] [gateway] [METRIC metric]]
```

The syntax is explained as follows:

- -f: This clears the contents of a routing table first.
- -p: This makes a route persistent even after rebooting the system when used with the ADD command. By default, routes are not preserved when the system is rebooted. If it is followed by the PRINT command, it lists the permanent entries.
- command: This indicates a command for processing the routing table; it can have the following values:
  - o PRINT: Lists the contents of the routing table.
  - o ADD: Adds an entry to the routing table.
  - o DELETE: Deletes an entry from the routing table.
  - o CHANGE: Modifies an entry.
- destination: This specifies the target network.
- netmask: This specifies the network mask.
- gateway: This specifies the next hop.
- METRIC: This specifies the metric.

An example:

```
route -p add  10.0.0.32 mask 255.255.255.240  192.168.1.2
```

In UNIX there are no permanent entries in the routing table. After rebooting, static entries are always fed into the routing table by the route command (by an automated procedure).

The repertoire of commands of the route command in UNIX is different as well. There is usually no Print command, but on the contrary there is a flush command (deleting the routing table) and a monitor command causing a *live* listing of changes in the routing table to a standard output (can be stopped by *Ctrl-C* key combination). For example:

```
route add -net 10.0.0.32/28 192.168.1.2
```

With the CISCO routers, static entries are added to the routing table by adding the entry into the router's configuration. For example:

```
ip route 10.1.1.0    255.255.255.0    192.169.1.1
```

This adds an entry routing the network 10.1.1.0/24 to the router (gateway) 192.169.1.1. The default entry, routing everything else to the router 192.168.1.2 is added by:

```
ip route 0.0.0.0    0.0.0.0    192.168.1.2
```

7.4 Routing Protocols

Routing protocols are application protocols used not by users (persons), but by routers to fill their routing tables automatically by mutual communication.

There are two independent divisions of routing protocols:

- **Link State Protocols (LSP)** and **Routing Vector Protocols (RVP)** divide routing protocols from algorithm point of view.

- **Interior Gateway Protocols (IGP)** and **Exterior Gateway Protocols (EGP)** divide routing protocols from organizational point of view. IGP is suitable for routing inside an autonomous system and EGP for exchanging routing information between autonomous systems.

7.4.1 Routing Vector Protocols

RVP is based on exchange of the contents of neighboring routers' routing tables. A vector is one entry in a routing table (vector size is a metric or cost). If we obtain the individual vectors from a neighbor's routing table, we can compile the vectors that are missing from the routing table and add them into it. However, we must not forget to increase the metric of such added entries.

The most often used routing protocols are RIP and RIP2. Their metric is the number of hops.

7.4.1.1 RVP Principle

We can explain the RVP principle describing particular steps of filling routing tables of neighboring routers.

In the first step (see Figure. 7.6.), imagine we switched on all the routers at the same moment. Immediately after switching them on, the particular routers only have routes (items in routing table) created according to their own configuration in their routing tables, i.e., they only know networks they are physically connected to.

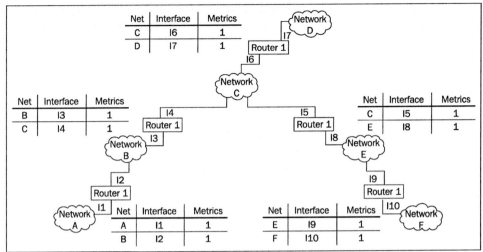

Figure 7.6: The first step of filling routing tables

Within the second step (see Figure 7.7), the neighboring routers mutually exchange their routing tables. If a router receives a routing table from its neighbor, it first adds 1 to the metrics of all routes. Then the router takes one item from the obtained routing table after another and tests if the same item is present in its own routing table. If it does not find a match, the router adds this new item into its routing table. If the same route is found, the router compares metrics of the two matching ones. Then, it writes the route with the lower metric into its routing table. In our case, the networks with the metric 2 are inserted.

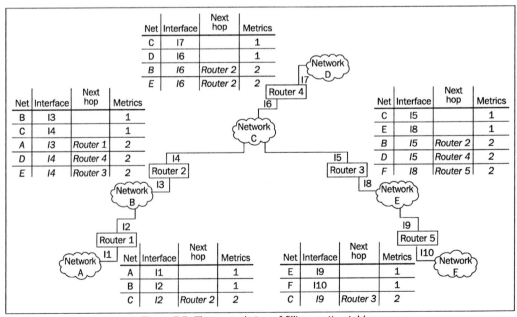

Figure 7.7: The second step of filling routing tables

Within the third step (see Figure 7.8), the neighboring routers exchange their routing tables again (the exchanged routing tables already have routes from step two). In our case the networks with the metric 3 are inserted.

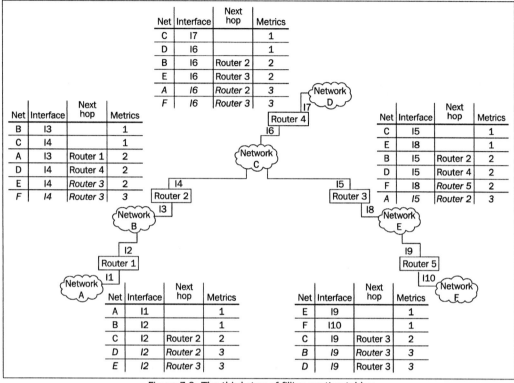

Figure 7.8: The third step of filling routing tables

Within the fourth step, the last one in our case (see Figure 7.9), the networks with the metric 4 are inserted. Note that all our routers have already completed routing tables. Because the network topology can change, routers do not store the dynamically created routing information into their tables permanently, but only for a short time (the time interval is usually 2-5 minutes according to a concrete routing protocol).

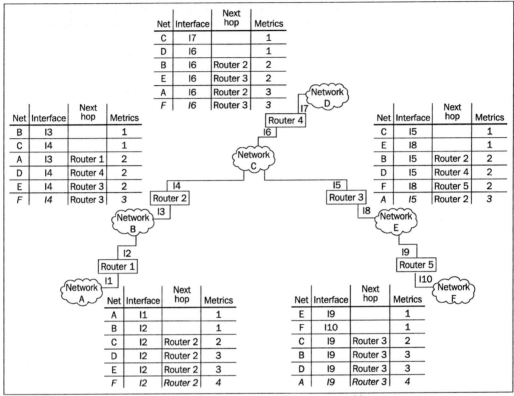

Figure 7.9: The fourth step of filling routing tables

This algorithm is called a **vector-distance algorithm** or a **Bellman-Ford algorithm**. Particular implementations or particular routing protocols using this algorithm are called protocols of the **Routing Vector Protocol (RVP)** type.

Probably the most known flaw of the RVP protocols is the slow convergence (or count to infinity) problem. Its principle is described in the figure shown below:

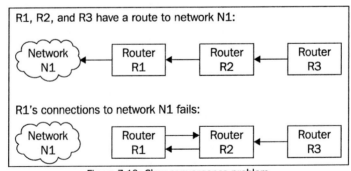

Figure 7.10: Slow convergence problem

Router R1 is directly connected to N1 (metric 1). It periodically advertises this information (route) to its neighbors. So router R2 learns this information from router R1 (metric 2). Correspondingly router R3 will learn this information from router R2 (metric 3).

Now suppose that R1's connection to network N1 fails. Router R1 changes its routing tables, stating that network N1 is inaccessible. After this router R1 receives from router R2 its routing information, stating that network N1 is accessible through router R2 (metric 2); R1 increases the metric to 3 and stores into its routing table that the network N1 is accessible through R2.

After some time, the information about network N1 stored in router R2's routing table expires. But after a while it receives an advertisement from router R1 that it knows a route to network N1 with metric 3. R2 increases the metric to 4 and stores it into its own routing table.

The result is that the information about the route to network N1 in routing tables oscillates. We have two solutions:

- The RVP protocols sets up an upper limit of metric. For example, the RIP and RIP2 protocols, using a number of hops as a metric, have an upper limit 16 (the metric 16 means that the network is unreachable). So the upper limit for the metric of an accessible network is 15.

- If a router receives routing information from some router, it does not advertise this routing information back to it (this technique is called split horizon update).

Another unpleasant feature of these protocols is the fact that these protocols do not support load balancing of parallel lines.

Since RVP protocols are designed for smaller WAN, the question always has to be asked whether the change of the network configuration will be dynamic enough, or if the routers will work better configured manually using static entries.

7.4.1.2 RIP and RIP2

RIP and RIP 2 are examples of RVP protocols. In UNIX, RIP is implemented by the *routed* or *gated* daemons.

In RIP neighboring routers exchange the contents of their routing tables via *broadcast*. One disadvantage is that routing table entries of protocol RIP do not include the network masks. Thus, the RIP protocol can be used only when networks with the standard mask are used.

This disadvantage has been eliminated from the RIP 2 protocol that transports not only a network address, but also a mask. RIP 2 spreads the contents of the routing tables usually via a multicast with the 224.0.0.9 IP-address.

A router advertises its routing tables every 30 seconds. The recipient keeps the received information live for 180 seconds. If the information is not updated within this time interval, it expires.

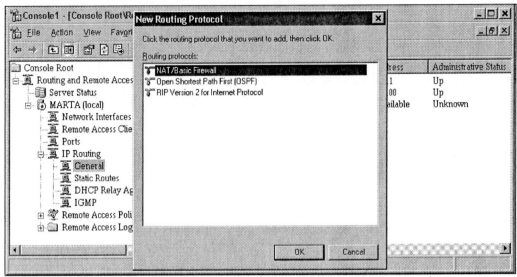

Figure 7.11: In Windows 2000/2003 Server, routing protocols are activated
from the Routing and Remote Access program.

These protocols are simple and easy to implement. One disadvantage is that the vector exchange may oscillate in larger networks causing a situation when some more remote networks may be available at one moment and not available a moment later. By larger networks, we mean networks with metrics higher than 10.

Probably the most important advantage of RIP protocols and of all other RVP protocols is that no configuration is required. You just start them and they run. On the other hand, LSP protocol configuration requires an experienced network administrator.

7.4.2 Link State Protocols

The principle on which LSP protocols are based on is entirely different. To be able to understand the LSP principle, we must make a short excursion into graph theory first.

A graph is a set of dots called *vertices* or *nodes* connected by links called *edges* or *arcs*. Two vertices are considered *adjacent* if an edge exists between them. In the Figure 7.12, vertices A and C are adjacent, but vertices A and B are not. The set of *neighbors* for a vertex consists of all vertices adjacent to it. In the example graph, vertex N3 has two neighbors, vertex J and vertex G. A *path* is a sequence of vertices in which each vertex is adjacent to both the preceding and succeeding vertices. The edges are evaluated by metric (costs). For example, in Figure 7.12 the edge from vertex A to vertex B has metric 6.

In our case, vertices of the graph are routers (or LANs) and edges are represented by lines between them. We can draw our network as a graph (see Figure 7.12). Let us imagine that the router A has to decide in which direction it is to send an IP datagram for vertex G. From the graph point of view, our task is to find out the shortest path from the vertex A to the vertex G.

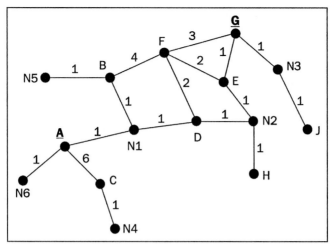

Figure 7.12: Graph G

The task of finding the shortest path in a graph can be solved with Dijkstra's algorithm. Edsger Wybe Dijkstra (1930-2002), a Dutch computer scientist, developed the algorithm. The algorithm's principle is shown in the Figure 7.13. With the help of this algorithm, we will create step-by-step a subgraph S of the graph G. For the purpose of this algorithm, we will rate the vertices of the graph G stepwise. At each vertex of the subgraph S, we will also record a name of a neighbor from which we have reached this vertex. Initially, rate all vertices of the graph G by infinity. Within the first step (1), the subgraph contains only the initial vertex (A) and its rating is set to 0. On each step, proceed as follows:

- For each new vertex U of the subgraph S (initially this is only the vertex A), move through all its neighbors that are not already elements of S. For every such vertex V, add the rating of U to the metric of the edge between U and V (do not change the metric of this edge). If the obtained value (denote it by x) is lower than the current rating of V, set the rating of V to x and record the name of the vertex U at V.

- Choose all neighbors of the subgraph S that have the lowest rating of all neighbors of S (this can be just one vertex). Add these vertices to the subgraph S.

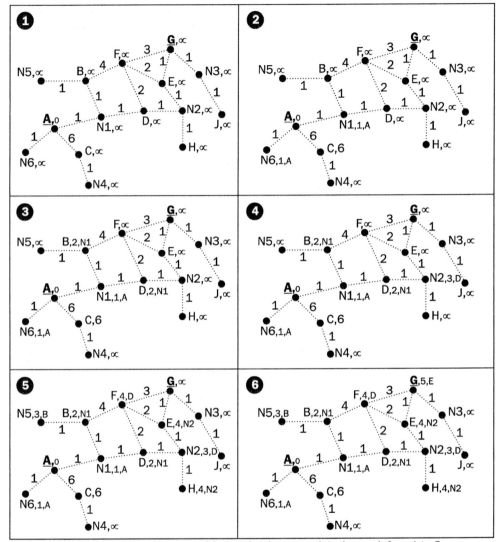

Figure 7.13: Successive steps of finding the shortest path in the graph from A to G

You can see here how to find out the subgraph of the shortest path from the vertex A to the vertex G in six steps:

1. The subgraph S contains only the vertex A (S={A}) and its rating is zero. All other vertices have sets rating to infinity.

2. We are looking for all neighbors of the subgraph S, i.e., of the vertex A. We find the vertices C, N6, and N1, rate these vertices, and record from which vertex we have reached them. Vertices N6 and N1 have the lowest rating (equal to 1), so we will add these vertices into the subgraph S. The result is S={A, N1, N6}.

3. Now, the new vertices of the subgraph S are N1 and N6. They have the neighbors D and B, which are not the elements of S. We rate these vertices (by adding the rating of N1 to the metric of the connecting edge D and B) by the value 2. Since the rating of the vertex C is 6, we add vertices D and B into the subgraph S. The result is S={A, B, D, N1, N6}.

4. Continuing in the same way, the result of the fourth step is S={A, B, D, N1, N2, N5, N6}.

5. Similarly, in the fifth step S={A, B, C, D, E, H, N1, N2, N5, N6}.

6. In the fifth step, we found the shortest path from A to G within the subgraph S. We can reconstruct this path by following the recorded vertices names, namely, A, N1, D, N2, E, and G.

7. We can continue until the subgraph S contains all the vertices of the graph G (S={A, B, C, D, E, F, G, H, J, N1, N2, N3, N4, N5, N6}).

We can also create a tree for these steps. In this tree, we can see how the particular vertices were added:

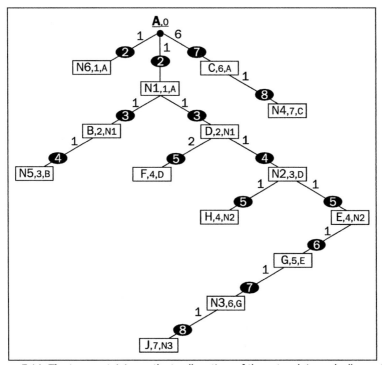

Figure 7.14: The tree containing paths to all vertices of the network is gradually created

Based on the tree graph shown earlier, we can easily create the routing table of router A:

Network	Next Hop	Network Interface	Metric
N1	Local interface	I3	0
N2	D	I3	3
N3	D	I3	6
N4	C	I2	7
N5	B	I3	3
N6	Local interface	I1	1

Table 7.2: Routing table

From the tree graph, it is clear that if router A wants to send an IP datagram to vertex G, it must forward it to vertex N1 first.

In Figure 7.15, you can see the network topology from which the graph G was created. We will also describe all network interfaces for the router A.

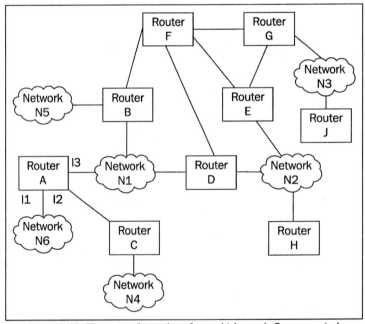

Figure 7.15: The network topology from which graph G was created

Correspondingly, all our routers can create their own routing tables. If your are confused as to what we need to create the routing tables, then the answer is we need nothing more than the complete topology of our network. Every router is able to create its own routing table from it.

How can a router obtain the complete topology of our network? We proceed in the following way: every router finds out connections to its neighbors. It sends a number of queries (n) by broadcast or multicast. If its neighbor is up (that means if it receives at least k responses; $1 \leq k \leq n$), it considers that the connection (edge of graph) exists.

Now, every router knows its neighbors. The next phase is called a flooding procedure. In this phase, the router sends information about its neighbors to all other routers.

All the routers use the same data to create their routing tables, i.e., all routers have the same data. This is a main difference from the RVP protocol, where routers learn from one another including possible mistakes due to which oscillations may arise.

The important thing is that the network topology can change dynamically (line off, line up, etc.). So the information about network topology must be updated regularly.

This algorithm is called **Shortest Path First** (**SPF**). Routing protocols based on this algorithm are called **Link State Protocol** (**LSP**) protocols.

Particular implementations of LSP bring various improvements in this process. We will mention two:

- It is not recommended to flood broad networks with large volumes of information from routers. This is why these networks are divided into areas, and the approach mentioned above is applied within one area at a time. On the borders between neighboring areas, there are border routers exchanging information on the whole areas

- If there are several routers within one common network (for example, a LAN), they mutually agree on one designated router, which takes care of routing.

LSP protocols are far more stable than RVP protocols and are applicable to even very broad networks. The disadvantage is that the network has to be designed, i.e., divided into areas by an expert and its configuration is not trivial either. If LSP is used without enough experience, it may happen that some links will not route data while others will be overloaded.

OSPF and IS-IS protocols are examples of LSP protocols. The feature in which they differ is the interpretation of the term *area*. The area is a logical grouping of routers, and its information may be summarized towards the rest of the network. The OSPF protocol is designed for IP routing only. The IS-IS protocol supports simultaneous routing by several protocols (for example, IP, IPv6, and DECnet). It is true that the IS-IS protocol must be configured by an expert.

7.4.2.1 OSPF

OSPF is an abbreviation of Open Shortest Path First, i.e., Open SPF The word Open is very important because this protocol was created by the **Internet Engineering Task Force** (**IETF**) initiative. The goal was to create a license-free specification. The consequence of this was a massive spread of this protocol. Unfortunately the approach of the biggest competitor IS-IS was different from the OSPF, which is why the IS-IS is not so widespread.

ES-ES is standardized by ISO/IEC 10589, and it is possible to find the official name of this standard at http://www.iso.org/:

> Information technology -- Telecommunications and information exchange between systems -- Intermediate System to Intermediate System intra-domain routing information exchange protocol for use in conjunction with the protocol for providing the connectionless-mode network service (ISO 8473).

OSPF implements many new features as follows: type of services routing, load balancing for equal-cost parallel lines, mutual authentication of communicating routers, distribution of external routing information (this means external networks outside the autonomous system), and so on.

An OSPF network is divided into particular areas. Routers located in area boundaries are called border routers. A flooding is processed only within a particular area. The border routers exchange summaries of routing information.

The topology of particular areas is very interesting. The core of the OSPF topology is a backbone area with routers having complete routing information. The other areas must be connected directly to this backbone area.

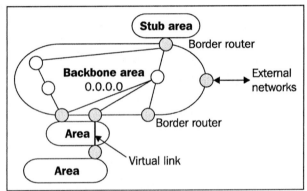

Figure 7.16: Topology of OSPF networks

A special kind of area is called a stub area. Inside the stub area, there is no spreading of the routing information of external networks, because all routing from this stub area can be done through the *default* route, directed to the backbone area. An area can be configured as a stub when there is a single exit point from the area, or when the choice of exit point need not be on external network basis.

The areas connected through more than one line enable load balancing. In this case, we are not talking about stub areas, because these areas must have full routing information. We call them backboneless areas or simply areas.

OSPF does not support direct connection of backboneless areas other than through the backbone i.e., transversal lines between backboneless areas are not allowed. The exception to this rule are areas not directly connected to a backbone area, but connected through a virtual link leading through another (transit) area. But even if virtually, this type of remote area is also *directly* connected to a backbone area. Routers on both ends of a virtual link are border routers. (Transit areas must not be stub areas too.)

Every OSPF router has its own, 4B-long unique identification. Correspondingly, every area also has its own 4 B-long, unique identification. This identification is similar to an IPv4 address. For example, a border area always has the 0.0.0.0 identification.

7.4.3 IPG and EGP

IGP protocols are to be used within autonomous systems. The above mentioned RIP, RIP2, OSPF as well as IS-IS protocols are all IGP protocols.

Internet providers need to exchange routing information as well. For the exchange of routing information between autonomous systems, Internet providers use the EGP protocols. The BGP protocol (Border Gateway Protocol) has also been used recently.

EGP protocols differ from IGP protocols mainly by allowing consideration of routing policies (i.e., billing policy).

7.4.4 Aggregation

Aggregation is the process of combining several entries in a routing table into a single one. It is useful, for example, in network promotion outside an autonomous system.

Several entries can be merged into one if the networks aggregated into one entry make up a super-network. Automatic aggregation is a dream rather than a reality. As non-assigned addresses are usually skipped in a provider's super-networks, all the IP addresses of the autonomous system cannot be aggregated into one or a few entries. Aggregation is in practice accomplished manually by promoting all assigned IP addresses outside the autonomous system.

7.4.5 Redistribution

The question mark in Figure 7.17 marks a router exchanging routing information in BGP, OSPF, and RIP protocols simultaneously and which may have a few static entries in its routing table.

It is not evident whether the information (routing table entries) acquired by a particular routing protocol should be promoted to other routing protocols, i.e., whether they should be redistributed. A routing table entry thus has to include the information of which protocol it was created by. Redistribution means transferring the routing information obtained by one routing protocol to another routing protocol.

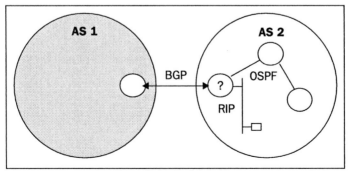

Figure 7.17: Redistribution

7.5 Neutral Exchange Point

If we want to establish a new Internet provider outside the U.S., we will have to solve two basic communication problems.

The first problem is to establish a connection with America, i.e., we must give our clients access to the world's Internet information sources. If we want to be an Internet provider in a geographically distant country, we will have to consider the great costs of transatlantic or transpacific connection lines. The solution could be to use the services of some of the international Internet providers. They already have running transatlantic or transpacific connection lines and you can connect to them. Initially this seems to be an acceptable solution. From the point of view of routing, the partner Internet providers run transit (built-in) autonomous systems (AS) through which we will be able to transfer our IP datagrams to various areas throughout the world.

We have an international connection now, but we must realize that we live in a specific country where a specific custom is followed, and most problems our citizens face are also national. This means that our citizens, i.e., our potential Internet clients will want to communicate mostly among themselves within their national community. In other words, our clients will also want to communicate with clients of our national competitors. If we are connected to the Internet only through an international connection line (for example, to the US), all the communication between our clients and clients of our national competitors will be routed through the US even if they live next door. From an economic point of view, this obviously would not be very feasible.

Thus, we need to resolve communication with our national competitors i.e., we need to resolve IP datagram exchange between our AS and those of our competitors. But negotiations with competitors are always difficult.

The solution is to establish a consortium of national Internet providers, which will establish a Neutral Exchange Point NIX through which all NIX members will exchange their IP datagrams. From a technical point of view, this can be accomplished by having a common LAN to which all NIX members connect their routers. Then, they can simply connect their routers with their particular AS.

8

IP Version 6

The original IP version 4 protocol, specified by RFC 760 in January 1980, was replaced by RFC 791 in September 1981. IP version 6 was originally specified by RFC 1883 in December 1995. Presently, IP version 6 uses the RFC 2460 specification. IP version 6 was therefore referred to as IP the Next Generation (IPng).

Although the IP version 4 was robust at the time of its publication in 1981, it did not anticipate several Internet advances including:

- The recent exponential growth of the Internet and the impending exhaustion of the IP version 4 address space
- The need for simpler configuration
- The requirement for security at the IP level
- The need for better support for real-time delivery of data, also called quality of service

IP version 6 has not only enlarged the IP address size from 4 to 16 bytes, but also offers a revamped view of the IP datagram. Fields such as the header checksum as well as other infrequently used fields are now optional rather than mandatory for the base header.

The IP version 6 datagram consists of a 40 byte-long base header followed by various extensions. Although a 40-byte basic header may seem rather large, keep in mind that the source and destination IP addresses alone consist of 32 bytes.

The base header structure is shown in the following figure:

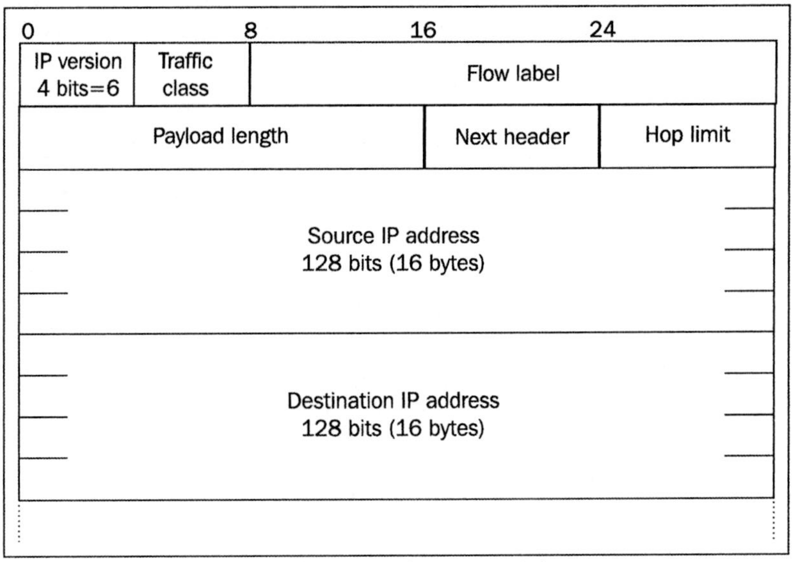

Figure 8.1: Base header of IP version 6 datagram

The **IP version** field has the value 6 rather than the value 4 found in IP version 4.

The **Traffic class** field contains four bits; therefore, it can have a value ranging between 0 and 15. It indicates priory and congestion control. Congestion control means that in the case of a network overload, the router is forced to discard certain IP datagrams. This field prioritizes which datagrams are less important and therefore more quickly discarded. In essence, datagrams of lesser value are discarded before those of higher value.

The 0-15 interval is divided into two parts:

- Interval 0-7 is for congestion-controlled usual traffic in which:
  - 0 is unspecified data
  - 1 is background traffic (e.g., news)
  - 2 is automatic traffic (e.g., mail)
  - 4 is user-initiated transmission of big amounts of data (e.g., FTP files)
  - 6 is interactive traffic (e.g., Telnet, X windows, etc.)
  - 7 is network management traffic (routing protocols, SNMP)
- Interval 8-15 is for noncongestion-controlled traffic real-time transmission (such as audio). Datagrams of lower value are thrown away before datagrams of higher value. This is valid only for the 0-7 interval since the 8-15 interval is processed separately. This is only in theory; in practice, there are Traffic class field fulfilled usually by zeros.

The **Flow label** field is introduced in IP version 6. Along with the source address it identifies individual data flows on the Internet. Until now, routing was done based solely on the destination address. A drawback of Internet routing is that individual datagrams are transmitted separately, i.e., if the flow of IP datagrams goes between two applications, then the routers along the way deal with each passing datagram on individual basis. For example, if you transmit a file of several MBs, the flow involves thousands of datagrams. Thus, each router along the way must deal with each of them individually. If there is no change in the network topology, then the router has to solve the same task for thousands of datagrams with the same result.

A solution to this is labeling datagrams of the same flow. Streamlining in this way allows the router to save memory by simply solving the task (to which interface the datagram is to be sent) for the first datagram of the flow. As for the ensuing datagrams, the router simply searches its cache. If it finds no matches, it solves the routing task for that particular datagram as well.

The datagrams of the same flow are automatically sent to the interface selected for the first one. The flow is identified based on the source address and the data flow label field. An item is stored in the router cache for no longer than six seconds. The danger is that the user could restart his or her computer, restarting its operating system again, and, coincidentally, the system might end up generating the same label for a different data flow. However, it is assumed that the user will not restart his or her computer before 6 seconds have elapsed.

Another possibility is the use of data flow labels for the provision of the guaranteed bandwidth. The routers on the way from the source to the destination are configured so as to provide data flows of a particular label with a corresponding bandwidth. When datagrams reach the router, they are stored in the queue. Under normal circumstances, the queue is First In First Out (FIFO) type. The router may not process in this way. The router may give priority depending on the concrete data flow. In such cases, the 6 second limit does not apply. This is only in theory; in practice, there are Flow label field fulfilled usually by zeroes.

The **Payload length** field specifies the total length of the IP datagram excluding the base header. Since the field has two bytes, the maximum length of the datagram transferred might be 65,535 bytes. It is also possible, however, to use a larger datagram from the next header of the router information that enables sending even larger datagrams (jumbograms).

0	**Hop-by-Hop Header**
4	IP protocol
6	TCP protocol
17	UDP protocol
43	**Routing Header**
44	**Fragment Header**
45	IRP Protocol
46	RRP protocol
50	**Encapsulating Security Payload**
51	Authentication Header
58	**ICMP protocol**
59	**No next header follows**
60	**Destination Options**

Table 8.1: Next headers in IP version 6 datagram

The **Next header** field specifies the next header type. Table 8.1 shows some of the possibilities the field offers. Section 8.1 deals with other types of next headers.

In Table 8.1, only items shown in bold are part of the IP protocol. All other items belong to higher-layer protocols.

The **Hop limit** field essentially corresponds to the TTL item (Time to Live of a datagram) in IP version 4. It can be used in one of the following two ways:

- To detect routing loops (to discard lost IP datagrams). The hop limit is decreased every time the IP datagram passes through a router. When it reaches 0, the datagram is considered lost and, subsequently, discarded.

- To find the shortest path through the Internet (similar to the `traceroute` command). The aim is to find the nearest member of a particular multicast group. Initially, a datagram is sent to the multicast with the hop limit set to 1. If no member responds, than a datagram with the hop limit set to 2 is sent, and so on.

8.1 Next Headers of IP Version 6 Datagram

Next headers can follow the base header.

The **Next header** field in the base header shows, which data type (header) follows the base header. Headers form chains. The chain contains only those headers that are necessary as opposed to IP version 4 that often carries extraneous information in its header.

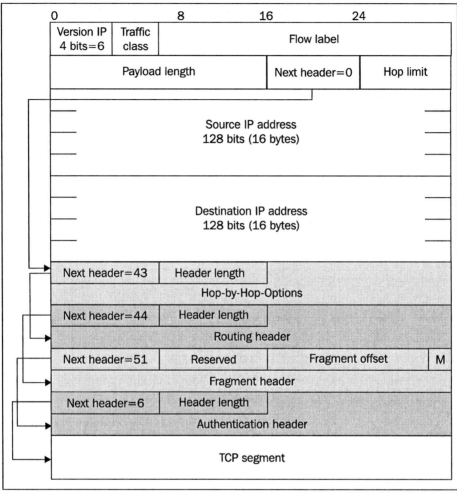

Figure 8.2: An example of IP version 6 datagram structure with arrows showing the order of header processing

The Next header field is followed by the header length field. This field specifies the shift that is necessary in order to reach the next header. The base header does not have a header length field since it is always 40 bytes long. The length is not used with fragment headers either since this header is always 8 bytes long.

8.1.1 Hop-By-Hop Options

This Next header contains individual pieces of information (options) that are aimed at routers transferring the datagram. Each router transferring the datagram must look at and process these options.

The option (see Figure 8.3) consists of the **Type** field (1 B long), the **Length** field of 1 B and the field containing the **Option** itself.

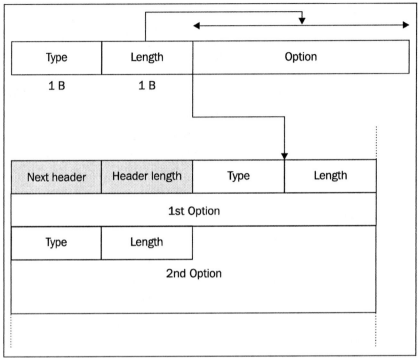

Figure 8.3: The structure of one of the options of the next header hop-by-hop options

The Type field consists of eight bits:

aabxxxxx

The aa bits inform the router what it is expected to do with the datagram if the option is not recognized. There are several possibilities:

- 00. "If you do not recognize this option, then skip over this option and continue processing the header."
- 01. "If you do not recognize this option, then discard the datagram and do not proceed to any other steps."
- 10. "If you do not recognize this option, then discard the datagram and inform the source of this using the ICMP protocol."
- 11. "If you do not recognize this option, then discard the datagram and if it is not addressed to a multicast, inform the source of this situation using the ICMP protocol."

The b bit indicates whether the router is allowed to change the option:

- 0. "The option value can or cannot be changed."
- 1. "The option value can be changed in transit."

Table 8.2 shows some of the options. The *padding* options serves for a simple alignment of the header length at multiples of 4-byte units.

Type in Decimal Units	Type in Binary Units	Option	Length	Alignment
0	00000000	Padding 1 byte long	1	N/A
1	00000001	Padding n bytes long	2+n	N/A
194	11000010	Large datagram (Jumbogram)	2+4	4

Table 8.2: Some options from the information header for routers

Padding is aimed at the alignment of the header length. The IP version 6 Jumbograms options (RFC 2675) uses alignment. That is why this option must terminate at a four-byte boundary:

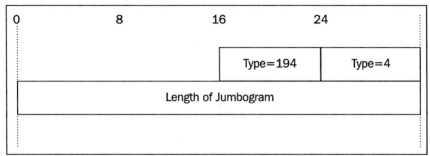

Figure 8.4: The IP version 6 Jumbograms length option has a maximum of four bytes

If the IP version 6 Jumbograms option is used, the datagram length in the base header is set to zero and the length indicated in this option is used. While the base headers uses a length of 2 bytes (i.e., the datagram can have up to 64 KB), the 4 bytes of the Jumbogram option provide for a maximum length of up to 4 GB.

8.1.2 Routing Header

As of now, the routing header Next header uses only the option (Type=0), which is source routing. The source specifies the IP addresses of the routers that are used in transmitting the datagram:

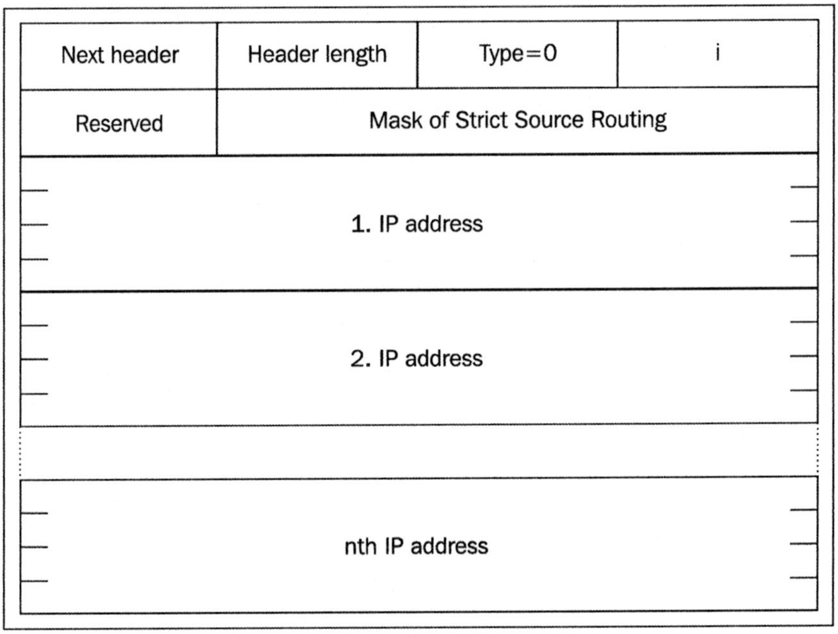

Next header	Header length	Type=0	i
Reserved	Mask of Strict Source Routing		

1. IP address

2. IP address

nth IP address

Figure 8.5: Source routing option

The lower part of the header contains the IP addresses of routers that the source wants to use for routing the datagram.

The **Mask of Strict Source Routing** field contains 24 bits (0-23 from left to right). Each bit corresponds to one hop and indicates whether the next router contained in the header must be the neighboring one (strict routing) or if other routers can occur between. For example, if the bit is set to 1, then the router employs strict routing for the following hop.

The **i** field indicates how many IP address (routers) from Source routing option was left. Each processing router that is listed in the header decreases the value of this field by 1.

The problem is, however, that if the datagram is to be routed via a particular router, the destination address must also contain the IP address of that next router. Therefore, the destination address always contains the IP address of the following router that is to be used for transmitting. The real destination address is then stored in the header of the routing information among other routers listed. The following figure shows the cycle of IP addresses in the **source routing information** header.

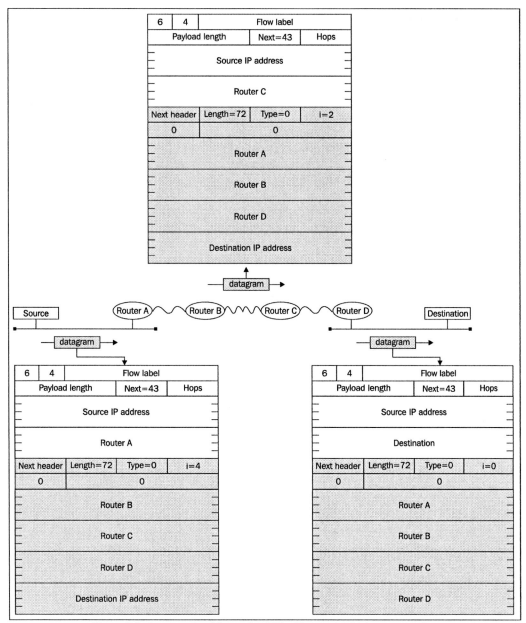

Figure 8.6: An example of the cycle of IP addresses in strict source routing

8.1.3 Fragment Header

Only the operating system source is capable of fragmenting IP datagrams in IP version 6. On the other hand, the routers along a datagram's delivery path are not allowed to fragment as they are in IP version 4.

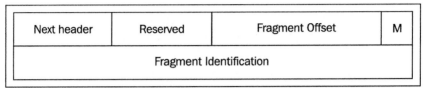

Figure 8.7: Fragment header

Unlike IP version 4, each IP datagram does not contain any identification (e.g., in the base header). Identification of the IP datagram is necessary for fragmenting so that the destination user knows which fragments are a part of the same datagram. In IP version 6, the datagram identification is only contained in the next header; therefore, it is not a part of each IP datagram.

The **Fragment Offset** field is used for putting the datagram together. By using this field, the destination user finds out the order that the fragments received should be in. The Fragment Offset field does not indicate the offset in bytes, but in multiples of eight bytes (8-byte units); therefore, fragments need to be divided into portions divisible by eight.

The **M** (more fragment) field indicates the last fragment. The one-bit M flag is set to 1 (1 = more fragments), except in the last fragment, where it is set to 0 (0 = last fragment).

8.1.4 Authentication Header

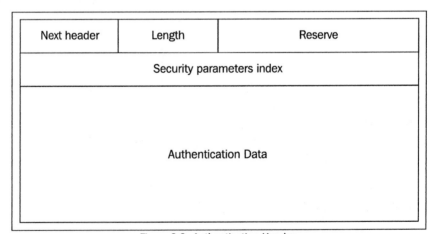

Figure 8.8: Authentication Header

The Authentication header uses IPsec for ensuring data integrity and also enables the source user to authenticate data in order to verify that they have been sent. The datagram is protected against any potential modifications in the IP datagram along its delivery path such as by a hacker.

The basic authentication is done by using the MD-5 (RFC 1321) algorithm for calculating a hash. The authentication uses a hash calculated from the non-variable IP datagram fields and a shared secret. The shared secret is a 128-bit long string (if it is shorter, it is padded with zeros). However, this string must first be exchanged between the source and destination in some other way. Note that each party may have more than one shared secret. The Security Parameters Index (SPI) points to corresponding shared secret.

8.1.5 Encapsulating Security Payload Header

While Authentication header ensuring data integrity, the Encapsulating Security Payload Header enables encryption of the transferred data.
It must be the final Next header in the IP datagram if the subsequent data is encrypted, otherwise following headers will be unavailable for processing by the routers transmitting the IP datagram.

The first four bytes, similar to the Authentication header, are an index for the table where the cryptographic material is stored such as encryption type, encryption mode, encryption keys, etc.

The following figure is an example of encrypted data structure for DES encryption in the CBC mode:

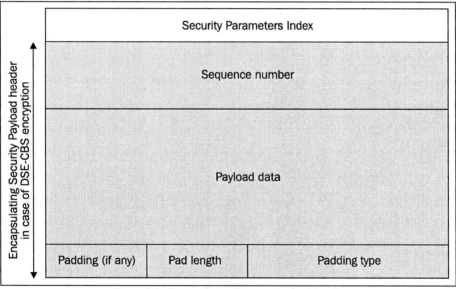

Figure 8.9: Encapsulating Security Payload header

There are three ways to utilize the Encapsulating Security Payload header:

- The end parties (source and destination) do the encryption or decryption.
- Either the source or the destination does not support encryption. In this case, a router encrypts or decrypts the data instead of the source or destination that does not support encryption. This router is referred to as the security gateway.

- Both the source and destination do not support encryption and security gateways do it for both of them:

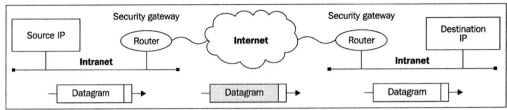

Figure 8.10: Security gateway

It is useful to utilize a security gateway in order to differentiate between the intranet and the Internet. Intranet traffic does not require encrypting while the transmission between two parts of a company via the Internet might require it.

8.2 ICMP Version 6 Protocol

Just as an ICMP protocol is used for diagnostics and error signaling in IP version 4, IP version 6 uses an ICMP version 6 protocol. For IP version 6, the ICMP protocol is specified by RFC 2463.

The ICMP version 6 protocol offers different functionality than the previous version of ICMP. For example, ICMP version 6 deals with the translation of IP addresses into link addresses. (The IP version 4 protocol uses separate protocols for that purpose, namely, ARP and RARP.)

With regard to packet structure, the ICMP packet has a higher-layer protocol; thus, the base header of the IP protocol as well as Next headers, if necessary, precedes it:

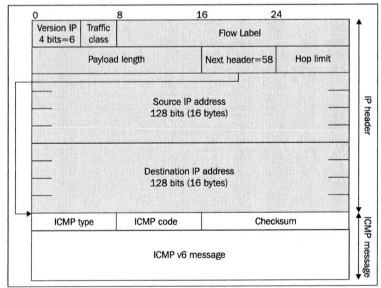

Figure 8.11: ICMP version 6 packet structure

The **ICMP type** field contains the message type (approximate classification of the message) and the **ICMP code** field specifies the detailed classification of the message.

RFC 2461 and RFC 2463 specify types and codes of ICMP messages that are listed in Table 8.3:

Type	Code	Description
1		Destination unreachable
	0	No route to destination
	1	Communication with destination administratively prohibited
	3	Address unreachable
	4	Port unreachable
2	0	Packet too big
3		Time exceeded
	0	Hop limit exceeded in transit
	1	Fragment reassembly time exceeded
4		Parameter Problem
	0	Erroneous header field encountered
	1	Unrecognized Next header
	2	Unrecognized IP version 6 option encountered
128	0	Echo request
129	0	Echo reply
133	0	Router solicitation
134	0	Router advertisement
135	0	Neighbor solicitation
136	0	Neighbor advertisement
137	0	Redirect message

Table 8.3: Types and codes of ICMP messages

ICMP message types are divided in two intervals:

- The 0 to 127 interval for error messages
- The 128 to 255 interval for informational messages

The function of the ICMP messages (shown in Table 8.3) within the 0–129 interval is similar to the ICMP messages in the IP version 4 protocol. Therefore, it is worth taking a look at the remaining message types.

8.2.1 Address Resolution

In Figure 8.12, station A with the address of FE80::220:AFFF:FE42:4636 wants to send an IP datagram to station B. However, the IP datagram must be inserted in the link frame. Station A knows station B's IP address (FE80::2A0:24FF:FE47:1EC), but also needs to have the link address of station B once the link frame has been established.

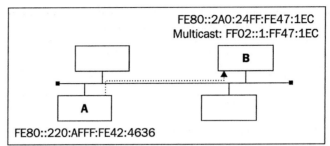

Figure 8.12: Station A wants to send an IP datagram to station B

Two ICMP messages can be used to resolve the neighboring link address on the local network:

- Neighbor Solicitation: Station A solicits the link address of station B via multicast.
- Neighbor Advertisement: Station B return its link address to station A.

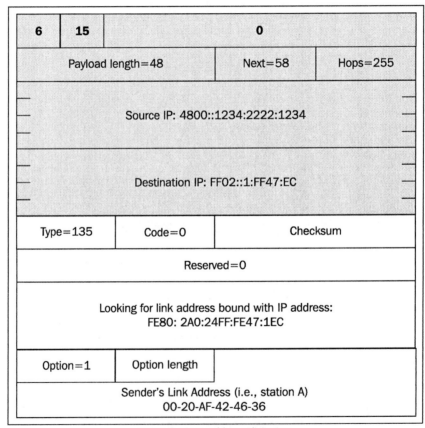

Figure 8.13: Neighbor solicitation

The maximum number of hop fields indicates 255 for a neighbor solicitation. If this request is sent through routers (i.e., from a different network), then the value of this field would decrease below 255, and, therefore, the destination party would know that it is an invalid request from another network rendering this request impossible. (The Link addresses are unique only within the LAN.)

The base header has a special purpose IP address (FF02::1:FF47:1EC) in the destination field. It is a multicast that has been constructed exclusively for this ICMP message. It is composed of the FF02:0:0:0:0:1:FF/104 prefix, with the remaining 24 bits taken by the lowest 24 bits of the IP version 6 address. As described in Section 8.3.3, in the case of unicasts, these 24 bits will contain the three lowest bytes of the link address (assigned by the network card producer). The ICMP type field has the value of 135. The code field has the value of 0, but routers can warn that by setting the code field to 1.

The ICMP message body contains the required IP address, and the option with the link address of the requesting party (the sender).

In ICMP messages, the options always consist of three fields:

- One-byte option field containing the option type (e.g., source link address indicates 1 in the option identification field for requests, 2 for answers)
- One-byte length field containing the option length
- The option itself

The Microsoft Network Monitor statement is worth taking note of as well:

```
+ ETHERNET:  EType = IP version 6
   IP6: Proto = ICMP6; Len = 32
        IP6: Version = 6 (0x6)
        IP6: Traffic Class = 0 (0x0)
        IP6: Flow Label = 0 (0x0)
        IP6: Payload Length = 32 (0x20)
        IP6: Next Header = 58 (ICMP6)
        IP6: Hop Limit = 255 (0xFF)
        IP6: Source Address = fe80::220:afff:fe42:4636
        IP6: Destination Address = ff02::1:ff47:1ec
        IP6: Payload: Number of data bytes remaining = 32 (0x0020)
   ICMP6: Neighbor Solicitation; Target = fe80::2a0:24ff:fe47:1ec
        ICMP6: Type = 135 (Neighbor Solicitation)
        ICMP6: Code = 0 (0x0)
        ICMP6: Checksum = 0x6665
        ICMP6: Reserved
        ICMP6: Target Address = fe80::2a0:24ff:fe47:1ec
      + ICMP6: Source Link-Layer Address = 00 20 AF 42 46 36
```

The answer is called a **Neighbor advertisement**. Let's take a close look at this message (see Figure 8.14). The base header of the IP datagram contains the value of 1 in the hop limit field, which prevents the answer from being sent to a different network. Furthermore, the destination IP address is not a multicast, but rather the IP address of the requesting party.

The body of the ICMP message contains three cryptic bits (flags): R, S, and O. The body also contains the station's IP address and option 2 contains the requested link address. If a router is the source party, the Router flag R is set to 1.

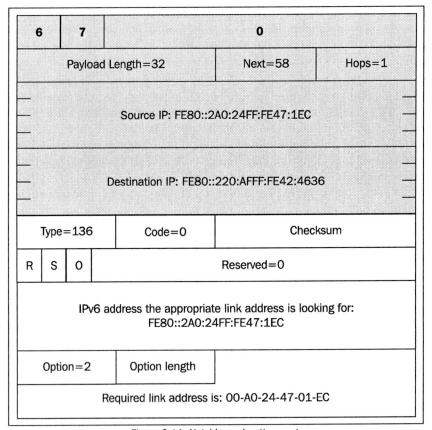

Figure 8.14: Neighbor advertisement

If it is an answer to a solicitation (i.e., if the ICMP message follows receipt of a neighbor solicitation message), the solicited flag (S) is set to 1.

If the source party wishes to stress that the destination user should rewrite the values saved in cache, the override flag (O) is set to 1.

The destination party saves the information from neighbor advertisement in cache, obviating the need to repeat the neighbor solicitation process when sending the responding IP datagram.

In Windows XP, it is possible to display the contents of this cache by entering the ipv6 nc command.

Here is the completed Network Monitor statement:

```
+ ETHERNET:  EType = IP version 6
+ IP6: Proto = ICMP6; Len = 32
  ICMP6: Neighbor Advertisement; Target = fe80::2a0:24ff:fe47:1ec
      ICMP6: Type = 136 (Neighbor Advertisement)
      ICMP6: Code = 0 (0x0)
      ICMP6: Checksum = 0xAD0E
      ICMP6: 0............................... = Not router
      ICMP6: .1.............................. = Solicited
```

```
ICMP6:  ..1............................ = Override
ICMP6:  Target Address = fe80::2a0:24ff:fe47:1ec
ICMP6:  Target Link-Layer Address = 00 A0 24 47 01 EC
    ICMP6:  Type = 2 (0x2)
    ICMP6:  Length = 1 (0x1)
    ICMP6:  Target Link-Layer Address = 00 A0 24 47 01 EC
```

8.2.2 Router Discovery

If a station needs to communicate outside a LAN, than a router address is necessary. To do this, the station needs to have the *default route* and save it to its routing table.

Routers make this information public on a regular basis by sending a multicast to all computers in the LAN (FF02::1) via an ICMP message known as **Router advertisement**.

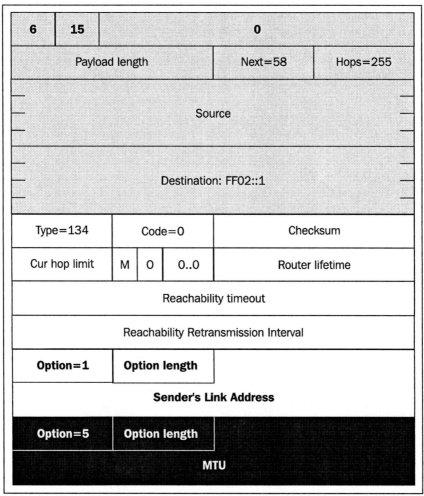

Figure 8.15: Router advertisement message format

After the router advertisement has been received, the station creates the *default route* for its routing table by simply setting the source IP address of this message as the default route.

The ICMP message Router advertisement contains the following fields:

- The ICMP message **Type** field with the value set to 134 and the **Code** field set to 0.
- By using the **Hop limit** field, the stations receive a recommended value that is to be entered into the Hop limit field in the base header of IP datagrams.
- The **M** and **O** bits (flags) are used for higher-layer protocols involved in the automatic configuration of the station (such as the DHCP protocol).
- The **Router lifetime** field contains the time in seconds that the station should use for keeping the *default* route in its routing table. If the value is set to zero, it means to delete this default route from the routing tables.
- The **Reachability timeout** suggests a time limit to place on neighbor information that a station understands. If a station fails to be contacted by a neighbor within this time period, it can suspect that the neighbor in no longer reachable. The **Reachability Retransmission Interval** limits the frequency of neighbor solicitations for a destination.

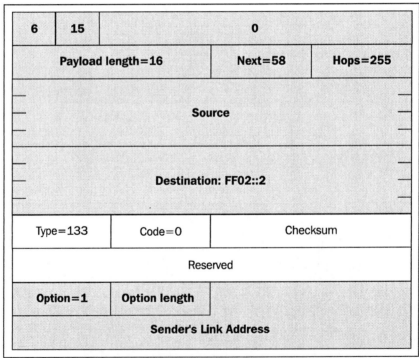

Figure 8.16: Router Solicitation message format

Additionally, the ICMP message for a neighbor advertisement may also contain certain options. Figure 8.15 shows the Sender's Link Address and MTU options.

We have seen the Sender's Link Address option when dealing with neighbor advertisement messages. In this case, it should prevent the station from sending another ICMP message in order to ask the router for its link address. The MTU specifies the maximum link frame size supported.

The station itself may issue a **Router solicitation** message as soon as it connects to the network, which allows it to find routers without having to wait for the next Router advertisement message. This message (see Figure 8.16) is sent by the station via multicast to all routers (FF02:2). The router then uses the neighbor advertisement function that contains the unique address of the requesting party. The router should not use a multicast.

8.2.3 Redirect

The following contingency is also shown in Figure 5.11.

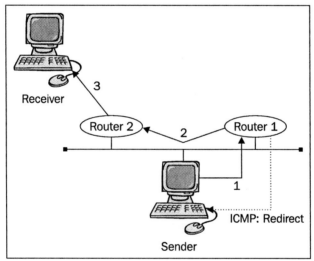

Figure 8.17: ICMP Redirect Message

Consider the situation where there are several routers on a LAN, and a source computer sends an IP datagram to a destination computer, as shown in Figure 8.17. Since the sender's routing table does not contain direct routing to Receiver through Router 2, it will use the default route that can be acquired, for example, from an ICMP message containing a **Router advertisement**, which results in routing via router 1. Router 1 will receive the datagram but it must forward to Router 2 through the same interface. During this process, Router 1 informs the Sender of this fact via a redirect ICMP message. The Sender will receive this message, and use it to make a new entry in its routing table that indicates the destination can be reached directly via Router 2.

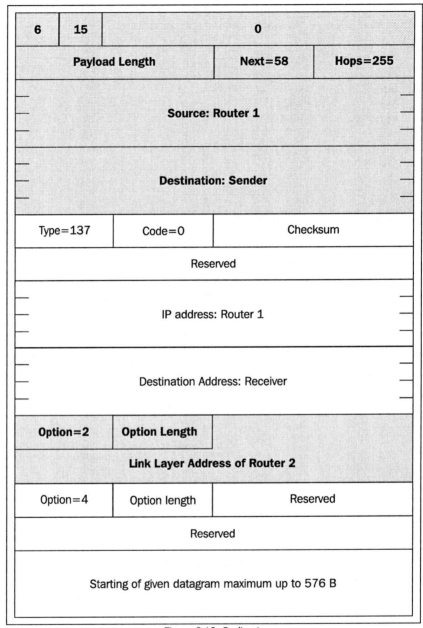

Figure 8.18: Redirect

The Redirect ICMP message is shown in Figure 8.18. It should be noted that the code field contains 0 if the destination of the ICMP message is a computer and 1 if the destination is a router.

8.3. IP Addresses

IP addresses in IP version 6 protocols have 16 bytes (128 bits). We recognize three types of addresses:

- **Unicast**: A unique address of a network interface (an analogy to IP version 4 interface address).

- **Anycast**: New type of address, an address referring to a group of network interfaces. An IP datagram containing the anycast type of address will be delivered to one of the interfaces listed (the closest one within the network topology). These addresses are assigned from unicasts address space.

- **Multicast**: A group address (an analogy to IP version 4 multicasts).

There are no broadcasts!

8.3.1 Types of Address Inscription

Three principal types of address inscription are used:

- hhhh:hhhh:hhhh:hhhh:hhhh:hhhh:hhhh:hhhh where h is one hexadecimal digit (0 to F) representing 4 address bits.

  Example: ABCE:3:89AD:134:FEDC:E4D1:34:4321(the initial 0s do not need to be indicated).

- An abbreviated type using a double colon. The double colon can appear only once in an address. The double colon replaces any number of groups consisting of four zeros.

  Example: The address 12A1:0:0:0:0:5:15:500C:44 can be abbreviated as 12A1::5:15:500C:44, the address 1234:0:0:0:0:0:0:14 as 1234::14, and a loop, i.e., the address 0:0:0:0:0:0:0:1 as ::1.

- hhhh:hhhh:hhhh:hhhh:hhhh:hhhh:hhhh:d.d.d.d with the last four characters expressed similarly to an IP version 4, i.e., each byte is expressed by a decimal number. This form of inscription is suitable for environments using IP version 4 and IP version 6 addresses together.

  Examples: ::195.47.103.12 and 12::A54:147.123.25.4

Network addresses are indicated similarly to IP version 4 addresses as a prefix followed by a slash and the number of bits forming the address, e.g., 80:1::1/64. RFC 4291 and RFC 2450 specify the allocation of version 6 IP addresses.

Network Address	Description
0:0:0:0:0:0:0:0	Unspecified address not assigned to any interface; if used, then it indicates that no address has been assigned to the interface
0:0:0:0:0:0:0:1	Loopback; corresponds to 127.0.0.1
...	
2000::/3	Globally unique addresses (unicasts)
2001:0000::/23	IANA
2001:0200::/23	APNIC (Asia and Pacific)
2001:0400::/23	ARIN (America)
2001:0600::/23	RIPE NCC (Europe)
2002::/16	"6 to 4" (see RFC 3056)
...	
1111 1110 10$_2$/10 (Such as FE80 ::)	Unique addresses within local networks or neighbors interconnected via link (Link-Local Unicast); corresponds to 169.254.0.0/16
1111 1110 11$_2$/10 (Such as FEC0 ::)	Unique address within one company (Site-Local Unicast); corresponds to 10.0.0.0/8
FF::/8	Multicasts

Table 8.4: Some parts of the IPng address space (for more details see http://www.iana.org/)

8.3.2 Multicasts

The first byte of a multicast prefix contains only binary 1s, i.e., hexadecimal FF:

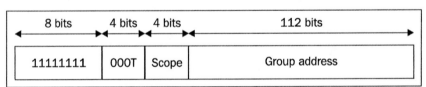

Figure 8.19: Multicast address

The second byte is divided into halves. The first half contains only one important bit, **T**, indicating if it contains a 0 that the multicast is permanently assigned (**well-known multicast**), and if it contains 1 that it is only temporarily assigned (**transient multicast**).

The second half of the second byte specifies the scope of the group forming the multicast. It can have different values such as:

- 1: Interface-local scope
- 2: Link-local scope
- 5: Site-local scope
- 8: Organization-local scope
- E: Global scope

There can also be dedicated multicasts. A few of them are (where xx equals to scope):

- FFxx::1: Multicasts for all stations (both computers and routers)
- FFxx::2: Multicasts for all routers
- FFxx::9: Multicasts for all routers using the RIP protocol

For example, the FF02::2 multicast is aimed at all routers on the LAN.

8.3.3 Unicasts

IP version 6 unicast addressees (similarly as IP version 4 addressees) are maintained by **Internet Registries (IR)**. Internet Registry is an organization that is responsible for distributing IP address space to its members or customers and for registering those distributions. IRs are classified according to their primary function and territorial scope within the hierarchical structure depicted in the following figure:

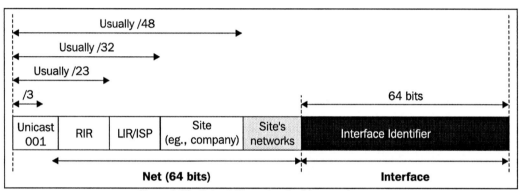

Figure 8.20: Unicast IP version 6 address assignment

The first three bits (001) determine the unicast. The following bits identify RIR, which have allocated address space from IANA (http://www.iana.org/). RIR allocates parts of its address space to individual ISP acting as LIR. Individual ISP assigns address space to its customers (to individual sites).

The **Interface address** (or the interface identification) has 64 bits. The preferred method of interface addressing is derived from interface addressing according to IEEE EUI-64 base on Link Layer Address (see Section 4.6.1 in Chapter 4) containing 8 bytes (64 bits). It consists of three bytes identifying the producer and five bytes assigned by the producer. The conversion of an EUI-64 address into an IP version 6 interface address is simple (see Figure 8.21), since only one bit is changed. It is the second lowest bit of the first byte. This bit specifies the address as either a unique worldwide address or as a locally administered one.

On the link layer, however, we usually use a six-byte address according to IEEE 802 (three bytes identifying the producer and three bytes assigned by the producer). We have to make the six-byte IEEE 802 address into an eight-byte IEEE EUI-64 address. The conversion is simple: two bytes of $FFFE_{16}$ are inserted between the third and forth byte:

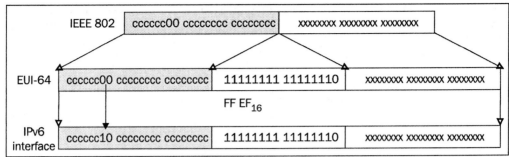

Figure 8.21: Conversion of an IEEE 802 address into an address used in IP version 6

An example:

The manufacturer of my network card assigned it the link address of 00-A0-24-47-01-EC. Using EUI-64 conversion, it changes to 00-A0-24-FF-FE-47-01-EC. The IP version 6 protocol will then use the interface address of ::2A0:24FF:FE47:1EC.

8.4 Windows 2003

Microsoft has implemented IP version 6 as a separate protocol stack independent of the IP version 4 protocol stack. Windows XP implements IP version 6 experimentally (the IP version 6 protocol stack can be installed (activated) by the `ipv6 install` command). Windows 2003, with SP 1 installed, implements it officially; it is possible to add it the same way you are used to add other network protocols with the help of the Control Panel menu. Unfortunately, this step is the only one you can do in Windows' window. Other setup must be done through the `netsh` program. Some programs support the IP version 6 protocol directly (`ping`, `tracert`, `netsh`, `ipconfig`, FTP, Telnet, Internet Explorer, etc.).

It is a good idea to run the `netsh` program without parameters. In this case, it works in a way that is similar to working with Cisco router configuration. We will see a command line:

`netsh>`

Now, let's go through the IP version 6 statement context:

`netsh> interface ipv6`

Within the IP version 6 installation, several interfaces are usually configured (and a new one for every new network card inserted into a computer). The following statement gives us information about configured interfaces:

`netsh interface ipv6>show interface`

```
    Querying active state...

    Idx  Met   MTU    State         Name
    ---  ----  -----  ------------  -----
      5     0   1500  Connected     Local Area Connection
      4     2   1280  Disconnected  Teredo Tunneling Pseudo-Interface
      3     1   1280  Connected     6to4 Pseudo-Interface
      2     1   1280  Connected     Automatic Tunneling Pseudo-Interface
      1     0   1500  Connected     Loopback Pseudo-Interface
```

Besides the long names of individual interfaces (the fifth column of the abstract above), you can see an interface index in the first column. If we want to specify not only an IP address, but also a local network interface, we must state the IP version 6 address followed by the interface index. The delimiter between the IP version 6 address and the interface index is the % character. For example:

```
C:\>ping fe80::c0a8:641e%5
```

Let's go back to the abstract of particular interfaces. Every interface can have one or more IP addresses. The next IP address for the interface number five (fe80::192.168.100.30 is represented in full hexadecimal form as fe80::c0a8:641e) can be added by the following statement:

```
netsh interface ipv6 add address 5 fe80::192.168.100.30
    Ok.
```

Now we can list assignments of IP addresses to particular interfaces:

```
netsh interface ipv6>show addr
    Querying active state...


    Interface 5: Local Area Connection

    Addr Type  DAD State   Valid Life   Pref. Life   Address
    ---------  ----------  ------------ ------------ ----------------------------
    Manual     Preferred      infinite     infinite fe80::c0a8:641e
    Link       Preferred      infinite     infinite fe80::20c:29ff:fe0d:4660

    Interface 4: Teredo Tunneling Pseudo-Interface

    Addr Type  DAD State   Valid Life   Pref. Life   Address
    ---------  ----------  ------------ ------------ ----------------------------
    Link       Preferred      infinite     infinite fe80::5445:5245:444f

    Interface 2: Automatic Tunneling Pseudo-Interface

    Addr Type  DAD State   Valid Life   Pref. Life   Address
    ---------  ----------  ------------ ------------ ----------------------------
    Link       Preferred      infinite     infinite fe80::5efe:192.168.100.30

    Interface 1: Loopback Pseudo-Interface

    Addr Type  DAD State   Valid Life   Pref. Life   Address
    ---------  ----------  ------------ ------------ ----------------------------
    Loopback   Preferred      infinite     infinite ::1
    Link       Preferred      infinite     infinite fe80::1
```

9
Transmission Control Protocol

Transmission Control Protocol (TCP) is an upper-layer protocol from the IP point of view. The first question that always occurs to a beginner is "*Why do we need two protocols, IP and TCP?*"

While IP transmits data between individual computers on the Internet, TCP transfers data between two actual applications running on these two computers. IP is used for data transfers between computers. An IP address is the address only of a computer's network interface, while TCP uses a port number as its address. If we were to compare this to a standard postal system, the IP address would be the building address and the port number (the address in TCP) would be the name of an actual resident in the building.

TCP is connection oriented. In other words, this is a service that establishes a connection between two applications, i.e., creates a virtual circuit for the time of connection. This is a full duplex circuit; data is simultaneously transferred in both directions independently as shown in Figure 9.1. The transferred bytes are numbered. Lost or damaged data is requested again. The integrity of the transferred data is ensured by a checksum.

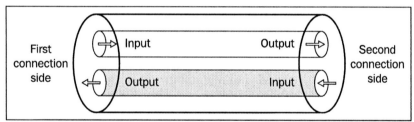

Figure 9.1: TCP creates a fully two-way link between the ends of the connection

In other words, an application that uses TCP does not have to worry about data getting lost during transfer or being modified by a transfer error. This safeguard is only effective against technical errors. It does not attempt to protect data from intelligent attackers, who could modify the data and also recalculate the checksum. The protocols in the TCP/IP family that deal with protecting data transfers from this type of attack are, for example, the SSL and S/MIME application protocols.

The ends of the connection (*source* and *destination*) are specified with the port number. This number is two-byte, so its value can vary between 0 and 65535. Port numbers often express the fact that they are TCP ports with a backslash and the protocol name (tcp). UDP uses a different set of ports than TCP (also 0 to 65535); so for example, port 53/tcp has nothing in common with port 53/udp.

On the Internet, the target application is addressed (unambiguously defined) with an IP address, a port number, and the protocol used (TCP or UDP). IP transfers an IP datagram to a specific computer. Various applications run on this computer. The operating system uses the target port number to recognize to which application it should deliver the TCP segment.

Ports are similar to mailboxes in an apartment building, as shown in Figure 9.2:

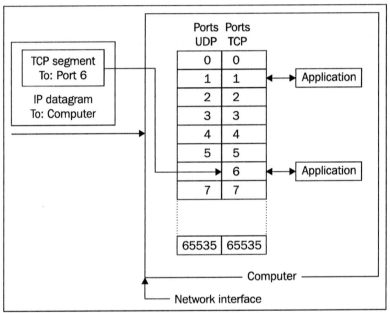

Figure 9.2: TCP and UDP ports

The basic unit of transfer in TCP is called a TCP segment, sometimes also called a TCP packet. Why a segment? An application running on one computer uses TCP to send data to an application running on a different computer.

For example, the computer may need to transmit a 2 GB file through TCP. TCP segments are wrapped in IP datagrams, which use only 16 bits to specify their length, so a TCP segment can only have a maximum length of 65535 minus the length of the TCP header. The transferred 2 GB must therefore be split into segments that fit inside TCP packets. We therefore figuratively call them TCP segments instead of TCP packets.

A TCP segment is inserted into an IP datagram. IP datagrams are inserted into a link frame. If the size of the TCP segment is too big to be entered into an IP datagram without exceeding the maximum capacity of the link frame (MTU), the IP has to perform fragmentation on the TCP datagram (see Figure 9.2).

Fragmentation increases overhead, which is why we try to create segments that are not long enough to require fragmentation. Note that the TCP header is transported in the first IP fragment only.

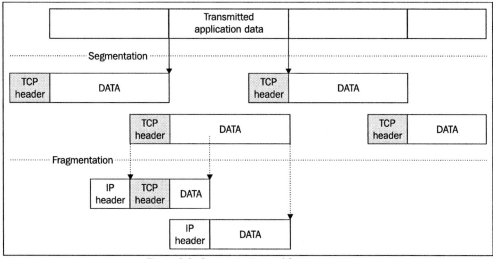

Figure 9.3: Segmentation and fragmentation

9.1 TCP Segments

The structure of a TCP segment is illustrated in the following figure:

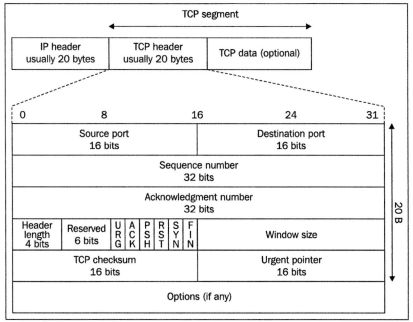

Figure 9.4: TCP segment

The **source port** is the port of the TCP segment source while the **destination port** is the port of the TCP segment destination. The five entries, source port, destination port, source IP address, destination IP address, and TCP protocol, unambiguously identify the particular connection on the Internet at any given time.

A TCP segment is part of the data flow between the source and the destination. The **sequence number** is the sequence number of the first byte of a TCP segment in the data flow from the source to the destination (TCP transfers bytes from the sequence number of the transferred byte to the length of the segment). The data flow in the opposite direction has an independent (different) numbering of its data. Since the transferred byte sequence number is 32 bits long, after reaching a value of 2^{32}-1, it cyclically attains a value of 0 again. Numbering usually does not start from zero (nor from some predefined constant number). Rather, numbering should start from a randomly chosen number. When the SYN flag is set, the source operating system always starts counting from scratch, thereby generating a new starting transferred byte sequence number called an **ISN** (Initial Sequence Number).

Conversely, the **acknowledgment number** expresses the number of the next byte that the destination is ready to accept. In other words, the destination confirms that it correctly received everything up to the acknowledgement number minus one.

Header length specifies the length of the TCP segment header in multiples of 32 bits (4 bytes), similar to the format of IP headers.

Window size specifies the maximum increment of the sequence number that will be still accepted by the destination.

Urgent Pointer is valid only if the URG flag is set. This points to the last byte of the urgent data. In some applications, the urgent pointer to the one byte beyond the last byte of urgent data. For example, this mechanism is used by the Telnet protocol.

The Telnet application protocol transfers data between a client and a server. Besides normal application data, the data flow can also contain the IAC (Interpret As Command) command, meaning "interpret the following data as a Telnet command". The IAC command begins with the IAC flag (decimal value 255) followed by the appropriate command. One example of this command is ABORT (abort process).

FTP control channel is controlled by the Telnet's commands (refer to Chapter 13 for more details). With the help of the Telnet commands, the FTP client may abort a file transfer from the server. From the user's point of view, it's easy to press the appropriate interrupt key. Pressing the interrupt key generates the following:

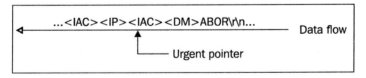

Figure 9.5: Urgent Pointer (the parentheses contain the Telnet's command)

At first, three bytes of urgent data (<IAC><IP><IAC>) is generated in the TCP stream, which the urgent pointer points to the next byte containing the Telnet's Data mark command <DM>. The <DM> byte is followed by the FTP command ABOR. When the FTP server receives the urgent data on the control channel, it reads the control channel, ignores any Telnet command, and looks for the FTP command ABOR.

The following flags can appear in the flag field:

- **URG**: TCP segment contains urgent data.

- **ACK**: TCP segment has a valid acknowledgment number field (set in all segments except the first segment with which the client establishes connection).

- **PSH**: This flag means push function. By means of this function, TCP allows a sending application to specify that the data must be *pushed* immediately. When an application requests the TCP to push data, the TCP should send the data that has accumulated without waiting to fill the segment. TCP segments sent in such a way are marked by PSH flag.

- **RST**: Reset the TCP connection.

- **SYN**: This flag means synchronize sequence numbers. Source is beginning a new counting sequence. In other words, the TCP segment contains the sequence number of the first sent byte (ISN).

- **FIN**: No more data from the sender. If we compare this to working with files, then the FIN flag would be the end of file (EOF). Receiving a TCP segment with the FIN flag does not mean that transferring data in the opposite direction is not possible. Because TCP is a fully duplex connection, the FIN flag will cause the closing of connection only in one direction. In this direction, however, no more TCP segments with the PSH flag will be sent (with the exception of possible retransmission).

In the rest of this chapter, we will write combinations of set flags by using the first letter of each flag's name. If a certain flag is not set, we will use a dot in place of its name. So for example, if a TCP segment only has the ACK and FIN flags set, we would write .A...F.

The IP header **checksum** is calculated from the IP header only. From the point of view of data transfer integrity, it is important that the checksum in a TCP segment header is also calculated from the transferred data. This checksum is calculated not only from the TCP segment itself, but also from certain IP header items. The checksum requires an even byte-count, so if the byte-count results in an odd number, one padding byte is added to the end.

The checksum is calculated from the fields shown in Figure 9.6. This structure serves only to calculate the checksum. In any case, this type of structure would never be transmitted over the Internet! This structure is sometimes called **pseudoheader**.

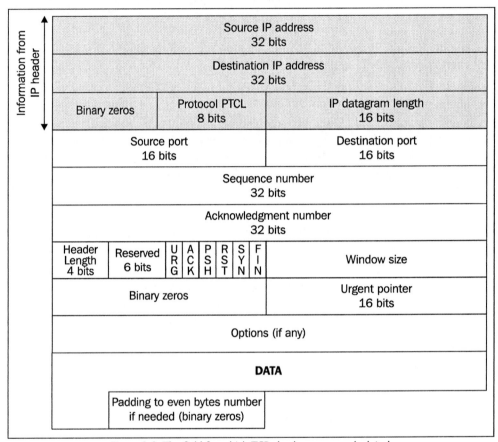

Figure 9.6: The field for which TCP checksums are calculated

Finally, in the following figure, you can see IP and TCP headers:

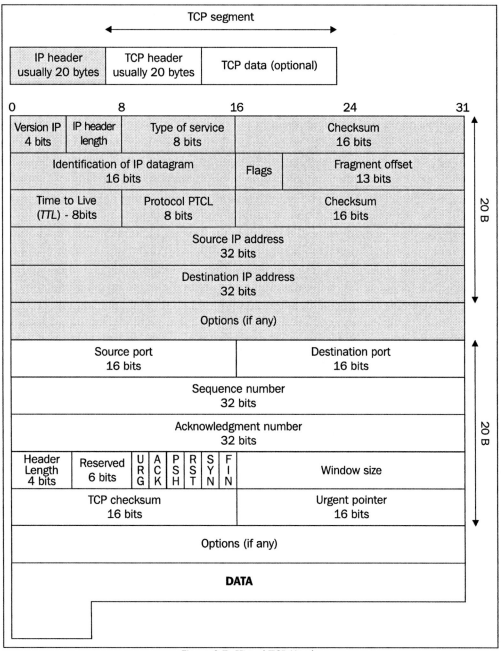

Figure 9.7: IP and TCP Header

9.2 TCP Header Options

Mandatory TCP header items take up 20 B. These mandatory items are followed by optional items. An optional item is made up of the optional item type, optional item length, and value. The length of the TCP segment must be a multiple of four. If the header length is not a multiple of four, it is padded with NOP (no operation) options.

Since the header length field of the whole TCP segment is only four bits long, this field can only contain a maximum value of $1111_2 = 15_{10}$. The header length is determined in multiples of four, so the header can have a maximum length of 15x4=60 bytes. Mandatory items take up 20 bytes, so at the most only 40 bytes are left for optional items.

Figure 9.8 shows some TCP header options and their structure. The most interesting item is the Maximum Segment Size (MSS) optional item. Using this item, both sides of a connection can agree on a maximum segment size at the beginning of the connection.

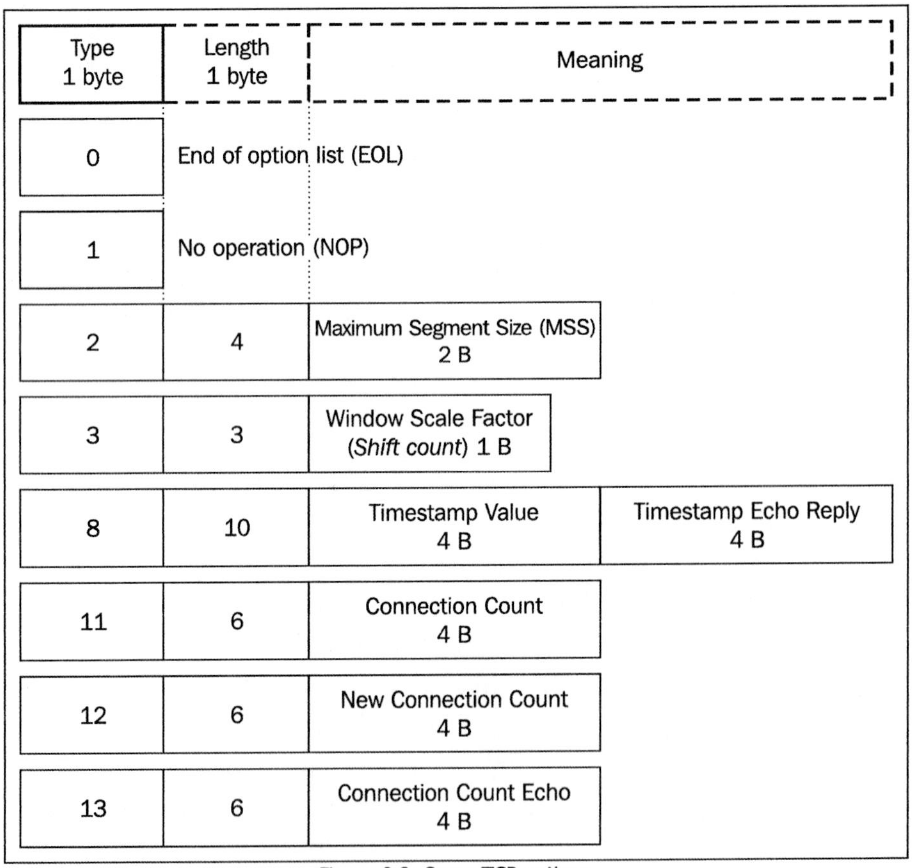

Type 1 byte	Length 1 byte	Meaning	
0		End of option list (EOL)	
1		No operation (NOP)	
2	4	Maximum Segment Size (MSS) 2 B	
3	3	Window Scale Factor (*Shift count*) 1 B	
8	10	Timestamp Value 4 B	Timestamp Echo Reply 4 B
11	6	Connection Count 4 B	
12	6	New Connection Count 4 B	
13	6	Connection Count Echo 4 B	

Figure 9.8: Some TCP options

An example of a TCP segment sniffed by Network Monitor is shown. The following TCP segment has the SYN flag set. The segment header only specifies one optional item, the Maximum Segment Size, which has a value of 1460.

```
+ FRAME: Base frame properties
+ ETHERNET: ETYPE = 0x0800 : Protocol = IP:  DOD Internet Protocol
  IP: ID = 0x4030; Proto = TCP; Len: 44
      IP: Version = 4 (0x4)
      IP: Header Length = 20 (0x14)
    + IP: Service Type = 0 (0x0)
      IP: Total Length = 44 (0x2C)
      IP: Identification = 16432 (0x4030)
    + IP: Flags Summary = 2 (0x2)
      IP: Fragment Offset = 0 (0x0) bytes
      IP: Time to Live = 128 (0x80)
      IP: Protocol = TCP - Transmission Control
      IP: Checksum = 0x63DF
      IP: Source Address = 194.149.104.198
      IP: Destination Address = 194.149.104.203
      IP: Data: Number of data bytes remaining = 24 (0x0018)
  TCP: ....S., len:    4, seq: 145165778-145165781, ack: 0, win: 8192,
      TCP: Source Port = 0x05B2
      TCP: Destination Port = 0x1151
      TCP: Sequence Number = 145165778 (0x8A70DD2)
      TCP: Acknowledgement Number = 0 (0x0)
      TCP: Data Offset = 24 (0x18)
      TCP: Reserved = 0 (0x0000)
      TCP: Flags = 0x02 : ....S.
          TCP: ..0..... = No urgent data
          TCP: ...0.... = Acknowledgement field not significant
          TCP: ....0... = No Push function
          TCP: .....0.. = No Reset
          TCP: ......1. = Synchronize sequence numbers
          TCP: .......0 = No Fin
      TCP: Window = 8192 (0x2000)
      TCP: Checksum = 0xF3ED
      TCP: Urgent Pointer = 0 (0x0)
      TCP: Options
          TCP: Option Kind (Maximum Segment Size) = 2 (0x2)
          TCP: Option Length = 4 (0x4)
          TCP: Option Value = 1460 (0x5B4)
```

9.3 Establishing and Terminating a Connection with TCP

The core of IP was the IP datagram description. Since IP is a datagram-oriented (connectionless) service, there was not much of a need to prepare for cases in which the IP datagram was not delivered. At most, IP can signal this status using ICMP. Signaling with ICMP is only done out of good will in IP. In practice, we often run across cases where signaling with ICMP is restricted because it is not desirable, for example, for security reasons.

TCP uses IP for transferring data over the Internet, even though it establishes a reliable stream-oriented service over this protocol. It must solve the problems of establishing and closing a connection, confirming received data, and re-requesting lost data, and also solve problems with keeping the communication paths passable. The TCP segment description is obviously only one small part of TCP. A larger part of the protocol is the description of TCP segment exchange (handshaking) between both ends of the TCP connection.

9.3.1 Establishing a Connection

TCP allows one side to establish a connection. The other side either accepts the connection or refuses it. From the point of view of the application layer, the side that is establishing the connection is the client and the side waiting for a connection is the server. There are other application models than the server-client model, but to keep things simple, we will use the client for the side that is initializing connection and the server for the side that is waiting for a connection.

As an example, let us say the client wants to establish a connection with the server running on the *Server* computer on port 4433. (In practice, we would write that the client wants to establish a connection with the *Server:4433* server.) The client uses port 1458 for the connection. While the server port must be a well-known port (so that the client knows which one it is), this rule does not apply to the client port. It is also possible, of course, for a client to always use a fixed port—in our example, it is port 1458.

It is more common, however, for a client not to rely on a concrete port number. It asks the operating system to assign it one of the free ports for the duration of the connection. Let us assume that the operating system assigns port 1458 to the client. The operating system thus assigns a port number higher than 1023. These ports are known as client or unprivileged ports as opposed to port numbers that are lower than 1024 that only privileged users (like the root user in UNIX) can request to use. For our example, it is not important whether the client specifically requested port 1458 or just wanted any port and 1458 was assigned to it by the operating system.

Windows 2000/XP usually only assigns client's ports up to port 5000. If we want to change this number, we have to rewrite the value of the MaxUpserPort key in the HKEY_LOCAL_MACHINE\SYSTEM\CurrentControlSet\Services\Tcpip\Parameters registry folder. This key is of REG DWORD type and is also valid for UDP ports.

Ports lower than port 1024 are known as privileged ports. These ports are most commonly used by servers because, as a rule, servers are initialized by privileged users or are initialized during the operating system startup as if they were initialized by privileged users. Our server does not use a privileged port; it uses port 4433 (4433>1203). Any operating system user can initialize this kind of server (if, of course, the appropriate port is open and is not already allocated to another process).

Servers normally use a well-known port number. The IANA organization assigns these numbers to server authors. You can view assigned port numbers at http://www.iana.org/.

The client begins establishing a connection by sending the first TCP segment (segment 1) as shown in Figure 9.9). In this segment the source port is 1458 and the destination port is 4433. The client encapsulates this TCP segment into an IP datagram whose source IP address is "Client" and whose destination IP address is "Server". So far everything is pretty clear. But what do the other TCP segment fields look like?

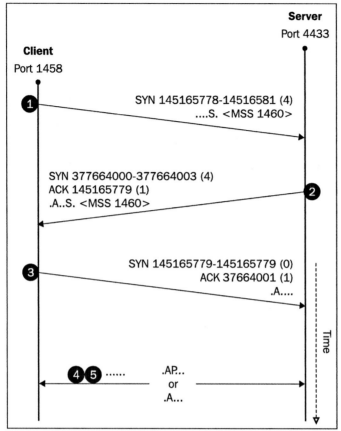

Figure 9.9: Establishing a connection

The client generates a random number between 0 and 2^{32}-1, which it uses to send as the Initial Sequence Number (ISN). In our case, we generated ISN=145165778. The SYN flag (....S.) in the TCP segment sets because the client has just created an Initial Sequence Number and inserted it in the Sequence number header field.. During this connection, the sequence number will always be incremented by the sent byte number so it cannot be generated again. Therefore the client cannot set the SYN flag in any other TCP segments during this connection.

Segment 1 is the first segment in the TCP communication, and therefore cannot confirm any received data. The acknowledgement number field does not have a valid meaning (being filled in with a binary zero) and thus even the ACK flag cannot be set (ACK is set in each following TCP segment until the end of the connection). A TCP segment with the SYN flag set and no ACK flag set is very specific. This setup is diagnostic for the first TCP segment in a connection. If you want to prohibit clients from establishing connection from a certain direction, all you have to do is filter out all TCP segments from that direction that have the SYN flag set and ACK flag isn't set together. In this case, the attacker does not stand a chance. This mechanism is often used to protect an intranet from the Internet.

Another part of segment 1 is the option MSS in the TCP header. MSS can be a part of the segment 1 or the segment 2 or both. This option informs the other side about the maximum length of the TCP Data field in the TCP segment that the sender wants to receive so that IP datagrams will not need fragmenting. This option can only appear in a TCP segment that has the SYN flag set (in other words, in the first two segments).

MSS usually uses 536 bytes by default. This value is used for connections outside of the local network (over a WAN). Our example uses an Ethernet II connection within a local network. For the Ethernet II link protocol, the maximum data part of a frame is 1500. If from this 1500 we subtract 20 for the IP header and another 30 for the TCP header, we come to the value 1460 (from our example).

Since we used MS Network Monitor for the sniffing, it appears in the segment 1 as if we had used segment 1 to send bytes with sequence numbers from 145165778 to 14516581. In other words, as if we had sent 4 bytes of data. The first three segments do not carry any data. Segment 1 only contains a four-byte optional item from the TCP header that specifies the maximum length of received segments <mss 1460>. MS Network Monitor adds the length of the optional header items to the data length. We often write optional header items in angular brackets.

The following is the MS Network Monitor output (only the TCP summary line is listed):

1. Segment client to server
    ```
    TCP: ....S., len: 4, seq: 145165778-145165781, ack: 0, win: 8192, src:
    1458  dst: 4433
    ```

2. Segment server to client
    ```
    TCP: .A..S., len: 4, seq: 377664000-377664003, ack: 145165779, win:33580,
    src: 4433  dst: 1458
    ```

    The second segment already confirms data received; it has the ACK flag set. It confirms one byte of data received. From the MS Network Monitor abstract, it appears that the segment is confirming one byte from the optional header items, but this is not the case. It is only confirming the SYN flag. Like the FIN flag, the SYN flag appears as if it consisted of one byte. This is actually caused by the fact that the acknowledgment number of the confirmed byte expresses the number of the next byte that the source may send. Thus the source may send ISN+1.

    Beginning with the second segment, all segments will confirm received data (that is, they will have the ACK flag set).

3. Segment client to server
    ```
    TCP: .A...., len: 0, seq: 145165779-145165779, ack: 377664001, win: 8760,
    src: 1458  dst: 4433
    ```

    The third segment also confirms the SYN flag, so it is as if it was confirming one byte. The third segment and the following ones cannot contain the MSS optional header item.

    With the third segment, connection establishment ends. Therefore we can say that TCP requires *three-phase handshaking* for establishing a connection and (as we will see in section 9.3.2) *four-phase handshaking* for closing a connection.

4. Segment client to server

```
TCP: .AP..., len:84, seq: 145165779-145165862, ack: 377664001, win: 8760,
src: 1458  dst: 4433
```

You may be surprised to find that the fourth segment is sent by the client to the server. You probably expected the fourth segment to be sent by the server to the client. It does not make any difference. As soon as either side receives the first ACK, it can begin transmitting. TCP is after all a full duplex connection, and our client was already getting impatient because of all the data it had to send. The fact that the TCP segment carries application data that may be transferred forthwith is signaled by setting the PSH flag.

5. Segment server to client

```
TCP: .AP..., len:79, seq: 377664001-377664079, ack: 145165863, win:33580,
src: 4433  dst: 1458
```

At all times during a connection, the connection is in a "state". During connection establishment, the following states can occur:

- Server:
    - LISTEN: The server is ready to connect with clients.
    - SYN_RCVD: The server has received the first TCP segment (SYN flag set) from the client.
- Client:
    - SYN_SEND: The client sent the first TCP segment (SYN flag set).

If the connection is established, the client and the server go into ESTABLISHED state. In this state, both ends can transmit data simultaneously. This is illustrated in Figure 9.10 overleaf.

In both Windows and UNIX, you can easily print out the current connections on your computer and their states using the following command:

```
netstat -a
```

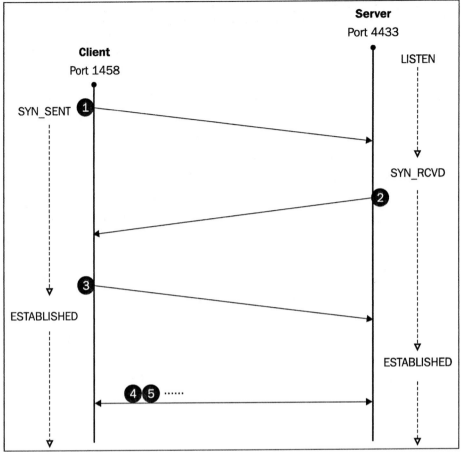

Figure 9.10: Connection establishment

9.3.2 Terminating a Connection

While in a client-server architecture, it is usually the client that establishes the connection, but either side can close the connection. The first side to send a TCP segment with the FIN (end of connection) flag carries out an **active close**, and the second side has no choice but to carry out a **passive close**.

Theoretically, it is possible to close the connection simultaneously. If one side carries out an active close of the connection, then it can no longer send data. The other side can, however, continue to send data until it also ends the connection. The state between the connection's active close and its passive close is called a **half close**. A TCP segment with the FIN flag set is similar to an end-of-file marker (EOF) as it happens in the file reading.

Four TCP segments are required for properly closing a connection. Like the SYN flag in connection establishment, the FIN flag confirms as if it takes up 1 B of data.

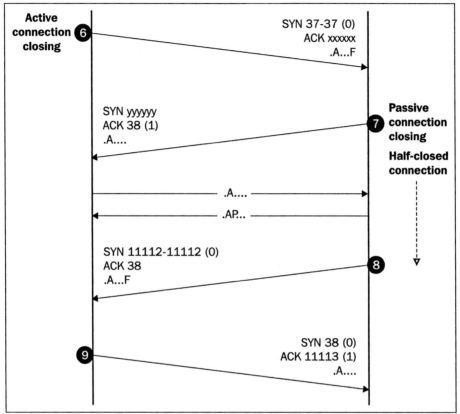

Figure 9.11: Ending a connection

In the above figure, segment 6 begins the active close of the connection with the set FIN flag. Segment 7 confirms the connection closure by the left side; in other words, it carries out a passive close. Most importantly, if segment 8 also contained the FIN flag, it would cause the entire connection to begin closing. Figure 9.11 shows a common example (for example, used by the rsh program), in which segment 7 does not contain the FIN flag, because the right side wants to continue the connection. In other words, it wants to use a half closed connection to transmit application data. The side that closed the connection cannot send any more data. When the second party has sent what it wanted to, it sets up the FIN flag in the last segment (8) and waits till the termination of connection is confirmed (9).

The following states are possible during connection termination (see Figure 9.12):

- FIN_WAIT1: This means the side finds it has sent all data (and needs to signal the end of the file), so it sets the FIN flag in the TCP segment, i.e., it signals the active close of the connection by segment 6.

- CLOSE_WAIT: This means that the second side received the active close of the connection, and it has no choice but to send segment 7 signaling that it is going into the passive close of the connection. The connection is then in CLOSE_WAIT state.

- FIN_WAIT2: This is the state that comes after the side that initiated active close receives segment 7 from the other side confirming the active close of the connection. This side remains in FIN_WAIT2 state until the other side sends a TCP segment with the FIN flag (in other words, until it goes into the TIME_WAIT state).

- LAST_ACK: This means that the other side has already sent all data and signals the complete close of the connection with segment 8.

- TIME_WAIT: This means that all data from both sides has been transferred. It is only necessary to confirm that the connections are completely closed. By sending the TCP segment 9, the complete connection close is confirmed.

  This segment is not confirmed, and the side that sent it must therefore wait in TIME_WAIT state for two minutes. (Some TCP/IP implementations shorten this period to as little as 30 seconds. In Windows, this timeout is set up using REG_DWORD named TcpTimedWaitDelay under HKEY_LOCAL_MACHINE\SYSTEM\CurrentControlSet\ Services\TcpIp\Parameters). This time period should be close to twice the time to live of a TCP segment in the network. The reason for this is simple: segment 9 could get lost in the network and the other side could ask for it to be repeated. If the connection was already closed, then it would be impossible to repeat the segment.

- CLOSED: This means that the second side received confirmation that the connection was completely closed and goes into CLOSED state. The side that sent segment 9 also goes into the CLOSED state after the appropriate time has elapsed.

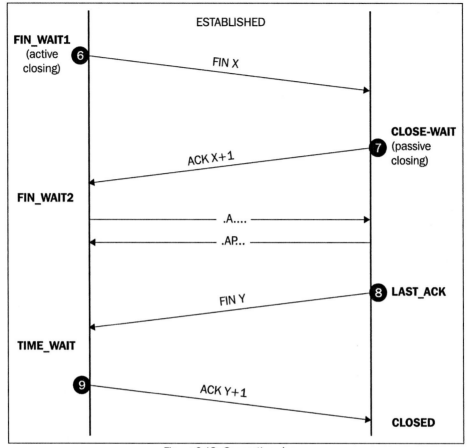

Figure 9.12: Connection closure

9.3.3 Aborting a Connection

A connection can be aborted by setting the RST (Reset) flag in a TCP segment header. A connection can be aborted in the following two cases:

- The client requests a connection with a server on a port on which no server is up running. This is different from UDP. If a UDP datagram is sent to a port on which no server is running, the system responds with an ICMP port unreachable message.

- The second case is when it is prohibited to continue in an existing connection. We can also divide this situation into two cases:

    o A proper connection close is a relatively long affair (for example, an application is forced to wait in TIME_WAIT state). After sending all of its data, the application wants to close the connection faster and uses a connection refusal. In practice, we often find that instead of segment 9, a segment with the RST flag is sent.

Another variation is that segment 9 is followed by a confirmation of segment 9 using a TCP segment with the RST flag set. Using this method, however, the connection can only be closed if both sides have exchanged all data.

o   One of the communicating sides finds that the other side is untrusted and immediately closes the connection. An example of this is SSL, which provides secure communication (encrypted and authenticated). If one side cannot authenticate itself or cannot use strong encryption algorithms as required by the other side, the connection is immediately terminated by setting the RST flag.

9.4 Determining the Connection State

You can list all the actual TCP and UDP connections using the netstat command with the –a parameter.

```
$ netstat -an
    Active Internet connections (including servers)
    Proto Recv-Q Send-Q  Local Address            Foreign Address          (state)
    tcp        0      0  194.149.105.18.22        194.149.103.204.24695    TIME_WAIT
    tcp        0      0  194.149.105.18.3099      194.108.145.128.25       SYN_SENT
    tcp        0  34472  194.149.105.18.3079      195.47.32.245.25         ESTABLISHED
    tcp        0      0  *.22                     *.*                      LISTEN
    tcp        0      0  *.25                     *.*                      LISTEN
    tcp        0      0  *.53                     *.*                      LISTEN
    udp        0      0  *.53                     *.*
    udp        0      0  127.0.0.1.53             *.*
```

> If the switch –n is used, it means that the IP addresses will not be replaced with DNS names by reverse translation.

The first two lines are the list header. The columns have the following meanings:

- The Proto column contains the name of the protocol used (TCP or UDP).

- The Recv-Q column displays the number of bytes in the connection input queue (waiting to be processed by an application).

- The Send-Q column displays the number of bytes in the output queue (waiting to be sent).

- The Local Address column contains the address of the local network interface separated from the local port number with a dot. Severs that are waiting for a connection can have an asterisk instead of an IP address. The asterisk indicates that the server is waiting for a connection on all of its network interfaces.

- The Foreign Address column contains the IP address and port number of the remote side of the connection. Asterisks indicate that the server is waiting for a connection from any IP address and port number.

- The (state) column displays the above-mentioned connection state.

For servers, the following combinations can appear:

Local Address	Foreign Address	(state)	Description
IP1.port1	IP2.port2	LISTEN	Server is awaiting connection to its IP1 network interface with a particular client where the client's IP address is IP2 and port port2.
IP1.port1	IP2.port2	Excluding LISTEN	Server is establishing connection / is connected / is ending connection with a particular client.
IP1.port1	*.*	LISTEN	Server is awaiting connection to its only IP1 network interface with any client.
*.port1	*.*	LISTEN	Server is awaiting connection to any of its network interfaces with any client.

Table 9.1: Server connection state

In the previous example the following line:

```
tcp       0     0  194.149.105.18.22       194.149.103.204.24695  TIME_WAIT
```

indicates that the server running on port 22/tcp of the local computer (i.e., the sshd program) confirmed complete connection closure (TIME_WAIT) with the computer having the IP address 194.149.103.204, and the client was assigned port 24695 for this connection.

The following line:

```
tcp       0     0  *.53                    *.*                    LISTEN
```

indicates that the server on port 53/tcp of the local computer (the named program) is waiting for a connection with any client on all of its network interfaces.

9.5 Response Delay Techniques

Interactive applications like Telnet and Character-at-a-time mode are complicated precisely because they are interactive. This means that if you press the *B* key on your keyboard, the character B is encapsulated in a TCP segment (20+1=21 B), the TCP segment is entered into an IP datagram (20+21=41 B) and this IP datagram then travels over the Internet as segment 1 (see Figure 9.13) until it reaches the server (of course, everything is also entered into link frames from router to router).

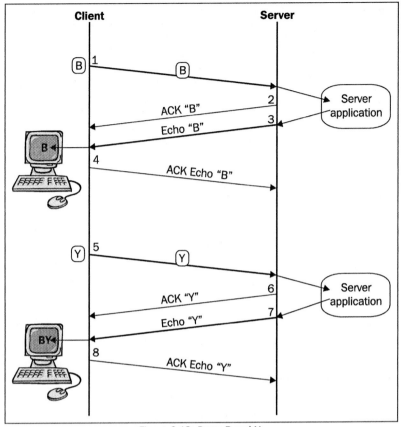

Figure 9.13: Press B and Y

The server:

- Confirms receiving the character. In other words, if it does not have any data to send; it sends a non-data segment (40 B), i.e., segment 2.
- Passes character B to the server application for processing. The server application must send character B back (segment 3) so that the client software can display character B on the client's monitor (using remote echo). Echo is necessary to give the user sitting on the client side the feeling that the application is interactive. The client receives the echo (character B) and does the following:
  - Displays it on the monitor.
  - Sends a confirmation that it received the echo to the server with segment 4. If it does not have any other data to send, it sends the confirmation with a non-data TCP segment.

If the application works in this way, then pressing one key on the keyboard means that 82 B must be transmitted in both directions (not counting the overhead of the link layer). The 82 B is made up of 41 B to send the character and another 42 B to confirm it.

The previous figure illustrates the situation in which the *B* and *Y* keys (the first two letters in the string BYE) are pressed. It is easy to see that we need to reduce the amount of data transferred in both directions, thereby reducing the chance of congestion in the connection path. The goal is to reduce the transfer of non-data segments. (In figure 9.13, segments 2, 4, 6, and 8 does not contain any data.)

Here we will mention the two strategies: **Delayed Acknowledgements** and **Nagale Algorithm**. The *Delayed Acknowledgement* strategy is based on the assumption that received data acknowledgement do not need to be sent immediately, but can be acknowledged after a small delay. During this delay, other data that needs to be transmitted may appear and acknowledgement may be sent together.

The foundation for this principle is that the operating system counts down timer with 200 ms usually tick. (The maximum length of a tick cannot exceed 500 ms.) After each tick, the system checks to see if there is anything to acknowledge. If several things need to be sent, they are sent all at once.

In Figure 9.14, the client using 200 ms delayed the acknowledgements tick.

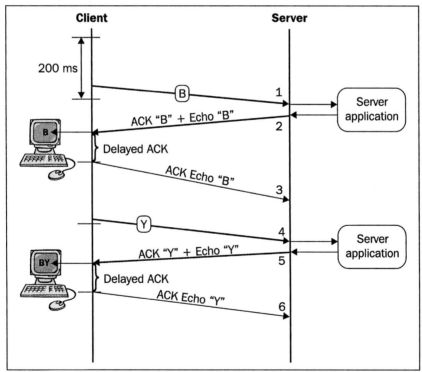

Figure 9.14: 200 ms delay

For small datagrams (called *tinygrams*), we can achieve even greater reductions using the **Nagle algorithm**, as shown in Figure 9.15. This algorithm states the following:

- TCP connection can have only one outstanding segment that has not yet been acknowledged.
- Data is collected and sent in a single segment when the acknowledgment arrives.

In this case, the client software does not wait for another tick. Instead, it waits until some data arrives from the other side; the acknowledgement sends only the data segments (they say: "*the ACK piggybacks the data*"). This algorithm synchronizes the response time with the capacity of the connection lines (controls the data flow). In other words, if the line is more loaded, then the response takes longer and the answer is also delayed.

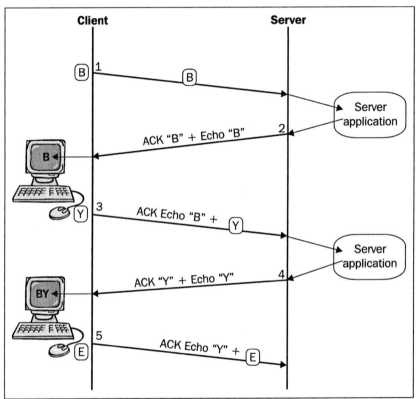

Figure 9.15: The Nagle algorithm

The Nagle algorithm is useful for programs like Telnet, but it is undesirable for programs like X-server. If we used it for X-server, then the mouse motion would be jerky on our monitor. For applications that transmit large amounts of data (like HTTP, the FTP data channel, etc.), both the response delay technique also loses its utility.

9.6 Window Technique

Now we can look at the problem that arises when a client needs to send large amounts of data. The client (or server) can send data to the other side without its reception being confirmed up to an amount that is called a **window** (or WIN in short). The WIN determines the opposite (destination) site of connection.

In Figure 9.16, let us imagine that the client has established a connection with the server and they have mutually agreed on an Maximum Segment Size (MSS) of 1 K (or 1024 B) and a mutual window size of 4 K (or 4096 B).

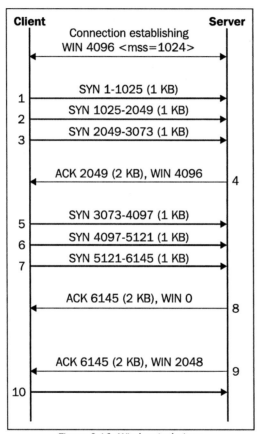

Figure 9.16: Window technique

The window technique is easier to understand from the figure above:

- The client begins transmitting data and sends segments 1, 2, and 3.

- The server returns a confirmation (segment 4) from the server that confirms segments 1 and 2.

- The client in return sends segments 5, 6, and 7, but the server has not had enough time to process the data and its buffer has been exhausted.

- Segment 8 therefore confirms that segments 3, 5, 6, and 7 were received, but at the same time, it closes the window for the client. In other words, the client cannot continue sending data. After the server processes part of the data, it allows the client to proceed with transmitting data again.

- Segment 9 does not fully open the window; it only opens 2 K because not all of the data in the buffer memory has been processed and there is no space for more.

Let us examine how the client sees the window after receiving segment 4:

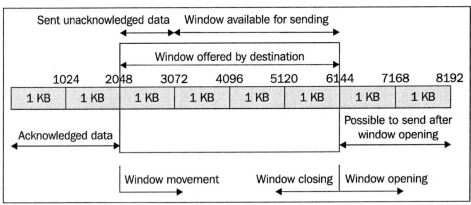

Figure 9.17: Window

The first 2 K is already confirmed. The window has been moved behind byte 2408. The client no longer needs to keep this confirmed data in its memory. Data that has been sent, but not confirmed, (segment 3) takes up 1 K. The client can therefore send 3 K of data without any further confirmation.

As data is sent, the window gradually moves as data is acknowledged as shown in the following figure:

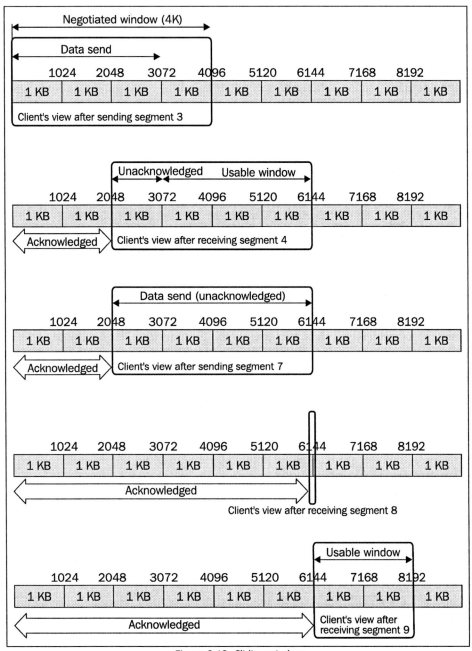

Figure 9.18: Sliding window

9.7 Network Congestion

A window (WIN) is the amount of data that the destination is able to receive. Although the window size is determined by the destination, the problem also extends to the source. If the source is on a fast network and the destination is on a slow network, then the source could literally jam up the network with data up to the window size. Since the network would not be able to transfer such large amounts of data, the network would get congested and the data that the network is not able to deliver would be thrown away. Routers enter IP datagrams into buffer memory, but even buffer memory is limited.

Data loss is always bad and our goal is to avoid it whenever possible. That is why we also define a window on the source side. This window tries to specify how much unconfirmed data the source can send before the network gets congested. The source-side window is called the **congestion window** (or CWND for short). The source gradually increases the CWND, but cannot increase it unlimitedly. The threshold after which network congestion is likely to occur is called **SSTHRESH**. However, we want to use the Internet to its fullest potential, so we want to find the greatest possible CWND that is a bit higher than the SSTHRESH. It only makes sense to measure the SSTHRESH in multiples of the segment size (*segsize*).

Figure 9.19: Network congestion

The source must always send amounts of unconfirmed data that do not exceed the window declared by the destination (WIN), but that also do not exceed the CWND. In other words, the maximum amount of unconfirmed data that it can send is the lesser value of WIN and CWND.

9.7.1 Slow Start

The question is how to define the maximum CWND. The source sets the CWND dynamically. First, it sends one segment and waits for its confirmation. If it receives confirmation, it sends two segments. If it receives a confirmation again, it sends four segments and so on. We are dealing with the 2^n series, which is exponential.

Understandably, after a few rounds, the source will reach the window size (WIN) or will flood the network and will not receive confirmation because congestion occurs. In other words, it has to send the segments again because a segment got lost. At this point, the CWND is reduced by half and this value is entered as the SSTHRESH value. (If the SSTHRESH is smaller than two segments, then its value is set to two segments.)

It is necessary to distinguish how it was determined that the segment was not confirmed. We were assuming that the segment got lost somewhere on route. The destination did not receive the segment, so it is still confirming the last received segment. After the destination repeats its confirmation for the last received segment three times, the source decides the segment as lost and resends it. However, it is also possible that the source does not receive any confirmation at all (even for any previous segment) within the defined time limit. In this case, the CWND is set to the size of one segment (*segsize*) and the SSTHRESH is set to twice the size of a segment (2xsegsize), and the slow start is started over from the beginning.

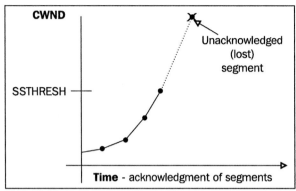

Figure 9.20: Slow Start

9.7.2 Congestion Avoidance

For each connection, the source keeps the actual values of the MSS, WIN, CWND, and SSTHRESH variables. MSS is set by the destination when the connection is established (the segment that has this options is marked with the SYN flag). WINDOW is dynamically set by the destination during the connection; it specifies the amount of data that can fit into the buffer memory.

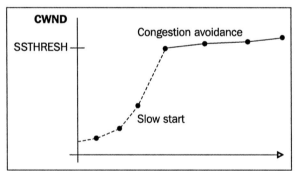

Figure 9.21: Congestion avoidance

When sending a segment, the source cannot sit around thinking about what to do. It must make decisions quickly based on the variables it has.

1. If CWND is less than or equal to SSTHRESH, then we are dealing with a slow start. It is therefore possible to try to send double the amount of data.

2. If CWND is already larger than SSTHRESH, then sending double the amount of data would probably cause congestion. In this case the CWND is only increased by segsizexsegsize/CWND+segsize/8 counted in integers. This *minor increase* of the CWND is called the **Congestion Avoidance Algorithm**.

9.7.3 Segment Loss

Not even the algorithm discussed previously can prevent TCP segment loss. Segment loss can be caused by changing situations in the communication paths, breakdowns along a communication path, and so forth.

If CWND is considerably large, then repeating the entire unconfirmed window when dealing with the loss of a single segment would be very unpleasant, since it would enormously increase the overhead of the system. This is why we use the **Fast Retransmit Algorithm**.

How can the source determine that the TCP segment was in fact lost? (For now we will not deal with the possibility that the source did not receive any confirmation at all from the destination.) The destination determines that the segment was lost because it receives other segments, but never receives the lost segment. In other words, it is missing data in the received data sequence and receives segments out of order. When it receives segments out of order, the destination is forced to resend (duplicate) its confirmation of the last correctly received segment.

However, TCP segments are wrapped in IP datagrams. Each IP datagram travels over the Internet independently and theoretically on a different route. Some routes are faster than others. It can therefore occur that one segment takes a slower route and naturally arrives at the destination after the following segment. In the meantime, the destination has already sent its duplicated confirmation.

Receiving one duplicated answer is therefore considered a commonplace occurrence. It is different when a segment actually gets lost. The destination does not receive the segment at all and receives the next segment. It carries out the duplicate confirmation of the last correctly received segment. It then receives the next segment, which is also out of order because the destination still has not received the missing segment. The confirmation is duplicated again. The destination then receives another segment that is out of order, repeats the duplication again, and so forth.

The source gradually receives the first duplicate from the destination, then the second, but still thinks that everything is normal. Once it receives the third segment, it thinks, "Something must have happened so I think I will retransmit the segment that the destination thinks is lost." It then resends the lost segment. The destination receives the missing segment, and since the destination did not throw away any of the subsequent segments (which were originally received out of order), it confirms that it received all of the delivered segments.

This fast retransmit algorithm allows the source to repeat only those segments that were lost instead of repeating all of the unconfirmed data. Repeating all of the unconfirmed data is necessary only when the fast retransmit algorithm does not succeed in the given time period.

9.8 The Window Scale Factor

The window declared by the destination has 2 B allocated in the TCP header. The destination can therefore declare a window that is between 0 and 65535 B. These windows are too small for gigabyte networks. One solution is to use the window scale factor optional item in the TCP segment header. This option can only be used in segments that initialize a connection (segments with the SYN flag).

Using the window scale factor item, both sides of the connection agree to scale the window by a factor of 0 to 14. Let us call this factor n. The agreed factor can be different in each direction.

The window scale factor is used in an interesting way. If the source proposes a window of size k big and proposes to scale it by n, then the destination understands that the window proposed by the source is $k \times 2^n$ (that is, it increases the width of the window by n bits).

The largest declared window possible is $65535 \times 2^{14} = 1073725440 = 1G\text{-}16384$. Thus with this window, the maximum amount we can declare is almost 1GB.

But why is there a limit to the size of the window? The answer is simple. Transmitted data bytes are numbered from 0 to 2^{32} (=4 GB). When the number 2^{32} is reached, we start over again from zero. If we increased the window to 8 GB, for example, the source could send up to 8 GB of unconfirmed data. If, however, the destination wants to repeat any part of that 8 GB (for example, the segment starting somewhere around 2GB), then the source would not know whether to send the segment beginning with 2 GB or the one beginning with 6 GB, because both would have the same sent byte sequence number. (We start counting from zero again when we reach 4 B.)

Even when using a window with a size of hundreds of MBs (which is permitted), it can happen that a segment will arrive over the Internet from a previously confirmed window, but will have a number used in the current window. This problem can be solved using another optional entry in the TCP segment header called **time stamp**. This entry can appear in any segment. The source enters an explicit increasing sequence (time). The destination then enters its time stamp in the reply and repeats the last received time stamp. In this way, we can determine which segments are old and which ones are current, as well as recognize old lost segments.

10
User Datagram Protocol

User Datagram Protocol (UDP) is a simple alternative to TCP. UDP is a connectionless service, it does not establish a connection, in contrast to TCP. The source party sends a UDP datagram to the destination party and then stops worrying about the datagram getting lost (this is a job for the application protocol).

UDP datagrams are enveloped in an IP datagram as shown in the following figure:

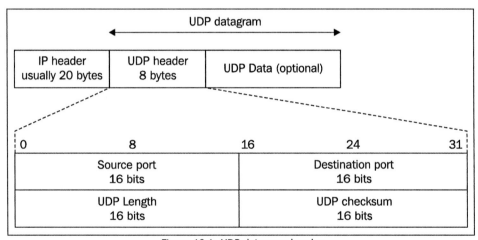

Figure 10.1: UDP datagram header

As you can see from the figure above, a UDP header is very simple. It contains the numbers of both the source and destination ports completely analogous to TCP. Again, it is important to mention that the port numbers of the UDP protocol have nothing to do with the port numbers of TCP. UDP uses an independent set of port numbers.

The **UDP Length** field indicates the length of UDP datagram (header length + data length). The minimum length is 8, i.e., a UDP datagram containing just the header and no data.

An interesting thing is that the checksum field does not need to be filled in. The calculation of the checksum is therefore not compulsory in UDP.

The overall appearance of UDP datagram including its IP header is shown in the following figure:

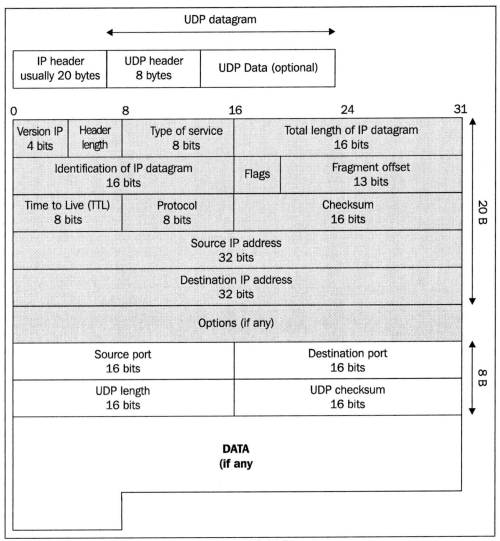

Figure 10.2: UDP

In the past, the checksum calculation was disabled in some computers, especially in computers that have the **Network File System (NFS)** installed. The reason for this was to speed up the response time of the computer.

Especially in the case of important servers, it is necessary to check that the checksum calculation is enabled. It could be dangerous, especially, for DNS servers since the checksum would then be calculated on the link layer only. But some link protocols such as SLIP do not calculate a checksum, so even a technical problem could cause damage to the application data without giving the destination user the chance of ever discovering the mistake.

If the checksum is calculated, then, as with TCP, the structure (pseudoheader) shown in Figure 10.3 is used for calculating it:

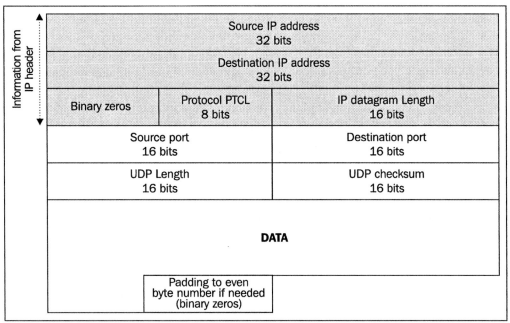

Figure 10.3: Pseudoheader for calculating the checksum of UDP datagrams

10.1 Fragmentation

Fragmentation in IP can also be used for UDP datagrams, but we should do our best to avoid fragmentation in UDP.

DNS could serve as a classic example. A DNS client sends a query via UDP to a server. If the server's answer exceeds the 512 B limit, all the extra data is cut short and the TC Flag in application data is set to indicate this message truncation (TC). Should the client request more information, it repeats the request using TCP which will also be used by the server for returning a complete answer.

An example of UDP datagram:

```
+ FRAME: Base frame properties
+ ETHERNET: ETYPE = 0x0800 : Protocol = IP:  DOD Internet Protocol
  IP: ID = 0x9CCE; Proto = UDP; Len: 74
      IP: Version = 4 (0x4)
      IP: Header Length = 20 (0x14)
    + IP: Service Type = 0 (0x0)
      IP: Total Length = 74 (0x4A)
      IP: Identification = 40142 (0x9CCE)
    + IP: Flags Summary = 0 (0x0)
      IP: Fragment Offset = 0 (0x0) bytes
      IP: Time to Live = 30 (0x1E)
      IP: Protocol = UDP - User Datagram
```

```
IP: Checksum = 0x803D
IP: Source Address = 194.149.104.203
IP: Destination Address = 192.36.148.18
IP: Data: Number of data bytes remaining = 54 (0x0036)
UDP: Src Port: DNS, (53); Dst Port: DNS (53); Length = 54 (0x36)
UDP: Source Port = DNS
UDP: Destination Port = DNS
UDP: Total length = 54 (0x36) bytes
UDP: UDP Checksum = 0x13A0
UDP: Data: Number of data bytes remaining = 46 (0x002E)
+ DNS: 0x7E01:Std Qry for 130.204.212.195.in-addr.arpa. of type Dom. name ptr
INET addr.
```

10.2 Broadcasts and Multicasts

It might seem at first glance that UDP is poor relative of TCP. So is there anything that UDP can do that TCP cannot? What is special about UDP is the fact that the destination of a UDP datagram does not have to be just a unique IP address, i.e., the network interface of a particular computer. The destination might also be a multicast; even a broadcast as well.

Though broadcasts can be addressed, addressing multicasts is much more interesting. For example, each client establishes a connection with the server in the Real Audio application. On the other hand, in the Progressive Real Audio application, the data is transmitted via multicasts, i.e., a huge amount of the transmission path capacity is saved. This is exactly the case where the UDP protocol serves you best.

11

Domain Name System

All applications that provide communication between computers on the Internet use IP addresses to identify communicating hosts. However, IP addresses are difficult for human users to remember. That is why we use the name of a network interface instead of an IP address. For each IP address, there is the name of a network interface (computer)—or to be exact, a domain name. This domain name can be used in all commands where it is possible to use an IP address. (One exception where only an IP address can be used is the specification of an actual name server.) A single IP address can have several domain names affiliated with it.

The relationship between the name of a computer and an IP address is defined in the **Domain Name System (DNS)** database. The DNS database is distributed worldwide. It contains individual records that are called **Resource Records (RR)**. Individual parts of the DNS database called **zones** are placed on particular name servers. That is, DNS is a worldwide distributed database.

If you want to use an Internet browser to browse to www.google.com with the IP address 64.233.167.147 (Figure 11.1), you enter the website name www.google.com in the browser address field.

Just before the connection with the www.google.com web server is made, the www.google.com DNS name is translated into an IP address and only then is the connection actually established.

It is practical to use an IP address instead of a domain name whenever we suspect that the DNS on the computer is not working correctly. Although it seems unusual, in this case, we can write something like:

    ping 64.233.167.147
or:

    http://64.233.167.147
or send email to:

    dostalek@[64.233.167.147]

However, the reaction can be unexpected, especially, for the email, HTTP, and HTTPS protocols. Mail servers do not necessarily support transport to servers listed in brackets. HTTP will return to us the primary home page and the HTTPS protocol will complain that the server name does not match the server name in the server's certificate.

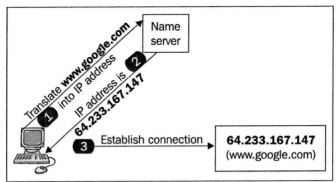

Figure 11.1: It is necessary to translate a name to an IP address before establishing a connection

11.1 Domains and Subdomains

The entire Internet is divided into domains, i.e., name groups that logically belong together. The domains specify whether the names belong to a particular company, country, and so forth. It is possible to create subgroups within a domain that are called **subdomains**. For example, it is possible to create department subdomains for a company domain. The domain name reflects a host's membership in a group and subgroup. Each group has a name affiliated with it. The domain name of a host is composed from the individual group names. For example, the host named bob.company.com consists of a host named bob inside a subdomain called company, which is a subdomain of the domain com.

The domain name consists of strings separated by dots. The name is processed from left to right. The highest competent authority is the root domain expressed by a dot (.) on the very right (this dot is often left out). **Top Level Domains (TLDs)** are defined in the root domain. We have two kind of TLD, **Generic Top Level Domain (gTLD)** and **Country Code Top Level Domain (ccTLD)**. Well known gTLDs are edu, com, net, and mil which are used mostly in the USA. According to ISO 3166, we also have two letter ccTLD for individual countries. For example, the us domain is associated with the USA. However ccTLD are used mostly outside the USA. For example, United Kingdom uses uk, India uses in, the Czech Republic uses cz, and so on. A detailed list of ccTLDs and their details can be found at http://www.iana.org/cctld/cctld-whois.htm.

The TLD domains are divided into subdomains for particular organizations, for example, coca-cola.com, mcdonalds.com, google.com. Generally, a company subdomain can be divided into lower levels of subdomains, for example, the company Company Ltd. can have its subdomain as company.com and lower levels like bill.company.com for its billing department, sec.company.com for its security department, and head.company.com for its headquarters.

The names create a tree structure as shown in the figure:

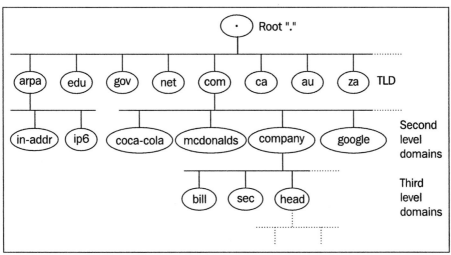

Figure 11.1a: The names in the DNS system create a tree structure

The following list contains some other registered gTLDs:

- The .org domain is intended to serve the noncommercial community.
- The .aero domain is reserved for members of the air transport industry.
- The .biz domain is reserved for businesses.
- The .coop domain is reserved for cooperative associations.
- The .int domain is only used for registering organizations established by international treaties between governments.
- The .museum domain is reserved for museums.
- The .name domain is reserved for individuals.
- The .pro domain is being established; it will be restricted to credited professionals and related entities.

11.2 Name Syntax

Names are listed in a dot notation (for example, abc.head.company.com). They have the following general syntax:

```
string.string.string .........string.
```

where the first string is a computer name, followed by the name of the lowest inserted domain, then the name of a higher domain, and so on. For unambiguousness, a dot expressing the root domain is also listed at the end.

The entire name can have a maximum of 255 characters. An individual string can have a maximum of 63 characters. The string can consist of letters, numbers, and hyphens. A hyphen cannot be at the beginning or at the end of a string. There are also extensions specifying a richer repertoire of characters that can be used to create names. However, we usually avoid these additional characters because they are not supported by all applications.

Both lower and upper case letters can be used, but this is not so simple. From the point of view of saving and processing in the DNS database, lower and upper case letters are not differentiated. In other words, the name newyork.com will be saved in the same place in a DNS database as NewYork.com or NEWYORK.com. Therefore, when translating a name to an IP address, it does not matter whether the user enters upper or lower case letters. However, the name is saved in the database in upper and lower case letters; so if NewYork.com was saved in the database, then during a query, the database will return "NewYork.com.". The final dot is part of the name.

In some cases, the part of the name on the right can be omitted. We can almost always leave out the last part of the domain name in application programs. In databases describing domains the situation is more complicated:

- It is almost always possible to omit the last dot.
- It is usually possible to omit the end of the name, which is identical to the name of the domain, on computers inside the domain. For example, inside the company.com domain it is possible to just write computer.abc instead of computer.abc.company.com. (However, you cannot write a dot at the end!) The domains that the computer belongs to are directly defined by the domain and search commands in the resolver configuration file. There can be several domains of this kind defined.

11.3 Reverse Domains

We have already said that communication between hosts is based on IP addresses, not domain names. On the other hand, some applications need to find a name for an IP address—in other words, find the reverse record. This process is the translation of an IP address into a domain name, which is often called **reverse translation**.

As with domains, IP addresses also create a tree structure (see Figure 11.2). Domains created by IP addresses are often called reverse domains. The pseudodomains IP6.arpa for IPv6 and in-addr.arpa for IPv4 were created for the purpose of reverse translation. The latter domain name has historical origins; it is an acronym for *inverse addresses in the Arpanet*.

Under the domain in-addr.arpa, there are domains with the same name as the first number from the network IP address. Thus the in-addr.arpa domain has subdomains 0 to 255. Each of these subdomains also contains lower subdomains 0 to 255. For example, network 195.47.37.0/24 belongs to subdomain 37.47.195.in-addr.arpa. This actual subdomain belongs to domain 47.195.in-addr.arpa, and so forth. Note that the domains here are created like network IP addresses written backwards.

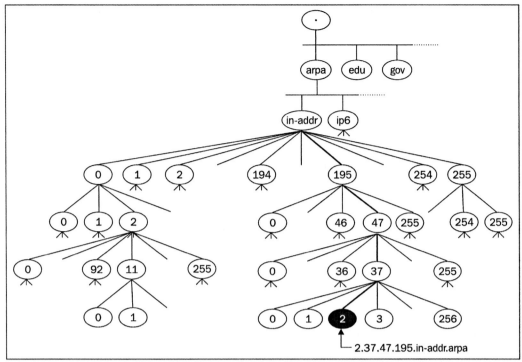

Figure 11.2: Reverse domain to IP address 195.47.37.2

This whole mechanism works if the IP addresses of classes A, B, or C are affiliated. But what should you do if you only have a subnetwork of class C affiliated? Can you even run your own name server for reverse translation? The answer is yes. Even though the IP address only has four bytes and a classic reverse domain has a maximum of three numbers (the fourth numbers are already elements of the domain—IP addresses), the reverse domains for subnets of class C are created with four numbers. For example, for subnetwork 194.149.150.16/28 we will use domain 16.150.149.194.in-addr.arpa. It is as if the IP address suddenly has five bytes! This was originally a mistake in the implementation of DNS, but later this mistake proved to be very practical so it was standardized as an RFC.

11.4 Resource Records

Information on domain names and their IP addresses, as well as all the other information distributed via DNS is stored in the memory of name servers as **Resource Records (RRs)**.

A name server (also referred to as a DNS server) loads data into its memory in several ways. Authoritative data are read from files on a disk or obtained via a zone transfer query from another server's memory. Nonauthoritative data are obtained by the server from other servers' memory as it answers individual DNS queries.

If a DNS client needs to obtain information from a DNS, it requests RRs from the DNS according to its requirements, i.e., a client can request from a domain server an A type RR with the IP addresses of the particular domain name. A client can be a resolver or a name server that cannot resolve the query on its own.

Each RR has the same structure in DNS protocol. The RR structure is shown in the following figure:

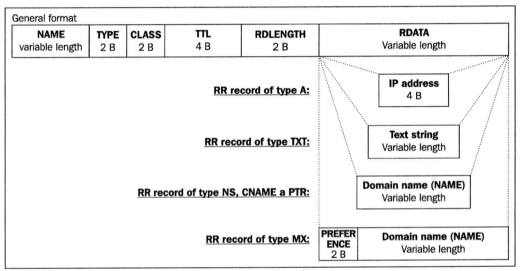

Figure 11.3: Resource Record structure

Each RR field consists of:

- **NAME**: Domain name.
- **TYPE**: Record type.
- **CLASS**: Record class.
- **TTL**: Time to live. A 32-bit number indicating the time the particular RR can be kept valid in a server cache. When this time expires, the record has to be considered invalid. The value 0 keeps nonauthoritative servers from saving the RR to their cache memory.
- **RDLENGTH**: A 16-bit number specifying the length of the RDATA field.
- **RDATA**: The data stored as a string of variable length. The format of the field depends on the RR type and class.

Note that the RR format in DNS protocol is in binary notation, i.e., it is opaque to users. This is the form in which RRs are propagated through the network via DNS protocol. On the other hand, users will want to insert their RRs and zone files in text format. As it is simple to convert binary notation to text format, individual fields are converted to text and separated by a space or a tab or a combination of these characters. Individual strings in domain names are spaced by a dot.

Type	Name	Description of the RDATA field
A	Host Address	32-bit IP address.
NS	Authoritative Name Server	The domain name of the name server, which is the authoritative name server for the particular domain.
CNAME	Canonical name for an alias	A domain name specifying a synonym to the NAME field.
SOA	Start Of Authority	Each zone data file must have exactly one SOA record. This consists of 7 fields.
PTR	Domain name pointer	Domain name. The record is used for reverse translation.
HINFO	Host information	Consists of two strings of characters. They contain descriptions of the hardware and thesoftware used in the NAME computer respectively.
MX	Mail exchange	Consists of two fields. The first is an unsigned 16-bit containing the preference value and the second is the domain name of the exchange server.
TXT	Text string	Text string containing a description.
AAAA	IP6 address	128-bit IP address (IP version 6).
WKS	Well known service description	A description of well known server services in TCP and UDP. It consists of three parts: 32-bit address, protocol number, and service ports.
SIG	Security signature	A description record used for authentication in Secure DNS.
KEY	Security key	A public zone key used as a signature in authentication.
NXT	Next domain	Name of another domain. Authenticating a nonexistent domain name and type.
A6	A6 host address	Can contain up to three fields: prefix length, part of an IP version 6 address, and prefix name.

Table 11.1 The most common types of RR

11.5 DNS Protocol

The DNS protocol works with several types of operations. The most commonly used operation is a DNS QUERY. It is a query that enables the obtaining of one or more records from the DNS database. The DNS QUERY operation was for a long time the only operation possible in the DNS system. New modifications to the DNS protocol have brought new kinds of operations, for example, DNS NOTIFY and DNS UPDATE.

The DNS protocol operates on a query/answer basis. A client sends a query to a server and the server answers it. DNS protocol uses name compression in order to make DNS packets as compact as possible.

The DNS protocol is an application-layer protocol and, as such, it does not carry out packet transfer on its own. The packet transfer is delegated to a transport protocol. Unlike the overwhelming majority of other application protocols, DNS protocol uses both UDP and TCP. Each query and the answer to it are transferred by the same transport protocol.

With translation queries (i.e., RR queries), UDP is preferred. Where a DNS answer is longer than 512 B, the answer includes only a 512 B part of the information, and the truncation (TC) bit is set in the header to mark that the answer is incomplete. The complete answer can be requested by the client via TCP.

For zone transfer, for example, between a primary and a secondary name server, TCP is used. Name servers wait for queries both on the 53/UDP port and the 53/TCP port.

> Some UDP implementations do not fill in the checksum field in the UDP packet header and take advantage of this option. This feature can be useful, for example, for NFS, but it is precarious with DNS. A network failure can result in a meaningless answer, especially where SLIP has been used on the way between a server and a client. Therefore make sure before a name server installation that your system is set to fill in the checksum in UDP packets.

11.6 DNS Query

The DNS QUERY operation consists of a query and an answer. A query contains a request for an RR (or several RRs) from the DNS database. The answer either contains the particular RR or is a denial. The RR contained in an answer can be the ultimate answer or help the client to formulate another DNS QUERY to achieve the aim, i.e., to formulate another iteration.

11.6.1 DNS Query Packet Format

DNS query uses the same packet format for both queries and answers as shown in the following figure:

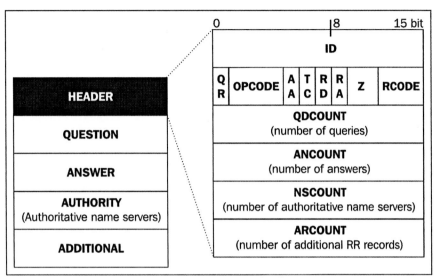

Figure 11.4: DNS Query packet format

A packet can consist of up to five sections. Each packet has to contain the HEADER section.

The term 'query' is used in two senses:

1. A DNS QUERY operation. A basic DNS protocol operation through which records (RR) are searched for in DNS databases.

2. The DNS QUERY operation always consists of a query (sent by a client) and an answer to it sent to the client by the name server. The client is either a resolver or a name server that cannot provide the answer on its own. A resolver usually marks its query with a tag showing it is a recursive query, i.e., it asks the name server to retrieve a final answer. In contrast, if the query is sent by a name server, it is usually marked with a tag showing it is an interactive query, i.e., the name server asks another name server to help it with the translation, but does not send a recursive query as it is able to arrive at what it needs by iteration.

11.6.2 DNS Query Packet Header

The packet header is obligatory and is contained both in the query and in the answer.

The first two bytes (16 bits) of a header contain a query identifier (**query ID**). A query ID is generated by a client and copied into the answer by a server. The ID is used to match a query with an answer. It identifies uniquely which particular query goes with which particular answer. The ID allows a client to send several queries at a time without waiting for an answer.

The next two bytes of a header contain the control bits. The significance of the control bits is shown in the following table:

Field	Number of bits	Value
QR	1	0 if the message is a query 1 if the message is an answer
Opcode	4	The query type is the same both for the query and the answer: 0: standard query (QUERY) 1: inverse query (IQUERY) 2: status query (STATUS) 4: notify query (NOTIFY) 5: update query (UPDATE)
AA	1	0 for non-authoritative answer 1 for authoritative answer
TC	1	1: the answer was shortened to 512 bytes; if a client needs to obtain the whole answer, the query must be sent again via TCP
RD	1	1 if Recursion Desired is set (this bit may be set in a query and is copied into the response). If RD is set, it directs the name server to pursue the query recursively.
RA	1	1 if Recursion Available is set (this bit is set or cleared in a response and denotes whether recursive query support is available in the name server).
Z	3	Reserved for future use
Rcode	4	The result code of an answer 0: No error (Noerror) 1: Format error, cannot be interpreted by the server (FormErr) 2: Server cannot answer (ServFail) 3: The query name does not exist (i.e., Nonexistent Domain), this answer can be released by authoritative name servers only (NXDomain) 4: Query type not supported (NotImplemented) 5: The server refuses to answer, for example, for security reasons (Query Refused)

Table 11.2 Significance of the individual control bits in a DNS packet header

The next four 2-byte fields in a packet header hold the number of records contained in the individual sections following the header:

- **QDCOUNT** specifies the number of RR in QUESTION section
- **ANCOUNT** specifies the number of RR in ANSWER section
- **NSCOUNT** specifies the number of RR in AUTHORITY section
- **ARCOUNT** specifies the number of RR in ADDITIONAL section

The following example shows a DNS packet found in a network:

```
Frame 2 (318 bytes on wire, 318 bytes captured)
Ethernet II, Src: Cisco_8e:1f:80 (00:15:63:8e:1f:80), Dst: Fujitsu_79:5d:0e
(00:0b:5d:79:5d:0e)
Internet Protocol, Src: 160.217.1.10 (160.217.1.10), Dst: 160.217.208.142
(160.217.208.142)
User Datagram Protocol, Src Port: domain (53), Dst Port: 1337 (1337)
```

```
Domain Name System (response)
    Transaction ID: 0x000c
    Flags: 0x8180 (Standard query response, No error)
        1... .... .... .... = Response: Message is a response
        .000 0... .... .... = Opcode: Standard query (0)
        .... .0.. .... .... = Authoritative: Server is not an authority for
domain
        .... ..0. .... .... = Truncated: Message is not truncated
        .... ...1 .... .... = Recursion desired: Do query recursively
        .... .... 1... .... = Recursion available: Server can do recursive
queries
        .... .... .0.. .... = Z: reserved (0)
        .... .... ..0. .... = Answer authenticated: Answer/authority portion
was not authenticated by the server
        .... .... .... 0000 = Reply code: No error (0)
    Questions: 1
    Answer RRs: 3
    Authority RRs: 6
    Additional RRs: 6
    Queries
        www.google.com: type A, class IN
    Answers
        www.google.com: type CNAME, class IN, cname www.l.google.com
        www.l.google.com: type A, class IN, addr 72.14.207.99
        www.l.google.com: type A, class IN, addr 72.14.207.104
    Authoritative nameservers
        l.google.com: type NS, class IN, ns d.l.google.com
        l.google.com: type NS, class IN, ns e.l.google.com
        l.google.com: type NS, class IN, ns g.l.google.com
        l.google.com: type NS, class IN, ns a.l.google.com
        l.google.com: type NS, class IN, ns b.l.google.com
        l.google.com: type NS, class IN, ns c.l.google.com
    Additional records
        a.l.google.com: type A, class IN, addr 216.239.53.9
        b.l.google.com: type A, class IN, addr 64.233.179.9
        c.l.google.com: type A, class IN, addr 64.233.161.9
        d.l.google.com: type A, class IN, addr 64.233.183.9
        e.l.google.com: type A, class IN, addr 66.102.11.9
        g.l.google.com: type A, class IN, addr 64.233.167.9
```

11.6.3 Question Section

DNS query packets mostly contain only one section: it is a question section for one question (QDCOUNT=1). The question section consists of three fields:

- **QNAME** contains a domain name. In DNS protocol the dot (.) notation is not used with domain names. Each part of a domain name (commonly stated between dots) is preceded by a byte containing the length of the string. The domain name is concluded by a zero marking its end (zero length of the string). An example of the content of this field in a query for the info.pvt.net domain name translation is as follows: $04_{16}info03_{16}pvt03_{16}net00_{16}$. The lengths of strings are in binary notation.

- **QTYPE** specifies the RR type required in the answer. The most common types of queries are shown in the following table:

Type	Value (in decimal notation)	Description
A	1	IP address version 4
NS	2	Authoritative name servers

Type	Value (in decimal notation)	Description
CNAME	5	The canonical name for an alias
SOA	6	Marks the start of a zone of authority
WKS	11	A well known service description
PTR	12	A domain name pointer
HINFO	13	Host information
MX	15	Mail exchange
TXT	16	Text strings
SIG	24	For a security signature
KEY	25	For a security key
NXT	30	Next Domain
AAAA	28	IP6 Address
CERT	37	CERT
A6	38	IP address version 6
AXFR	252	Transfer of an entire zone
IXFR	251	Incremental transfer
*	255	A request for all records

Table11.3 Query type values

- **QCLASS** stands for query class:

Numerical value (in decimal notation)	Description
1	IN: Internet
3	CH: Chaos
4	HS: Hesiod
255	*: all classes (as QCLASS only)

Table 11.4 Query Classes

An example of a DNS packet found in a network is as follows (the question section is shown in bold):

```
Frame 2 (318 bytes on wire, 318 bytes captured)
Ethernet II, Src: Cisco_8e:1f:80 (00:15:63:8e:1f:80), Dst: Fujitsu_79:5d:0e
(00:0b:5d:79:5d:0e)
Internet Protocol, Src: 160.217.1.10 (160.217.1.10), Dst: 160.217.208.142
(160.217.208.142)
User Datagram Protocol, Src Port: domain (53), Dst Port: 1337 (1337)
Domain Name System (response)
    Transaction ID: 0x000c
    Flags: 0x8180 (Standard query response, No error)
    Questions: 1
    Answer RRs: 3
    Authority RRs: 6
    Additional RRs: 6
    Queries
```

```
www.google.com: type A, class IN
    Name: www.google.com
    Type: A (Host address)
    Class: IN (0x0001)
Answers
Authoritative nameservers
Additional records
```

11.6.4 The Answer Section, Authoritative Servers, and Additional Information

Along with a header section and a repeated question section, answer packets contain another three sections: an answer section, an authoritative servers section, and an additional information section. The answer itself is included in the answer section. The authoritative name server section holds the names of the name servers in NS Type of RR. The additional information section usually holds IP addresses of authoritative name servers. Records in these sections are common resource records similar to name server cache records and use the same format as:

- **NAME**: The domain name, the same format as in the QNAME question section.

- **TYPE**: The record type, the same format as in the QTYPE question section.

- **CLASS**: The record class, the same format as in the QCLASS question section.

- **TTL**: RR expiry date, i.e., the time an answer can be kept in cache as valid.

- **RDLENGTH**: RDATA section length.

- **RDATA**: the right side of the RR (an IP address or a domain name).

An example of a DNS packet with answer, authoritative servers, and additional information sections is as follows:

```
Ethernet II, Src: 00:15:f2:20:25:26, Dst: 00:0e:35:e1:fb:4c
Internet Protocol, Src Addr: 10.0.0.138 (10.0.0.138), Dst Addr: 10.0.0.1
(10.0.0.1)
User Datagram Protocol, Src Port: domain (53), Dst Port: 3718 (3718)
Domain Name System (response)
    Transaction ID: 0x0003
    Flags: 0x8180 (Standard query response, No error)
    Questions: 1
    Answer RRs: 5
    Authority RRs: 6
    Additional RRs: 6
    Queries
        www.google.com: type A, class IN
    Answers
        www.google.com: type CNAME, class IN, cname www.l.google.com
        www.l.google.com: type A, class IN, addr 64.233.183.104
        www.l.google.com: type A, class IN, addr 64.233.183.147
        www.l.google.com: type A, class IN, addr 64.233.183.99
        www.l.google.com: type A, class IN, addr 64.233.183.103
    Authoritative nameservers
        l.google.com: type NS, class IN, ns c.l.google.com
        l.google.com: type NS, class IN, ns d.l.google.com
        l.google.com: type NS, class IN, ns e.l.google.com
        l.google.com: type NS, class IN, ns g.l.google.com
        l.google.com: type NS, class IN, ns a.l.google.com
        l.google.com: type NS, class IN, ns b.l.google.com
    Additional records
        a.l.google.com: type A, class IN, addr 216.239.53.9
```

```
         b.l.google.com: type A, class IN, addr 64.233.179.9
         c.l.google.com: type A, class IN, addr 64.233.161.9
         d.l.google.com: type A, class IN, addr 64.233.183.9
         e.l.google.com: type A, class IN, addr 66.102.11.9
         g.l.google.com: type A, class IN, addr 64.233.167.9
```

The answer section and the additional information section in the example above are in bold.

12
Telnet

Telnet is one of the oldest application protocols used within the Internet, and its origin is tied with the ARPANET network. Telnet's history dates back to 1969 when the word "Telnet" came into being as an acronym for **Telecommunications Network Protocol**. RFC 764 standardized Telnet in 1980, and RFC 854 replaced it in 1983.

Usage

Telnet protocol is used to emulate a conventional character terminal (for example, the legendary VT100) in TCP/IP-based computer networks.

A 'conventional terminal' is an I/O device used for human-computer communication. A conventional terminal is hardware consisting of a keyboard and an output device, namely, a printer or a display. A conventional terminal is usually connected to a computer via a serial asynchronous link (IBM terminals are a different story and therefore not mentioned in this book).

It is possible to emulate a conventional terminal in the HyperTerminal program (previously known as Terminal) in Windows XP PCs. Beginners often ask the question, "*What is the difference between HyperTerminal and Telnet? They both do the same job!*" The question always catches us unprepared. The difference is fundamental. While HyperTerminal changes a PC into a console when connected to a computer via a serial link (i.e., using either a null modem or a pair of modems), Telnet emulates a console via TCP/IP. The answer to the earlier question is as follows: Using HyperTerminal, you communicate through a COM port on a particular computer without TCP/IP; Telnet communication is through a network card (except when a computer is connected to a TCP/IP network using SLIP or PPP). Since this answer doesn't seem sufficient to beginners, another argument is at hand: Each user using HyperTerminal needs a separate socket (serial COM port) on the server side, whereas if Telnet is used, the server can do with a single interface (for example, Ethernet) shared by all participants.

Using Telnet is not limited to working on a remote computer only. Network administrators appreciate Telnet when testing protocols such as FTP, POP3, SMTP, HTTP, NNTP, and so on. Although many readers might possibly be using the Telnet protocol on a day-to-day basis, it may seem that an entirely different protocol than the Telnet that is being discussed here. This is not the case; Telnet is a relatively complicated protocol, which provides us with a convenient environment for daily use.

Support from Operating Systems

UNIX, Windows, and other operating systems supporting TCP/IP support the Telnet protocol. While *clients* have been implemented into the Windows operating system since Microsoft started supporting TCP/IP, *servers* have been implemented from Windows 2000 onwards.

Security

With security-sensitive servers, it is necessary to make sure immediately after installing the server that a Telnet server is not running. If the Telnet server is running, it must be stopped immediately and steps taken to ensure that it does not start after rebooting the system. On the other hand, the Telnet client can be found to be useful many a time. Telnet over SSL/TLS is currently not popular. Where secure communication is necessary, SSH is preferred.

User Sector

System administrators appreciate the use of Telnet as they can perform remote system administration via Telnet. The times when ordinary users used the Telnet program have irretrievably passed.

12.1 The NVT Protocol

NVT is an acronym for **Network Virtual Terminal**. NVT is a subset of the Telnet protocol, i.e., it is as if the Telnet protocol consists of two layers: the lower layer called NVT and the upper layer called the main Telnet protocol. The NVT protocol deals with data presentation, i.e., it provides answers to questions such as into which byte should the letter A be transformed in order to be interpreted as A again at the other end of the network connection, or which Telnet protocol command should be generated when the well-known *Ctrl + C* (^c) combination of characters is keyed in for abnormal termination of a program run from the console.

It is precisely the NVT protocol that is used (to a limited extent) for data presentation in a number of other protocols such as FTP, POP3, SMTP, NNTP, HTTP, etc. **Multipurpose Internet Mail Extension** (**MIME**) is basically an extension of this philosophy. This is also the reason why the NVT protocol is discussed in such detail. It is a presentation by the NVT protocol (testable by the Telnet program) or some other data presentation that is used in the application layer of Internet protocols.

The question is which other kinds of data presentation used in the Internet are available—the answer is simple. One would tend to expect that there are no other types of presentation. This, however, is not the case namely for binary oriented protocols important for encrypted communication. The DER (or BER) coding is used in SNMP protocol as well as *secure* communication protocols. The TLS (or SSL) protocol is the only one that has a presentation of its own.

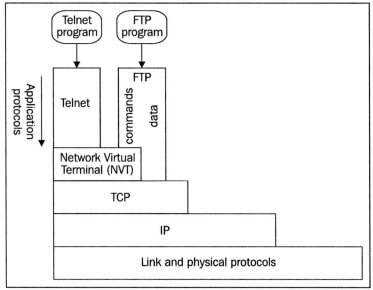

Figure 12.1: Network architecture of the NVT protocol

Figure 12.2 shows the philosophy underlying the use of the Telnet protocol. Either the client works on computer A either from a classical terminal from which the client controls the Telnet program running on computer A (computer A has, for example, a UNIX or Windows operating system), or the client is sitting at computer A (equipped with, for example, MS Windows) and is running the Telnet program on it.

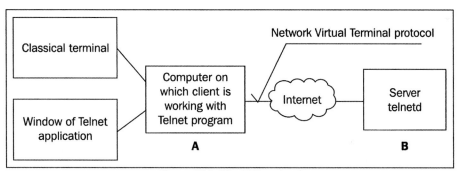

Figure 12.2: The NVT protocol

Now let's assume a client seated at computer A needs to work on computer B. The client starts the Telnet program using the name of the computer he or she wants to connect to, i.e., B. The Telnet program establishes communication with well-known port 23 of computer B via TCP. At that port, the Telnet protocol server (the telnetd program) is waiting.

The problem is that the representation of data in computers A and B may differ, i.e., computer A may use, say, ASCII coding while the coding used by computer B may be entirely different. To accommodate this, the NVT protocol specifies the representation of the data being transferred in the network. The data representation is called an **NVT protocol**. This means that the Telnet protocol prescribes neither to computer A nor to computer B which data representation they are to use locally (for example, when saving data on disks), but specifies which data representation is to be used by both computers when sending data to or receiving data from the network.

This is why the Telnet protocol does not care which representation of data is used by computers A and B. Computer A is obliged to send data in the NVT representation using TCP protocol. Similarly, computer B converts data from NVT to its own representation.

The basis of representation of data in the NVT protocol are the 128 initial characters of ASCII coding (the highest bit (8th bit) equals zero). The first 32 characters are control characters (new line (NL), carriage return (CR), bell (BEL), etc.). CR and NL character pairs stand for the end of the line.

Here is a superb example of how the NVT protocol is used. Let us suppose that both A and B use the UNIX operating system. The character for the end of line is NL in UNIX. If the end of line is sent from computer A, it must replace the single character NL in the TCP segment by two characters, CR and NL. Conversely, computer B must replace the pair of characters, CR and NL, by only NL. If computer B receives just the NL character (without CR), then it has received data not representing the end of line, but something else.

12.2 Telnet Protocol Commands

The **IAC (Interpret As Command)** character's decimal value is 255 (FF in the hexadecimal notation) and is of special significance. If a character of this value is to be transmitted, it must be doubled. The IAC character is interpreted as the beginning of a Telnet protocol command.

This means the IAC character may be followed by the commands listed in the following table:

Command			Significance
Decimal Notation	Hexadecimal Notation	Symbol	
236	EC	EOF	End of file
237	ED	SUSP	Suspend process
238	EE	ABORT	Abort process
239	EF	EOR	End of record
240	F0	SE	Sub option end
241	F1	NOP	No operation
242	F2	DM	Data mark (usually mark urgent data in TCP segment)
243	F3	BRK	Break process
244	F4	IP	Interrupt process
245	F5	AO	Abort output
246	F6	AYT	Are your there?

Command			Significance
Decimal Notation	Hexadecimal Notation	Symbol	
247	F7	EC	Escape character (escape to the command line)
248	F8	EL	Erase line
249	F9	GA	Go ahead
250	FA	SB	Sub option beginning
251	FB	WILL	See Table 12.2
252	FC	WONT	
253	FD	DO	
254	FE	DONT	
255	FF	IAC	Data byte with decimal value 255

Table 12.1: Telnet protocol commands

Let us go back to Figure 12.2 and consider the commands in the previous table. If the user wants to stop the process by any of the commands ABORT, BREAK, or INTERRUPT, he or she selects the appropriate key at the console. As the command is keyed in, the corresponding process termination command is generated (for example, IAC ABORT, i.e., FF EE). However, the question is whether the corresponding commands are to be interpreted locally on computer A (i.e., whether they are used for generating IAC Telnet protocol commands), or whether this information is to be transmitted to server B for interpretation.

Both alternatives can occur in practice. In UNIX, local interpretation of commands and IAC command generation can be set in the command line of the Telnet program by the following command (not available in the Microsoft Client):

telnet> toggle localchars

The toggle command toggles (between TRUE and FALSE) various flags that control how Telnet responds to events. In our case, it serves the localchars flag. If this flag is TRUE, then the flush, interrupt, quit, erase, and kill characters are interpreted locally and transformed into appropriate Telnet commands. The result depends on the chosen Telnet communication mode (see Section 12.2.3). Local interpretation in the *character-at-a-time* mode is rarely used. On the other hand, this setting is ignored in the *line* mode. Local interpretation is *always* used in the line mode.

Individual Telnet IAC commands can also be sent *manually* from the command line. This is done using the send command. For example, a process can be terminated using the BRK command (available in Windows XP):

telnet> send BRK

The AYT command ("*Are you there server?*"), which is a variation on the ping command is very interesting. If the communication with the server is all right, the server responds with YES (available in Windows XP):

telnet> send AYT
    [yes]

The server returns the [YES] string. If the string is not shown, it means there is something wrong in the communication with the server or the communication has not been established at all.

The Telnet protocol uses the following commands as a basic tool for negotiation of mutual communication options by the sender and the recipient:

- WILL command: The sender suggests it would like to use an option.
- DO command: The sender instructs the recipient to use a particular option.
- WONT command: The sender informs the recipient it will not use a particular option.
- DONT command: The sender instructs the recipient not to use a particular option.

Six different communication situations can occur and are explained in the following table:

Sender	Recipient	Description
WILL	DO	Sender wants to enable option. Recipient confirms use of option.
WILL	DONT	Sender wants to enable option. Recipient disallows use of option by sender.
DO	WILL	Sender wants the receiver to enable option. Recipient agrees.
DO	WONT	Sender wants the receiver to enable option. Recipient declines.
WONT	DONT	Sender wants to disable option. Recipient must confirm it.
DONT	WONT	Sender wants receiver to disable option. Recipient must confirm it.

Table 12.2: Basic compound command communication pattern

A number of options can have parameters. A list of some of the options is shown in the following table (for a detailed list see, e.g., RFC 2400):

Option Name	Decimal Number	Hexadecimal Number	Description	RFC
ECHO	1	1	If, for example, the A key is keyed from the console, we expect the 'A' character to appear on the screen to confirm that we did press the A key. The character can be sent to the screen locally by the console or by the server via the Telnet protocol. The ECHO option is a request for the server.	857
SUPPRESS GO AHEAD	3	3	This option suppress half-duplex mode.	858
STATUS	5	5	This verifies the current status of the Telnet options.	859

Option			Description	RFC
Name	**Decimal Number**	**Hexadecimal Number**		
TIMING MARK	6	6	This option provides a mechanism for a user or a process at one end of a Telnet connection to be sure that the previously transmitted data has been completely processed, printed, discarded, or disposed. Currently most often used for communication in line-at-a-time mode.	860
TERMINAL TYPE	24	18	This option can have the following parameters: 1=SEND: the server requests the client to send the client's current terminal type. 0=SENDING: the client is stating the name of its current terminal type. A string including the terminal type immediately follows the 0 option.	1091
NAWS	31	1F	Negotiation of terminal window size (i.e., the client informs the server of the number of lines and columns of its terminal window). This option can have two 2-byte parameters: number of columns and number of lines.	1073
TSPEED	32	20	Terminal connection speed (classical terminal serial line). This option can have two parameters: sending speed and receiving speed.	1079
LFLOW	33	21	Data flow control (i.e., ^S and ^Q processing—interrupting and restarting terminal output); this option can have the following parameters: 0=OFF (used, e.g., by the VI editor), 1=ON, 2=RESTART-ANY, 3= RESTART-XON	1372
LINEMODE	34	22	LINEMODE is a Telnet mode that processes terminal characters on the client side of a Telnet connection. This option can have a number of parameters.	1184
XDISPLOC	35	23	Negotiates the X-display location of a Telnet client when a user runs the Telnet client under the X-windows system.	1096
OLD ENVIRON	36	24	This option means Environment variables. This option has been superseded by the RFC 1872 standards.	1408
NEW ENVIRON	39	27	This option means Environment variables. This option has a number of parameters (see RFC 1572). Two parameters, DISPLAY and PRINTER, are transmitted in practice.	1572
STARTTLS	46	2E	Telnet starts the TLS.	
KERMIT	47	2F	Telnet Kermit.	
EXTOP	255	FF	Extended option list.	861

Table 12.3: Telnet protocol options

As an example, we may use a compound command for terminal type. If the server knows the type (and therefore the attributes) of the terminal the user is seated at, it can offer him or her the full-screen mode of the *vi* editor. One of the options on how to enquire about the terminal type is to initiate the request for terminal type by the server. In the first step, it asks the client whether it is able to convey the terminal type by using the DO-WILL communication (provided the client's answer is positive). In the next step, the server sends out a compound command (including the parameters) requesting a string containing a particular type of parameters. The compound command with parameters must always contain SB and SE.

An example of such communication is shown in the following table (bold text is used for hexadecimal values followed by the command):

Client		Server	Description
	←	**FF FD 18** <IAC DO TERMINAL-TYPE>	The server instructs the client to send its terminal type.
FF FB 18 <IAC WILL TERMINAL-TYPE>	→		The client agrees to provide its terminal type.
	←	**FF FA 18 01 FF F0** <IAC SB TERMINAL-TYPE SEND> <IAC SE>	The server instructs the client to send its terminal type using the parameter 01 (SEND).
FF FA 18 00 76 74 31 30 30 FF F0 <IAC SB TERMINAL-TYPE SENDING> vt100 <IAC SE>	→		The client sends its terminal type, namely, vt100 using the parameter 00 (SENDING).

Table 12.4: Client-server communication

12.2.1 Signal for Synchronization

The Telnet protocol uses the Data Mark command (<IAC DM> sequence) as SYNCH signal. This sequence causes the other end to discard all previously typed (but not yet read) input. This sequence is send as TCP urgent data (urgent pointer points to <DM>).

The following command can enforce the synchronization sent from the command-line of the Telnet program:

```
telnet> send synch
```

12.2.2 The Telnet Command Line

Users of the Telnet program work within a local operating system and are connected to the operating system of a remote computer, thanks to the Telnet protocol. Apart from communicating with the remote operating system, a user may use the Telnet command line. A user can access the command line in two possible ways:

- The user runs the `telnet` command without any parameters. After this, no connection is established, and the Telnet command line is at the user's disposal.

- During an established session with a remote system, a user can access the command line by using an escape sequence. The escape sequence is usually the ^] character (i.e., pressing the *CTRL* and *]* keys simultaneously). By selecting this character, the user calls the Telnet program command line on his or her local computer:

`telnet>`

or

`Microsoft Telnet>`

in Windows 2000/XP. A user can then run Telnet program commands in the command line.

Communication can be established by the following command:

`telnet> open server [port]`

The TCP port is optional; if not stated, the default port is port 23. This, however, involves a small problem. Establishing communication (for example, in UNIX) with an default port in terms of the Telnet protocol is different from establishing communication with another port. This is because if a client is establishing communication with an default port, it can more or less take for granted that there is a Telnet protocol server waiting at port 23, i.e., the client may go ahead with sending IAC commands (SUPPRESS-GO-AHEAD, WILL TERMINAL TYPE, WILL FLOW, and so on) as the server will most probably interpret them.

If, however, the user uses the Telnet program for communication for example, with an SMTP server, the SMTP server might be unable to interpret commands such as WILL-TERMINAL-TYPE. This is why when establishing communication with another port, the Telnet program only establishes the communication at the TCP level and waits for the server to respond. If the server comes up with IAC commands (for example, IAC DO TERMINAL-TYPE), the client knows it is communicating with a Telnet server and also sends IAC commands to the server. If the server does not return any IAC command, the Telnet program assumes there is no Telnet server and does not bother the server with IAC commands. (If the user wants the client to communicate using IAC commands at an explicit port from the start, the client should put the - character in front of the port number.)

Similarly, the `close` command ends communication.

The `set` command sets Telnet program variables, for example:

`telnet> set escape ^G`

This command sets escape sequences to ^G (also available in Windows XP).

The following command redirects the output of debugging information to a specified file (in Windows XP, use the `set logfile` command).

`telnet> set tracefile file`

The `toggle` command, among other things, prints the debugging information (not available in the Microsoft Client). The debugging information is very interesting in terms of understanding the Telnet protocol. Some functions of the Telnet protocol using the `toggle` command are demonstrated here. We start by listing the IAC commands in text form sent by the Telnet command:

telnet> toggle options

This will display subsequent Telnet commands. For example:

```
SENT DO SUPPRESS-GO-AHEAD
```

This means that the client has sent the IAC command DO-SUPPRESS-GO-AHEAD (i.e., FF DD 03 in hexadecimal notation).

Another type of listing is the listing of the entire data packet (without the link protocol header, IP header, and TCP headers) obtained by the command:

telnet> toggle netdata

This command will continue to list the transmitted data. An example of a listing of a packet is as follows:

```
> 0x0    fffa2000393630302c39363030fff0fffa230074312e7076742e637a3a302e30
> 0x20   fff0fffa270000444953504c41590174312e7076742e637a3a302e30fff0fffa
> 0x40   180044545445524dfff0
```

The > character means that the client sends the packet to a server. Similarly, the < character would mean reception of a packet from the server. The center column beginning with 0x0 defines the offset of the first character on the line from the beginning of the packet listing in hexadecimal notation. The right-hand side column contains the actual data.

The `status` command enables us to obtain the current relation setting.

The `send` command enables us to manually send an IAC command. Another command that deserves mentioning is `getstatus`; the client uses the IAC STATUS SEND command to request status information from the server. This command is not available in the Microsoft Client.

```
telnet> send getstatus
    Sent suboption STATUS SEND         (sending request for status)
    RCVD IAC SB
    Received suboption STATUS IS        (the server supports:
    WILL ECHO                            - character mode
    WILL SUPPRESS GO AHEAD
    WILL STATUS                          - respond to request for status
    DO TERMINAL TYPE                     - process client's terminal type
    DO NAWS                              - process client's windiow size
    DO TSPEED                            - process client's line speed
    DO LFLOW                             - process data flow control
    DO LINEMODE                          - line mode
    DO XDISPLOC                          - client's X-server location
    DO NEW-ENVIRON                       - environment variables consistent
    with RCF-
                                        1572
```

12.2.3 Communication Modes

The mode command enables changing communication modes.

For communicating in the Telnet protocol, one of thsee four modes can be employed:

- **Half-duplex**: This mode is analogous to radio communication and consists in the communication of two subjects using a shared frequency. If one participant of the communication is transmitting a signal, the other participant must listen. The participant continues to transmit the signal until it is terminated, usually by saying "*over*", which means a switchover from emission to reception. Similarly, the Telnet protocol uses the <IAC GA> command instead of "*over*". This mode has become outdated.

- **Character-at–a-time**: This is the most popular mode at present. This mode is usually the default one at both clients and servers. The client sends characters one by one to the server (the characters are usually sent in separate TCP segments, i.e., each character is surrounded by at least 20 bytes of an IP header and at least 20 bytes of a TCP segment header.

  The switchover to 'character at a time' is done by the following dialog:

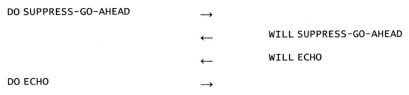

  This shows that both SUPPRESS-GO-AHEAD and ECHO options are active.

- **Line at a time**, or **'kludge' line**: This mode is derived from 'character-at-a-time'. 'Character-at-a-time' requires the SUPPRESS-GO-AHEAD and ECHO options to be simultaneously active. 'Line-at-a-time' is analogous to 'character-at-a-time' with one of the two options stated inactive at a time.

  The client executes the ECHO option locally. Keying in a password is a problem as we do not wish the password to be shown on the screen. Therefore, the server switches to 'character at a time' before the password is keyed in; the server sends WILL ECHO command and the client confirms it with DO ECHO. After keying in the password, the server returns to the original mode by sending WONT ECHO, which is confirmed by DONT ECHO by the client.

- **Linemode**: The entire input line (including potential modifications) is processed at the client end and the line is sent to the server only when this is done. The switchover to linemode is done as follows:

Linemode also has a problem with entering a password, which is dealt by a temporary switchover to character-at-a-time mode (as in 'line-at-a-time' mode). The use of the *vi* editor is dealt with in a similar way.

12.3 Example of Windows NT Client Communication

Our example describes Microsoft Windows NT Telnet protocol client communication with a server using the True64 UNIX operating system. In Windows NT (or 2000), the `toggle` command is not available. For this reason, the debugging list cannot be used to analyze the Telnet protocol.

This should not discourage Windows users. We should recall that the MS Network Monitor program is available in Windows. MS Network Monitor helps in capturing the individual Telnet protocol packets as shown in the following figure:

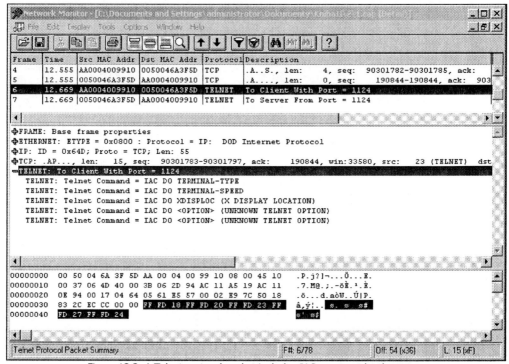

Figure 12.3: A Telnet protocol packet includes IACs sent out by the server

Let us assume that the communication is started at the TCP level. Microsoft Client does not start the communication using the IAC Telnet protocol, not even at the default port, but waits to see whether the server uses Telnet protocol.

Table 12.5 shows an exhaustive listing of this communication. For example, the communication data shown in Figure 12.3 are broken down to five separate IACs. Each IAC is listed in hexadecimal notation and is followed by the equivalent text.

Client		Server	Description
		FF FD 18 `<IAC DO TERMINAL-TYPE >`	The server instructs the client to send its terminal type.
		FF FD 20 `<IAC DO TSPEED>`	The server instructs the client to send its line speed.
	←	FF FD 23 `<IAC DO XDISPLOC>`	The server instructs the client to send its window's location (for X-Windows).
		FF FD 27 `<IAC DO NEW-ENVIRON>`	The server instructs the client to send variables of its environment (SET command listing in Windows).
		FF FD 24 `<IAC DO OLD-ENVIRON>`	The server instructs the client to send its environment variables (outdated option).

FF FB 18
`<IAC WILL TETMINAL-`
`TYPE>`
	→		The client agrees to provide a terminal type (response to DO).

FF FC 20
`<IAC WONT TSPEED>`
FF FC 23
`<IAC WONT XDISPLOC>`
FF FC 27
`<WONT NEW-ENVITON>`
FF FC 24
`<WONT OLD-ENVIRON>`
	→		The client refuses to provide its line speed (user does not work at classical terminal).
			
			The client refuses to provide its window's location (user does not use X-Windows).
			
			The client refuses to provide its environment variables.

	←	FF FA 18 01
		`<IAC SB TERMINAL-TYPE`
		`01>`
		FF FO
		`<IAC SE>`
			The server requests the terminal type from the client. As the option is used with a parameter, it must be bracketed by SB and SE.

FF FA 18 00 76 74 31 30 30
`<IAC SB TERMINAL-`
`TYPE 00> vt100`
FF FO
`<IAC SE>`
	→		The client sends the server its terminal type, i.e., vt100. As the option is used with a parameter, SB and SE must be used.

	←	FF FB 03
		`<IAC WILL SUPPRESS -GO-`
		`AHEAD>`
			The server does not wish to use half-duplex.

		FF FD 01 `<IAC DO ECHO>`	The server wants client to ECHO.
		FF FD 1F `<IAC DO NAWS>`	The server wants client to use NAWS.
		FF FB 05 `<IAC WILL STATUS>`	The server requests STATUS.
		FF FD 21 `<IAC DO LFLOW>`	The server wants client to use LFLOW.

Client	Server	Description
FF FD 03 <IAC DO SUPPRESS-GO-AHEAD> →		The client confirms not using half-duplex mode.
FF FB 01 <IAC WILL ECHO>		The client agrees to ECHO.
FF FC 1F <IAC WONT NAWS>		The client refuses NAWS.
FF FC 05 <IAC DONT STATUS> →		The client denies STATUS.
FF FC 21 <IAC WONT LFLOW>		The client refuses LFLOW.
	FF FE 01 <IAC DONT ECHO> ←	The server does not want the client to ECHO.
	FF FB 01 <IAC WILL ECHO>	The server wants to ECHO itself.
FF FC 01 <IAC WONT ECHO> →		The client will not ECHO.
	← Login:	
FF FD 01 <IAC DO ECHO> →		The client agrees that the server will ECHO.
User name →		
	← Password:	

Table 12.5: Client-server Telnet protocol communication (Windows NT client)

12.4 Example of UNIX Client Communication

Let's say our client is started in an X-Windows window within the True64 UNIX system. The server is True64 UNIX as well.

An example of this communication is shown in the following figure:

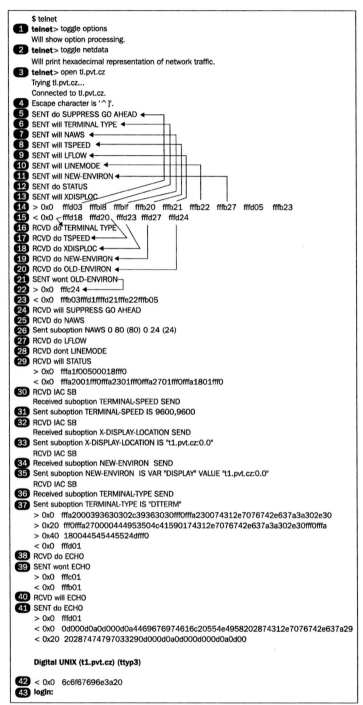

```
      $ telnet
 1  telnet> toggle options
      Will show option processing.
 2  telnet> toggle netdata
      Will print hexadecimal representation of network traffic.
 3  telnet> open tl.pvt.cz
      Trying tl.pvt.cz...
      Connected to tl.pvt.cz.
 4  Escape character is '^]'.
 5  SENT do SUPPRESS GO AHEAD
 6  SENT will TERMINAL TYPE
 7  SENT will NAWS
 8  SENT will TSPEED
 9  SENT will LFLOW
10  SENT will LINEMODE
11  SENT will NEW-ENVIRON
12  SENT do STATUS
13  SENT will XDISPLOC
14  > 0x0   fffd03   fffbl8   fffblf   fffb20   fffb21   fffb22   fffb27   fffd05   fffb23
15  < 0x0   fffd18   fffd20   fffd23   fffd27   fffd24
16  RCVD do TERMINAL TYPE
17  RCVD do TSPEED
18  RCVD do XDISPLOC
19  RCVD do NEW-ENVIRON
20  RCVD do OLD-ENVIRON
21  SENT wont OLD-ENVIRON
22  > 0x0   fffc24
23  < 0x0   fffb03fffd1ffffd21fffe22fffb05
24  RCVD will SUPPRESS GO AHEAD
25  RCVD do NAWS
26  Sent suboption NAWS 0 80 (80) 0 24 (24)
27  RCVD do LFLOW
28  RCVD dont LINEMODE
29  RCVD will STATUS
      > 0x0   fffa1f00500018fff0
      < 0x0   fffa2001fffOfffa2301fffOfffa2701fffOfffa1801fff0
30  RCVD IAC SB
      Received suboption TERMINAL-SPEED SEND
31  Sent suboption TERMINAL-SPEED IS 9600,9600
32  RCVD IAC SB
      Received suboption X-DISPLAY-LOCATION SEND
33  Sent suboption X-DISPLAY-LOCATION IS "t1.pvt.cz:0.0"
      RCVD IAC SB
34  Received suboption NEW-ENVIRON  SEND
35  Sent suboption NEW-ENVIRON  IS VAR "DISPLAY" VALUE "t1.pvt.cz:0.0"
      RCVD IAC SB
36  Received suboption TERMINAL-TYPE SEND
37  Sent suboption TERMINAL-TYPE IS "DTTERM"
      > 0x0    fffa2000393630302c39363030fffOfffa230074312e7076742e637a3a302e30
      > 0x20   fffOfffa270000444953504c41590174312e7076742e637a3a302e30fffOfffa
      > 0x40   180044545445524dfff0
      < 0x0    fffd01
38  RCVD do ECHO
39  SENT wont ECHO
      > 0x0    fffc01
      < 0x0    fffb01
40  RCVD will ECHO
41  SENT do ECHO
      > 0x0    fffd01
      < 0x0    0d000d0a0d000d0a4469676974616c20554e4958202874312e7076742e637a29
      < 0x20   20287474797033290d000d0a0d000d000d0a0d00

      Digital UNIX (t1.pvt.cz) (ttyp3)

42  < 0x0   6c6f6f696e3a20
43  login:
```

Figure 12.4: Client/server communication in UNIX

We first start the Telnet program without a parameter and thus get the Telnet program command line. From here we start a listing of debugging information both of IAC in text form (1) and of all application data in hexadecimal notation (2).

We use the open command to establish communication with t1.pvt.cz server. The Telnet program sets the escape sequence as ^]. As the port number was not specified in the open command, the client (unlike Windows NT Client) assumes it is establishing connection with a Telnet protocol server. This is why immediately after the connection is established, the client sends these IAC commands of the Telnet protocol to the server:

- (5) The client does not want to communicate in half-duplex.
- (6) The client wants to send the server its terminal type.
- (7) The client wants to send the number of rows and columns of its window.
- (8) The client wants to send its terminal's line speed.
- (9) The client wants to negotiate data flow control with the server.
- (10) The client wishes to work in the linemode.
- (11) The client wants to send environment variables in line with RFC 1572.
- (12) The client requests the status.
- (13) The client wishes to send its X-server location to the server.

The client sends the commands (5 to 13) to the server in the packet shown on line 14. The server responds with IAC command in the packet shown in hexadecimal notation on line 15. The individual IAC on both lines are separated by spaces. The packet on line 15 contains the following IAC commands:

- (16) The server requests the client to send the terminal type (in response to line 6).
- (17) The server asks the client to send its line speed (in response to line 8).
- (18) The server wants the client to send the information of its X-server location.
- (19) The server requests the environment variables according to the new specifications.
- (20) The server requests the environment variables according to the old specifications.

On line 21, the client refuses to send environment variables according to the old specifications; the packet in hexadecimal notation is shown on line 22. The server responds with a packet (23) that includes the following commands:

- (24) The server will not communicate in half-duplex (in response to line 5).
- (25) The server requests the client to send the number of lines and columns of its terminal.
- (26) Contains the instant response including two 2-byte parameters:
  - The first parameter (first two parameter bytes) has 0 in the first byte and 80_{10} (50_{16}) in the second byte, i.e., the client informs the server it has 80 columns available.
  - The second parameter informs the server there are 24 lines available.
- (27) The server supports data flow control.

- (28) The server does not support the linemode.
- (29) The server supports the transmission of status information.

The next packet sent by the server contains the following commands:

- (30) The server requests the terminal speed of the client. The client immediately responds on line 31 saying that the sending and receiving speed is 9600 b/s.
- (32) The server requests the X-server location of the client. The client responds on line 33 that the location is t1.pvt.cz:0.0.
- (34) The server asks for the environment variables. The client sends only the value of the "DISPLAY" environment variable (see line 35).
- (36) The server requests for the terminal type. The client says on line 37 that the terminal type is "DTTERM".

The server tries to suggest 'line-at-a-time' by asking whether the client wants to do ECHO on line 38. The client refuses 'line-at-a-time' mode (39).

On line 40, the server suggests to ECHO to which the client responds positively on line 41.

Now the tiring IAC sequence ends, and the server identifies itself on line 42 and invites the user to key in the login (43) and password.

13

File Transfer Protocol

File Transfer Protocol (**FTP**) is an application protocol suitable for file transfers in a computer network based on TCP/IP. Like the Telnet protocol, FTP too has a very rich history. It dates back to RFC 114 released on April 16, 1971. Now it is standardized by RFC 959 and amended by RFC 2228 and RFC 2640.

Usage
FTP is used for file transfers in computer networks using TCP/IP protocol.

Support from Operating Systems
UNIX, Windows, and other operating systems supporting TCP/IP support FTP as well asTelnet protocol. The FTP client is also an integral part of all web browsers.

Security
FTP is neither less nor more secure than Telnet. Because it is intended for file transfers, anonymous servers that do not have high security requirements often use it.

Telnet over SSL/TLS is currently not very popular. Where secure communication is necessary, the SSH protocol is used. The client program for file transfer over SSH protocol is named scp.

User Sector
There are basically three groups of FTP users:

1. Users and system administrators working on the operating system of a particular server.
2. Ordinary users mostly use FTP for data download from FTP servers via Internet browsers. In this case, an anonymous FTP server is used.
3. Many intermediate users utilize FTP in special graphical clients for Windows (for example, WS_FTP) or as part of a graphical application of the "Commander" type (for example, Norton Commander, Windows Commander, etc.).

13.1 Architecture

The architecture of the FTP protocol is as follows:

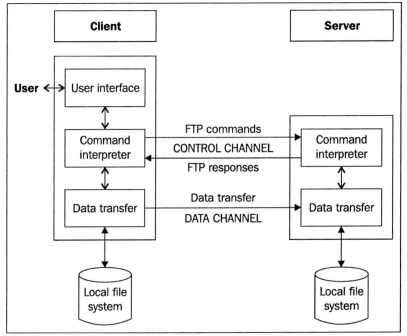

Figure 13.1: The FTP architecture

A user works with a user interface that is represented either by the command line of the FTP program, a GUI FTP utility, or an Internet browser.

The user interface is usually created according to the working of the operating system in which it is implemented. The user interface gives requests to the layer of the command interpreter. Then the command interpreter communicates with the server using commands defined by the FTP protocol. Section 13.4 contains an overview of these commands. However, the user can make use of an even richer range of commands since the command interpreter usually interprets several commands for working with the local file system of the client (for example, the lcd command that is used to set the current directory on the client side).

If both the client and the server layers of the command interpreter in the command channel agree on data transmission between the client and the server, a request for data transmission is given to the data transmission layer. The data transmission layer works with the local file system. It is able to *read* a file and *write* transferred data (into the file system).

FTP protocol architecture is special as it uses two channels of the client-server type:

- **Control channel**: Using this channel, a client sends its requests to a server, for example, for directory listing or file downloading. This channel uses NVT presentation protocol. By default, a server expects requests of the command channel at the well-known 21/TCP port.

- **Data channel**: Using this channel, the required data (either directory listing or file content) is transferred. A data channel is a bit special because the role of a server and a client can be switched. Therefore, we distinguish two modes of FTP protocol communication: active and passive.

When the data channel is open, concrete data transmission features are always set up. The following four FTP protocol options can be set up:

- Type of transferred data. FTP protocol distinguishes up to four types of transferred files (however, only ASCII and binary are usually implemented):
  - **ASCII**: This is the default type of a transferred file. The transferred data is represented in the NVT protocol, i.e., a sender converts the transferred data into NVT and a receiver converts it from NVT to the coding in the receiver's operating system. A command channel also uses this way of transferring data.
  - **EBCDIC**: This is used if both ends of the connection are systems using EBCDIC code.
  - **Binary type**: This transfers data as continuous flow of bytes. This type is commonly used for binary data transmission.
  - **Local file type**: This is usually not implemented today. It is intended for binary data transmission between systems with different data representation.

- Format option (this option can be set only for ASCII or EBCDIC file types):
  - **Non-print**: File does not contain format characters.
  - **Telnet format control**: File contains vertical format characters for printing as they are defined in the Telnet protocol.
  - **FORTRAN control**: First character of each line contains the FORTRAN language format control character.

- Structure of a transferred file. This option can be as follows:
  - **File structure**: A file is a stream of bytes (default value).
  - **Record structure** (only for ASCII or EBCDIC type transfers): In this case, the structure of a transferred file may contain records. The transferred file contains the control characters EOR (end of record) and EOF (end of file). Both control characters are preceded by the FF escape sequence (a semantic byte of value FF must be doubled). The escape sequence is followed by either 01 (for EOR) or by 02 (for EOF). The combination of EOR and EOF at the end of the file can be reduced to FF 03.
  - **Page structure**: This is supported in some operating systems. Each page is transmitted with a page number so that the pages can be received in random order.

- Transmission mode. This specifies how a file is transferred:
  - **Mode stream**: This is the default value. A file is transferred as a stream of bytes. In the case of file structure, the receiver knows it is an end of the file if the sender closes the data channel. In the case of record structure, the FF 03 characters indicate the end of the file.
  - **Block mode**: Transfers data in blocks. Each block contains an information header field.
  - **Compressed mode**: This mode enables compression of transferred data.

We can display the status of an established FTP connection by the status command:

```
ftp> status
    Connected to infoserv.ripe.net.
    No proxy connection.
    Mode: stream; Type: binary; Form: non-print; Structure: file
    Verbose: on; Bell: off; Prompting: on; Globbing: on
    Store unique: off; Receive unique: off
    Case: off; CR stripping: on
    Ntrans: off
    Nmap: off
    Hash mark printing: off; Use of PORT cmds: on
    Interpretation of "|" in filenames: off
```

Here is an explanation of the highlighted line:

- Mode: stream: The transmission mode is mode stream.

- Type: binary: The type of transferred data is binary (continuous byte flow).

- Form: non-print: The format option is non-print (transferred data does not contain format characters for output, for example, at a printer).

- Structure: file: The structure of the transferred data is file structure.

13.2 Active Mode of FTP Protocol Communication

Active mode is the basic mode of FTP protocol communication. The most frequently asked question is how the user can influence the option of the communication mode. The answer is hard to give because an FTP client developer must enable this option. Only some clients have such an option; Linux clients support the proxy command, but Windows clients doesn't support the proxy command. On the other hand, most Internet browsers use passive mode. However, servers usually support both communication modes.

At first, we will briefly show a scenario of active communication in the following table:

Step	FTP communication
1.	C:\WINDOWS\system32>ftp ftp.ripe.net Connected to hawk-ftp.ripe.net. 220 FTPD Server (RIPE NCC FTP server)
2.	User (hawk-ftp.ripe.net:(none)): anonymous 331 Anonymous login ok, send your complete email address as your password.

Step	FTP communication
3.	Password:
4.	230-Welcome 194.149.105.131, 230- 230-This is the ftp-server of the RIPE Network Coordination Centre (NCC). ... 230- 230 Guest login ok, access restrictions apply.
5.	ftp> debug Debugging On.
6.	ftp> dir ---> PORT 194,149,105,131,4,11
7.	200 PORT command successful.
8.	---> LIST
9.	150 Opening ASCII mode data connection for file list
10.	-rw-r--r-- 1 ftpuser ftpgroup 2826 Nov 18 2004 About-ripe drwxr-x--x 2 ftpuser ftpgroup 4096 Dec 9 2004 cdforlinx ...
11.	226 Transfer complete. ftp: 1384 bytes received in 2,53Seconds 0,55Kbytes/sec. ftp>

Table 13.1: Active mode

Here is a description of the steps shown in the above table:

1. A client wants to establish connection with the ftp.ripe.net server for control channel. At first, the client will ask the port management of its local computer for a free port allocation. Any one of the ports above 1023 (client port) is allocated to it. This port is used for the TCP connection with the server port 21/TCP. In this way the command channel is set up, and the FTP service is ready for a new user.

2. The FTP service asks for the username.

3. The FTP service authenticates the user by a user password.

4. Once the user is logged in, the FTP service prints out its banner.

5. Since we want to describe the FTP protocol communication in detail, we type debug, an FTP client command. This command has no influence on the communication between a client and a server. The FTP client will only output detailed information of the FTP protocol communication. For example:

   --> PORT 194,149,105,131,4,11

   This means the client sent to the server (-->) an FTP protocol command, PORT 194,149,105,131,4,11.

6. Now we can execute the `dir` command for a detailed listing of the current working directory on the server. To send a directory listing from the server to the client, a data channel must be created. For establishing a data channel, the server changes its role. This change of role is the basic characteristic of active mode of the FTP.

The FTP client asks the port management of its operating system for the allocation of a free port and then starts the TCP server on this port for the data channel. Port 1035 (expressed decimally) is allocated to the FTP client. The hexadecimal value of 1035 is 04 0B. However, FTP protocol states every byte decimally, i.e., 4 and 11. Another way of calculating is 4 x 256 + 11=1035.

With the help of the PORT command, the FTP client sends six decimal numbers containing its IP address (194.149.105.131) and the port (1035=4,11), i.e., it sends 194, 149, 105, 131, 4, 11.

7. The server acknowledges the PORT command.

8. The client software translates the client `dir` command into the FTP protocol LIST command. The user types the client command. FTP commands are transferred in the FTP control channel in NVT representation (i.e., in ASCII).

9. The FTP server establishes TCP connection with the FTP client using the IP address and port from the PORT command. Notice that it is the FTP *server* that establishes a connection and not the FTP client (see 1), but the server and the client have exchanged their roles in the data channel. The FTP server indicates that it has established a TCP connection with the FTP client and opens the ASCII mode data channel for transferring the directory listing.

10. The server transfers the directory listing through the data channel.

11. The server indicates through the control channel that the transfer of the directory listing is complete (and closes the data channel).

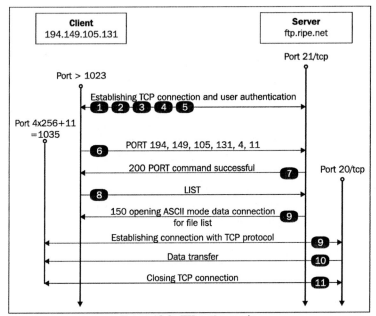

Figure 13.2: FTP active mode

In this kind of FTP active mode, the data channel is established from the FTP server to the FTP client. In TCP terminology, the FTP server is the TCP client for the data channel, and the FTP client is a TCP server.

13.3 Passive Mode of FTP Protocol Communication

In some cases, it is possible that a data channel cannot be established from an FTP server to an FTP client (for example, firewalls may deny such a connection). In such cases, we can use the passive mode of communication, where a client creates connections for both the command and data channels. This can be very useful if we want to protect, for example, our network by packet filtration at the access router or a firewall.

In the case of active mode, we cannot use the Telnet program for FTP protocol survey, because we would have to run the Telnet program at the server to create the data channel. In contrast, in the case of the passive mode, we can use the Telnet program instead of the FTP program. In this case, we must directly use the FTP protocol commands as described in Table 13.1.

We will briefly clarify the basic principles of passive FTP communication again at the ftp.ripe.net server (see Figure 13.3):

	Passive FTP Communication
1	`C:\>telnet ftp.ripe.net  21` `220 FTPD Server (RIPE NCC FTP server)`
2	`user ftp` `331 Anonymous login ok, send your complete email address as your password.`
3	`pass libor.dostalek@siemens.com`

4	`230-Welcome 194.149.105.131,`
	
	`This is the ftp-server of the RIPE Network Coordination Centre (NCC).`
	`...`

5	`pasv` `227 Entering Passive Mode (193,0,0,215,237,221).`
6	`list` `150 Opening ASCII mode data connection for file list`

	Client Starting Next Telnet Session

7	`C:\>telnet 193.0.0.215 60893`
	`-rw-r--r--   1 ftpuser   ftpgroup   2826 Nov 18 2004   About-ripe`
	`drwxr-x--x   2 ftpuser   ftpgroup   4096 Dec  9 2004   cdforlinx`
	`drwxrwxr-x   2 ftpuser   ftpgroup   4096 Feb 21 2005   erx`
	`lrwxrwxrwx   1 ftpuser   ftpgroup      7 Jul  1 2003   fyi -> rfc/fyi`
	`...`
	
	`Connection to host lost.`
	`(60893 = 256 x 237 + 221)`

Client Starting Next Telnet Session	
8	`226 Transfer complete.`
9	`quit` `221 Goodbye.`
10	`Connection to host lost.`

Table 13.2: Passive mode

The explanation of the table above is shown in the following list:

1. We establish a connection with the `ftp.ripe.net` server via the command channel. We use the well-known 21/TCP port reserved for FTP servers.

2. A user authentication follows. Since we are not using an FTP client, but only a Telnet program, we must directly type the FTP protocol commands. We type the FTP `user` command with the username parameter (here, the username is `ftp`).

3. For the password, we use the FTP `pass` command and enter the password as its parameter.

4. In the case of successful authentication, the server returns its welcome banner.

5. This part is critical. Here the client says that the communication has to proceed in the passive mode (by the FTP `pasv` command), i.e., we want the server to allocate a port for the data channel. In passive mode, the server does not use port 20, but asks its port management for a free port. In our case, the port 60893=256x237+221 is allocated. This time it is the server that returns the `PORT` command, its IP address, and the number of the allocated port to which the client has to establish the connection.

6. Now we can type the FTP `list` command for the directory listing.

7. The server expects the connection for the data channel to be established, so we must quickly run another Telnet program in a different window and establish a connection with the server, but this time at port 60893. This way we can immediately see the output of the data channel.

8. The server indicates through the control channel that the transfer of the directory listing is complete (and closes the data channel).

9. Now, we can quit the control channel.

10. Here, the server indicates that the connection is closed.

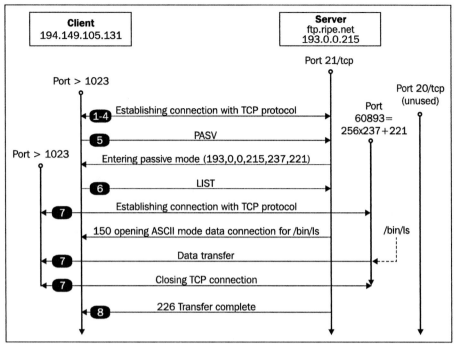

Figure 13.3: FTP passive mode

13.4 FTP Commands

Users usually use user programs like ftp.exe. User programs have a user interface (generally a command line) that allow users to input user commands. The most fundamental function of a user program is converting a user command to an FTP command that is transmitted over a network. The FTP command always contains a keyword (for example, USER). This keyword can be followed by parameters separated by a space. The command is terminated with the CR (carriage return) and LF (new line) characters. FTP commands are always in ASCII.

FTP Command (transferred by network)	Usual user command	Description
USER username	user	Username.
PASS password		Password.
ACCT account	account	Apart from a username, some servers can also require an account name, which can be used for accessing some data.
CWD	cd	Change working directory (at server)
CDUP	cdup	Parent directory will by set as working directory (at server).
SMNT path	–	File system mount.

FTP Command (transferred by network)	Usual user command	Description
QUIT	quit	Terminates a user session and if file transfer is not in progress, the server closes the control channel.
REIN	–	Reinitialization—user is logged off, but connection through command channel remains. A command USER can follow.
PORT port	–	See text.
PASV	passive	Passive mode.
TYPE code	ascii, binary	Transferred file type specification (first parameter) and file transfer format option (second parameter. Example: TYPE A N. ASCII type without printing format characters must be set up.
STRU structure	form	Specifies the structure of transferred file. E.g. STRU F. Transferred file structure must be set to 'file structure'.
MODE mode	mode	Transmission mode. E.g. MODE S means stream mode setting.
RETR path	get	Downloads file from server.
STOR path	put	Transfers file to server.
STOU path	rununique + get	Similar to STOR, however, transferred file will have an explicit name in directory (ftp will not replace existing file, but it will change a name).
APPE path	append	Transfer file to server. If there is already a file with the same name, the file is not replaced, but it is extended with the transferred data.
REST data mark		Restart of data transfer.
RNFR path	rename	Rename of file will be performed by two FTP commands.
RNTO path		Command RNFR checks whether file exists at server, and commands RNTO sets new name of file.
ABOR		Tells the server to abort the previous FTP command and any associated transfer of data. This command uses the Telnet synchronization command Data Mark.
DELE path	delete	Delete file.
RMD path	rmdir	Remove directory.
MKD path	mkdir	Make directory.
PWD	pwd	Print working directory.
LIST [path]	dir	List directory content.
NLIST [path]	ls	Detailed list of directory content.

FTP Command (transferred by network)	Usual user command	Description
SITE string		Command for other server services. Which services a particular server provides, one can learn by the command: SITE HELP. E.g. SITE IDLE identifies setting of inactive connection limits.
SYST	system	Find out the type of operating system at the server.
STAT [path]	status	This command causes a status response to be sent over the control connection as a reply. The command may be sent during a file transfer.
HELP [command]	remotehelp	Output supported commands at server.
NOOP		Empty command (no command).

Table 13.3: FTP commands (transferred by network)

It is necessary to distinguish between the user commands of an FTP program and FTP protocol commands. For example, for directory listing, a user types the dir command, which is converted into the FTP LIST command.

On the other hand, the FTP program has many internal user commands that often have nothing to do with network communication, but serve to make things comfortable for the user. Such commands are, for example, as follows:

- hash command: Using this command a user can set the client software so that after transmitting 1 or 2 KB of data through the data channel, a hash sign (#) appears on the display. Thus, the user would know that the data is really being transferred and the program has not hung.

- lcd command: The user can change the working directory of the local system by using this command. Sometimes more commands concerning the local system are implemented. For example, lpwd command on Linux; lpwd command changes working directory on local machine. Generally, we can execute all (external) commands of the local system by adding an exclamation mark before the command at the command line.

- literal command: This command is very important. By using this command, one can send any FTP protocol command, for example, any argument of the literal command is directly inserted into the TCP protocol. For example, literal PWD.

- Commands starting with an m character: This character creates a special group. These commands enable the use of wildcard characters for multiple choices, such as the asterisk (*) character in file names. Thus it is possible to transfer several files by one command. However, it is necessary to realize that these commands only generate, on behalf of the user, several FTP commands that are gradually executed. By the first command, the remote directory listing is obtained, on the basis of which individual commands are generated. After all, it is only a feature of the *client* software and is not another set of FTP commands.

The problem with the transmission between different operating systems (for example, Microsoft and UNIX) is the fact that Microsoft usually uses upper case for file names, while UNIX uses lower case . The question is whether to convert letters in file names, i.e., either from upper case to lower case or lower case to upper case). This conversion is generally controlled by the case user command.

- Apart from the previously stated FTP commands, experimental commands starting with the x character can be also used, for example, xCWD is the experimental analog of the command CWD (for detailed information, see RFC 1123).

13.5 Proxy

It should be noted that the proxy described here does not relate to a proxy we will meet in the field of HTTP. The principle is that a client can mediate file transfer between two FTP servers, for example, between the ftp.ripe.net server and the ftp.pvt.cz server.

First, the client creates the command channel with the ftp.ripe.net server. Using the proxy command, the client creates other channel (called a 'proxy-channel') with the ftp.pvt.cz server. The ftp.pvt.cz server allocates a port where it will wait for the connection for the data channel (the server sends the IP address and the allocated port number to the client by the command channel). The point is the server can think it is waiting for the connection from the client. Nevertheless, the client gives the IP address and the allocated port to the ftp.ripe.net server. Now the ftp.ripe.net server can establish the connection for the data channel with the ftp.pvt.cz server and can input data it wants to send through the created data channel. In this case, the client must give the RETR command (read file) to one server and the command STOR (write file) to the other server.

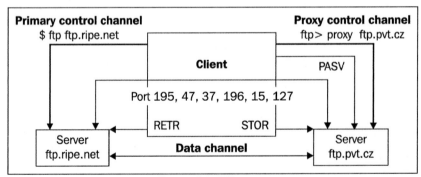

Figure 13.4: FTP proxy

And finally, the listing of the communication in debugging mode:

```
ftp> ftp.ripe.net

    Connected to ftp.ripe.net.
    220 ftp.ripe.net FTP server (Version wu-2.6.1(1) Tue Jul 18 14:18:18 CEST
    2000) ready.

    Name (ftp.ripe.net:root): ftp
    331 Guest login ok, send your complete email address as password.
```

Password:
230 Guest login ok, access restrictions apply.
Remote system type is UNIX.
Using binary mode to transfer files.

ftp> debug
Debugging on (debug=1).

ftp> proxy open ftp.pvt.cz
Connected to ftp.pvt.cz
220 ftp.pvt.cz FTP server (Digital UNIX Version 5.60) ready.

Name: ftp
--> USER ftp
331 Guest login ok, send ident as password.

Password:
--> PASS XXXX
230 Guest login ok, access restrictions apply.
--> SYST
215 UNIX Type: L8 Version: Digital UNIX V4.0 (Rev. 878)
Remote system type is UNIX.
Using binary mode to transfer files.

ftp> proxy get file
--> TYPE I
ftp.pvt.cz:200 Type set to I.
--> PASV
ftp.pvt.cz:227 Entering Passive Mode (195,47,37,196,15,127)
--> TYPE I
ftp.ripe.net:200 Type set to I.
--> PORT 195,47,37,196,15,127
ftp.ripe.net:200 PORT command successful.
--> RETR file
ftp.ripe.net:150 Opening BINARY mode data connection for file (2093 bytes).
--> STOR file
ftp.pvt.cz:150 Opening BINARY mode data connection for file (0.0.0.0,0).
ftp.pvt.cz:226 Transfer complete.
ftp.ripe.net:226 Transfer complete.
local: file remote: file
ftp>

Proxy FTP is not implemented in Windows XP clients.

13.6 Return Codes

The server replies to individual FTP protocol commands set by the client with a message with a three-digit return code followed by text clarifying the return code. The three-digit return code has the form xyz where:

x takes any of these following values:

- 1: A positive preliminary reply when starting some action. Before the client can send another command, one can expect a message about the termination of the action.

- 2: A positive completion reply (the requested action has been successfully completed). The client can send commands.

- 3: A positive immediate reply after which the client has to perform a concrete action. For instance, after entering a username, a password is required.

- 4: A transient negative completion reply. This means the command was not accepted and the requested action did not take place, but the error condition is temporary and the action may be requested again.

- 5: A permanent negative completion reply, for example, on an unsupported command.

y can take any of these following values: 0 for syntax errors, 1 for informative message, 2 for connection error, 3 for authentication error, 4 for unspecified error, and 5 for a file system error.

z specifies the error in detail.

Here are some examples:

```
125 Data connection already open; transfer starting.
230 User logged in, proceed.
331 User name okay, need password.
452 Insufficient storage space in system.
502 Command not implemented.
```

13.7 Abnormal Termination of Data Transfer

Abnormal termination of a data transfer is practically the only use of the Telnet protocol commands (NVT protocol) by FTP.

In Table 13.3, we can find the ABOR command that is used for an abnormal termination of the previously executed command. It could happen that the server would sequentially process individual client commands one by one. In such a case, the ABOR command would be processed after the completion of the previous command. But we would usually want to terminate the previous (running) command sooner, i.e., to process the command ABOR immediately when the server receives it. This can be achieved as follows:

The client software is generally sensitive to some key sequence for abnormal termination, for example, *Ctrl* + *C* (graphical clients can have a single button for termination). After pressing *Ctrl* + *C*, the client would like the server to stop sending data into the data channel. The client accomplishes this with two actions:

1. With the help of an NVT protocol command, the interrupt process client command (<IAC IP>), it sends a signal to a server. The <IAC DM> (data mark) command, which is a signal for synchronization (SYNCH), follows the <IAC IP> command. The FTP protocol data are encapsulated into a TCP segment. This TCP segment has the URG flag set and the 'Urgent Pointer' TCP header field filled in pointing to the data mark command (<IAC DM>). For more details, refer to Sections 9.1 and 12.2.

2. It executes the ABOR FTP command (a command of the FTP protocol).

Overall, the client sends 10 bytes of data:

```
<IAC IP><IAC DM>ABOR CR LF
```

A particular implementation of the FTP client sets the urgent data flag and sends the IAC commands. The implementation depends on the software developer of the FTP client.

13.8 Anonymous FTP

Not all FTP servers use the "anonymous server" principle. An anonymous server enables us to access clients without client authentication.

Since the FTP protocol did not take into account anonymous servers, FTP anonymous users have to set a username and password during their access to an FTP server. Generally, either the string anonymous or the string ftp is used as a username. Both strings have the same meaning. A user email address is often demanded as a password. This helps the anonymous server operator to create statistics concerned with access to the server.

Some anonymous servers allow access only to clients whose computers have the appropriate PTR record in the DNS. This restriction, however, has very disputable significance.

An anonymous FTP server serves users for downloading file, i.e., companies can offer free information using an anonymous FTP server. Anonymous FTP servers can be accessed very easily using Internet browsers.

If anonymous FTP servers are connected to Internet, they are exposed to a high risk of attack. That is why anonymous FTP server implementations frequently perform the trick shown in the following figure to increase their safety:

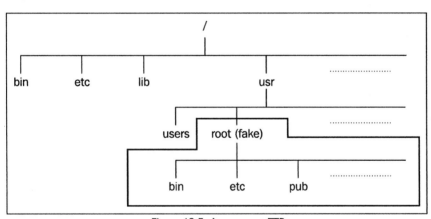

Figure 13.5: Anonymous FTP

During the startup of an FTP server, the system changes the root directory into a *fake* root directory that the FTP server wants to make accessible. This means the server operating system will intentionally pretend that the fake directory is the root directory containing FTP server data. Thus, the anonymous users logged into this server will not be able to access other directories of the server operating system.

It is necessary to point out here that the server will not be able to access even the directories in which, for example, the ls program (used for directory listing) is placed. Therefore, we must not forget to add, for example, the bin directory with the ls program into the *fake* root directory. It is also usually necessary to add the etc directory with the fake passwd file. It is, however, not necessary to allow total access to the fake bin directory—only an 'execute right' is given to the users for executing the `ls` program. The `ls` program *must not* use the shared libraries of the operating system; it must have statically compiled. Statically compiled programs are incomparably larger than the dynamically linked ones. Therefore, it is interesting to display the size of the `ls` program placed in the directory where it is used in the operating system, and the size of the `ls` program used by the anonymous FTP server.

An anonymous FTP server must *never* be started under the super user mode. For anonymous user access, a user (or user group) is given minimal access to the server operating system. Generally, an anonymous FTP server is used only for reading files; therefore, the administrator of the anonymous FTP server usually removes the write privilege from all directories.

In practice, an anonymous FTP server is sometimes also used for file exchange among users. Here, it is necessary for anonymous users to have write access. Mostly, write permission is allowed only for one directory. Conversely, the write permission is set for that particular directory, but read permission of the directory (not for files in this directory) is removed. Thus, a user can copy data in that directory, but nobody will be able to open the content of the directory. Instead, one user will agree with another user for file exchange, using another channel (for example, a phone line).

14

Hypertext Transfer Protocol

The **Hypertext Transfer Protocol (HTTP)** protocol is a significantly young protocol. Its origin dates back to the year 1990. Its predecessor was the Gopher protocol (today nearly forgotten). The other turning point is HTTP protocol version 0.9, which has many implementations. The new version 1.1 (RFC 2616) is more complicated.

Usage
HTTP protocol serves for information searching on the Internet (or intranet).

Security
HTTP itself supports many authentication methods (such as username and password, Kerberos, etc.). Netscape introduced securing communication by means of HTTP Secure Socket Layer (SSL). SSL became the base for the Internet standard Transport Layer Security (TLS). SSL/TLS is based on PKI with ITU-T X.509 certificates.

HTTP communication using SSL or TLS (HTTP over SSL/TLS) is called **HTTPS**. It is interesting that the client authentication can be done either by means of the HTTP protocol or by means of the SSL/TLS layer.

User Segment
Today, HTTP protocol is the most used protocol on the Internet. In fact, some Internet users even identify the Internet with the HTTP protocol.

> The components of HTTP are the proxy and tunnel specifications. That is why the Internet has no problems through firewalls. Due to this, HTTP protocol became a popular protocol for tunneling other protocols (RTSP, ICQ, Napster, etc.).

14.1 Client-Server

A client-server relationship is the basic architecture of communication in HTTP protocol. If a direct TCP connection between a client and a server is established, the user types the **Uniform Resource Identifier (URI)** he or she wants to survey into the browser:

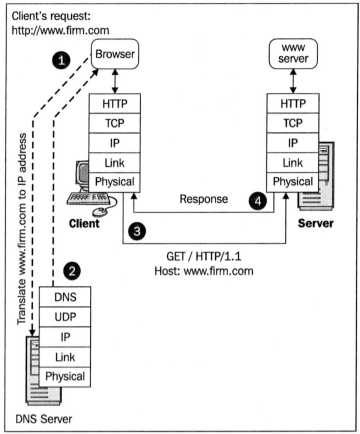

Figure 14.1: HTTP architecture

As shown in the previous figure, the client first takes the server name from the URI and with the help of DNS, translates it into the IP address (1 and 2). Then the client establishes a TCP connection with the obtained IP address of the server. The browser inputs the HTTP request into the newly created channel (3), and the server responses with an HTTP response (4) within the same TCP connection. Then, the browser displays the response to the user.

It is important that the browser displays the web pages to the user. Every web page usually consists of many objects and every object must be downloaded by a separate HTTP request from the web server. In the older versions of the HTTP protocol, a new TCP connection was always established for each request. Only the basic text of the web page is downloaded by the first request; the basic text usually contains many references for objects necessary for properly displaying the web page. Thus, in the next step, separate TCP connections with the web server are established simultaneously to download each individual object. This process creates transmission peaks in the transmission channel.

HTTP protocol version 1.1, by default, assumes that only one TCP connection will be established between the client and server for the entire web page. It is possible to close the connection after one or more requests. The client can send several requests within one TCP connection without waiting for the response to the previous request (this process is known as **pipelining**).

By default, HTTP protocol version 1.1 assumes that more requests and responses will be entered into the established connection. If you explicitly want to close the connection, it is necessary to put the following header field into the HTTP header:

```
Connection: Close
```

HTTP communication always consists of requests and responses. The relation between a client and a server is always created only by a request and a response to this request. The older version of the HTTP protocol even established a TCP connection only for one request-response cycle. The newer version uses the already established connection for more request-response cycles. However, these cycles are independent even if several request-response cycles go through one TCP connection.

The fact that the HTTP protocol does not engage in a dialogue longer than one request and the immediate response is a certain limitation of the HTTP protocol. In practice, the following situation can occur: A user wants to make a purchase using the HTTP protocol at a virtual department store on the Internet. The user chooses the goods and adds them into the virtual shopping basket that the user virtually carries with him or her while shopping. However, the user (client) might choose more goods during the next client-server relation. The problem is how to store the information about the anonymous client that he or she already has some goods in his or her shopping basket. We will deal with this problem later in Section 14.11.

The following figure illustrates how a Telnet program establishes a connection with the www.fiji.gov.fj server at the well-known HTTP port 80:

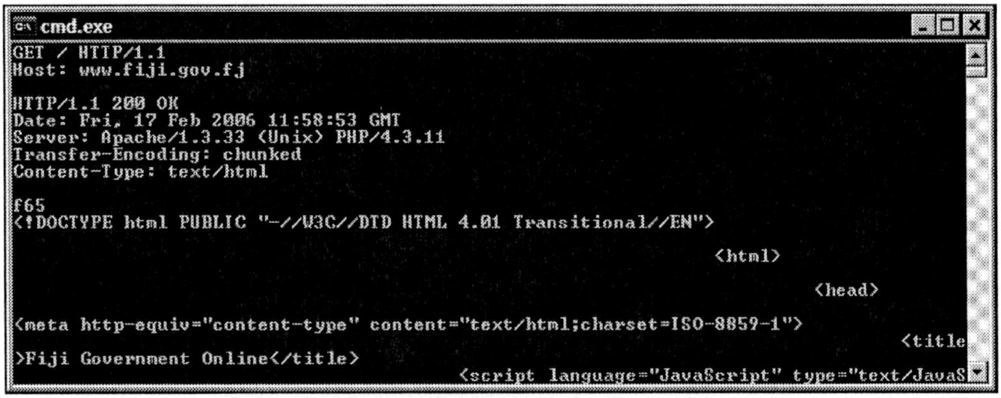

Figure 14.2: An example of HTTP communication for experts

A request is sent to the HTTP protocol as follows:

```
GET / HTTP/1.1
Host: www.fiji.gov.fj
```

The response was immediate:

```
HTTP/1.1 200 OK
```

In the previous figure overleaf, the first line requests the content of the root directory by the GET method, and the second line shows the name of the virtual web server. The blank third line separates the HTTP header field from data.

Windows XP users: Press the Telnet's escape keys *Ctrl +]* without delay before issuing the GET command. You would then receive the Microsoft Telnet prompt. At this prompt, input the set localecho Telnet command and press *Enter* and then issue the GET command.

Surprisingly, such a communication with a web server is not sufficient for some users; they demand information to be graphically displayed as shown in the following figure:

Figure 14.3: An example of HTTP communication for normal users

However, this type of display is significantly more complicated. In the figure above, the browser displays the text formatted in the HTML language. This text contains only references to pictures, so that every picture from the web page can be downloaded from the web server using independent request-response communication. These communications are independent (though they go through one TCP connection), i.e., the picture can also be used in other web pages or can be downloaded separately.

Another limitation of the HTTP protocol is the client-server architecture itself. This architecture does not allow for sending asynchronous events from a server to a client. Thus, it is difficult to create applications of stock exchange type using the HTTP protocol, because in the case of share price change, the stock exchange application immediately needs to inform the client of this fact. However, the stock exchange site is on a server, and a working server cannot initiate a TCP connection. Unfortunately, in the case of the HTTP protocol, the server can inform the client only when the client sends some request to the server.

> GSM (mobile) has solved this problem. GSM uses WAP protocol, which includes a variation of HTTP protocol. This variation of HTTP has a **WAP Push** function. This function exchanges the role of an HTTP client and an HTTP server for a short period. During this period, a mobile phone plays the role of a server on which information is posted from a system (out of the GSM network) playing the client's role.

A user usually sets the browser (client) so that the responses (web pages) will be displayed to the user and, if possible, stored in a cache to reduce the response time and network bandwidth consumption on future equivalent requests. When repeating the request, the information can be displayed to the user from the local cache.

As usual, caching has problems with fresh information. Various strategies are used to overcome the problem of when to display cached information and when the client should transfer information from the server . It is possible for a client to ask a server by HTTP: "*Have you changed the web page?*" Only if the reply is "*Yes*" will the page be transferred from the server. Some responses of the server can be marked not to be stored into the cache. The client must contact the target server even if it has a cached copy of the data being requested.

Storing data into cache is very complicated; Section 14.10.7 deals with this problem. Nowadays we have very sophisticated algorithms for working with a cache. Thanks to dynamic web pages, secured connections, and also due to a higher throughput of communication lines, the importance of a cache is gradually declining.

An Internet browser is not only an HTTP client. Usually, browsers have integrated FTP client and also Gopher client.

The HTTP protocol introduces proxies, gateways, and tunnels. Any number of these intermediate systems can come between a client and a server. From a TCP protocol viewpoint, a TCP connection is always established between two neighbor nodes (i.e., a TCP connection between the client and the first proxy, between the first proxy and the second proxy, and so on). In order to describe a proxy, a gateway, and a tunnel, we will describe a network scheme with only one intermediate system between a client and a server. Later, we will find out that nothing important changes if there is more than one intermediate system.

Intermediate systems are often used where it is not possible to establish a TCP connection directly between a client and a server, for example, at the firewall that separates an intranet from the Internet.

14.2 Proxy

A proxy is a system that consists of two parts:

- The *server* part of a proxy accepts client requests and passes them to the client part of the proxy. In backward communication, the responses pass from the client part of the proxy to the origin client.

- The *client* part of a proxy receives request from the server part of the proxy, establishes a TCP connection with the target server, and sends the request to the target server on behalf of the client.

Figure 14.4 shows how a proxy appears to a user. The important function of a proxy lies hidden in the middle of the proxy, i.e., between the server and the client part. It is as follows: A proxy understands the application protocol (in our case, the HTTP protocol), and it can perform several operations with the accepted request from the client. The operations are as follows:

- It can store responses into its cache (for example, a disc). If a proxy receives the same request in the future (for example, from another client), then it can return this request more quickly directly from the proxy cache without establishing a connection with the target server. This might look effective, but there is one essential question: "*How do we know that the cached data is fresh?*"

- It can modify a request (or response), i.e., change data of the application protocol.

- It can decide whether the client is authorized to perform such a request.

A proxy can verify if a client is authorized to perform a request in several ways, as follows:

- A proxy can check that the client does not access any prohibited server. For example, an employer can set a proxy server black list. The servers from this list will be inaccessible to the employees. In practice, it is common that employers forbid access to, for example, www.playboy.com. (However, there is almost no sense in doing this, as employees will find 10 other servers with even more interesting themes about which the employer does not know.)

- A proxy can check whether the user is authorized to use a proxy. In such a case, it requires user authentication. The most frequent types of user authentication are as follows:
    - The IP address of the user's PC. This authentication is not too safe; therefore, it is used to restrict intranet clients from using the proxy (for example, not allowing access to the Internet through the proxy).
    - User name and password.
    - User name and onetime password.
    - Kerberos based authentication
    - User's certificate based authentication

- A proxy running on a firewall can ask the operating system to check from which network interface the user proxy request comes, i.e., whether the user is accessing the proxy from an intranet or from an Internet network interface. Of course, the standard TCP/IP implementation in operating systems does not know this. This is one of the differences between a standard operating system and an operating system with a firewall installed.

- If a proxy knows where the request came from (whether from the intranet or Internet), it can use different authentication mechanisms for requests from the intranet and Internet. For instance, from the intranet, it accepts all requests—while from the Internet, it requires a onetime password for authentication.
- A proxy can also check the transferred data for spyware and similar malicious codes.

A functioning proxy is shown in the following illustration:

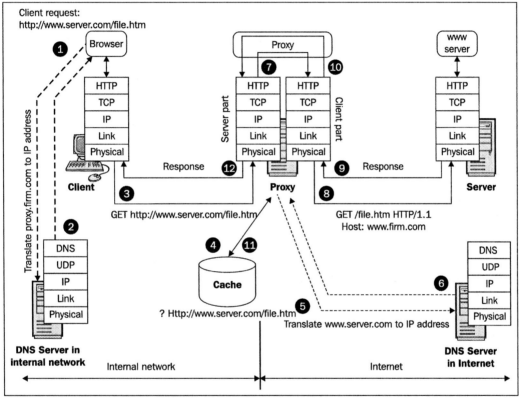

Figure 14.4: Proxy

At the beginning, a user (client) types the URI he or she wants to view into a browser. For instance, the client types the following request:

```
http://www.server.com/file.htm
```

However, the client handles this request by means of a proxy, i.e., the browser finds out the application protocol from the URI and forwards the request to the proxy server that has been configured for that protocol.

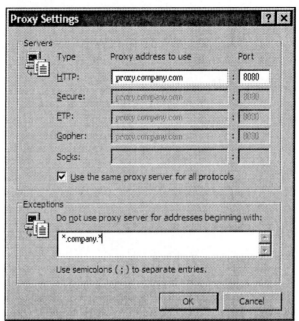

Figure 14.5: Configuration of a proxy, a gateway, and a tunnel in an Internet browser

In Figure 14.4, the first step shows that the client translates the proxy DNS name into the IP address (1 and 2). Now, the client can establish a TCP connection with the server part of proxy at the port stated in the Proxy Settings window (see Figure 14.5). The client will insert its HTTP request in the newly created TCP connection (3):

```
GET http://www.server.com/file.htm HTTP/1.1
Host: www.server.com
```

The proxy looks in its cache to check whether the response to this request already exists (4). If the response to the request is not found in the cache, the proxy sends the request to its client part to handle it. The client part parses the URI. The proxy takes the server name (www.server.com) from the URI request and translates it into an IP address from a DNS server (5 and 6). Since the proxy has access to the Internet, it can have this request translated in the Internet.

First, the client part of proxy rewrites the request as shown:

```
GET /file.htm HTTP/1.1
Host: www.server.com
```

Next, the client part of the proxy establishes a TCP connection with the target server and delivers the request on behalf of the client (8). The server response is received by the client part of proxy (9). The proxy stores the response into the cache if the proxy policy allows it (11). Finally, the proxy delivers the response to the client (12), and it is displayed to the user and, eventually, it is stored into its local cache as well.

In Figure 14.5, the configuration of an Internet browser is shown. The proxy for the HTTP protocol is configured in this window. Furthermore, proxies or gateways for the FTP and Gopher protocols can be configured here too. The Secure option is used for a tunnel configuration of SSL/TLS.

You can try this if you are working behind a company's firewall with the help of Telnet program. First, you find the DNS name (or the IP address) and the TCP port of your company's HTTP proxy (see Figure 14.5). As an example, the proxy address used is proxy.company.com and the port number is 8080.

Now use the Telnet program as follows:

```
C\> telnet proxy.company.com 8080
```

In the Telnet window, input an HTTP request with an absolute URI. For example:

```
GET http://www.packtpub.com HTTP/1.1
Host: www.packpub.com
<Enter><Enter>
```

You obtain the home page of www.packpub.com on you company's intranet.

> **Windows XP users**: Press the Telnet's escape keys *Ctrl +]* without delay before issuing the GET command. You would then receive the Microsoft Telnet prompt. At this prompt, input the set localecho Telnet command and press *Enter* and then issue the GET command.

14.3 Gateway

A **gateway** is an intermediate node that works similarly to a proxy. The main difference is that a gateway changes one application protocol to the other protocol. The most common type of a gateway has a server part that accepts HTTP requests from clients and changes them into FTP communications as shown in the following figure:

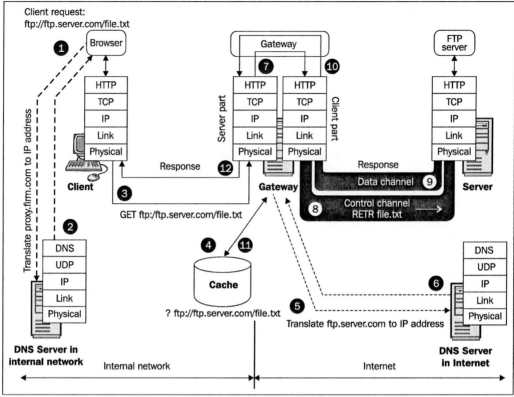

Figure 14.6: Gateway

An interesting feature of the FTP gateway is that if a user wants to display the content of a directory, the gateway finds out only the directory content as listed by the list command of the FTP protocol. Such a directory listing is not an HTML formatted web page. However, the gateway must display this directory content to the client in a web page style. To accomplish this task, the gateway must have icons for a file, a directory, etc. With the help of these icons, the gateway creates a web page containing the directory content and it is displayed to the client. The logical result is that if you display the directory content through a proxy from one supplier and later on through a proxy from another supplier, the graphic design may be displayed differently.

This is not surprising, because if a browser establishes a connection directly with a target server (without proxy), the directory content received through the FTP protocol must be similarly converted into a graphic form. Hence, the listing of the same directory displayed by various browsers (or another version of the same browser) can have a different graphic design.

You can perform the following example for any FTP server on the Internet. Follow the steps shown in the previous example of an HTTP proxy and use the following:

```
C\> telnet proxy.company.com 8080
```

In the Telnet window, input an HTTP request with absolute URI. For example:

```
GET ftp://ftp.rfc-editor.org/ HTTP/1.1
Host: ftp.rfc-editor.org
<Enter><Enter>
```

You obtain a root directory listing of the `ftp.rfc-editor.org` FTP server on you company's intranet.

14.4 Tunnel

A **tunnel** is an intermediate system that does not need to understand the contents of transferred data. Even encrypted application data can be transferred through a tunnel. It is used by the SSL or TLS protocols. A tunnel is configured in the Secure option in Figure 14.5.

A tunnel is explained in the following figure:

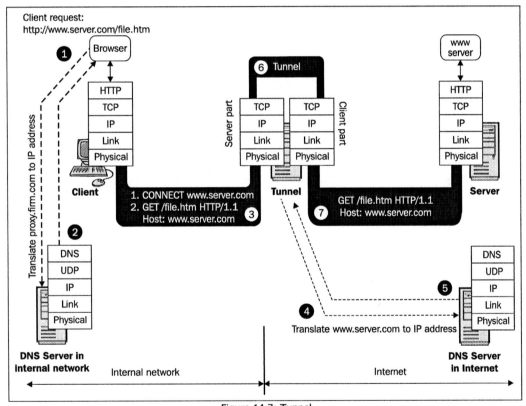

Figure 14.7: Tunnel

The client translates a tunnel name into an IP address (1 and 2). The client establishes a TCP connection with the server part of tunnel. Into this created channel, the client usually inserts the CONNECT command with the DNS name and, optionally, the port of the target server (3). The tunnel translates the target server's DNS name into the IP address (5 and 6) and establishes a TCP connection with the target server at the port stated in the CONNECT command.

Now, the tunnel has created two dual carriageway connections. We can imagine the direction of the connection as shown using two pipes in the following figure:

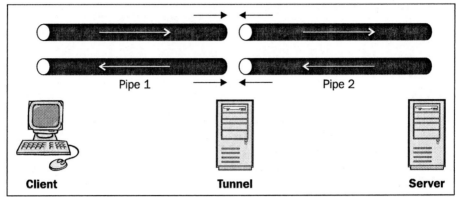

Figure 14.8: A tunnel welds both connections together

In the previous figure, one pipe serves for the *outgoing* connection and another for the *incoming* connection (duplex line). A tunnel simply welds two pipes together. After welding, the tunnel will mechanically pass data between the server part and the client part of tunnel with no knowledge about the content of passed data, for example, SSL/TLS data are enciphered. Everything that comes from the client is mechanically sent through the "welded" pipes to the target server. Similarly, everything that comes from the server is sent to the client. Within such a connection, the client can start establishing an encrypted connection by the SSL/TLS protocol.

It is quite logical that if a tunnel cannot read the transferred data, it also cannot control what data a client downloads from a server. For example, tunnels do not know how to prohibit downloading Java applets or ActiveX components from the target server. The tunnel does not cache the transferred data.

For practice purposes, you can solve the following problem: We have created an application with the client-server architecture, and there is a user who wishes use this application. However, the user is in the internal network separated by a firewall and our server is on the Internet. It is easy to change the application to first establish a connection through the tunnel and then type the CONNECT server:port HTTP/1.1 command. The tunnel will establish a connection with the server:port target and weld both connections together. Now the client has already established connection with the target server. Of course, the client will operate if the tunnel (for example, for SSL/TLS as configured in the Secure field in Figure 14.5) is started up at the firewall.

If you are aware of a Telnet server on the Internet (for example, computer.firm.com), then you may experiment with the tunnel on your firewall. First, however, note the content of the Secure field shown in Figure14.5.

```
c:\> telnet proxy.company.com 8080
    Connecting To proxy.company.com ...

    CONNECT computer.firm.com:23

    HTTP/1.1 200 Connection established
```

```
Proxy-agent: Apache/1.3.14 (UNIX)

FreeBSD/i386 (computer.firm.com) (ttyp4)

login:
```

(The proxy sends the second line of the code, the client sends the highlighted third line, and the server sends the remaining part.)

The result would depend on your skills and the skills of your firewall administrator. If you are not aware of any Telnet servers, then use an HTTP server and port 80 (or without any port). In this case, use the GET method.

There exist insidious programs that provide many Internet services though tunnel. But a firewall administrator's nightmare are worms that sniff intranet network traffic and send confidential information through the tunnel outside the company.

14.5 More Intermediate Nodes

There are many possible combinations of intermediate systems on the way from a client to a target server.

It is quite common to use 'Proxy on Proxy' in companies that have an intranet separated into several secure zones. For example, the first secure zone is for employees, and the second secure zone is for production servers. The zone for production servers is interconnected with the employee secured zone through an internal firewall. Next, the employee zone is connected through another firewall to the Internet. Both firewalls may run proxies and tunnels.

In the case of a double proxy, the target server name must be translated to its IP address at the last proxy before the target server. Similarly, it is a good idea to place a gateway at the end of the node chain as shown:

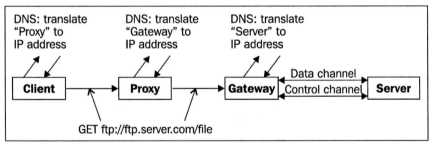

Figure 14.9: A chain of intermediate systems

Note that intermediate systems are before the Internet. This is a limitation of HTTP. If the intermediate system was after the Internet (on the target server side of Internet), then would be impossible to configure the proxy in a browser (as the client would not know the DNS name or IP address of a remote proxy). Such proxies are called **reverse proxies**.

A reverse proxy is useful when a web server provider would like to protect its server with a firewall or would like to use some hardware accelerators before the web servers. Different manufacturers offer different solutions because the reverse proxy is outside the HTTP specification. The real problem with a reverse proxy is how to pass user authentication through the reverse proxy. There are many solutions. One of them is to authenticate users against the reverse proxy and pass user identification from the reverse proxy to the target server in additional HTML header lines. These header lines usually begin with the `iv-` string (i.e., Identity Verification).

14.6 Uniform Resource Identifier

A **Uniform Resource Identifier (URI)** is an object identifier in a web world. A URI can be any of the following: **Uniform Resource Name (URN)**, **Uniform Resource Locator (URL)**, and **Uniform Resource Characteristic (URC)**. In this book, we will only discuss the URL.

Individual application protocols have their own URI scheme. A URI is specified by RFC 1738 as:

```
<scheme>:<scheme-specific-part>
```

where `<scheme>` can be, for instance, `http` (HTTP protocol), `ftp` (FTP protocol), `mailto` (SMTP protocol), `nntp` (NNTP protocol (news groups)), `telnet` (Telnet relation), `file` (local file), `imap` (IMAP protocol), `ldap` (LDAP protocol), or `pop` (POP3 protocol).

The schemes (but not in the whole URI) are not case sensitive, i.e., `ftp` is the same as `FTP` or `Ftp`.

Only ASCII characters occur in a URI. If you must use a non-ASCII character, it must be replaced with the % character followed by the hexadecimal code of the character. In the hexadecimal code of the character, we can write both upper and lower case for the hexadecimal digits A to F. The special characters (;, /, ?, :, @, =, and &) are reserved for special usage, i.e., if they are to be used in some string, they must be replaced with % and their hexadecimal code.

14.6.1 The http Scheme

Syntax:

```
http://<user:password>@<server>:<port>/<path>?<query string>#<fragment>
```

A username and a password are used for client authentication. Generally, it is *not* recommended to set a password in a URI. If a password is not set, then HTTP protocol will start an additional dialogue to request it. In the dialogue window, the password is not displayed during typing (individual letters of the password are replaced with asterisks or dots). In this case, a colon must not follow the username.

If a username (or username and password pair) is set, the @ character must precede the server name. A TCP port is stated after a colon. If we want to use the well-known port 80 for HTTP, we state neither a colon, nor the port number. The path contains a file identification consisting of directories separated by a slash and a file name.

A question mark (?) is followed by query string. A hash (#) specifies a reference to a web page fragment. A web page can be larger than the size of the monitor screen. Using a scrollbar, we can browse a web page. A web page can be also separated into labeled fragments; these labels are identified as <fragment>. If we want to display a particular fragment in a window without moving the scrollbar, we use a reference to this fragment.

Example:

1. A request from an anonymous client for a root directory content of the server.company.com server is shown as:
   http://server.company.com

2. The root directory content of the server.company.com server is requested by the user novak. If the server demands a password for this user, a consequent dialogue with the server will be called by:
   http://novak@server.company.com

3. An anonymous user starts the forms.exe program from the cgi-bin directory. The field1=%20&field2=value2 string passes to the forms.exe program by the QUERY_STRING system variable. It uses a form with two fields: field1 and field2. field1 contains a space (ASCII code 20_{16}) and field2 contains the value value2:
   http://server.company.com/cgi-bin/forms.exe?field1=%20&field2=value2

4. An anonymous user wants to display the content of the document document.html from the /adr1/adr2/adr3 directory. The user wishes to display the paragraph5 fragment directly.
   http://server.company.com/adr1/adr2/adr3/document.html#paragraph5

14.6.2 The ftp Scheme

Syntax:

ftp://<user>:<password>@<server>:<port>/<d1>/<d2>/.../<dn>/<file>;type=y

This syntax containing a username, password, and a server name is similar to the HTTP syntax. The only difference is that if a username is not set, the user "anonymous" will be automatically used instead. If a user's email address is known, it is used as a password. The well-known port for FTP is 21. The type of the transferred file(s) can be either i or a; however, these parameters are not used in practice.

The basic question is how to interpret the /<d1>/<d2>/.../<dn>/<file> string. The answer is simple: FTP uses the CWD command. The commands CWD d1, CWD d2, up to CWD dn are successively executed by the FTP protocol. Then, the RETR file command is executed.

This procedure does not allow specifying an absolute path (a path from the root directory) easily, because inserting a slash is problematic (see second example).

Example:

ftp://ftp.company.com/etc/passwd

CWD etc and RETR passwd FTP commands perform this request.

If we want to execute the CDW /etc command, we must set:

ftp://ftp.company.com/%2Fetc/passwd

because the hexadecimal value of a slash is 2F.

14.6.3 The mailto Scheme

Syntax:

```
mailto:<rfc822-addr-spec>
```

This scheme has only one parameter, which is an email address to which the mail message has to be sent.

Example:

```
mailto:libor.dostalek@siemens.com
```

14.6.4 The nntp Scheme

Syntax:

```
nntp://<server>:<port>/<newsgroup-name>/<article-number>
```

For more details, refer to Chapter 16.

14.6.5 The telnet Scheme

Syntax:

```
Telnet://<user>:<password>@<server>:<port>/
```

In this scheme, the following can be left out: the final slash, the username, and the password.

14.6.6 The file Scheme

Syntax:

```
file://<server>/<path>
```

This scheme is usually used as a reference to data in a local disk. Instead of a computer name, an empty string (or a `localhost` name) is used. When specifying files this way, we most frequently state three consecutive slashes. The path is then the whole specification of a file. The pipe character is used instead of colon because the colon has a special meaning as password and/or port separator in a URI.

Example:

```
file:///C|/WINNT/system32/file.txt
```

The situation is interesting in operating systems where the directory structure is different from Windows or UNIX operating system. As an example, let us consider the OpenVMS operating system. For this operating system, we will express, for example, the DISK$USER:[MY.NOTES]-NOTE123456.TXT file.

```
file:///disk$user/my/notes/note12345.txt
```

14.6.7 The pop Scheme

Syntax:

```
pop://<user>;auth=<auth>@<host>:<port>
```

For more details, see RFC 2384.

RFC 2192 specifies the imap scheme, and RFC 2255 specifies the ldap scheme.

14.7 Relative URI

If a URI does not start with a scheme name, then this is called a 'relative URI'. A relative URI is always related to some base, i.e., to some absolute URI. This base can be the URI of the displayed document or even the URI of the previous document. If there is no such URI, an implicit URI of the application can be used.

A relative URI can contain . or .. characters; they are a reference to a working or parent directory respectively. A relative URI is parsed in several independent parts: a server name, a path including a file name, a request, and a fragment. Individual parts are separated by the following characters: # (fragment), ? (query string), and so on.

Let's take the base (which is the absolute URI) and replace its parts by a relative URI from right to left. Hence, in the displayed http://www.company.com/path/file.htm page, the following hypertext references (relative URIs) can be found:

- #paragraph1 that can be translated to the following absolute URI:
  http://www.company.com/path/file.htm#paragraph1.

- file2.htm that can be translated to the following absolute URI:
  http://www.comapny.com/path/file2.htm.

- ../file3.htm that can be translated to the following absolute URI:
  http://www.company.com/file3.htm.

14.8 The HTTP Request

The HTTP request (and response) structure reminds us of an email structure. At first sight, we see the difference only in the first line. The first line of a request contains a **method**, and the first line of a response contains **status line**.

An HTTP request consists of the following (see Figure 14.10):

- A method: HTTP version 1.1 supports the following methods: GET, POST, HEAD, OPTIONS, TRACE, CONNECT, PUT, and DELETE. The PUT and DELETE methods are not always implemented.

- A header: This consists of individual header fields. Every header field starts with a keyword (for example, Host). A colon followed by a space terminates the keyword. After a space, the header field parameters can follow. The whole header field is always terminated by an end of line (CR+LF). Only one header field is compulsory, namely, the Host header field.

- A blank line: I.e. CR+LF twice; the first CR+LF ends the last line of a header field. (CR is a cursor return character ($0D_{16}$), and LF is a new line character ($0A_{16}$)).

- The transferred data (optional).

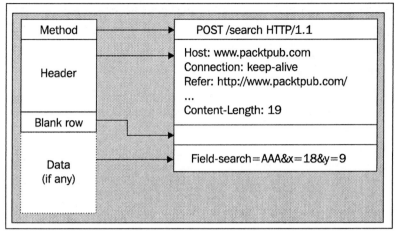

Figure 14.10: HTTP request

In HTTP protocol version 1.1, the method always has the following form:

`<Method's name> <URI> HTTP/1.1`

In the current version of HTTP, it is obligatory to include the third item (version number) in the form HTTP/1.1 for version 1.1. If the version number (along with the HTTP string) is missing, then HTTP version 0.9 is assumed. (In the case of an HTTP request, version 0.9 of HTTP does not support the header line Host:, and the HTTP response will not contain a status line.)

An example of the GET method of HTTP version 1.1:

`GET / HTTP/1.1`

Personally, it is surprising to see that web servers do not accept an 'absolute URI' as a parameter (an absolute URI begins with the name of scheme and a server name, for example, begins with the http://server... string). If the browser cuts the method name and server name from a URI, then you obtain a relative URI. An absolute URI is accepted only by proxies and gateways (tunnels do not require URIs at all; tunnels only require the target server name and the port (optional)).

Another interesting topic is that HTTP methods *require* a URI. However, common users write only the server name in their browser's location field, but the browser will cut the server name from the URI so that nothing remains. In this case, the browser itself adds the slash (root directory) after the server name.

14.8.1 The GET Method

GET method is used to retrieve information stored on a server. With the help from the query string of a URI (after the question mark), a request for desired information may be defined. The GET method can theoretically also contain data, however, it is rarely used because data is transferred as a part of the request especially in this case.

The GET method is often used with the combination of conditional header lines that are as follows: If-Modified-Since, If-Unmodified-Since, If-Match, If-None-Match, or If-Range header field. The result is a "conditional GET" that is helpful primarily in the case of static web pages. A conditional GET method requests that the web page be transferred only under the circumstances described by the conditional header lines. A conditional GET method is intended to reduce unnecessary network bandwidth usage by allowing cached web pages.

Let us see some examples by means of the Telnet program for Windows XP. We will connect to the server www.packtpub.com at port 80:

```
C:\> telnet www.packtpub.com 80
```

> **Windows XP users**: Press the Telnet's escape keys *Ctrl +]* without delay before issuing the GET command. You would then receive the Microsoft Telnet prompt. At this prompt, input the set localecho Telnet command and press *Enter* and then issue the GET command.

In the following examples, sentences in bold are client commands, the text in italics are comments, and the remaining text is the server response.

In the first example, we ask the server to list its root directory content. Web servers are usually configured for not returning a file list of web server's root directories. They usually give back the content of an index file (for example, index.html, default.htm, and so on), if present, which is a server's home page.

Example 1:

```
GET / HTTP/1.1
Host: www.packtpub.com
```
(An empty line separates a request header and a request body)
(The request body is empty)

```
HTTP/1.1 200 OK
Date: Tue, 20 Dec 2005 19:23:09 GMT
Server: Apache
Cache-Control: must-revalidate
Pragma: no-cache
Content-Type: text/html; charset=UTF-8
```
(A blank line separates a response header and a response body)

```
<!DOCTYPE html PUBLIC "-//W3C//DTD HTML 4.01 Transitional//EN">
<html>
<head>
<meta http-equiv="content-type" content="text/html; charset=UTF-8">
<title>Packt Publishing Book Store</title>
<link href="http://www.packtpub.com/rss.xml"
...
```

In HTTP protocol version 1.1, the Host header field is mandatory; therefore, even our request must contain this header field. The Host header field contains the server name.

The response, apart from the status line, contains several interesting header fields:

- Date: Shows the date and time of the start of the response.
- Server: Contains information about the software used by the target server to handle the request.
- Cache-Control and Pragma: With the help of these header lines, the server specifies how to manage a web page in a cache. In this case, we do not save the web page in cache.
- Content-Type: This header line indicates the media type of the transferred data.

Example 2:

Now we will use the www.iana.org web server in the same way:

```
GET / HTTP/1.1
Host: www.iana.org

HTTP/1.1 200 OK
Date: Tue, 20 Dec 2005 19:59:03 GMT
Server: Apache/1.3.27 (UNIX)  (Red-Hat/Linux)
Last-Modified: Thu, 04 Nov 2004 19:34:30 GMT
ETag: "1acad9-153a-418a8446"
Accept-Ranges: bytes
Content-Length: 5434
Connection: close
Content-Type: text/html

<HTML>
  <HEAD>
    <META HTTP-EQUIV="Content-Type" CONTENT="text/html; charset=iso-8859-1">
    <META NAME="Author" CONTENT="IANA">
    <META NAME="Keywords" CONTENT="IANA, ICANN, domains, ip address, protocol,
parameter, Internet authority">
...
```

This web server primarily provides static web pages. Static web pages are ripe for caching. From a caching point of view, consider the following two header lines:

- Last-Modified: Indicates the date and time at which the target server believes the web source (web page) was last modified.
- ETag: This header line provides the current value of the entity tag of the web source (web page). An entity tag is an unambiguous identifier of the web page. Entity tags are used for comparing two or more web source from the same resource (the same web server).

These two header lines will be useful in conditional GET requests. The conditional GET requests use the following conditional header fields: If-Modified-Since, If-Unmodified-Since, If-Match, If-None-Match, and If-Range. A conditional request causes the requested data to be transferred only if the condition of the request is true. The If-Match and If-None-Match header lines evaluate the response version (ETag), while the If-Modified-Since and If-Unmodified-Since headers evaluate the last modification date.

Example 3:

In example 2, we received the response with the "1acad9-153a-418a8446" entity tag (it is necessary to use quotation marks). Therefore, we can ask the server to return the web source if only this source was changed:

```
GET / HTTP/1.1
Host: www.iana.org
If-None-Match: "1acad9-153a-418a8446"

HTTP/1.1 304 Not Modified
Date: Tue, 20 Dec 2005 20:29:29 GMT
Server: Apache/1.3.27 (UNIX)  (Red-Hat/Linux)
Connection: close
S: ETag: "1acad9-153a-418a8446"
Connection to host lost.
```

From the code, we can see that the web source identified by the "1acad9-153a-418a8446" entity tag was not modified and hence was not transferred.

Example 4:

The If-Modified-Since header field means that the client would like to transfer the web source (web page) from the web server only if the particular source has been modified. However, not the web source identification, but the last modification time is decisive.

```
GET / HTTP/1.1
Host: www.iana.org
If-Modified-Since: Tue, 20 Dec 2005 19:59:03 GMT

HTTP/1.1 304 Not Modified
Date: Tue, 20 Dec 2005 20:41:50 GMT
Server: Apache/1.3.27 (UNIX)  (Red-Hat/Linux)
Connection: close
ETag: "1acad9-153a-418a8446"
Connection to host lost.
```

Since the particular page has not been modified, the server returns only the header field informing us that the page has not been modified.

14.8.2 The POST Method

The POST method is useful for sending data (for example, an HTML form) to a server. However, there is a hitch in using the POST method with the Telnet program. The problem is that in an HTTP request, an empty line follows the data sent by a client to a server. In doing so, the server must recognize how much data the client will send. From a keyboard, we cannot type the data quickly, and the server does not wait for us. A solution to this problem is to inform the server about the number of bytes to be sent in the header. For this purpose, the Content-Length header line is used. (In contrast, a browser puts both the header and data into one TCP segment so that the server can deal with of the whole request.)

Example 5:

```
POST /cgi-bin/ping HTTP/1.1
Host: test.company.com
Content-Length: 29
```
                    (A blank line separates a header from a message body)

```
filed1=info&field2=&pfield3=3
```

```
HTTP/1.1 100 Continue
```

```
HTTP/1.1 200 OK
Date: Thu, 21 Dec 2000 07:21:11 GMT
Server: Apache/1.2b10
Transfer-Encoding: chunked
Content-Type: TEXT/HTML
```

```
188
<HTML>
  <HEAD>
```

Now we count the number of bytes the data part of our request has and add the Content-Length header field into the header. The impatient server informs us by the HTTP /1.1 100 Continue message ("*Go on quickly!*") that it will process our request (this usually does not happen to a browser, because it is fast enough to supply the server quickly with the data). As for the response, the Transfer-Encoding:chunked header field is interesting. This header field notifies that the server it is sending the message in parts (chunks). This form of response consists of individual parts, each starting with a row containing the hexadecimal value of the data ($188_{16}=392_{10}$). The last part of a zero byte must be always stated. The last part is followed by a blank line, which can be followed by header fields of the HTTP response footing (rarely used in practice).

Furthermore, we would like to mention the data filed1=info&field2=&pfield3=3 that we sent to the server. These are three fields of a web form. The first field of a web form is called field1 and the user fills it by the value info. The user did not fill the second field called field2. Finally, the third field called field3 is filled by the digit 3. The individual fields are separated from one another with the & character; this is a special character separating web page fields.

It is important to note that by using the POST method, the data is sent in the data part of the HTTP request. If we want to send the same form content of using the GET method, the request method would look like as follows:

```
GET /cgi-bin/ping?filed1=info&field2=&pfield3=3 HTTP/1.1
Host: test.company.com
```

In this case, we do not need the Content-Length header field, because data is sent as a query string in the URI. If a CGI script on the server side processes the data, one script would have to be used for the GET method and another for the POST method. The GET method CGI script obtains the transferred data through the QUERY_STRING system variable. In contrast, the PUT method CGI script obtains the transferred data through standard input. (Of course, it is also possible to write a script that can process both the standard input and the QUERY_STRING variable alternatively.)

14.8.3 The HEAD Method

The HEAD method is similar to the GET method except that the server does not return a message body in the response.

Example 6:

```
HEAD / HTTP/1.1
Host: www.iana.org
```

```
HTTP/1.1 200 OK
Date: Tue, 20 Dec 2005 21:17:06 GMT
```

```
Server: Apache/1.3.27 (UNIX) (Red-Hat/Linux)
Last-Modified: Thu, 04 Nov 2004 19:34:30 GMT
ETag: "1acad9-153a-418a8446"
Accept-Ranges: bytes
Content-Length: 5434
Connection: close
Content-Type: text/html
Connection to host lost.
```

14.8.4 The TRACE Method

The TRACE method is an HTTP analog of the tracert ICMP command in Windows XP. This time, however, we will not find out how many routers are between our computer and the target computer, but we can find out the number of intermediate systems (proxies or gateways).

If we communicate through a proxy or gateway, we must not forget that we have to enter the complete absolute URI (http//info.pvt.net) into the TRACE method.

Example 7:

```
TRACE http://info.pvt.net HTTP/1.1
Host: info.pvt.net

HTTP/1.0 200 OK
Date: Wed, 20 Dec 2000 17:24:04 GMT
Server: Apache/1.2b10
Content-Type: message/http

TRACE / HTTP/1.0
Host: info.pvt.net
Cache-Control: Max-age=259200
Via: 1.1 proxy.pvt.com:8080 (Squid/1.1.22)
```

The statistics, in which we are so interested, are in the via header field. In this header, proxies or gateways are listed. In our example, we communicate only through one proxy.

Cache-control is an interesting header. In our case, it indicates that information may be kept for up to 259,200 seconds in the cache.

14.8.5 The OPTIONS Method

The OPTIONS method represents a request for information about the communication options available on the Request-URI. This method allows the client to determine the options and/or requirements associated with a resource of the capabilities of a server without implying a resource action or initiating a resource retrieval. If we ask for the server in general rather than to a specific resource, we will have to use an asterisk instead of a URI:

Example 8:

```
OPTIONS * HTTP/1.1
   Host: www.packtpub.com

   HTTP/1.1 200 OK
   Date: Tue, 20 Dec 2005 21:35:09 GMT
   Server: Apache/2.0.54
   Allow: GET,HEAD,POST,OPTIONS,TRACE
   Content-Length: 0
   Content-Type: text/plain; charset=ISO-8859-1
```

The server informs us it supports the GET, HEAD, POST, OPTIONS, and TRACE methods.

14.9 The HTTP Response

The HTTP response starts with a status line in the following form:

`<Version> <Result code> <Reason-Phrase>`

Here, `Version` is the HTTP protocol version in which the response is formulated. `Result code` specifies the success or failure of an operation, and `Reason-Phrase` is intended for the user. A header formed from the header fields follows the status line again. A blank line that separates the header from the message body terminates the header. If the header contains the `Transfer-Encoding:chunked` header field, there can be once again an empty line after the data followed by the footer, which is formed again by the header fields. In practice, a case where the footer is used has not been observed.

Here is an example of a status line (positive response):

`HTTP/1.1 200 OK`

`Result code` consists of three digits. The first digit determines the response type:

- 1xx: Informative response and the process continues
- 2xx: Process successful
- 3xx: Redirecting, i.e., further process will concern another URI
- 4xx: Client error (for example, a syntax error in the request)
- 5xx: Server error (for example, a CGI-script error)

14.9.1 An Overview of Result Codes

100 Continue
101 Switching Protocols
200 OK
201 Created
202 Accepted
203 Non-Authoritative Information
204 No Content
205 Reset Content
206 Partial Content
300 Multiple Choices
301 Moved Permanently
302 Found
303 See Other
304 Not Modified
305 Use Proxy

307 Temporary Redirect

400 Bad Request

401 Unauthorized

402 Payment Required

403 Forbidden

404 Not Found

405 Method Not Allowed

406 Not Acceptable

407 Proxy Authentication Required

408 Request Time-out

409 Conflict

410 Gone

411 Length Required

412 Precondition Failed

413 Request Entity Too Large

414 Request-URI Too Large

415 Unsupported Media Type

416 Requested range not satisfiable

417 Expectation Failed

500 Internal Server Error

501 Not Implemented

502 Bad Gateway

503 Service Unavailable

504 Gateway Time-out

505 HTTP Version not supported

If the Reason-Phrase does not fit into the status line, then it continues into the warning header field. It is an extension of the status line. The warning header field has two parameters, the warn-code and the note, separated by a space.

Most often, the warning header field is used to complete the information given from cache and not from the target server. It can happen that the cache returns some stale information because, for example, the proxy is not able to establish an upstream connection with the server (the result codes are from 110 to 112).

An overview of the result codes used in the `warning` header field:

Warning Code	Warning Note
110	Response is stale
111	Revalidation failed
112	Disconnected operation
113	Heuristic expiration
199	Miscellaneous warning

Table 14.1: HTTP response warning codes

14.10 Other Header Fields

Now we discuss about some other header fields.

14.10.1 Accept Header Field

Using the `Accept`, `Accept-Charset`, `Accept-Encoding`, and `Accept-Language` header fields, the client notifies of its capabilities in its request. Each of these header fields can contain several parameters separated by commas. These parameters, in every instance, can have a quality (q) associated with them, which can be stated after a semicolon. The quality is a number between 0 and 1. The higher the quality of the property, the more it is preferred by the client and it is 1 (the default value is q=1). An asterisk can be used to specify all the possible choices of the property.

Using the `Accept` header field, the client specifies supported media types. For example:

`Accept: text/*;q=0.3, text/html, image/jpeg;q=0.7, model/vrml, */*;q=0.1`

This code states that the client prefers:

1. any text with quality `0.3`
2. `text/html` with quality `1`
3. `image/jpeg` with quality `0.7`
4. `model/vrml` with quality `1`
5. any medium with quality `0.1`

Using the `Accept-Charset` header field, the client specifies the supported character sets:

`Accept-Charset: iso-8859-5, unicode-1-1;q=0.8, *;q=0.1`

This code states that the client prefers the `iso-8859-5` character set (with quality as 1). Furthermore, with quality `0.8`, it supports the `unicode-1-1` character set, otherwise it supports any character set with quality `0.1`.

Using the `Accept-Encoding` header field, the client specifies the supported types of data compression:

`Accept-Encoding: compress;q=0.5, gzip`

The client prefers the gzip method; however, with quality `0.5`, it also supports the compress method.

Using the Accept-Language header field, the client specifies the supported languages:

```
Accept-Language: cz, en;q=0.5
```

The client prefers the Czech language (cz), but also supports the English language (en).

The Accept-Ranges header field uses the server in its response to the client. (see Example 2 in Section 14.8.1).

14.10.2 Client Authentication

A client can enter a username and password directly into the URI; however, this is not common. When a client does not set its authentication information, a dialog is more common. In this case, the server will return:

```
HTTP/1.1 401 Unauthorized
WWW-authenticate: auth_method realm="string", optional auth.parametrs
```

The first parameter (auth_method) is the type of authentication that the server demands. The realm string will be displayed to the client so it knows to which object it has to authenticate. Finally, some authentication methods can use additional parameters. The Basic authentication method does not use additional parameters.

RFC 2617 distinguishes two authentication types: Basic and Digest. Both methods use authentication by username and password.

The Basic authentication transmits the unsecured name and password in text form throughout the network. The authentication dialog then proceeds, for example, as follows:

```
GET /file HTTP/1.1
Host: server.company.com

HTTP/1.1 401 Unauthorized
WWW-authenticate: Basic realm="server.company.com"
... other header lines

GET /file HTTP/1.1
Host: server.company.com
Authorization: Basic RG9zdGFsZWs6cGFzc3dvcmQNCg==

HTTP/1.1 200 OK
...
```

Here, the client after receiving the HTTP/1.1 401 Unauthorized message performs authentication by the Basic authentication method (username and password). Nevertheless, the server can offer several objects, and we can use different authentication for each of them. Therefore, the server returns the realm string so the browser can display on the user's dialog window to which object (server) it has to set the username and password. A string is created from the username and password entered by a client by placing a colon between them (for example, Dostalek:password). In the Authorization header field, the string is not transmitted directly, but is encoded by Base64:

```
Base64(Dostalek:password)="RG9zdGFsZWs6cGFzc3dvcmQNCg=="
```

Anyone who sniffs the Authorization header field, on the way from the client to the server, only needs to apply decoding Base64 to the RG9zdGFsZWs6cGFzc3dvcmQNCg== string (for example, by an OpenSSL program) and will see the password. The authentication of the Digest type tries to prevent this. This authentication type also uses the user password; however, it does not transmit the password itself, but a hash (calculated, for example, by the MD5 algorithm) from the following:

- A Nonce number generated by the server as a hash from the clock stamp, response identification (`ETag`), and the private key of the server.
- An Opaque number generated by the server. The *nonce* and *opaque* numbers are delivered to the client in the `WWW-Authenticate` header field as extra parameters.
- Username.
- User password.
- String from the `realm` parameter.
- Required URI.

RFC 2831 brings further possibilities of authentication. In addition, some firewalls use the Basic authentication; however, they use a one-time password generated by the authentication calculator (authentication token).

Microsoft is launching the **Simple and Protected Negotiate (SPNEGO)** authentication method. In this method, the server answers with a `WWW-Authenticate` header field containing the Negotiate authentication method. The client in its response adds the `Authorization` header field with two parameters. The first parameter is an authentication method named Negotiate, and the second parameter is a SPNEGO token containing a Kerberos ticket or NTLM credentials.

Using a Kerberos ticket is a good solution because it allows Windows domain users to do single sign-on on UNIX servers. An IBM reverse proxy (WebSeal) also supports this method.

14.10.3 Proxy Authentication

Client to proxy authentication is quite similar to client to server authentication. If a proxy requires authentication, it will send the following response:

```
407 Proxy Authentication Required
proxy-authenticate: auth_method realm="string", optional auth.parametrs
```

The client is authenticated using the `Proxy-Authorization` header field. The `Proxy-Authenticate` and `Proxy-Authorization` headers have the same syntax as the `WWW-Authorization` and `Authenticate` headers.

14.10.4 Content Header Field

`Content` header fields are intended for media type specification. They are based on MIME type specifications; however, they are not quite compatible with MIME itself (MIME is discussed in Section 15.3). HTTP protocol does not support, for example, the `Content-Transfer-Encoding` header field nor, of course, the `Mime-Version` header field.

The `Content-Type` header field is analogous to the `MIME` header field with the same name. It describes the type of data to be transferred. For example:

```
Content-Type: text/html; charset=ISO-8859-4
```

This header field specifies that the data to be transferred is text formatted in HTML and uses the ISO-8859-4 character set.

The Content-Length header field contains the length of the data to be transferred.

The Content-Encoding header field specifies the compression algorithm.

```
Content-Encoding: gzip
```

The Content-Language header field specifies the language. For example:

```
Content-Language: en
```

The Content-MD5 header field contains the MD5 hash algorithm from the data to be transferred.

The Content-Range header field is used if a message contains only a part of the data to be transferred. For example, if the server response is too long, the server will divide the data into several parts:

```
HTTP/1.1 206 Partial content
Content-Range: bytes 21010-47021/47022
```

(The total length of a message follows the slash)

```
Content-Length: 26012
```

The Content-Location header field contains a URI with the data to be transferred. This header field is important particularly when the required data is stored in several locations. This header field is not associated with redirection!

The client uses the Referer header field (so spelled) to notify the server from where it received the information of the required URI. The server can statistically interpret data obtained from this header field at regular intervals. However, browsers usually fill the URI of the displayed page into the Referer header field. If it is correct, the hypertext link is shown on the displayed web page. However, if the user explicitly enters a new URI into the location window, then the Referer header field can be misleading (i.e., it would contain the previously displayed web page).

For example, if the page of a charitable organization is displayed in your browser, and you enter www.playboy.com into the dialogue window, the link to the charitable organization will get into the Referer header field, and it will appear in the Playboy statistics that this charitable organization has a reference link to their pages.

14.10.5 Redirection and Temporary Unavailability of Objects

It can happen that the required object is relocated to another URI (for example, to another server or into another directory). In such a case, the server will return the status line with a 3xx result code followed by the header field:

```
Location: new-URI
```

where new-URI specifies the location of the required information.

For example:

```
HTTP/1.1 301 Moved Permanently
Location: http://www.company.com/file
...
```

However, it can also happen that the object has not been moved, but is temporary unavailable. The server can notify the client not only of the bad news (that the object is not available), but by using the Retry-After header field, it can give the client advice on when to ask for the object again. For example, it may advise the client to repeat the request after one minute:

```
HTTP/1.1 503 Service Unavailable
Retry-After: 60
...
```

The Retry-After header field can be of importance even in the case of redirection:

```
HTTP/1.1 301 Moved Permanently
Location: http://www.company.com/file
Retry-After: 10
...
```

In this case, the server informs the client to perform redirection after 10 seconds.

14.10.6 Cache

We must realize that caches can be found in the following places: clients, proxies, gateways, and servers. A cache is not found in a tunnel since a tunnel does not know what it transfers.

A cache is either shared or private. A shared cache stores information independent of which user it is intended for. If the information is dependent on the user (for example, client authentication information, personal inquiry, and so on), it must not be stored into the shared cache; however, it can be stored into a private cache.

A cache can accelerate the response rate of a communication. However, the basic problem is how to prevent the cache from responding with stale data. If the server does not want anything unusual out of the cache, it usually fills in the Date, Last-Modified, and Expires header fields in a response. If the server needs anything unusual, it will also fill in the Cache-Control header field. A client can also use this header field in its request.

The Expires header field determines the date and time of expiration of the information, after which it is considered stale; before this time, the information is considered fresh. The cache counts the time in seconds for which information can be considered as fresh (*freshness lifetime).*

The age of the information is maintained in the cache, i.e., the time the information was stored in cache or traveled through the network. The age is stated in seconds. If the information is retrieved from the cache, then it is not from the original source (from the target server). The Age header field is used for stating the age of the information.

Example 9:

A response containing the following header fields arrives on December 23, 2005 at 19:11:22:

```
Date: Sat, 23 Dec 2005 19:11:22 GMT
Expires:  Sat, 23 Dec 2005 22:11:22 GMT
```

In this case, the age is 3600 seconds and *freshness lifetime* is 7200 seconds. If this information is immediately handovered (December 23, 2005 at 19:11:22), the following header field would be added to it:

```
Age: 3600
```

A problem arises with information that does not contain the Expires header field. Here, it depends on the implementation. A bit of consideration of the usage of the Date and Last-Modified header fields appears to be quite useful. The difference in the values stated in the Date and Last-Modified header fields represents the time the information has remained unmodified on the server. Then it may be reasonable to maintain this information in the cache for a time that is, let's say, 10% of this difference.

The Cache-Control header field can have many directives. The *client* can set in the Cache-Control header field the following directives:

- no-cache: The response must not be retrieved from a cache.
- no-store: Sensitive information is probably used, therefore it must not be stored.
- max-age=s: The client does not want information older than 's' seconds.
- min-fresh=s: The client only wants information that will be considered as fresh for at least the next 's' seconds (whose freshness lifetime is no less than its current age plus the 's' seconds).
- max-stale=s: The client is ready to accept even stale information, but not information stale by more than 's' seconds.

In its response, the *server* can state the following directives:

- public: The response can be stored even into a shared cache.
- private: The response can only be stored into a private cache (the response contains private information and another user can have other information from the same URI).
- no-cache: The response must not be stored into a cache.
- no-store: The response must not be stored on a disk (it can, for example, contain sensitive information). An exception is the storage on a disk (outside cache) specified explicitly by the user (for example, by clicking the right mouse button).
- must-revalidate: By this request, the server requires all intermediate caches to refresh.
- proxy-revalidate: This has the same meaning as the must-revalidate directive, except that it does not apply to private (non-shared) client (browser) caches. Thus, for example, the information for client authentication can be maintained in the client cache (a client need not repeatedly insert the authentication information).
- max-age=s: The server explicitly specifies the maximum time for which information can be maintained in cache. If the server includes the max-age=0 directive in its response, it will force all the intermediate caches to refresh their information.
- s-maxage=s: Analogous to max-age, however, it applies only to a shared cache.

It is also necessary to mention that HTTP protocol version 1.0 supported only one header field, namely, Pragma: no-cache.

The server commanded uses this header field for not storing the response into the cache. Therefore, if the data is not to be stored into cache, this header field is used for backward compatibility (not all intermediate proxies and gateways may support HTTP version 1.1).

14.10.7 Software Information

A client can use the User-Agent header field in its request to inform the server about the software under which it is running. The server can use this information for statistical purposes. The server also uses the User-Agent header field for response formulation if it wants to employ some special properties of the client software. For example, applications running on the server can query if the client is using MS Explorer, and if so the application can send ActiveX components to the client.

The server can use the Server header field in its response to inform the client of the software under which it is running.

14.11 Cookie

The HTTP protocol uses only the request and the immediate response to that request. It is not possible to keep a running session between the client and the server. It is not possible to keep any information between two requests to the server.

Netscape solved this problem by establishing a simple relation, during which it is possible to pass information from the server response to the subsequent request(s). The server writes a small piece of data called a **cookie** into its response. The Cooke is written in the Set-Cookie header line. The client repeats this cookie in the next request to this server in the Cooke header line. This creates a session that is not intended as a persistent TCP connection, but as a logical session created from HTTP requests and responses.

The main server initiates a session. In subsequent requests, the target server may use a cookie to determine the current state of the session. It may send back the Set-Cookie response header with the same or different information to the client, or it may not send the Set-Cookie header at all. The target server may end a session by sending the client a Set-Cookie header with the Max-Age=0 parameter. The client can then repeat this information in its next request.

In the following figure, the Microsoft's Internet Explorer menu in which a user can configure a cookie usage is shown:

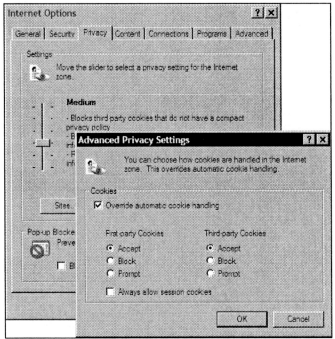

Figure 14.11: Cookie settings (Internet Explorer)

The client, for example, can shop at a virtual department store by using a cookie. The client passes through the virtual department store and chooses goods into his or her shopping basket. However, the information on what the client has in the shopping basket must be maintained somewhere. This information on the client relation status with the department store will be maintained in cookies.

The process is explained in the following steps (all details of the request and response headers are omitted):

1. The client enters the virtual department store `www.department.store.com` and identifies him or herself via a `http://www.department.store.com/shop/login` form, i.e., the client sends the following HTTP request:
   ```
   POST /shop/login HTTP/1.1
   ...
   ```

2. The server assigns an identification to the client using the `Set-Cookie` header field:
   ```
   HTTP/1.1 200 OK
   Set-Cookie: Customer="007"; Path="/shop"
   ...
   ```

3. The client chooses goods from the jacket department by using forms:
   ```
   POST /shop/jacket HTTP/1.1
   Cookie: Customer="007"
   ...
   ```

4. The server returns the identification of chosen goods:

```
HTTP/1.1 200 OK
Set-Cookie: Goods="jacket_05"; Path="/shop"
...
```

5. The client can continue choosing; however, he or she must choose the shipping and payment method at the final stage:

```
POST /shop/transport HTTP/1.1
Cookie: Customer="007"; Goods="jacket_05"
...
```

6. The server returns the identification of the chosen shipping and payment method:

```
HTTP/1.1 200 OK
Set-Cookie: Transport="cash on delivery"; Path="/shop"
...
```

7. The client arrives at the cash register and wishes to confirm the purchase order (we will not consider payment here):

```
POST /shop/transport HTTP/1.1
Cookie: Customer="007"; Goods="jacket_05"; Transport="cash on delivery"
...
```

8. Finally, the server confirms the purchase order, and the relation is terminated:

```
HTTP/1.1 200 OK
...
```

A complication of cookie usage is present in the client's freedom to pass through the virtual department store and, in the middle of shopping, switch to an entirely different server, which, coincidentally, can also use cookies, and some of the data in its the URI can even be the same (for example, part of the path).

Therefore, the client must record a cookie for each server. But different applications may be running on the same server—all using cookies—so the client must separately record individual communications with the help of cookies. The client must distinguish individual communications according to the following:

- A server name must not contain a period in the name, i.e., it must not be the server name with a subdomain. (In our case, the server is www.)
- A server port restricts the port to which a cookie may be returned in a Cookie request header. (In our case, it is 80, the well-known port of an HTTP server.)
- A domain name specifies the domain for which the cookie is valid. (In our case, it is .department.store.com.)
- A path specifies the subset of URLs on the target server to which this cookie applies. (In our case, it is /shop.)

The path and domain tell a browser that the cookie has to be sent back to the server when requesting URLs of a given domain and path.

14.11.1 Set-Cookie and Set-Cookie2 Header Fields

As we mentioned earlier, Netscape introduced the cookie. In 1997, RFC 2109 standardized the cookie. This standard requires the mandatory version parameter, but this parameter is usually not used.

In 2000, a new standard was issued as *RFC 2965 – HTTP State Management Mechanism*. This standard introduced new Set-Cookie2 and Cookie2 header lines. Both header lines Set-Cookie and Set-Cookie2 have a similar syntax:

- Cookie name=value. For example, goods="jacket_05". The header field must contain at least one occurrence of this parameter.
- Version=1, i.e., the version of the cookies protocol. This header is required, but is not used in proxies.

The following parameters are officially optional:

- Comment=comment: This may contain comments.
- Discard: A cookie may not be maintained after the termination of a client program (browser).
- Domain=domain: This specifies a domain to which the cookie refers.
- Max-Age=seconds: This specifies maximum time for which the client can maintain this information. The target server may end a session by sending the client a Set-Cookie header with a Max-Age=0 parameter.
- Path=path: This specifies the subset of URIs on the server to which this cookie applies.
- Port=port: This specifies the server port from which the cookies were sent.
- Secure: This specifies the request to a client to communicate through a secured channel whenever it sends back a cookie.

14.11.1.1 Cookie Header Field

A Cookie header field has the following syntax:

Cookie: $Version=1; par1; par2; ...

where par$_x$ has the following syntax:

Cookie name=value [; $Path=path] [; $Domain=domain] [; $Port=port]

The square brackets in the above code means optional options.

15
Email

Electronic mail (email) is one of the oldest and also one of the most widely used Internet services. Mail communication is performed by many application protocols (SMTP, POP3, IMAP4, etc.), and this chapter describes these protocols.

Support from Operating Systems

At present, email is implemented probably in all existing operating systems. Logically, operating systems of end-user stations implement clients of particular protocols while server operating systems implement mail servers. As was described in the case of TCP/IP protocol, a mail server is far beyond the client-server architecture. It is better to use the more appropriate term Mail Transfer Agent (MTA) instead of mail server.

Security

Two types of security are used for email:

- **End-to-End security**: A sender secures the entire path through which an email travels (from the sender to the receiver). In this case, an electronic signature (for integrity and non-repudiation of the email) and/or electronic envelope (for privacy of the email) is used. End-to-End security is based on the S/MIME protocol and its extension ESS.

- **Peer-to-Peer security**: This is mostly used between an end user and a neighboring mail server. In this way we prevent an unauthorized person from drawing our mails from our mailbox or some snooper from sniffing our mails. In the case of outbound mails, a mail server can check the client's identity to know who is sending spam through it. The SSL/TLS protocol is also used for securing Peer-to-Peer email communication,.

User Sector

We would hardly find any users not using email.

15.1 Email Architecture

The basic idea of the email architecture (see Figure 15.1) on the Internet dates back to the mid seventies. Nowadays, the standard RFC 821 from 1982 is the basis of the mail communication on the Internet. (RFC 822 describes the form of an email message.) At that time, users were sitting at terminals from which they started mail clients. A mail client has nothing in common with network communication. In essence, a mail client is only a specialized text editor. This text editor can display to the user the message content from the mailbox; it can also work with the messages in the mailbox. It can also do the same with the user's private mailboxes. Furthermore, it is possible to receive and send messages by means of the mail client. Sending a message does not mean any network communication, only storing the message into a message queue.

The queue of messages is regularly scanned by the SMTP client, which establishes a connection with the remote SMTP server, to which it delivers the message. The remote SMTP server accepts the message and checks whether it is intended for a local user. If the accepted message is intended for a local delivery, it tries to deliver the message to the inbox of the local user. If it is not, it then stores the message into the mail queue, and the whole process repeats again.

If the recipient is an address of a local system user, the SMTP server will store the accepted message into the recipient's mailbox. Here it is necessary to mention that the mail server usually has a privileged access to all the users' mailboxes in its system. In other words, the SMTP server is generally started up under a privileged user. If an attacker breaks into the mail server, he or she can receive an unlimited access to the system. Therefore, the following procedure is much better: the mail server runs under another user than the superuser. Then the user accesses the mailboxes using group privileges.

In the system, each user has, as a rule, one mailbox known as INBOX, where the SMTP server stores the user's incoming mail. The mailbox is not a file called INBOX, but its name is usually the same as the username. The name INBOX was established by the IMAP4 protocol.

Moreover, the user can also establish private mailboxes, where he or she moves the incoming mail from the INBOX mailbox. The SMTP server does not operate the private mailboxes. They are generally established under the home directory of the user. The aim is to force the user not to archive the incoming mail in the *system's* mailbox, i.e., INBOX. Some mail clients also achieve this aim. If the user displays the incoming mail, then they automatically transfer it into a private mailbox, which they call INBOX or inbox, in the home directory of the user.

The Internet mail has one fundamental property due to the storage of outgoing mail into a queue and incoming mail into a mailbox. It is a fact that the user can send email that the recipient does not have to collect from his or her mailbox until he or she wants. Therefore, it is not necessary to immediately establish a connection with the recipient system at the time of mail dispatch. The recipient system can even be switched off at the time when the sender sends a message. If the SMTP client does not succeed in sending the mail, it will leave the mail in the queue. Of course, the message will not be in the queue forever. The system administrator usually has set a maximum time the item will stay in the queue, typically set at 2 to 7 days. After this time, the mail is returned to the sender as undelivered.

It is still more complicated! The SMTP client may not send a message for many reasons. It is up to proper configuration to differentiate between two scenarios:

- At the time the mail could not be delivered onward, but after a certain time it may be possible (for example, the target system name was translated in DNS, but the system was not available).

- The message cannot be delivered due to an error, which cannot be removed (for example, the remote system name is correct, but the stated recipient does not exist in the system). In such a case, it is necessary to delete the message from the queue and to return it immediately to the sender.

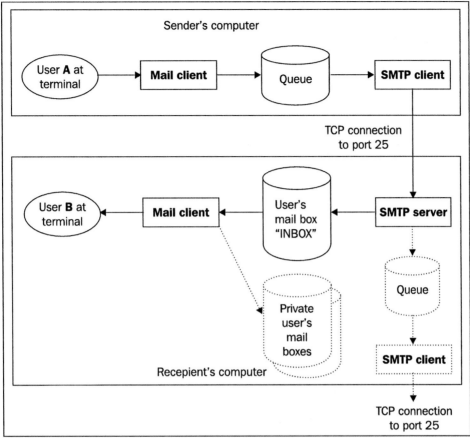

Figure 15.1: SMTP architecture

In the figure above, user A wants to send an email message to user B. User A will type the message using a mail client. Finally, he or she will send the message; however, the message only gets stored into a queue. The SMTP client scans through the queue until it gets to the message. It tries to deliver the message to the recipient's system; if it does not succeed, it will leave it in the queue.

When the server receives the message, it investigates if the message recipient is a local system user; if he or she is a local system user, it stores the message into the recipient's mailbox. If the recipient is not a local system user, it stores the message in the queue for further dispatch. Afterward, the recipient can process the accepted message with his or her mail client.

The arrival of personal computers caused a great change in the use of email. At its core, email remains the same; however, nowadays users do not want to sit at a mail server terminal (even if it is emulated by the Telnet protocol on their PC), but want to use applications on their PC. The question is how to send and receive mail from a PC.

While one can easily use the SMTP protocol again for sending emails, the SMTP protocol is not suitable for mail server to PC mail delivery. Why not? The recipient's PC is generally switched on for only several hours a day. Apart from this time, the mail would stay in the sender's queue, and the recipient system would appear to be unavailable. Another problem is that an SMTP server would have to run on the recipient's PC. Therefore, another strategy was chosen, as shown in the following figure:

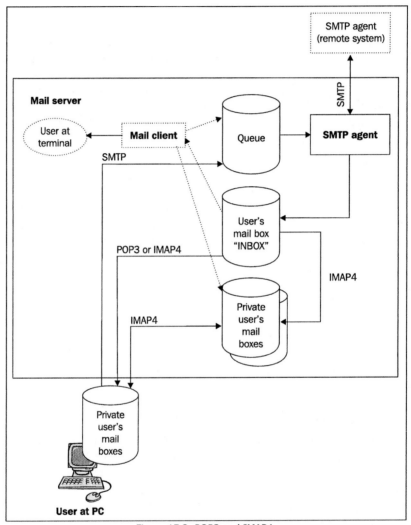

Figure 15.2: POP3 and IMAP4

The user has an incoming mailbox (INBOX) on the mail server. From the SMTP protocol viewpoint, the mail server is the endpoint system. The only problem is how to take the delivery of messages in the INBOX using your PC.

Two protocols are available for using the user's mailbox on the mail server (both of which are supported by Microsoft and other manufacturers as well):

1. **Post Office Protocol version 3 (POP3):** This is a very simple protocol where the user works offline. The user downloads incoming mail from the mail server onto his or her PC and terminates the TCP connection with the server. Only after the mail is downloaded does the user work with the individual mail messages. If the user wants to send mails, he or she will use the SMTP protocol.

2. **Internet Message Access Protocol version 4 (IMAP4):** This is a complicated protocol that enables the user to work not only offline, but also online. The user can establish a connection with the mail server for a longer time and can be continuously informed by the server of changes in his or her mailbox. The IMAP protocol also enables the user to work with private mailboxes on the server directly from the PC. By means of the IMAP4 protocol, it is also possible to synchronize mailboxes on the PC to those on the server. Thus, the mailboxes on the server remain as a backup of mailboxes on the PC. If the user wants to send mail, he or she will again use the SMTP protocol. Using the IMAP protocol is particularly practical when we sometimes want to work from our PC and at other times from a server terminal.

Another choice is to operate a web server on the mail server, which enables users to access their mailboxes via the Web.

The question is when to choose POP3 and when to choose IMAP4. For the big Internet providers, POP3 protocol is very advantageous because the mail does not stay on the server:

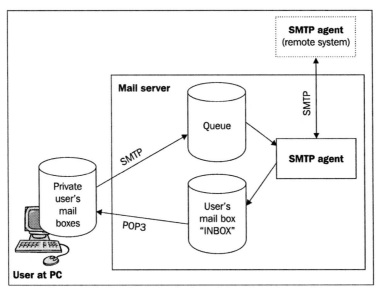

Figure 15.3: Email solution for large Internet service providers

Users download mails to their PCs. When we imagine hundred thousand users, all permanently having their mail on the server, we realize that no disk capacity is sufficient for such an immense amount of data. This can only be possible for small providers, who can offer to selected clients the premium service of private mailboxes on the server.

In contrast, the IMAP4 protocol is advantageous for smaller companies because it performs the backup of the mailboxes. In addition, it is easier to back up one disk system rather than each user doing it individually.

Nevertheless, the loss of the content of mailboxes can cause great economic damage. Therefore, it is necessary when using the POP3 protocol to back up mails either on the server or on the PC, for example, by using a CD-R.

In the figures, we do not use the word "mail server", but "SMTP agent". The reason is that there is always an SMTP client for sending mail and an SMTP server for mail reception together. Additionally, the mail client software must, at regular intervals, scan through the queue, and try to send items in this queue to a service (or a daemon) that is running. This daemon behaves as a client from the TCP protocol viewpoint only at the moment when an item in the queue is being dispatched.

The question is how to organize a company's mail on its internal network. If we have more than one mail server, the use of one central mail server identified as the **mail hub** will work well.

All the company's mail communications then pass through the central mail hub. Since the passage of all the company's mail messages is logged here, it is possible to centrally query if a piece of mail was received or sent. Similarly, as in a proxy, it is possible to check on the central mail hub whether the mail messages contain malicious codes (viruses, spyware, etc.). In addition, we can have not only malicious code protection, but also antispam protection. If direct communication between individual systems was possible, then such protection would be necessary at each system, which could be economically unsupportable.

The postmaster is responsible for the mail server configuration. All configuration problems are concentrated at the central mail hub configuration. The local mail agent configuration is usually easy (they send everything to the central mail server). The default system settings set during the original system installation can often be used for the local mail agent configuration.

There are several choices on how to configure the central mail hub of the company. At the beginning, it is necessary to determine which mail addresses will be used by the employees. In essence, there are two philosophies:

1. Mail addresses of the type novak@shop.company.com or dvorak@toolroom.company.com
2. Mail addresses of the type Bob.Novak@company.com

In the first case, we divide the internal network of the company into DNS domains such as shop.company.com, toolroom.company.com, etc. For each domain, we operate a local mail server (local mail agent). In doing so, it is possible to operate several domains on one physical server.

From the Internet, the mail messages arrive for novak@shop.company.com at the central mail server. The central mail server is configured to deliver all emails to the domain shop.company.com to the s1.shop.company.com server.

At the s1.shop.company.com server, the user *Novak* has his mailbox (INBOX). The user *Novak* will thus probably have two mail addresses: novak@s1.shop.company.com and novak@shop.company.com. At the s1.shop.company.com server, the SMTP agent will probably be configured to accept both mail addresses for its local users.

In the second case, the mail message for the recipient, Bob.Novak@company.com, comes to the central mail hub. Here, this address is translated to the address novak@shop.company.com or to the address novak@s1.shop.company.com. Now, such an address is deliverable within the internal network.

The other possibility (for the central mail hub) is not to translate the recipient address and forward messages to local mail s1.shop.company.com without address translation. However, the local mail server must be configured to accept such addresses.

Address translation may cause problems with the implementation of secure mail (S/MIME) in the case of a digitally signed message. In this case, the sender's address must match the email address in the sender's certificate. In the case of an enveloped (enciphered) message, the recipient's address must match the email address of the recipient's certificate.

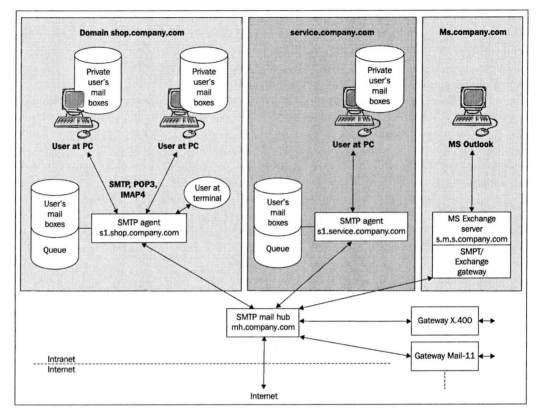

Figure 15.4: Mail hub

The user can have up to three mail addresses:

- novak@s1.shop.company.com
- novak@shop.company.com
- Bob.Novak@company.com

The central mail server is usually configured to rewrite the sender's address for mail going to the Internet so that every sender has only one address. Also, addresses of the type novak@s1.shop.company.com reveal something about the company's internal structure. This could be a potential information leak and could be used by attackers.

It does not matter much to the internal network if the user has more than one address. However, it is problematic during Internet conferences. For instance, closed conferences (on the basis of the listserv system) control the sender's address. If the user registers in the conference under one name and then sends a report under another name, the report can be rejected.

Nowadays, the preferred form of an email address on the Internet and the intranet is Bob.Novak@company.com.

15.1.1 DNS and Email

We have many potential email addresses, for example `novak@s1.shop.company.com`, `novak@shop.company.com`, `Bob.Novak@company.com`, or even `Bob.Novak@s1.shop.company.com`. We need to deliver all these addresses to the `s1.shop.company.com` server; a correctly formulated record in the DNS can achieve this. For example:

```
company.com.          IN MX 10 mh.company.com.
                      IN MX 20 mail.provider.com.
*.company.com.        IN MX 10 mh.company.com.
                      IN MX 20 mail.provider.com.
mh.company.com.       IN A   ...
mail.provider.com.    IN A   ...
```

MX records are used to direct mail to a particular mail server—in our case, the central mail server, `mh.company.com`. The first line says that all mail for addresses terminated by the `@company.com` string are to be delivered to the `mh.company.com` server. The second line then says that if, by chance, the `mh.company.com` server is not available at the moment, then mail has to be delivered to the `mail.provider.com` server from where it will be transferred to `mh.company.com` later.

The third line says that all mail terminated by the `company.com` string has to be directed to the `mh.company.com` server. If we do not want to transmit addresses of the type `novak@s1.shop.company.com`, `novak@shop.company.com` or `Frantisek.Novak@s1.shop.firm.com` on the Internet, but only addresses of the type `Bob.Novak@company.com` or `novak@company.com`, then we will not use the third and fourth lines with an asterisk (we assume that A records for intranet servers do not exist on the Internet, for example, A records for `s1.shop.company.com`).

Another choice is not to use the asterisk (*), but to list in DNS the second level subdomains, for which we want to deliver mail over the Internet:

```
company.com.              IN MX 10 mh.company.com.
                          IN MX 20 mail.provider.com.
shop.company.com.         IN MX 10 mh.company.com.
                          IN MX 20 mail.provider.com.
machine-shop.company.com. IN MX 10 mh.company.com.
                          IN MX 20 mail.provider.com.
ms.company.com.           IN MX 10 mh.company.com.
                          IN MX 20 mail.provider.com.
```

15.2 Mail Message Format

The mail message format is specified by the RFC 822 standard. Every email message contains a message header and a message body. The message header is separated from the message body by one blank line (CR LF CR LF). The header and the body of the message use only ASCII characters.

The header is formed from individual header fields. Every header field begins with a keyword followed by a colon. Parameters can be listed after the keyword. The header field ends at the end of a line (i.e., CR LF).

Spaces and tabs may be inserted between individual parts of the header field. The header field may continue on the next line. However, in such a case, the next line must begin with a space or tab (the keyword of the header field must be indented from the first position in the line).

The following characters have special significance, especially in an address:

- Semicolon (;) and colon (:) are important list delimiters. A colon follows the field name and, for example, semicolons separate recipients in the TO header field.

- Angular brackets (<>) have special meaning in an address. If the address contains a string within the angular brackets, then everything outside this string will be ignored; the address will be taken from the string within the angular brackets.

- Square brackets ([]) are significant in computer names; they show that the computer name should not be translated in the DNS.

- Parentheses (()) usually contain comments.

Here is an example:

```
From: Libor Dostalek
      <dostalek@siemens.cz>
To: Bob.Novak@company.com;
    Novak@[195.47.40.4] (raw IP-address)
```

15.2.1 Basic Header Fields

A review of basic header fields is as follows:

Header Field	Description
Received:	Every email server through which the message passes adds this header field to the beginning of an email message. Thus, all the Received header lines create a block of header fields on top of the message header. Therefore, if we read this block from bottom to top, we will discover the whole route, and through which email servers the message has passed. This header field may contain words such as:
	from (sending server).
	by (receiving server).
	via (physical path).
	with (network or mail protocol).
	id (receiver message identification).
	for (for whom the message is intended). For example, if the recipient is set as a distribution list, then the original recipient will be maintained, i.e., the distribution list).
From:	The sender who sends the email.
Sender:	Handled by, e.g.., secretary. This field contains, for example, information about a conference through which the message was received.
Date:	Posting date (date, time, and time zone).
Reply to:	To whom you send your replies.
In-Reply-To:	Replying to your message. Identification of the previous correspondence to which this message is an answer.
To:	Recipients (primary recipients of the message).
Cc:	Carbon copy (secondary recipients of the message).

Header Field	Description
Bcc:	Blind carbon copy (additional recipients of the message). This header field is erased before sending.
Message Id:	Message identification (unique identifier that refers to this version of a particular message).
Keywords:	Keywords or phrases describing the content separated by commas.
References:	Identify other correspondence which this message references.
Subject:	Subject (short summary of the message content).
Comments:	Comments about the message.
Encrypted:	Encryption (obsolete).
X-:	All header fields beginning with the string X- are user defined (here the word *user* means software developer, not software user). For example, X-Mailer is often used to identify the software used by the sender of the message.
Resent:	When automatic message forwarding is used (for example, return of an undelivered message by an intermediate mail server), the Resent- string will be add at the front of the original header field (for example, Resent-From or Resent-CC. etc.).

Example:

```
Received: from amphissa.erlm.siemens.de ([146.254.164.8])
          by cz.siemens.net
          with Microsoft SMTPSVC;
          Thu, 29 Dec 2005 08:14:58 +0100
Received: from tegea.erlm.siemens.de
          by amphissa.erlm.siemens.de
          with ESMTP
          id 1786215B526
          for <libor.dostalek@siemens.com>;
          Thu, 29 Dec 2005 08:14:58 +0100 (CET)
Received: from zetes.siemens.com (zetes.siemens.com [217.194.34.75])
          by tegea.erlm.siemens.de
          with ESMTP
          id CA10D1774B8
          for <libor.dostalek@siemens.com>;
          Thu, 29 Dec 2005 08:14:56 +0100 (CET)
Received: from imap.packtpub.com (unknown [217.207.125.60])
          by zetes.siemens.com (Postfix) with ESMTP
          for <libor.dostalek@siemens.com>;
          Thu, 29 Dec 2005 08:14:55 +0100 (CET)
Received: from paramita (unknown [203.122.53.88])
          by imap.packtpub.com (Postfix)
          with ESMTP
          id B6D24970B36
          for <libor.dostalek@siemens.com>;
          Thu, 29 Dec 2005 07:22:12 +0000 (GMT)
From: "Abhishek" <abhisheks@packtpub.com>
To: "'Dostalek Libor'" <libor.dostalek@siemens.com>
Subject: RE: TCP/IP DNS_Chapter 14
Date: Thu, 29 Dec 2005 12:44:44 +0530
Message-ID: <000001c60c47$8ce00220$0d00a8c0@paramita>
X-Mailer: Microsoft Office Outlook 11
Return-Path: abhisheks@packtpub.com

Message text
```

The header of this message must be divided into Received header fields and other header fields. The Received header fields were added to the beginning of the message by mail servers through which the message passed. Therefore, the order of Received header fields is important. The Received header field added by the first server will be in the last place; the preceding Received header field was added by the second server, and so on.

If we read the Received header fields from bottom to top, we will see that the message had been sent from a computer named paramita, and it was then handled by imap.packtpub.com. The message continued to zetes.siemens.com, and then was handed over to tegea.erlm.siemens.de, amphissa.erlm.siemens.de, and finally arrived at cz.siemens.net.

15.3 MIME

The SMTP message format was defined by the RFC 822 standard, and in 2001 the RFC 2822 standard superseded the RFC 822 standard. These standards are suitable to transfer data in the ASCII format. It soon became clear that this standard was not suitable for many users' needs; users wanted to send emails containing texts written with other character sets, formatted text, images, sounds, binary files, and so on. Recently, a new need is to send secure email with attached encrypted or electronically signed messages.

The users' needs quickly exceeded the limit of the RFC 822 standard and the **Multipurpose Internet Mail Extension (MIME)**, specified by RFC 2045-2049, was therefore introduced. Today, RFC 2048 has be superseded by RFC 4288 and RFC 4289.

The problem of sending emails containing other kinds of data than text in the ASCII code can be solved without MIME; the message just needs to be encoded into ASCII before sending. To read it, the recipient first has to decode the message. The sender and the recipient have to agree, via another means of communication, on the method of encoding the data into ASCII. The most commonly used encoding systems are Base64 and Quoted Printable or UUENCODE for UNIX. Experienced recipients will quickly recognize the encoding method and will therefore be able to select the most suitable decoding program before processing (such as reading) the received data.

For ordinary users, however, this procedure is unacceptable. Users do not want to be bothered with things like encoding; they want their mail client to handle these issues by itself. An ordinary user thus prefers the second choice, which consists of setting up a new brand of message header fields, labeling the content type of the transferred message body, and the algorithm used for encoding the data into ASCII before sending. In this way the whole process can be fully automated, and the user does not have to take any part in it. The MIME standard specifies the description in the additional message header fields.

The recipient's software can therefore recognize the type of encoding from the message header field and decode the message automatically. The sender's software also identifies the type of data transferred in the Content-Type header field; this helps the recipient's software to recognize the most suitable viewer for it. An appropriate viewer from the following is then opened:

- A text viewer for text
- An image viewer for images
- An appropriate player for sounds, videos, or animations

Header fields carry the additional information about the transferred data, and their names start with 'Content-' string specified by the MIME standard. MIME standard extends RFC (2)822, which preserves backward compatibility. MIME is designed to use the current email system to send messages containing text with diacritic signs, texts in different alphabets, images, sounds, and so on.

This standard has to deal with two principal issues:

- How to transform a message containing binary data, for instance, into a message conforming to the RFC (2)822 standard, i.e., one transferable by the regular transfer protocols.

- How to differentiate the different types of messages. In other words, MIME introduces a classification of the data (media type) transferred, which has become very useful even outside the scope of email. MIME defines the following header lines for mail messages, which specify content type and content transfer encoding.

15.3.1 MIME Header Fields

MIME works with the following header fields:

- **MIME-Version**: The presence of this header field in a message indicates that the message is structured according to MIME, i.e., according to RFC 2045-2049.

- **Content-Type**: Specifies the media type and subtype of data in the message body (text, audio, video, virtual reality, etc.).

- **Content-Transfer-Encoding**: Specifies either the encoding transformation used to convert the message into a format suitable for the transfer mechanism (for example, Base64) or the data format (for example, 8-bit).

- **Content-ID**: Specifies content identification. By means of content identification, it is possible to make a link to another mail message.

- **Content-Description**: Associates some descriptive text with a given body. An example of Content-Description: "Image of Prague Castle".

- **Content-*some string***: Reserved for future use in MIME.

- **Content-Disposition**: A header field specified by the RFC 2183 standard.

15.3.1.1 MIME-Version

This is the only header field in MIME not starting with the "Content-" string. This header field specifies the version of the MIME standard. The reason for implementing this header field is backward compatibility in the future. The MIME extensions according to RFC 2045-2049 are version 1.0. A new set of header fields might be introduced with a new version of MIME.

The HTTP protocol also uses header fields based on MIME, and many of them also start with the "Content-" string, but they are adapted to HTTP. The fact that HTTP header fields are not fully MIME-compatible is indicated by the absence of the Mime-Version header field in the HTTP message header.

A message composed according to RFC 2045-2049 must contain this header field. This header field thus reads:

```
MIME-Version: 1.0
```

The `MIME-Version` header field must precede all other MIME header fields in a RFC (2)822 header.

15.3.1.2 Content-Type

This header field describes the type of data in the message body so that the client receiving the message can select the appropriate way of presenting the message content. The form of the header field is:

```
Content-Type: type/subtype; parameters
```

The header field specifies the nature of the message body using the type and the subtype; additional parameters can be used if necessary. The parameters are formed as follows:

```
attribute=value; ...
```

There can be several parameters in random order separated by a semicolon.

The type indicates the nature of the data involved and whether the message contains text, an image, or, for instance, a general binary file (octet stream). The subtype then specifies the format of the text, image, and so on. Thus, the following example of a header field will inform the recipient that the message contains an image in JPEG format:

```
Content-Type: image/jpeg
```

Basic media types are defined in RFC 2046. There are two categories of media types:

- Discrete media types describing the type of data transferred. These include among others:
  - `text`
  - `application`
  - `image`
  - `audio`
  - `video`
- Composite media types specifying that the message is composed of several parts. These include among others:
  - `message`
  - `multipart`
  - `report`

Other media types may be registered. Registration procedures are described in RFC 4288 and RFC 4289. Experimental types can also be used, but they need to be differentiated from the standard types by the `x`-prefix before the type name. The names of types, subtypes, and parameters are not case sensitive. We will discuss more about the `content-type` header field in Sections 15.3.4 and 15.3.5 because it is a fundamental part of MIME.

15.3.1.3 Content-Transfer-Encoding

The data intended for sending by email is often 8-bit or binary. This kind of data usually cannot be sent directly; a transformation mechanism (encoding) thus needs to be applied to convert the data into ASCII code. In other words, the data is transformed into a 7-bit format. The Content-Transfer-Encoding header field is designed to indicate the type of encoding used in each case.

The Content-Transfer-Encoding header field can not only indicate the algorithm used to transform the data, but also inform about the 7-bit, 8-bit, or binary character of data that has not been transformed.

MIME defines two algorithms to encode data: Base64 and Quoted-Printable. The following are frequently used types of encoding specified in the Content-Transfer-Encoding header field:

- Quoted-Printable: The message body is transformed by the Quoted-Printable algorithm.
- Base64: The message body is transformed by the Base64 algorithm.
- 7-bit: The message body is not transformed; it is in short lines and contains only ASCII characters (*short lines* mean lines with 998 octets or less between CR LF line separation sequences).
- 8-bit: The message body is not transformed; the lines are short, but there can be characters not included in ASCII.
- Binary: The message body is not transformed, and the byte flow is not split into lines. Any sequence of octets is allowed.
- x-extension: Experimental encoding (i.e., for developers' needs).

The 8-bit, 7-bit, and binary values mean no encoding; they are only indications of the data type.

The Content-Transfer-Encoding header field refers to the whole body of the message. If the header field appears in a particular part of the message, it refers only to this part.

Example:

```
Content-Type: text/plain; charset=ISO-8859-2
Content-Transfer-Encoding: base64
```

This example is interpreted as follows: The original message body has been written in the ISO-8859-2 character set and has been transformed into ASCII by the Base64 algorithm.

15.3.1.4 Content-Disposition

The Content-Disposition header field determines whether the message body is intended for direct presentation to the recipient (inline) or not (attachment). Attachments are intended to be processed by the recipients themselves (such as a file to be saved to the hard drive). The header field can also contain further parameters:

- filename: Name of the file to be saved.
- creation-date: Indicates the date on which the file was last modified.
- read-date: Indicates the date on which the file was last read.
- size: An approximate size of the file in bytes.

An example of a message carrying sound to be played to the recipient is as follows:

```
Message-ID: 335A2639.C79@siemens.com
Date: Sun, 20 Apr 1997 16:20:41 +0200
From: Libor Dostalek dostalek@siemens.com
X-Mailer: Mozilla 3.01Gold (WinNT; I)
MIME-Version: 1.0
To: dostalek@siemens.com
Subject: (no subject)
Content-Type: audio/wav
Content-Transfer-Encoding: base64
Content-Disposition: inline; filename="ding.wav"
```

UklGRkYtAABXQVZFZm10IBAAAAABAAEAIlYAACJWAAABAAgAZGF0YSItAACgICAgICAgICA
gICAgICAgICAgICAgICAgICAgICAgICAgICAgICAgICAgICAgICAgICAgICAgICAgICAgICA
ICAgICAgICAgICAgICAgICAgICAgICAgICAgICAgICAgICAgIC ...

15.3.2 Standard Encoding Mechanisms

The encoding mechanisms convert 8-bit data into 7-bit (i.e., data only containing ASCII characters). MIME defines two encoding mechanisms: Quoted-Printable and Base64.

15.3.2.1 Quoted-Printable

This encoding mechanism is designed for message body mostly containing ASCII characters. The resulting encoded text stays readable to a great degree.

The encoding rules are as follows:

- ASCII characters are not encoded and are left unchanged. In addition, ends of lines are conserved. To be precise, bytes with a decimal value from 33 through 60 and from 62 through 126 are unchanged (ASCII characters from ! to < and from > to ~).

- The remaining bytes are replaced with an equal to sign (=) followed by a hexadecimal value of non-ASCII character. Thus, for instance, á is replaced by =E1.

- Byte values 9 and 32 are replaced by a tab and by a space respectively. These characters cannot end a line.

- Ends of lines are marked by CR LF (Carriage Return Line Feed).

- The encoded line can have a maximum length of 76 characters. If longer, a soft line break is inserted. A soft line break is the equal to sign (=) plus the end-of-linepair.

Example:

The string václav vopička will be encoded in Quoted-Printable as v=E1clav vopi=E8ka, where:

- á = E1 in hexadecimal
- č = E8 in hexadecimal

Using this method of encoding for a text composed only of characters other than ASCII, would make the text three times longer. Base64 encoding, however, prolongs a text by only a third.

15.3.2.2 Base64

Base64 is a mechanism used for encoding non-ASCII data. The encoded output is only one-third longer than the original. The encoding algorithm uses a Base64 table containing 64 signs (plus =). To encode 64 signs, 6 bits are needed ($2^6 = 64$). The = sign (65_{10}) is used for the special purpose of marking a padding at the end of the file.

From the point of view of encoding, the message is not viewed as a flow of eight-bit groups (octets or bytes), but as a flow of six-bits groups. Each group of six bits is then encoded according to the Base64 table as shown below:

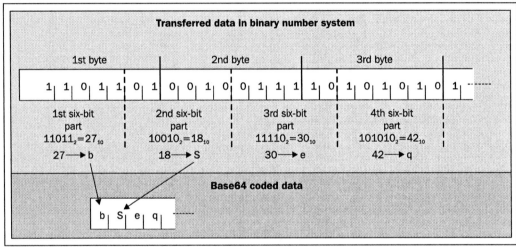

Figure 15.5: Base64 encoding

In the beginning, the text is divided into sequences of 24 bits (byte triplets). Each byte triplet is divided into 4 sixes of bits. The decimal value of each group of six bits is replaced by one sign in the Base64 table; the encoding proceeds from left to right. The corresponding sign from the Base64 table replace each six-bit group.

The following is the Base64 table:

Value	Encoded	Value	Encoded	Value	Encoded	Value	Encoded
0	A	17	R	34	i	51	z
1	B	18	S	35	j	52	0
2	C	19	T	36	k	53	1
3	D	20	U	37	l	54	2
4	E	21	V	38	m	55	3
5	F	22	W	39	n	56	4
6	G	23	X	40	o	57	5

Value	Encoded	Value	Encoded	Value	Encoded	Value	Encoded
7	H	24	Y	41	p	58	6
8	I	25	Z	42	q	59	7
9	J	26	a	43	r	60	8
10	K	27	b	44	s	61	9
11	L	28	c	45	t	62	+
12	M	29	d	46	u	63	/
13	N	30	e	47	v		
14	O	31	f	48	w	pad	=
15	P	32	g	49	x		
16	Q	33	h	50	y		

The target (encoded) text has to be organized into lines with the maximum length of 76 characters. All ends-of-lines signs and other signs not included in the Base64 table have to be ignored by the decoding program; they can indicate a transfer error.

If less than 24 bits are left at the end of the text after the division, zero bits are added from the right. This addition is indicated by the = sign.

The problem is that the length of the text does not necessarily have to be divisible by three. If the text is divided into groups of 3 bytes, then there are three possibilities:

- The last group has 3 bytes. There is no complication and no = signs are added at the end.
- The last group has 2 bytes (16 bits). The first 12 bits are encoded regularly according to the Base64 table. The remaining 4 bits are completed with two binary 0s to make 6 bits and the result is also encoded in Base64. At the end, however, = is added to signal the 2-bit filler.
- The last group has 1 byte (8 bits). The first 6 bits are encoded regularly according to the Base64 table. The remaining 2 bits are completed with four binary 0s and the result is encoded in Base64. At the end, two = signs are added to signal the 4-bit filler.

The principle is best understood from the following examples:

Example: The length of the source text is divisible by three.

```
8-bit input:       01101101  01001000  01111011   11100011  10101010  11110001
6-bit input:       011011 010100 100001  111011   111000 111010 101011  110001
Decimal:           27     20     33      59        56     58     43      49
Base64 (output):   b      U      h       7         4      6      r       x
```

Example: The last group is 2 bytes long.

```
8-bit input:       01101101  01001000  01111011   11100011  10101010
Padding:                                                                00
6-bit input:       011011 010100 100001  111011   111000 111010 101000
Decimal:           27     20     33      59        56     58     40
Base64 (output):   b      U      h       7         4      6      o     =
```

Example: The last group is 1 byte long.

```
8-bit input:     01101101  01001000  01111011  11100011
Padding:                                                 0000
6-bit input:     011011 010100 100001  111011  111000 110000
Decimal:         27     20     33      59      56     48
Base64 (output): b      U      h       7       4      w = =
```

15.3.3 Non-ASCII Text in Message Header Fields

Non-ASCII characters should never appear in a message header. If the header field contains such a character, the message can either be delivered correctly to the recipient or it can be stopped by a server on its way to the recipient; it can even be lost completely.

RFC 2047 deals with the issue of using non-ASCII characters in the header fields. Again, there are two principal issues:

- What do the signs represent? A hexadecimal F8 can represent the Czech ř in one character set and the Russian ш in another.

- How is it encoded into ASCII? Quoted-Printable or Base64 can be used, to mention the most common.

The syntax of a non-ASCII string in a header field will be as follows:

=?charset?encoding?string?=

As for the encoding, q will be used for Quoted-Printable and b for Base64.

For example:

If the sender intends to write his or her name in the From header field with diacritics, then this can be accomplished from the following example: A message from Václav Vopička, whose email address is vaclav.vopicka@company.cz:

From: =?iso8859-2?q?V=E1clav Vopi=E8ka?=Vaclav.Vopicka@company.cz

Václav does not like his name to be written without diacritics, so he puts it correctly in an escaped header field (From) and uses the ISO-8859-2 character set.

15.3.4 Discrete Media Types in Content-Type

The discrete media type tells the recipient's system what kind of software to use to open the message body. The software could be as follows: a text viewer, an image viewer, an audio player, a video player, or even software to show it in virtual reality.

15.3.4.1 text

The text type is designed for text messages. It is divided into the following subtypes:

- plain: See RFC 2045 and RFC 2046

- richtext: See RFC 1341 and RFC 2046

- enriched: See RFC 1896

- html: See RFC 2854

- `sgml`: See RFC 1874
- `c822-headers`: See RFC 1892
- `css`: See RFC 2318
- `xml`: See RFC 2376
- `directory`: See RFC 2425
- `calendar`: See RFC 2445
- `parityfec`: See RFC 3009

The `plain` subtype is primary; it identifies unformatted text. The other subtypes are used for formatted texts. The `html` subtype containing HTML markup is a good example.

When using the `text` type, the `charset` parameter can be used to indicate the character set. Examples of character sets are ASCII, ISO-8859-1, ISO-8859-2, Windows-1250, and so on.

For example:

```
Content-Type: text/plain; charset=ASCII
```

This is the implicit type. Thus, if the `Content-Type` is not present, it is implicitly understood that the message is written in the `text/plain` type and subtype and the character set used is ASCII.

For example:

```
Content-Type: text/html; charset=iso-8859-2
```

15.3.4.2 application

This type is used for data that needs to be processed by an application to be presented properly to the recipient. Generally, the subtype is the name of the application for which the data is designed. The user has to be informed in some way on how to process the received data, for example, in an accompanying message. The header field itself may not provide all the necessary information.

The subtypes are:

- `octet-stream`: This indicates that the body contains arbitrary binary data. The `type` parameter (type of binary data) can be used (carrying information for the recipient). The recommended action after receiving this kind of message is to save the data into a file without decoding and run the application.
- `Post-Script`: This indicates that the message body is a Postscript document.

Here are some other subtypes (other registered subtypes are available at `http://www.iana.org/assignments/media-types/index.html`):

- `sgml`: see RFC 1874
- `pgp-signature`, `pgp-encrypted` and `pgp-keys`: for PGP
- `pkcs7-mime`, `pkcs7-signature`, and `pkcs-10`: for S/MIME
- `msword`: text in the MS Word format
- `pkcs7-mime`: secured message by S/MIME

Example: An MS Word file, `file.doc`:

```
Content-Type: application/msword
```

```
Content-Disposition: attachment; filename="file.doc"
```

Example: Internally digitally signed message

```
MIME-Version: 1.0
Content-Type: application/pkcs7-mime;
  smime-type=signed-data;
  name="smime.p7m"
Content-Transfer-Encoding: base64
Content-Disposition: attachment; filename="smime.p7m"

MIAGCSqGSIb3DQEHAqCAMIACAQExCZAJBgUrDgMCGg....
```

15.3.4.3 image

The `image` type specifies an image, i.e., that the message body is an image. To show it properly, an appropriate viewer is needed. The subtypes include, among others:

- `jpeg`: See RFC 2045 and RFC 2046
- `gif`: See RFC 2045 and RFC 2046
- `tiff`: See RFC 2302

Example:

```
Content-Type: image/jpeg
```

```
Content-Disposition: inline; filename="file.jpg"
```

15.3.4.4 audio

The `audio` type specifies sound. To present the sound properly, an appropriate player is necessary. The subtypes include, among others, the following:

- `basic`: Mono sound with 8 kHz sampling frequency (implicit subtype)
- `32kadpcm`: See RFC 2421 and RFC 2422
- `L16`: See RFC 2586
- `telephone-event`: See RFC 2833
- `tone`: See RFC 2833
- `mpeg`: See RFC 3003
- `parityfec`: See RFC 3009
- `MP4A-LATM`: See RFC 3016

Example:

```
Content-Type: audio/wav
```

15.3.4.5 video

The message body is a video/mpeg, which is the implicit subtype.

Example:

Content-Type: video/mpeg

15.3.4.6 model

The model type is designed for multidimensional structures (such as virtual reality). The type is described in RFC 2077.

15.3.5 Composite Media Types in Content-Type

So far, we have only dealt with simple messages, i.e., those only having one part:

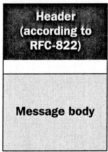

Figure 15.6: Structure of a standard message according to RFC (2)822

Now we will focus on messages composed of several discrete messages. Each discrete message can be further composed of message parts or it can be a single discrete message.

The message body can carry the following:

- Several message parts; then, a Content-Type: multipart header is used.
- A long message transported as several short messages (Content-Type: message).

15.3.5.1 multipart

The body of this type of message contains several different message parts. Each part of the message body starts with an initial delimiter followed by the part's headers (if any), a blank line, and the body of the message part itself. The final delimiter closes the last part.

The message parts are not interpreted according to RFC 822. Optionally, they can contain header fields (the blank line after the heading must always be inserted). If the message part has no header fields, then the implicit header fields of the message as a whole are used.

A **delimiter** is a special sequence of characters that cannot occur anywhere within the message parts. A delimiter is defined in the `boundary` parameter in the `Content-Type` header field of the multipart message.

The form of the parameter is `boundary=string`. The delimiter is then a line starting with two dashes (`--`) followed by the parameter string. The maximum length of a delimiter is 70 characters. The final delimiter has two extra dashes added to the end.

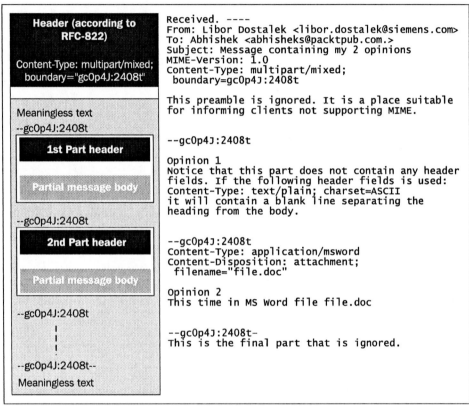

Figure 15.7: Multipart/mixed type of message

Here are some comments related to Figure 15.7:

`Content-Type: multipart/mixed; boundary="gcOp4J:2408t"`

This header field indicates that the message body is composed of several parts, while the message part headers do not have to be given. Each part starts with the following line:

`--gcOp4J:2408t`

The final delimiter determines that there are no more parts. The final delimiter is closed by two dashes:

`--gcOp4J:2408t--`

The following figure of MS Outlook shows the example from Figure 15.7:

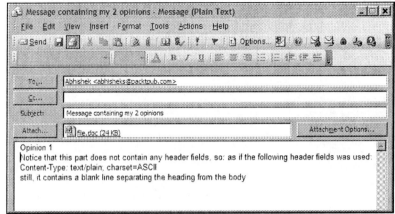

Figure 15.8: MS Outlook example created from Figure 15.7

The `multipart` type has the following subtypes:

- `multipart/mixed`: This is the primary subtype. It is intended for messages containing independent parts that need to be bound in a given order. A classical example of this subtype is an email message containing one or more attachments.

- `multipart/alternative`: This message subtype contains several parts, where all parts contain identical information and it is only the form that differs. For instance, the same message is first written in ASCII, then in ISO-8859-2 with non-ASCII characters, and then it is played (audio). The preferred form among the three is put to the end position. The recipient's software has to recognize which forms it is able to present and select the best of them.

Example:

```
From: angel@eden.org
To: devil@hell.org
Subject: Invitation
MIME-Version: 1.0
Content-Type: multipart/alternative; boundary=boundary42

In case your browser does not support MIME,
I'm just inviting you for a trip.
--boundary42
Content-Type: text/plain; charset=ASCII

  I'm even inviting you without diacritics.
  --boundary42
  Content-Type: text/html; charset=us-ascii

Join <H1>us</H1>
--boundary42
Content-Type: audio/basic
Content-Transfer-Encoding: base64

UklGRkYtAABXQVZFZm10IBAAAAABAAEAIlYAACJWAAABAAgAZGF0YSItAACgICAgICAgICA
gICAgICAgICAgICAgICAgICAgICAgICAgICAgICAgICAgICAgICAgICAgICAgICAgICAgICA
gICAgICAgICAgICAgICAgICAgICAgICAgICAgICAgICA
...
--boundary42--
```

The software creating a message of this type has to arrange the parts according to growing media quality. MS Outlook often uses this media type for text messages (plaint text and HTML).

- `multipart/parallel`: The client software is asked to present all parts simultaneously such as playing a sound along with an image.

- `multipart/report`: This subtype can be used, for example, for reporting mail system administrative messages.

- `multipart/signed` and `multipart/encrypted` are subtypes for S/MIME (secured MIME). The `multipart/signed` subtype is designed for digitally signed messages; it specifies a message composed of the following two parts:

  o Message body
  o External electronic signature (internally digitally signed message using discrete media type `application/pkcs7-mime`.)

```
MIME-Version: 1.0
Content-Type: multipart/signed;
  protocol="application/pkcs7-signature";
  micalg=SHA1;
  boundary="----=_NextPart_000_001C_01C4FBD7.AEA7F600"

This is a multi-part message in MIME format.

------=_NextPart_000_001C_01C4FBD7.AEA7F600
```
First part (message):

```
Content-Type: text/plain; charset="iso-8859-2"
Content-Transfer-Encoding: quoted-printable

My r=E9sum=E9 is Yes!
Libor
```

```
------=_NextPart_000_001C_01C4FBD7.AEA7F600
```
Second part (external signature):

```
Content-Type: application/pkcs7-signature; name="smime.p7s"
Content-Transfer-Encoding: base64
Content-Disposition: attachment; filename="smime.p7s"
```

MIAGCSqGSIb3DQEHAqCAMIACAQExCzAJBgUrDgMCGgUAMIAGCSqGSIb3DQEHAQAAoIILPDCCAnAw
ggHZoAMCAQICAgJCMA0GCSqGSIb3DQEBBAUAME4xCzAJBgNVBAYTAkNaMREwDwYDVQQKEwhQVlQg
YS5zLjEQMA4GA1UEAxMHQ0EtUFZUMTEaMBgGCSqGSIb3DQEJARYLb3B1ckBpY2euY3owHhcNMDAw
MzA5MDkwODI3WhcNMDUwODMwMDkwODI3WjBOMQswCQYDVQQGEwJDWjERMA8GA1UEChMIUFZUIGEu
...
6oNiNTdGSq3+toeOMx+cciMBG1QT5/VElbBsSUumVo79fq7DxjUYSP4SEAwCwWsfTjk3IwxloQAA
AAAAAA==
```

```
------=_NextPart_000_001C_01C4FBD7.AEA7F600-
```

Figure 15.9: An external electronic signature
```

(Notice: hexadecimalE9 is é in the ISO-8859-2 character set.)

- The `multipart/encrypted` subtype specifies a message in an electronic envelope (encrypted message), but it is not often used in practice.

15.3.5.2 message

The `message` subtype is designed to send an email message as the body of another email message (`message/rfc822`), to send a long message as several short ones (`message/partial`), or instead of sending the message body, to send only information about the location of the message on a server (`message/external-body`).

The few subtypes are as follows:

- `message/rfc822` specifies that the body contains a nested message, and its syntax complies with RFC 822. Unlike a message defined by RFC 822, it is not necessary for each body of a `message/rfc822` to include the `From`, `Subject`, and `To` header fields. MIME messages can also be nested.
- `message/partial` is designed to send long messages as several short ones, while the recipient's software can automatically show them as one (merged) message.
- `message/external-body` only gives information about the message located outside the received message. The location of the data is specified by the following parameters:
    - `access-type` specifies the server (protocol). The most common server types are `ftp`, `anon-ftp` (anonymous FTP-server), `mail-server` (list server), and `local-file` (file on a local machine).
    - `name` specifies the name of the file.
    - `site` specifies the name of the machine (server storing the file).
    - `expiration` specifies the expiration time.

Example: (taken from RFC 2046)

```
From:
To:
Date:
Subject:
MIME-Version: 1.0
Message-ID: <id1@host.com>
Content-Type: multipart/alternative; boundary=42
Content-ID: <id001@guppylake.bellcore.com>

--42
Content-Type: message/external-body; name="BodyFormats.ps";
              site=ţthumper.bellcore.comţ; mode=ţimageţ;
              access-type=ANON-FTP; directory=ţpubţ;
              expiration="Fri, 14 Jun 1991 19:13:14 -0400 (EDT)"

Content-type: application/postscript
Content-ID: <id42@guppylake.bellcore.com>

--42
Content-Type: message/external-body; access-type=local-file;
              name=ţ/u/nsb/writing/rfcs/RFC-MIME.psţ;
              site=ţthumper.bellcore.comţ;
              expiration="Fri, 14 Jun 1991 19:13:14 -0400 (EDT)"
```

```
Content-type: application/postscript
Content-ID: <id42@guppylake.bellcore.com>

--42
Content-Type: message/external-body;
             access-type=mail-server
             server=tlistserv@bogus.bitnett;
             expiration="Fri, 14 Jun 1991 19:13:14 -0400 (EDT)"

Content-type: application/postscript
Content-ID: <id42@guppylake.bellcore.com>

get RFC-MIME.DOC
--42--
```

In this example, the sender is sending three links for the same data. The first copy of the data can be found on an anonymous FTP server, the second on a local drive, and the third can be found in a list server's archive.

While identifying the whole message is optional (`id1@host.com`), the message parts' content must always be identified (`id42@guppylake.bellcore.com`).

It is also important to realize that the content of a message part is not data, but information about this message. The `Content-Type` header field is thus used in three different ways:

`Content-Type: multipart/alternative; boundary=42` specifies the media type of the message as a whole.

`Content-Type: message/external-body;` specifies the media type of the message part; this is a link.

`Content-Type: application/postscript` is not a header field, but the content of the message specifying to which type of data it is linked.

15.4 SMTP

The **Simple Mail Transfer Protocol (SMTP)** is a simple protocol. Individual commands are in the form of ASCII text (similar to the Telnet protocol). Therefore, it is easy to use the Telnet program, for example, to send an email using the SMTP protocol.

The client uses the TCP protocol to establish a communication channel to a server on a well-known port 25. The client will enter commands in this channel, and the server will reply with a three-digit code followed by an error description text.

Commands entered by the client are four-character words that are not case sensitive. A command may be followed by a parameter separated by a space. The command will end with the end of the line (CR LF).

The principle of the SMTP protocol may be shown by an example of sending an email using the Telnet program from Windows XP. (The highlighted code indicates the client's commands, and the remaining code indicates replies from the server.):

```
C:\> Telnet smtp.provider.com 25
    220 dns.terminal.cz ESMTP

    HELO libor.computer.org
    250 smtp.provider.com Hello libor.computer.org pleased to meet you
```

```
MAIL FROM: phantom@hell.org
250 phantom@hell.org... Sender ok

RCPT TO: dostalek@pvt.cz
250 dostalek@pvt.cz... Recipient ok

DATA
354 Enter mail, end with "." on a line by itself

I will come for you.
phantom
.

250 UAA91875 Message accepted for delivery

QUIT
221 dns.terminal.cz closing connection
```

After establishing a TCP connection, the server introduced itself (status code 220). The client was free to enter the HELO command and introduce itself. If I want to send an email, I begin the dialogue with the MAIL command. The parameter of this command must be FROM: followed by the email address of the sender (if you do not wish to divulge the sender's identity, then you can use the form FROM: <>). The server will verify the sender and use the status code 250 to inform me that the sender has been accepted.

Then I have to enter the recipient email address using the RCPT command. The recipient is entered as a parameter to the command after the word TO:. Once again, the server uses the status code 250 to accept the recipient. Now I can move on to sending the email by entering the DATA command. Status code 354 from the server will notify me that (if I did not know) the message is terminated with a period on a new line after which a new line must follow (i.e., CR LF. CR LF). The message is taken as it is (including the message header) and sent away. Once again, the server uses the code 250 to advise me when the message has been accepted.

Finally, I enter the QUIT command to terminate the connection. Such termination will be verified by code 221 from the server.

Command	Description
HELO client	The client introduces itself by the computer name. This command should be used at the commencement of a dialog with the server.
	`HELO libor.pvt.net 250 dns.terminal.cz Hello Libor.pvt.net, pleased to meet you`
MAIL FROM: sender	Sender's email address.
RCPT TO: recipient	Recipient's email address (this command is repeated for every recipient).
DATA	The message that you want to send.
RESET	The current translation will be terminated abnormally (all the information transferred in FROM and TO will be discarded).
SEND FROM sender	This is similar to the MAIL command, but the message will be shown on the recipient's terminal. (Not used).

Command	Description
VRFY address	This is used to query if the recipient knows the particular address listed. The server returns the full name of the user and the exact mail identification.
EXPN address	This is similar to VRFY, but it can work not only with individual users, but also with whole lists of users.
HELP	HELP 214-This is Sendmail version 8.9.3 214-Topics: 214- HELO EHLO MAIL RCPT DATA 214- RSET NOOP QUIT HELP VRFY 214- EXPN VERB ETRN DSN 214-For more info use "HELP <topic>"
QUIT	This is used to terminate a connection.
TURN	This switches the role of a client to a server and vice versa. If the server confirms this command, the client will expect the server to begin sending emails to the client. As this command is considered unsafe, it is not used. Its weak spot is that anyone, without authorization, could *suck* the email queue out of the server.

Table 15.1: SMTP commands

You probably noticed that some information such as Sender and Recipient is entered twice. These are first entered in the message header (in header fields) and then in the commands of the SMTP protocols (for example, in the MAIL and RCPT commands).

Data from the message header are of secondary importance as far as the message transport through the Internet is concerned. The SMTP not only transports the header, the empty line, and the text of the message, it also transports the so-called SMTP message envelope (do not confuse this with an electronic envelope!). The SMTP message envelope contains data from the MAIL and RCPT commands.

To transport the message between SMTP servers, the SMTP envelope is important. In the previous example, we used the Telnet program to send a message without any header fields (i.e., it did not even have the TO and FROM header fields). However, if you examine such a message after its delivery to the recipient, you will see that the mail server completed the FROM header field, i.e., it took the data from the SMTP envelope and used it to create the header field.

On the other hand, if you use a program to insert a message without an envelope into the email queue (or if you hand it over to the sendmail program directly), then information from header fields has to be taken into the envelope. Header fields in the header are of secondary importance, but they can sometimes come in handy for email transport.

This is why even a recipient addressed in the BCC header field receives a message addressed to him or her. The reason is simple; if a mail server loads a message and, for example, is creating the envelope for the first time, and encounters the BCC header field, it will take this header field out. However, that does not mean the information contained in the header field will be discarded; it will be inserted into the SMTP envelope. This will deliver the message to its recipient, but this recipient will not be mentioned in the header.

Here is a review of the status codes:

```
211 System status, or system help reply
214 Help message
220 <domain> Service ready
221 <domain> Service closing transmission channel
250 Requested mail action okay, completed
251 User not local; will forward to <forward-path>

354 Start mail input; end with <CRLF>.<CRLF>
421 <domain> Service not available,
450 Requested mail action not taken: mailbox unavailable
451 Requested action aborted: local error in processing
452 Requested action not taken: insufficient system storage
500 Syntax error, command unrecognized
501 Syntax error in parameters or arguments
502 Command not implemented
503 Bad sequence of commands
504 Command parameter not implemented
550 Requested action not taken: mailbox unavailable
551 User not local; please try <forward-path>
552 Requested mail action aborted: exceeded storage allocation
553 Requested action not taken: mailbox name not allowed
```

15.5 ESMTP

Extensions of the SMTP protocol led to the development of **Extended SMTP (ESMTP)**. The extension principle is specified in the RFC 1869 standard. The main problem concerning any extension is in its backward compatibility. In this case, the creators of ESMTP came up with a very smart solution.

While the SMTP protocol usually begins its dialogue with the HELO command, ESMTP uses the EHLO command. The server's reply will be either of the following:

- The client must have made a mistake in the command name. The client will immediately realize that the server is *SMTP-only* and carry on with the HELO command.

- Status code 250 (shows that everything is OK). The client will immediately notice that the server is of ESMTP type. Furthermore, the server's reply will contain the list of extension commands it supports:

```
EHLO libor.computer.org
250-dns.terminal.cz Hello libor.computer.org, pleased to meet you
250-EXPN
250-VERB
250-8BITMIME
250-SIZE 8388608
250-DSN
250-ONEX
250-ETRN
250 HELP
```

We still need to describe some of the extension commands. These commands are usually written as abbreviations of words characterizing their meaning (ONEX = One message transaction only).

VERB

The VERB (Verbose) command will cause the server to list all the details of the communication with next mail server.

For example:

```
C:\> Telnet smtp.provider.com 25
    220 smtp.provider.com ESMTP
    verb
    250 Verbose mode
    mail from: boss@company.com
    250 boss@company.com... Sender ok
    rcpt to: coworker@ompany.com
    250 coworker@ompany.com... Recipient ok
    data
    354 Enter mail, end with "." on a line by itself
    Unfortunately you are fired ...
        .

    050 dostalek@pvt.cz... Connecting to smtp.company.com. via esmtp...
    050 220 smtp.company.com SMTPXD version 141 ready at Thu, 28 Dec  ...
    050 >>> EHLO smtp.provider.com
    050 500 Command unrecognized
    050 >>> HELO smtp.provider.com
    050 250 smtp.company.com Hello smtp.provider.com, pleased to meet you
    050 >>> MAIL From:<boss@company.com>
    050 250 <boss@company.com>... Sender ok
    050 >>> RCPT To:<coworker@ompany.com>
    050 250 <coworker@ompany.com>... Recipient ok
    050 >>> DATA
    050 354 Enter mail, end with "." on a line by itself
    050 >>> .
    050 250 MAA14445 Message accepted for delivery
    050 coworker@ompany.com... Sent (MAA14445 Message accepted for delivery)
    250 MAA43965 Message accepted for delivery
    050 Closing connection to smtp.company.com.
    050 >>> QUIT
    050 221 smtp.company.com closing connection
```

This is a dialogue of a server with the subsequent server on the way to the recipient. The >>> string means sending the command.

8BITMIME

This extension is designed for the transfer of MIME messages containing 8-bit data. If the server does not confirm its support for this 8-bit transfer, the SMTP client may not send any message; the body of the message contains characters other than ASCII. However, it may encode the message, for example, by using Base64. This will transform the message into 7-bit characters.

The 8BITMIME extension extends the MAIL command by the BODY=8BITMIME parameter.

For example:

```
    MAIL FROM: phantom@hell.org  BODY=8BITMIME
    250 phantom@hell.org    ... Sender and 8BITMIME ok

    RCPT TO: dostalek@pvt.cz
    250 dostalek@pvt.cz … Recipient ok

    DATA
    354 Send 8BITMIME message, ending in CRLF.CRLF.
        ...
      .
    250 OK
```

SIZE

This extension is designed for specifying the maximum size of the message in bytes. The server returns a SIZE extension with a numeric parameter, which will provide decimal specification of the maximum message length to accept (message length includes line terminations, but not the DATA command itself).

Furthermore, the SIZE extension may be used as another parameter for the MAIL command that can specify the message length. In this way, the server can allocate corresponding memory space to save the message. On the other hand, the server may reject such a large message (for example, due to insufficient memory) before the data transfer starts.

ETRN

Especially small companies that have their mail servers behind a dial-up line will welcome this extension. In this case, the incoming emails remain on the mail server of the provider that is trying to delivery the messages to a company's mail server, which is not available for most of the time.

If the company is connected to a dial-up line, it expects the flow of incoming mail from the provider, yet nothing happens. The provider's mail agent will send the messages as soon as they come to the end of the queue. As the messages were lying there for a long time, the agent was allowed to extend its delivery retry periods. Or the agent may even be configured, in the case of a company (i.e., DNS domain), in such a way that it does not try to deliver the items until it receives the ETRN command.

The ETRN command has only one parameter, which is the domain, for which the server should start searching the queue. It is necessary to point out that, in contrast to the TURN command, if the ETRN command is executed by an attacker, then the mail queue is started in vain. If you use the TURN command, the attacker would receive the requested mail.

Extensions of the ETRN command are specified in RFC 1985.

15.5.1 Message Delivery Receipt

Electronic mail on the Internet does not guarantee delivery of messages. For several reasons, any message may get lost on its way through the Internet. Therefore, the sender may sometimes consider it prudent to have the message delivery confirmed. The recipient could handwrite the confirmation, but obviously we are more interested in the possibility of automating this task.

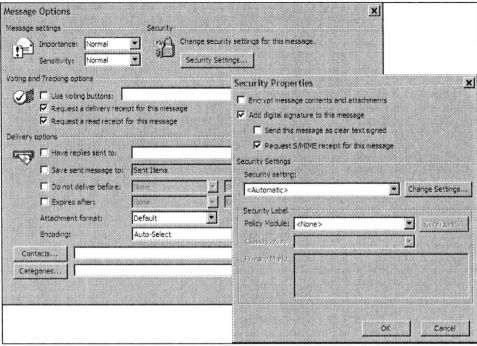

Figure 15.10: Message delivery reports setting in MS Outlook

Notification of the delivery of the mail to the recipient may be automated in two ways:

- By an extension of the ESMTP known as DSN that notifies of the delivery of the mail into the user's mailbox on the server. (In the figure above, the option is **Request a delivery receipt for this message**.)

- By a MIME extension executed via the `Disposition-Notification-To` header field. This extension notifies the opening of the message by the recipient. However, opening a message does not mean it has been read or understood by the recipient. (In the figure above, the option is **Request a read receipt for this message**.)

In fact, the difference between these two mechanisms is that the DSN extension is interpreted by the ESMTP server, i.e., the ESMTP server will generate the delivery report, whereas MIME is interpreted by the mail client only (for example, MS Outlook), and a delivery report will be generated by the mail client.

> S/MIME introduces a third kind of email notification where a recipient correctly verifies the digital signature of the email message. In the figure above, the option is **Request S/MIME receipt for this message**.

Whether your mail client supports one of these extensions, or even both, depends on the software manufacturer. If both these notifications are used, you will receive two messages. The first one says your mail has been delivered to the mailbox, and the second one indicates the recipient has opened your mail.

15.5.1.1 Delivery Status Notification

The **Delivery Status Notification (DSN)** extension enables message delivery notification. It extends the MAIL command for the SMTP protocol by the following two parameters:

- The RET parameter is used to indicate whether the notification report should contain the whole of the original message (RET=FULL) or the message header only (RET=HDRS).

- The ENVID parameter determines the message identification to enable the pairing of notifications with the original messages.

Furthermore, the DSN extension extends the RCPT command by two parameters:

- The NOTIFY parameter specifies a condition for generating a notification. Conditions may be as follows:
  - o   NOTIFY=NEVER (never send a notification)
  - o   NOTIFY=SUCCESS (send notification in case of successful delivery)
  - o   NOTIFY=FAILURE (send notification in case of delivery failure)
  - o   NOTIFY=DELAY (send notification in case of delayed delivery)

    SUCCES, FAILURE, and DELAY conditions may be combined, for example, NOTIFY=SUCCESS, FAILURE (send notification in case of successful or failed delivery)

- The ORCPT parameter determines the original recipient. The initial address may be changed, for example, during message *forwarding*. This parameter contains two values: address type (for example, rfc822) and a single address (for example, ORCPT=rfc822;dostalek@pvt.cz).

Notification is sent at the moment of delivery into the recipient's mailbox (INBOX), i.e., at the moment after which the message will be available via the POP3 or IPMA4 protocols.

Here is an example of the sent message:

```
MAIL FROM: skol00@t1.pvt.cz RET=HDRS ENVID=007
250 <skol00@t1.pvt.cz>... Sender ok
RCPT TO: dostalek@ica.cz NOTIFY=SUCCESS,FAILURE
    ORCPT=rfc822;dostalek@pvt.cz
250 <dostalek@ica.cz>...   Recipient ok
DATA
354 Enter mail, end with "." on a line by itself
```

The following is the message text:

```
250 QAA64601 Message accepted for delivery
```

In the previous example, the message has arrived at its recipient, and it was saved in its mailbox. This caused the notification report to be sent to the sender skol00@t1.pvt.cz . The interesting part is actually the notification report shown in the following table. This notification report is of multipart type; it comprises several separate parts:

Notification Report	Description

``
Received: from localhost (localhost)
 	
        by t1.pvt.cz (8.9.3/8.9.3)
        id   QAA31130;
        Thu, 28 Dec 2000 16:20:57 +0100 (MET)
Date: Thu, 28 Dec 2000 16:20:57 +0100 (MET)
From: Mail Delivery Subsystem <MAILER-DAEMON>
Message-Id: <200012281520.QAA31130@t1.pvt.cz>
To: <skol00@t1.pvt.cz>
MIME-Version: 1.0
Content-Type: multipart/report; report-type=delivery-status;
        boundary="QAA31130.978016857/t1.pvt.cz"
Subject: Return receipt
Auto-Submitted: auto-generated (return-receipt)
 	
This is a MIME-encapsulated message
 	
–QAA31130.978016857/t1.pvt.cz
``
	This is the header of the whole message. The message comprises three parts, separated by the boundary.

``
The original message was received at Thu, 28 Dec 2000 16:20:57
from server.ica.cz [195.47.13.11]
 	
    -- The following addresses had successful delivery notifications–
<dostalek@t1.pvt.cz> (successfully delivered to mailbox)
 	
    -- Transcript of session follows ---
<dostalek@t1.pvt.cz>... Successfully delivered
 	
–QAA31130.978016857/t1.pvt.cz
``
	The first part contains a text message for the user (in case the client is not able to process it automatically).

``` Content-Type: message/delivery-status Original-Envelope-Id: 007 Reporting-MTA: dns; t1.pvt.cz Received-From-MTA: DNS; server.ica.cz Arrival-Date: Thu, 28 Dec 2000 16:20:57 +0100 (MET) Original-Recipient: rfc822;dostalek@pvt.cz Final-Recipient: RFC822; <dostalek@t1.pvt.cz> Action: delivered (to mailbox) Status: 2.1.5 –QAA31130.978016857/t1.pvt.cz ```	The second part is intended for automatic processing by the client.

Notification Report	Description

`Content-Type: text/rfc822-headers`
 	
`Return-Path: <skol00@t1.pvt.cz>`
`Received: from server.ica.cz (server.ica.cz [195.47.13.11])`
`        by t1.pvt.cz (8.9.3/8.9.3) with ESMTP id QAA30941`
`        for <dostalek@t1.pvt.cz>; Thu, 28 Dec …`
`Received: from dns.terminal.cz (dns.terminal.cz [195.70.130.1])`
`        by server.ica.cz (8.9.2/8.8.7) with ESMTP id QAA25234`
`        for <dostalek@ica.cz>; Thu, 28 Dec ...`
`From: skol00@t1.pvt.cz Received: from [195.47.37.200]`
`        by dns.terminal.cz (8.9.3/8.9.3) with SMTP id QAA64601`
`        for dostalek@ica.cz; Thu, 28 Dec ...`
`Date: Thu, 28 Dec 2000 16:20:18 +0100 (CET)`
`Message-Id: <200012281520.QAA64601@dns.terminal.cz>`
 	
`—QAA31130.978016857/t1.pvt.cz—`
	The last part contains the header (header fields) of the original message (see RET=HDRS).

Table 15.2: Notification report

The `Content Type: multipart/report; report-type-delivery-status` message is specified by RFC 1894. The core of this message is its second part, `Content Type: message/delivery-status`, which is repeated for explanatory purposes:

```
Content-Type: message/delivery-status

Original-Envelope-Id: 007
Reporting-MTA: dns; t1.pvt.cz
Received-From-MTA: DNS; server.ica.cz
Arrival-Date: Thu, 28 Dec 2000 16:20:57 +0100 (MET)

Original-Recipient: rfc822;dostalek@pvt.cz
Final-Recipient: RFC822; <dostalek@t1.pvt.cz>
Action: delivered (to mailbox)
Status: 2.1.5

—QAA31130.978016857/t1.pvt.cz
```

The body of this message contains the following:

- Information about the message:
  - `Original-Envelope-Id`: Original identification of the message entered using the ENVID parameter.
  - `Reporting-MTA`: Mail agent that asks for a receipt; contains name type and name.
  - `Received-From-MTA`: The name of the mail server from which the message was received; contains name type and name.
  - `Arrival-Date`: Date and time of message delivery into the recipient's mailbox.
- Information about the recipient and about the message delivery:
  - `Original-Recipient`: The original recipient as specified by the sender.
  - `Final-Recipient`: The recipient who actually received the message.

- o Action: Action specifying the delivery results: Failed (the message was not delivered), Delayed (the message was delayed), Delivered (the message was delivered), Relayed (the message was transferred to another mail system through a gate), and Expanded (the message was send to recipients listed; *the recipient's address was a list, i.e., alias or mail list*).
- o Status: Contains three numbers separated by periods. These three numbers indicate the status of the message delivery. The first number (class) indicates whether the message has been delivered (2 means delivered, 4 means undelivered due to temporary failure, 5 means undelivered due to unrecoverable error). The second number (subject) specifies the cause of delivery problems (1 means address, 2 means mailbox, 3 means mail system, 4 means network, 5 means mail protocol, 6 means media type, 7 means security). The third number provides detailed specification of the real cause. See RFC 1893 for a detailed list of status codes.

15.5.1.2 The Disposition-Notification-To Header Field

This is an MIME extension (see Section 15.3). This extension is officially called **Message Disposition Notification** (**MDN**) (see RFC 2298). The header of the original message will include the header field:

```
Disposition-Notification-To: <e-mail>
```

where <e-mail> is the mail address for which the message notification is intended.

The notification report will be of multipart/report type again. The notification report will comprise the following parts:

- Readable message for the sender.

- The message/disposition-notification report containing extract information concerning the opening of the message by the client (also the reason for delivery failure). This part is primarily intended for automated processing by the mail client.

- The third optional part is the original message.

Example:

```
HELO Libor
250 dns.terminal.cz Hello Libor, pleased to meet you
MAIL FROM: dostalek@t1.pvt.cz
250 <dostalek@t1.pvt.cz>... Sender ok
RCPT TO: dostalek@t2.pvt.cz
250 <dostalek@t2.pvt.cz>...    Recipient ok
DATA
354 Enter mail, end with "." on a line by itself

MIME-Version: 1.0
Content-Type: text/plain
Disposition-Notification-To: dostalek@t1.pvt.cz
Subject: xx

message text
.

250 RAA39113 Message accepted for delivery
```

The recipient, dostalek@t1.pvt.cz, (i.e., the recipient from the `Disposition-Notification-To` header field) has received the notification report of the opening of the message by the recipient:

```
Received: from ...
Reply-To: <dostalek@t2.pvt.cz>
From: "Libor Dostalek" <dostalek@t2.pvt.cz>
To: <dostalek@t1.pvt.cz>
Subject: =?windows-1250?B?UPhl6HRlbm86IA==?= ... i.e. Coded by Base64 Subject:
          Read by xx
Date: Tue, 2 Jan 2001 17:26:33 +0100
Message-ID: <001601c074d8$c56bace0$940e11ac@cbu.pvt.cz>
MIME-Version: 1.0
Content-Type: multipart/report;
        report-type=disposition-notification;
        boundary="--=_NextPart_000_0017_01C074E1.273014E0"
In-Reply-To: <200101021625.RAA39113@dns.terminal.cz>

This is a multi-part message in MIME format.

---=_NextPart_000_0017_01C074E1.273014E0
Content-Type: text/plain;
        charset="iso-8859-2"
Content-Transfer-Encoding: 8bit

Your message

    Subject: xx
    Sent: 02-01-2001 17:25

    was read on 02-01-2001 17:26

---=_NextPart_000_0017_01C074E1.273014E0
Content-Type: message/disposition-notification
Content-Transfer-Encoding: 7bit

Reporting-UA: Klim.pvt.cz; Microsoft Outlook CWS, Build 9.0.2416 (9.0.2910.0)
Final-Recipient: rfc822;dostalek@t2.pvt.cz
Original-Message-ID: <200101021625.RAA39113@dns.terminal.cz>
Disposition: automatic-action/MDN-sent-automatically; displayed

---=_NextPart_000_0017_01C074E1.273014E0-
```

The body of the `message/disposition-notification` report contains the following header fields:

- `Reporting-UA` (UA = User Agent or the mail client): This header field contains the DNS name and the name of the software product.

- `Final-Recipient`: The recipient to whom the message is being issued.

- `Original-Message-ID`: Identification of the original message (from the `Message-ID` header field).

- `Disposition`: The syntax of this header field is `disposition-mode/disposition-type; disposition-modifiers`, where:
  - The `disposition-mode` can be as follows: `automatic-action` (the processing of the `Disposition-Notification-To` header field has been done automatically), `manual-action` (the processing of the `Disposition-Notification-To` header field has been a result of an explicit instruction by the user rather than some sort of automatically performed action, `MDN-sent-manually` (the notification was sent after explicit approval by the user), and `MDN-sent-automatically` (the notification was sent automatically).

- o The disposition-type can be as follows: displayed (the message was opened by the user), dispatched (the message was processed, i.e., printed out, forwarded, sent by fax, and so on without necessarily having been previously displayed to the user), processed (the message was processed by a server without being displayed to the user), deleted (the message was deleted), denied (the recipient does not wish to inform the sender about the way the message was processed), and failed (the message was not processed and an error occurred during processing).

15.6 POP3

Post Office Protocol version 3 (POP3) is a simple protocol that users can use to download emails from their mailbox on the mail server to local mailboxes on their PC. It is intended to work offline with the mail server. POP3 is specified in RFC 1939.

A client establishes connection with the well-known TCP port 110 of a server. After this connection has been established, the server introduces itself, and is in the Authentication state (i.e., waiting for an authentication from its user). For example:

```
+ OK QPOP (version 2.1.4-R4-b5a) at t1.pvt.cz starting <3774.978040846@t1.pvt.cz>
```

Basic authentication is done with a username and password. If authentication is valid, communication proceeds to the Transaction state, where clients can work with messages in their mailbox on the server. Even if clients, for example, delete some messages from the mailbox on the server, such deletions are not permanent during the transaction state. At the end of the session, clients will have to switch into the Update state, where the changes in their mailbox on the server become permanent.

The server always responds to the entered commands with a reply beginning either with the + mark if the response is positive or with the - mark in the case of an error report.

As commands are entered in ASCII, communication with the POP3 server is even simpler using the Telnet program, which also communicates in ASCII.

First, let's look at the individual commands (they are *always* made of four characters):

- Authentication state:
  - o The USER command is used to enter the user's name. For example:
    ```
    USER dostalek
    +OK Password required for Dostalek.
    ```
  - o The PASS command is used to enter the user's password (this command is optional). For example:
    ```
    PASS password
    +O dostalek has 2 message(s) (3605 octets)
    i.e. login was successful; you have 2 message on the server, these are
    3.605 bytes long in total.
    ```
  - o The QUIT command is used to terminate the connection.

- Transaction state:
  - The STAT command shows the number of messages in the mailbox and the total size of the mailbox:
    ```
    STAT
    +OK 2 3605
    ```
  - The LIST command returns the list of messages in the mailbox (one message on each line). Every message has its sequence number and size:
    ```
    LIST
    +OK 2 messages (3.605 octets)
    1 1.196
    2 2.409
    ```
  - The RETR command is used to download the message to a PC. The parameter will be the number of messages to be downloaded:
    ```
    RETR 2
    ```
  - The DELE command is used to delete a message in the mailbox on server. The parameter will be the number of messages to be deleted:
    ```
    DELE 2
    +OK Message 2 has been deleted.
    ```
  - NOOP is an empty command:
    ```
    NOOP
    +OK
    ```
  - The RSET command enables to regenerate messages deleted during the current session:
    ```
    RSET
    +OK Maildrop has 2 messages (3.605 octets)
    ```
  - The TOP command enables us to display the message beginning. Its syntax is:
    TOP message_number number of lines in the message body
- Update state:
  - Sessions are terminated once more by the QUIT command. At this moment, the physical deletion of all messages marked as deleted takes place.

Example (downloading a message from the server):

```
c:\> Telnet t1.pvt.cz  110
    +OK QPOP (version 2.1.4-R4-b5a) at t1.pvt.cz starting.
        <3774.978040846@t1.pvt.cz>

USER dostalek
+OK Password required for dostalek.

PASS password
+OK dostalek has 2 message(s) (3605 octets).

LIST
+OK 2 message (3605 octets)
1 1196
2 2409

RETR 2
+OK 1196 octets
X-UIDL: b27991db2a4199a85f593d76b58338c7
Received: from dns.terminal.cz (dns.terminal.cz [195.70.130.1])
by t1.pvt.cz (8.9.3/8.9.3) with ESMTP id XAA04273
for <dostalek@t1.pvt.cz>; Thu, 28 Dec 2000 23:21:10 +0100 (MET)

... message header and message body
```

Although there are various possible extensions to the POP3 protocol, POP3 servers are in practice usually designed as very simple ones. They enable a single connection between a mailbox and its user with only a POP3 protocol. After logging in, the user's mailbox on the server will be duplicated. The original mailbox will remain the same, and it will be able to accept further emails (e.g., via the SMTP protocol). A copy of the original mailbox will be used by the POP3 protocol. When the Update mode is entered, the two mailboxes once again converge into one.

After a user logs into the POP3 server, first a test will be conducted to check whether there is an existing mailbox copy. If so, it is expected that the user will work with his or her mailbox using the POP3 protocol and such login requests will be denied. Therefore, if the user cannot log into the POP3 server, we have to check whether there is an existing copy of the mailbox accidentally left from the previous login.

Another problem with POP3 on UNIX servers occurs at the moment when we would like to activate the C2 security mode (now called as Common Criteria mode) in the server operating system. The POP3 server may sometimes stop working after such an activation (no one is able to log in). The problem is that the POP3 server must find the passwords of the users in order to verify them. When transitioning into the C2 security mode, the passwords in the operating system may be relocated to a *safer place*. The POP3 server cannot work with such a safe saving of passwords and hence is not able log in any users.

15.7 IMAP4

The **Internet Message Access Protocol (IMAP)** version 4 is specified by RFC 3501. This specification is sometimes also called as 'IMAP4 rev1' because it is a revision of the initial form of the IMAP4 protocol specified in RFC 2060 and RFC 1730.

IMAP4 is a sophisticated protocol intended for use with mailboxes on a server using a PC in the online (or offline) mode. At the same time, we can work with our mailboxes from several applications. Some applications even establish two TCP connections with the IMPA4 server (for example, MS Outlook)—one connection for working with mailboxes and the other one for working with individual items (email messages). An IMAP4 protocol server uses the well-known port 143/TCP.

When IMAP4 is working with a mailbox (during an established TCP connection), another application can change the content of this mailbox (for example, the SMTP server records newly received mail in the mailbox). These events (for example, a new message coming into the mailbox) are reported by the server in the established connection. The client can actually find out about newly received mail by sending the empty command, NOOP, to the server. This will initiate the server to check whether any changes in the mailbox have been made. If so, the client will be informed about the particular changes.

If one application opens a mailbox for reading and writing and another application also wants to open the mailbox for reading and writing, the first application will have to change its mailbox to read-only. The first application will be immediately notified that the mailbox is now open for reading only, and if any changes in the mailbox need to be made, it has to be reopened. This kind of work with mailboxes is typical for servers using the IMAP4 protocol, but what about other applications?

In order to allow several applications to work with one mailbox, they should *not interfere with* one another, otherwise a collision occurs, and the IMAP4 server will terminate the connection. For example, incorrect behavior may often be simulated as follows: a mailbox opened for IMAP4 is simultaneously opened by a `mail` program on the server and changes are made to it—let's say a message is deleted (similar results would occur if we concurrently open the mailbox using either IMAP4 or POP3 protocol).

However, I have to describe first what the commands of the IMAP4 protocol actually look like. After the client has established a TCP connection with the server on port 143, the server will introduce itself. For example, a Telnet session running on Windows XP goes as follows:

```
C:\>Telnet server.company.com 143
* OK server.company.com IMAP4rev1 v10.170 server ready
```

The client can enter commands now; commands are entered in ASCII (similarly to for the Telnet, SMTP, and POP3 protocols, and so on). However, these commands are unlike those in POP3 protocol. The difference is not only in the command names, but especially in the usage of these commands. In the IMAP4 protocol, several commands can be entered, and their corresponding replies may come from the server in a random order. Therefore, the client numbers the entered commands, and the server repeats the number of the command to which it is responding. It is up to the client how he or she identifies (numbers) the commands. Commands are generally identified as a string (it does not even have to be a number), and the uniqueness of such identification is also the sole responsibility of the client.

After the connection has been established, we can show the format of commands and replies by using CAPABILITY command causing the server to tell the client what functionalities it can provide:

```
0000 CAPABILITY
*CAPABILITY IMAP4 IMAP4 REV1 SCAN SORT AUTH=LOGIN
0000 OK CAPABILITY completed
```

The client numbers its query with the string 0000, and it is followed by the command (in our case it is the CAPABILITY command). A command may be followed by its parameters (there are no parameters for the CAPABILITY command).

The server sends two kinds of replies:

- Unnumbered replies that have an asterisk instead of the command or reply number. These unnumbered replies in effect contain the information requested by the client. In our case, the server supports the following: the IMAP4 protocol, the IMAP4 revision 1 protocol, SCAN and SORT extensions, and user authentication with the LOGIN command (i.e., by name and password).

- Numbered replies that begin with the command number and inform about the outcome of the command.

A numbered reply comprises the following:

- Command number.
- Result, which can be as follows:
  - OK (command executed successfully).
  - NO (command execution failed).

- ○ BAD (command error, for example, command syntax error).

- ○ The result of PREAUTH may be the server's indication (after establishing the connection) that the client is logged in as an actual user without the necessity to log in using the LOGIN or AUTHENTICATE command.

- ○ The BYE response may be returned if the server does not want to communicate with the client any more. For example, the client may be logged in for a long time without any activity:

  `* BYE Autologout: idle for too long`

  Or this result may be a part of logout sequence during the termination of the connection:

  `5 LOGOUT`
  `* BYE p30x01 IMAP4rev1 server terminating connection`
  `4 OK LOGOUT completed`

  Or there was a login attempt by a client listed in the *blacklist*, therefore, the server sends the client the BYE result instead of the introduction.

- Other replies specifying text information.

The following figure shows the individual states of the IMAP4 protocol:

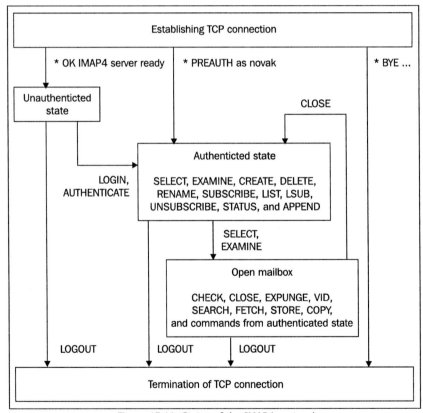

Figure 15.11: States of the IMAP4 protocol

Once a connection has been established, the Unauthenticated state occurs necessitating the authentication of the client (or the termination of the authentication by entering the LOGOUT command). An exception might be when the server informs the client immediately after establishing the connection that the client has been pre-authenticated (PREAUTH).

In the Authenticated state, the client may work with mailboxes on the server as with files (i.e., the client can create a mailbox, delete it, and rename it). The SELECT (or EXAMINE) command may enable the client to open a particular mailbox and switch to the 'Open mailbox' mode in which he or she can work with individual items inside the open mailbox (for example, items that will be transferred from the server to the client.).

The CAPABILITY, NOOP, and LOGOUT commands do not depend on the current state; therefore, it is possible to enter those anytime.

15.7.1 Unauthenticated State

15.7.1.1 LOGIN

The LOGIN command enables the user to log in using his or her name and password. After the successful execution of the LOGIN command, the Authenticated state will be initiated.

```
1 login user password
1 OK LOGIN completed
```

15.7.1.2 AUTHENTICATE

For other authentication mechanisms, instead of using a name and a password (for example, authentication using the Kerberos system), the AUTHENTICATE command is used. Generally, the client suggests an authentication scheme as a parameter for the AUTHENTICATE command. If the server supports this scheme, the reply will be a + mark meaning "*proceed with authentication*". The client then replies with some particular authentication information. If the authentication dialogue requires further communication between the server and the client, the server will reply with a line beginning with a + mark again.

All the authentication information transferred between the client and the server is encoded in Base64.

15.7.2 Authenticated State

15.7.2.1 CREATE, DELETE, RENAME, and LIST Commands

The CREATE command is used to create a mailbox as a file, the DELETE command initiates its deletion, the RENAME command is used to change the name of a file, and the LIST command serves for directory listing. Now we issue the LIST command:

```
2 LIST "" "*"
* LIST (\NoInferiors) "/" .profile
* LIST (\NoInferiors \UnMarked) "/" .login
* LIST (\NoInferiors \UnMarked) "/" .cshrc
* LIST (\NoInferiors \ Marked) "/" Drafts
* LIST (\NoInferiors \ Marked) "/" "Sent Items"
* LIST (\NoInferiors) NIL INBOX
2 OK LIST completed
```

Directory listing in the UNIX operating system can help us see approximately the same listing:

```
$ ls -a
.       ..      .cshrc      .login      .profile      Drafts      Sent Items
```

(There was no INBOX on my system. It is the *system* mailbox present in the `/var/spool/mail` directory and not in the home directory.)

The syntax of the LIST command is quite irregular. The LIST command has two parameters; the first parameter is a path, and the second one is the name of the mailbox. The mailbox name may include wildcard characters like an asterisk and the percentage sign. The asterisk expands everything, but the percentage sign only applies to the mailbox name and not to the directory structure (or the mailbox structure, if you wish).

In our directory, we create a `mail` subdirectory, and in this subdirectory, we create a `mailbox2` file. Here is the difference between the asterisk sign and the percentage sign:

```
1 list "" "%"
* LIST (\NoInferiors) "/" .profile
* LIST (\NoInferiors \UnMarked) "/" .login
* LIST (\NoInferiors \UnMarked) "/" .cshrc
* LIST (\NoInferiors \Marked) "/" Drafts
* LIST (\NoInferiors \Marked) "/" "Sent Items"
* LIST (\NoSelect) "/" mail
* LIST (\NoInferiors) NIL INBOX
1 OK LIST completed

1 list "" "*"
* LIST (\NoInferiors) "/" .profile
* LIST (\NoInferiors \UnMarked) "/" .login
* LIST (\NoInferiors \UnMarked) "/" .cshrc
* LIST (\NoSelect) "/" mail
* LIST (\NoInferiors \Marked) "/" Drafts
* LIST (\NoInferiors \Marked) "/" "Sent Items"
* LIST (\NoInferiors) "/" mail/mailbox2
* LIST (\NoInferiors) NIL INBOX
1 OK LIST completed
```

The server's reply to the LIST command gives information about each listed file (one file per line) comprising three entries:

- Attributes in parentheses. The possible attributes in parentheses are:
    - \NoInferiors: This is not a directory, i.e., there cannot be another item under this item within the mailbox structure (it is not possible to have any sublevels of hierarchy existing under this name).
    - \NoSelect: This file cannot be opened as a mailbox.
    - \Marked: This file is marked so that it could be opened as a mailbox.
    - \Unmarked: This file is not marked as a mailbox.
- Delimiters in the mailbox hierarchy (for example, in UNIX, the path to a file uses forward slash as a delimiter between directory names). The word NIL means there is no hierarchy.
- Mailbox name (file name).

Here is an example that uses the CREATE command to create a subdirectory in the home directory (~dostalek) with two mailboxes, MailboxA and MailboxB:

```
3 CREATE "~dostalek/MailboxA"
3 OK CREATE completed

4 create "~dostalek/MailboxB"
4 OK CREATE completed
```

Type the LIST command to verify whether the mailbox has been created:

```
5 list "" "*"
* LIST (\NoInferiors) "/" .profile
* LIST (\NoInferiors \UnMarked) "/" .login
* LIST (\NoInferiors \UnMarked) "/" .cshrc
* LIST (\NoInferiors \Marked) "/" Drafts
* LIST (\NoInferiors \Marked) "/" "Sent Items"
* LIST (\NoInferiors) "/" MailboxA
* LIST (\NoInferiors) "/" MailboxB
* LIST (\NoSelect) "/" mail
* LIST (\NoInferiors) "/" mail/mailbox2
* LIST (\NoInferiors) NIL INBOX
5 OK LIST completed
```

The same listing can be obtained by an operating system command:

```
$ ls Mailbox*
  MailboxA   MailboxB
```

However, a regular user would not be satisfied with such a listing—that's why the user's mail application shows it in a friendlier format. The following figure shows an example of the graphical interpretation of our listing in the MS Outlook Express window (MS Outlook has a similar window):

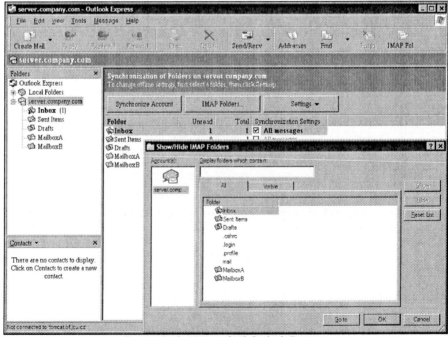

Figure 15.12: Listing of MS Outlook Express

The RENAME command can be used to change the name of MailboxB directory to MailboxC. For example:

```
6 RENAME MailboxB MailboxC
6 OK RENAME completed
```

Finally, the DELETE command is entered to erase the mailbox:

```
C: 7 DELETE MailboxC
S: 7 OK DELETE completed
```

We will create the MailboxB directory again in order to have at least two mailboxes on the server for further explanations.

15.7.2.2 SUBSRCIBE, LSUB, and UNSUBSCRIBE Commands

A client uses the SUBSCRIBE command to tell the server to mark a directory as a mailbox.

```
C: 1 subscribe MailboxA
S: 1 OK SUBSCRIBE completed
```

Now we can enter the LIST command to get a listing of the mailboxes:

While implementing our server, we will create a file in the user's home directory called .maliboxlist, which contains information about which mailboxes are marked:

```
$ cat $HOME/.mailboxlist
    INBOX
    Sent Items
    MailboxA
    MailboxB
    Drafts
```

The UNSUBSRIBE command serves to unmark a mailbox.

The LSUB command is similar to the LIST command, but it provides a list of marked mailboxes only.

15.7.2.3 STATUS

The STATUS command can be used to obtain information about a mailbox without opening it. The STATUS command has two parameters: the first parameter is the mailbox name and the second one (in parentheses) is the list of item statuses.

The status of an item in a mailbox may be as follows:

- MESSAGES: The server will return the number of messages in the mailbox.
- RECENT: The server will return the number of items with the \Recent attribute.
- UIDNEXT: The server will return the number of the message that will be received next.
- UIDVALIDITY: The server will return a unique identification (UID) of the mailbox.
- UNSEEN: The server will return number of items without the \Seen attribute.

In the following example, we will look at the INBOX status instead of the private mailbox status (/var/spool/mail/dostalek):

```
4 STATUS INBOX (MESSAGES RECENT UIDNEXT UIDVALIDITY UNSEEN)
* STATUS INBOX (MESSAGES 6 RECENT 0 UNSEEN 4 UIDNEXT 7
  UIDVALIDITY 978588855)
4 OK STATUS completed
```

15.7.2.4 SELECT and EXAMINE Commands

The SELECT command allows us to open the mailbox, i.e., switch to 'Open mailbox' mode. The EXAMINE command is similar to the SELECT command, but it opens the mailbox for reading purposes only. The mailbox name will be entered as a parameter:

```
5 select INBOX
* 6 EXISTS
* OK [UIDVALIDITY 978588855] UID validity status
* FLAGS (\Answered \Flagged \Deleted \Draft \Seen)
* OK [PERMANENTFLAGS (\Answered \Flagged \Deleted \Draft \Seen)]
  Permanent flags
* OK [UNSEEN 3] 3 is first unseen
* 0 RECENT
5 OK [READ-WRITE] SELECT completed
```

The server's reply is more complex; it comprises several kinds of lines:

- The line containing 6 EXISTS states that the currently open mailbox contains 6 messages.
- The OK [UIDVALIDITY 978588855] line states the unique ID of the mailbox.
- The FLAGS line contains parenthesized identification list of the flags (at a minimum, the system-defined flags) that are applicable for this mailbox:
  - \Seen: Message has been read.
  - \Answered: Message has been answered.
  - \Flagged: Message marked as urgent.
  - \Deleted: Message marked as deleted. The EXPUNGE command may be used to delete messages.
  - \Draft: Message is not finished yet.
  - \Recent: New message. This message will not be marked as \Recent after the next mailbox opening.
- The OK [PERMANENTFLAGS Answered \Flagged \Deleted \Draft \Seen)] line lists attributes, which the client may change and which will remain changed permanently even after a particular session has ended.
- The OK [UNSEEN 3] line specifies the number of the first unread message in the mailbox (i.e., all the messages preceding this one have been read).
- The 0 RECENT line shows the number of messages marked as \Recent.

15.7.3 Open Mailbox

Every mailbox has its unique identification, and the server returns it in the UIDVALIDITY parameter. This identification is independent of the mailbox name in the operating system.

Similarly, every email message in the mailbox also has its own identification, which is guaranteed to be unique as well. The identification sequence is an incremental one. By combining the mailbox and the message identifiers, we will get a unique identification of a particular message in the system.

This unique identification is guaranteed, but it is not very useful. That is why messages are sequentially numbered from one onwards within a mailbox. So if there is, for example, a message deleted using the EXPUNGE command, other messages in the mailbox must be renumbered.

15.7.3.1 COPY

The COPY command will copy messages from the open mailbox into the mailbox listed as the second parameter. The first parameter is the number of the message to be copied. We can list a range of messages instead of only one (for example, 3:6 is a range for messages number 3, 4, 5, and 6). The following example will copy messages numbered from 3 to 6 into the mailbox called Mailbox1:

```
3 COPY 3:6 Mailbox1
3 OK COPY completed
```

15.7.3.2 SEARCH

The SEARCH command can be used to search for messages in a mailbox. A search is performed according to the search criteria listed as parameters with the SEARCH command. If there are many search criteria listed, the search will select messages that fit all the criteria all at once (AND). However, we have to add that there is also the OR criterion, which assesses partial criteria by means of the OR operation. There is also an analogous negative criterion NOT.

The following is a list of criteria:

- Message range, for example, 3:6
- ALL (all the messages in the mailbox)
- ANSWERED (all the messages marked as \Answered)
- DELETED (all the messages marked as \Deleted)
- DRAFT (all the messages marked as \Draft)
- FLAGGED (all the messages marked as \Flagged)
- SEEN (all the messages marked as \Seen)
- NEW (all the message marked as \Recent, but without the \Seen mark)
- RECENT (all the messages marked as \Recent)
- UNANSWERED (all the messages not marked as \Answered)
- UNDELETED (all the messages not marked as\Deleted)
- UNDRAFT (all the message not marked as \Draft)
- UNFLAGGED (all the message not marked as \Flagged)
- UNSEEN (all the messages not marked as \Seen)
- BODY *string* (all the messages where the body contains a particular string)
- TO *string* (all the messages that contain a particular string in the TO header field)
- CC *string* (all the messages that contain a particular string in the CC header field)
- BCC *string* (all the messages that contain a particular string in the BCC header field)
- SUBJECT *string* (all the messages that contain a particular string in the Subject header field)

- FROM *string* (all the messages that contain a particular string in the From header field)
- HEADER *header field string* (all the messages containing a particular string in a particular header field)
- ON *date* (all the messages sent on a particular date)
- BEFORE *date* (all the messages whose internal date is older than a particular date)
- SINCE *date* (all the messages whose internal date is the same or later than a particular date)
- SENTBEFORE *date* (all the messages sent before a particular date)
- SENTON *date* (all the messages sent on a particular date)
- SENTSINCE *date* (all the messages sent on or after a particular date)
- LARGER *size* (all the messages larger than the listed byte size)
- SMALLER *size* (all the messages smaller than the listed byte size)
- UID *id* (all the messages with an explicit identification)
- NOT (the negation of search criterion)
- OR *criterion1 criterion2* (OR operator)

An example:

```
789 SEARCH UNSEEN NOT FROM dostalek SINCE 4-Jan-2000
* SEARCH 7 8
789 OK SEARCH completed
Result: Messagess 7 and 8 satisfy searching criteria.
```

15.7.3.3 FETCH

The FETCH command can be used to download a message or a part of it from a server. This command has the following syntax:

```
FETCH messages (what)
```

While the term messages means either a number or a message range (for example, 2:93), what means which part of the message will be obtained. We can use parentheses to specify various information that the server needs to get.

Here are some examples:

- BODY[*section*]: The server will return the content of the section listed in the square brackets. Sections are HEADER, HEADER.FIELDS (header fields whose names are listed in parentheses), HEADER.FIELDS.NOT, MIME, and TEXT (message text). For example:

```
89 FETCH 9 BODY[HEADER.FIELDS (FROM DATE)]
* 9 FETCH (BODY[HEADER.FIELDS ("FROM" "DATE")] {83}
Date: Fri, 5 Jan 2001 15:28:39 +0100
From: Libor Dostalek test user <dostalek>

)
89 OK FETCH completed
```

The FETCH command returns the Date and From header fields from message number 9. Data sent from the server is in parentheses (after the FETCH string). The first line of the

returned data repeats the data that has been returned by the server—BODY[HEADER
.FIELDS ("FROM" "DATE")] followed by the string {83}. Curly braces contain the length
of the following data that did not fit on this line. This means 83 bytes of data is being
sent, and the end of data is indicated by a closing parenthesis.

- BODY[*section*] <*from.to*>: This is analogous to the previous option, where the angular
  brackets contain the volume of data to be transferred. The following example will
  transfer the first 20 bytes from the data part of message number 6

```
90 FETCH 6 BODY[TEXT]<1.20>
* 6 FETCH (BODY[TEXT]<1> {20}
20 bytes of message
)
90 OK FETCH completed
```

- BODY.PEEK[*section*] <*from.to*>: This command is analogous to BODY, but it does not
  mark messages returned as \Seen.

- FLAGS: Returns attributes of the listed messages:

```
81 FETCH 9:10 FLAGS
* 9 FETCH (FLAGS (\Seen))
* 10 FETCH (FLAGS (\Seen))
81 OK FETCH completed
```

- RFC822: Returns the message in a format specified by RFC 822:

```
83 fetch 9 RFC822
* 9 FETCH (RFC822 {277}
Received: by P30X01.cbu.pvt.cz; (5.65/1.1.8.2/23Jun99-9.1MPM)
           id AA18388; Fri, 5 Jan 2001 15:28:39 +0100
Date: Fri, 5 Jan 2001 15:28:39 +0100
From: Libor Dostalek test user <dostalek>
Message-Id: 0101051428.AA18388@P30X01.cbu.pvt.cz
To: dostalek
Subject: Experiment

Message text
)
83 OK FETCH completed
```

- RFC822.SIZE: Returns the message length:

```
84 fetch 9 RFC822.SIZE
* 9 FETCH (RFC822.SIZE 277)
84 OK FETCH completed
```

- UID: Returns the message number.

- BODYSTRUCTURE: Returns the message structure. For example, a message containing
  text in two alternative forms (text and HTML), and an attached file in MS Word
  format has the following structure:

```
91 FETCH 11 BODYSTRUCTURE
* 11 FETCH (BODYSTRUCTURE ((("TEXT" "PLAIN" ("CHARSET" "iso-8859-2") NIL
NIL "QUOTED-PRINTABLE" 10 1 NIL NIL NIL)("TEXT" "HTML" ("CHARSET" "iso-
8859-2") NIL NIL "QUOTED-PRINTABLE" 345 10 NIL NIL NIL) "ALTERNATIVE"
("BOUNDARY" "-=_NextPart_001_0008_01C07734.EBEF7F00") NIL
NIL)("APPLICATION" "MSWORD" ("NAME" "file.doc") NIL NIL "BASE64" 26628 NIL
("ATTACHMENT" ("FILENAME" "file.doc")) NIL) "MIXED" ("BOUNDARY" "--
=_NextPart_000_0007_01C07734.EBEDF860") NIL NIL)
91 OK FETCH completed
```

Here is the message in the RFC 822 format to demonstrate the difference:

```
Message-Id: <000b01c0772c$8b1046e0$950e11ac@libor>
From: "Libor Dostalek" <dostalek@pvt.cz>
To: <dostalek>
Subject: test
Date: Fri, 5 Jan 2001 16:31:14 +0100
Mime-Version: 1.0
Content-Type: multipart/mixed;
        boundary="--=_NextPart_000_0007_01C07734.EBEDF860"

This is a message in MIME format containing several parts.
----=_NextPart_000_0007_01C07734.EBEDF860
Content-Type: multipart/alternative;
        boundary="--=_NextPart_001_0008_01C07734.EBEF7F00"
----=_NextPart_001_0008_01C07734.EBEF7F00
Content-Type: text/plain;
        charset="iso-8859-2"
Content-Transfer-Encoding: quoted-printable

Message text

----=_NextPart_001_0008_01C07734.EBEF7F00
Content-Type: text/html;
        charset="iso-8859-2"
Content-Transfer-Encoding: quoted-printable

<HTML>
<BODY bgColor=3D#ffffff>
<DIV><FONT face=3D"Arial CE" =size=3D2>
Message text
</FONT></DIV></BODY></HTML>

----=_NextPart_001_0008_01C07734.EBEF7F00-

----=_NextPart_000_0007_01C07734.EBEDF860
Content-Type: application/msword;
        name="file.doc"
Content-Transfer-Encoding: base64
Content-Disposition: attachment;
        filename="file.doc"

MS Word document encoded by Base64
----=_NextPart_000_0007_01C07734.EBEDF860-
```

15.7.3.4 STORE

The STORE command serves to change item attributes (see the SELECT command) in a mailbox. It is obviously possible to add, for example, the \Draft attribute. However, the most interesting attribute is \Deleted, which prepares the item for deletion. The EXPUNGE command will then delete the item.

The STORE command has three parameters:

- Item number or range of item numbers in a mailbox where the change of attributes occurs.

- The second parameter is one of the following keywords: FLAGS, +FLAGS or –FLAGS. By using the +FLAGS keyword, we add attributes, by using the –FLAGS word, we remove attributes listed as the third parameter, and by using the word FLAGS, we set item parameters to the parameters listed as the third parameter of the STORE command.

- The last parameter is a list of attributes enclosed in parentheses.

Examples:

```
35 store 9:10 +FLAGS (\Deleted)
* 9 FETCH (FLAGS (\Seen \Deleted))
* 10 FETCH (FLAGS (\Seen \Deleted))
35 OK STORE completed

36 store 10 -FLAGS (\Deleted)
* 10 FETCH (FLAGS (\Seen))
36 OK STORE completed

37 store 9 FLAGS (\Deleted)
* 9 FETCH (FLAGS (\Deleted))
37 OK STORE completed
```

15.7.3.5 EXPUNGE

The EXPUNGE command deletes items in the mailbox marked as \Deleted. There are 11 messages in our mailbox, and messages number 9 and number 10 are marked \Deleted. The EXPUNGE command will cause the following:

```
38 EXPUNGE
* 9 EXPUNGE
* 9 EXPUNGE
* 9 EXISTS
* 0 RECENT
38 OK Expunged 2 messages
```

You will probably think there is a mistake because messages 9 and 10 should have been erased, but message number 9 is erased twice. It works as follows: immediately after the deletion of message number 9, renumbering inside the mailbox will take place because messages inside the mailbox must be numbered by a continuous sequence of numbers. So the original message number 10 is message number 9 now. So the new message number 9 (initially number 10) must be deleted now.

15.7.3.6 CLOSE

The CLOSE command will help us to close the mailbox and switch to the 'Authenticated state' mode.

```
100 close
100 OK CLOSE completed
```

15.8 Mailing Lists

Electronic mail is sent to one or more recipients. The fundamental idea of a mailing list is that we want to send the information to several recipients—mailing list members.

Such request can be met in several ways: manually or by using a helpful application (for example, mailman, listserv, majordomo, etc.), or by the NNTP protocol described in the next chapter.

The procedure for the manual operation would be as follows: We create a group email address within the local mail client. This group address includes all the mailing list members. We send the mail messages to this group address. The problem is that every member of our mailing list must create a group address manually, and every member of the mailing list might forget to add some members to his or her group address. The forgotten addresses may vary from member to member. Group addresses can also be created on servers (called as *aliases*). The disadvantage of this is that the server administrator must maintain this group address manually.

A helpful application automates this. This is a server, and it has its own mailing list email address (let's say it is conference@company.com). Members of the mailing list will then send their contributions to conference@company.com, which will then distribute these contributions to all the mailing list members. Message headers generally include the Reply-To:conference@company.com header field so that recipients wanting to reply will simply select the Reply button in their mail application, and their contribution to the mailing list will be created automatically. Minor problems may arise when you wish to *flame* (verbally attack on the Internet) a particular member. You will realize this is not possible by simply pressing the Reply button, but that you have to copy the sender's name from the From header field and paste it into the To header field, otherwise you will be sending your spicy response to everyone.

Mailing lists are divided into open and closed lists and also into moderated or unmoderated lists. Anyone can become a member of an open mailing list as long by sending a mail to the mailing list mail address (let's say the mailing list address is conference-request@company.com) with a body that contains only one line:

SUBSCRIBE *mailing-list name surname*

You might be wondering why the command does not include your email address. The email address is actually taken from the header field of your email (from the From header field). Similarly you may sign out of the mailing list by using the following command:

UNSUBSCRIBE *mailing-list*

Some mailing lists use the SIGNUP or JOIN command instead of SUBSCRIBE. Therefore, it is advisable that you send an email containing the HELP string before you even start communicating with the mailing list. Then the mailing list will send you instructions including the description of the commands it accepts. If your email address changes, it is necessary to sign out of the mailing list before such a change and log in with your new address. Under these circumstances, if you do not manage to log out in time, you will need to send an email from the old address (for example, via the Telnet program as described in Section 15.4).

One cannot log into a closed mailing list so easily. It is necessary to contact the mailing list administrator, who will add you into the configuration file manually.

An unmoderated mailing list automatically forwards email messages from its members to everyone participating. Conversely, an email message sent to a moderated mailing list is displayed to the mailing list moderator first, who will judge whether the contribution will be distributed further or not.

Helpful applications, for example, mailman, listserv, majordomo, etc., have many functions. The most important one is the email message archiving. The mailing list will save email messages into an archive. Using commands sent by email, one can get to older email messages. By sending the HELP command, the syntax for these commands will be displayed. There will also be commands that we can use to find out about mailing lists provided by a particular server, and we can find out who the members are.

The retrieval of information from servers by using emails was very popular at the time when there were no web servers. To make life easier, current mailing list archives have gates for the HTTP protocol so the information in mailing list archives can be easily accessed. Another type of gate to mailing lists is a gate based on the NNTP protocol. Contributions to such a mailing list are then distributed to one of the NNTP forums.

The basic feature of a mailing list application is the fact that contributions are delivered to mailboxes of mailing list members. So if you are on a vacation for a month, you will not miss any contribution as all of them will be in your mailbox.

16
Forums

Whereas an email message is delivered to a recipient's mailbox, a news message is delivered to an NNTP server (news server) into a newsgroup (discussion forum or simply forum). A user must log in to the news server and must subscribe to some concrete newsgroup and work with news messages in the newsgroup.

News messages are in the newsgroups only for limited time. If the user is on holiday for a long duration, he or she might even miss some news contributions. In the case of email, the user would loose messages if the mailbox gets full.

Support from Operating Systems

While NNTP clients are mostly an integral part of mail clients (for example, Outlook Express), NNTP servers are usually not a part of installation sets of common operating systems. This is why the running of an NNTP server is not so easy, and it is usually the business of big ISPs.

Security

Securing news articles is not so common. It is possible to use the NNTP over SSL/TLS communication (in this case, we talk about NNTPS). News messages can also be hypothetically secured with the help of S/MIME. In practice, only an electronic signature could be used. The encryption of a news message is questionable because it is not clear which public key should be used for encrypting.

User Sector

The usage of news depends on a particular region. In some regions it is a very popular, while in others it is almost not used at all. News has problems, probably even more than emails, with unasked contributions (often very vulgar) that constantly lower its popularity.

Contributions to newsgroups or forums using the NNTP protocol are maintained on news servers (NNTP servers). Users can download a particular contribution and read it. Contributions on servers are maintained for a certain time period (several days) and then deleted; so if you do not get to read it, too bad.

Contributions are maintained on servers, but exchanging them between servers is also possible. This is a very complicated matter that is not managed by any protocol, but only by what is customary. Therefore, the configuration of such a news server is really an art. Configuration of news servers generally falls under the jurisdiction of the same wizards that take care of mail servers. One of the criteria when choosing an Internet provider is the up-to-date state of its news server.

The problem is in the distribution of contributions (news articles) among servers. From the global point of view, there are few significant channels for news. These channels are so huge that they can occupy a transmission bandwidth just for the connectivity of the provider. As news is quite expensive, we should not be surprised if the providers block access to their news servers for the clients of their competitors.

We can have private discussion groups on an intranet, which do not propagate into the Internet. Although the NNTP protocol itself does not support proxies, gates, or tunnels, intranet clients usually do not have a problem getting through the firewall to the provider's news server—there is a generic proxy on the firewall for such purposes, because clients are usually not required to access the Internet via more than one news server.

If you read a contribution in a discussion group, you have two options for replying. You can either reply using the NNTP protocol and send in your own contribution to the discussion group, or you can reply to the author yourself via SMTP (i.e., via email).

Users can either enter discussion groups as anonymous users or they need to be authenticated when entering a discussion group for users only. Authentication is possible by using a name and password or in more sophisticated ways such as secured access via SSL/TLS.

The most interesting feature is the names of discussion groups; they are similar to computer DNS names. For example, there can be a computer named `server.company.com`. The computer name includes the top-level domain (`com`) on the extreme right, then the second-level domain (`company`), and so on. This means every DNS name is read from right to left.

On the other hand, the names of discussion groups are read from left to right. The name `'alt.binaries.pictures.nature'` is read as follows: `'nature'` is a subset of group `'pictures'`, which is a subset of the group `'alt.binaries'`.

The top-level groups are as follows:

- `comp`: Discussion groups about computers
- `net`: Discussion groups about computer networks
- `alt`: Alternative (entertainment groups) like `alt.binaries` (contains binary data)

Individual national groups begin with country identification such as `de` for Germany, `cz` for the Czech Republic, and so on. Large corporations (like Microsoft) also have main groups.

16.1 Message Format

The format of the contribution is specified by RFC 1036. The format is similar to an email message format except that there are even more header fields. Therefore, we will only be interested in header fields that are specific to contributions. They are as follows:

- **Path header field**: This header field is analogous to the email 'Received header' field. While every mail server adds a new 'Received header' field at the beginning of the message, there is only one 'Path header' field. Names of news servers through which the message passes are added from the left and separated with an exclamation mark.
  PATH: news.nextra.cz!newsfeed1.online.no!nextra.com

  This means that the message went from the `nextra.com` server to the `newsfeed1.online.no` server and ended up on the `news.nextra.cz` server.

- **News group header field**: This header field indicates the discussion group for which the messages are intended. For example:
  Newsgroup: alt.binaries.pictures.nature

- **Message-ID header field**: This header field represents a unique identification of the contribution (message).

- **Expires header field**: This header field is an explicit expression indicating the message expiration date. If it is not stated, messages will be erased before or after expiration of a period set by the particular news server administrator.

- **Control header field**: If a message contains this header field, then it is a service message sent between news servers.

- **Approved header field**: This header field is used for moderated discussions and contains information concerning the person who allowed the distribution of the message within a discussion group.

- **Lines header field**: This header field contains the number of lines in the body of the contribution.

16.2 NNTP Protocol

The NNTP protocol is specified in RFC 977. The NNTP protocol server listens at a well-known port 199/TCP.

Once again, as the NNTP protocol commands are in ASCII, it is possible to use the Telnet program (for example, from Windows 2000/XP) to communicate with the news server:

`C:\WINNT>telnet news.provider.com 119`

After a connection is established, the server will introduce itself as follows:

`200 news.provider.com InterNetNews NNRP server INN 2.4.1 ready (posting ok).`

The first line of a reply is always a status line indicating how successful we were. The status line begins with a three-digit status code. The three-digit status codes are similar to those in the FTP and HTTP protocols:

```
100 help text follows
199 debug output
200 server ready - posting allowed
201 server ready - no posting allowed
202 slave status noted
```

```
205 closing connection - goodbye!
211 n f l s group selected
          (n = estimated number of articles in group,
           f = first article number in the group,
           l = last article number in the group,
           s = name of the group.)
215 list of newsgroups follows
220 n <a> article retrieved - head and body follow 221 n <a> article
                            retrieved - head follows
222 n <a> article retrieved - body follows
223 n <a> article retrieved - request text separately 230 list of new
                            articles by message-id follows
231 list of new newsgroups follows
235 article transferred ok
240 article posted ok
335 send article to be transferred.  End with <CR-LF>.<CR-LF>
340 send article to be posted. End with <CR-LF>.<CR-LF>
400 service discontinued
411 no such news group
412 no newsgroup has been selected
420 no current article has been selected
421 no next article in this group
422 no previous article in this group
423 no such article number in this group
430 no such article found
435 article not wanted - do not send it
436 transfer failed - try again later
437 article rejected - do not try again.
440 posting not allowed
441 posting failed
500 command not recognized
501 command syntax error
502 access restriction or permission denied
503 program fault - command not performed
```

The client of the NNTP protocol may find itself in two situations:

- The client is the end user, usually sitting at a PC, who would like to join a particular discussion, i.e., he or she wants to read messages and send contributions to the discussion.

- The client is a news server that wants to obtain new contributions from another server or wants to send new contributions to another server.

16.2.1 End User Communication

At first, the end user needs to find out which groups actually exist; this can be done using the LIST command:

```
LIST
215 Newsgroups in form "group high low flags".
alt.0099 0000000125 0000000125 y
alt.0d 0000009272 0000009269 y
alt.12hr 0000008408 0000008405 y
alt.12step.cuckold.jaime-de-castellvi 0000001787 0000001786 y
alt.12step.pedo.derek-mcmurray 0000001203 0000001202 y
alt.12step.sadomasochism.thewitch-dragon 0000002802 0000002801 y
alt.1d 0000029493 0000029483 y
alt.23is.strange 0000003566 0000003564 y
alt.2600d 0000002358 0000002358 y
alt.2600hz 0000004450 0000004450 y
alt.2d 0000005892 0000005892 y
...
```

The first line of the reply is the status line with the status code 215 (the process was successful, and the group list follows); the following lines list individual groups. Each newsgroup is sent as a line of text in the following format:

```
group last first p
```

where group is the name of the newsgroup, last is the number of the last known article currently in that newsgroup, first is the number of the first article currently in the newsgroup, and p is either y or n indicating whether posting to this newsgroup is allowed (y) or prohibited (n) and m indicates that the group is moderated.

The first group is alt.0099. At this moment the server has one messages for this group. The highest message number in this group is 125 and the lowest one is also 125. The ending letter y indicates that it is possible to add contributions into this group.

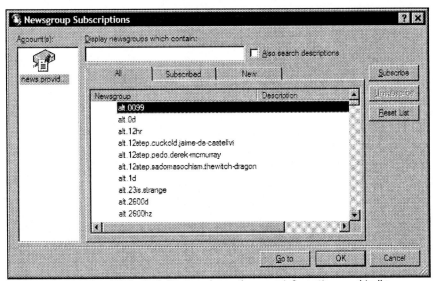

Figure 16.1: MS Outlook Express shows the same information graphically

If the client is interested in, for example, the discussion group called alt12.hr, he or she can use the GROUP command to find out the number of contributions in this group. At the same time, this command will set it up to work with this group.

```
GROUP alt12.hr
211 2 148 149 alt12.hr
```

The server replies with a status line (with status code 211) that it has two messages available for this group (numbers 148 and 149). The STAT command with message number as the message parameter will allow us to work with message number 148 in the alt12.hr group:

```
STAT 148
223 148 <91819$9mv$1@news.inet.tele.dk> status
```

After the status code (223), the STAT command returns the number of the contribution (148) and its identification in angular brackets. Now, the client may download the whole message using the ARTICLE command, the header using the HEAD command, and the message body using the BODY command.

```
ARTICLE
220 148 <918i9h$9mv$1@news.inet.tele.dk> article
Path: news.nextra.cz!newsfeed1.online.no!nextra.com
   !newsfeed.nettuno.it!enews.sgi.com
   !news.tele.dk!Tele.Dk.POSTED!not-for-mail
From: "Karel Hroch" <karel.hroch@cmail.com>
Newsgroups: alt12.hr
Subject: Some Subject
Date: Wed, 13 Dec 2000 20:22:13 +0100
Organization: Posted Courtesy of Tele Danmark
Lines: 13
Message-ID: <918i9h$9mv$1@news.inet.tele.dk>
NNTP-Posting-Host: p016.as-1006.contactel.com

News text
```

If the client wants to send a contribution to the discussion group, he or she will use the POST command (the message is ended with a period on a new line). There are special testing discussion groups for testing messages (for example, `alt.test`, `cz.test`, etc.) in order not to bother the users of *real* discussion groups. So we will send the contribution to the `cz.test` testing group:

```
POST
From: "Libor Dostalek" <dostalek@siemens.com>
Newsgroups: alt.test
Subject: TEST
Date: Fri, 20 Jan 2006 19:48:01 +0100
Organization: Cesnet, Czech NREN Operator
Lines: 3
Message-ID: <937kje$1fq7$2@news.cesnet.cz>

Test from Libor
.
340 Ok
240 Article posted
```

This time instead of using the Telnet program, we will use MS Outlook Express to look at the results:

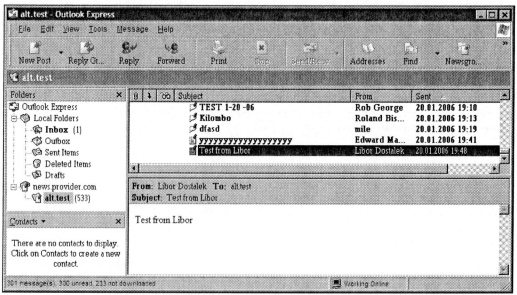

Figure 16.2: The contribution displayed by the MS Outlook Express application

16.2.2 Communication Among Servers

As far as the TCP protocol is concerned, this is once again a client-server communication. Again, there can be two scenarios:

- The NNTP server (as a TCP client) wants to obtain new groups (NEWGROUPS command) and new contributions (NEWNEWS command).

- The NNTP server (as a TCP client) wants to offer new contributions to the other party (IHAVE command).

New forums (new news groups) on the NNTP server is possible to learn with the help of NEWGROUPS command. The NEWGROUPS command has two mandatory parameters: date (in the YYMMDD format) and time (in the HHMMSS format). The question is, does the remote NNTP server have anything new since the specified date (in the first parameter in YYMMDD format) and time (in the second parameter in the HHMMSS format).

```
NEWGROUPS 060101 120000
231 New newsgroups follow.
free.it.ales.arti.cartoni 0 1 y
.
```

Since the listed time, the server has got one new forum free.it.ales.arti.cartoni (the report is similar to the one used in the LIST command).

New contributions (news articles) posted or received by the specified news group since the specified date will be listed with the help of NEWNEWS command. The first parameter of the NEWNEWS command is the name of the discussion group whose contributions are being requested. Other parameters are date and time.

Newsgroup name containing an asterisk (*) may be specified to broaden the article search to some or all newsgroups. The asterisk will be extended to match any part of a newsgroup name. The following example asks for all new contributions (news articles) for the main news group cz.

```
NEWNEWS cz.* 060101 200000
230 New news follows
<9907.32994-27222-512060803-978805386@seznam.cz>
<A05CF6DED9CDD41193EA0008C724357801AA00@exchange.diamo.cz>
937kje$1fq7$2@news.nextra.cz          ...
.
```

The server returns the unique identification of a new article. New articles can be downloaded using the ARTICLE command with the unique article identification parameter (in angular brackets):

```
ARTICLE <3A5735AB.B4F794B5@regionet.cz>
```

If we want to offer a contribution to another party, we can use the IHAVE command with the article identification parameter (in angular brackets). The other party will find out whether they have such an article and if not, will request this article.

```
IHAVE <937kje$1fq7$3@news.nextra.cz>
335 News to me!  <CRLF.CRLF> to end.
  sends news
.
235 Article transferred successfully.  Thanks.
```

In reality, news servers are actually configured to communicate only with selected news servers:

```
IHAVE <937kje$1fq7$3@news.nextra.cz>
480 Transfer permission denied
```

16.2.3 Session Termination

The NNTP protocol session is terminated using the QUIT command.

17

Lightweight Directory Access Protocol

Directory Access Protocol (DAP) was established by the **International Telecommunication Union (ITU)** in the X.500 series that looked for an electronic analog of a telephone directory book. DAP protocol was chosen for searching electronic directories, but it was too complicated for Internet implementation. Therefore, people dealing with the Internet simplified it and developed a new protocol. For naming the new protocol, they simply added the word 'Lightweight' at the beginning of DAP.

The architecture is simple: On the server, there is a particular directory (database), and an LDAP server that enables clients to access the database through the LDAP protocol.

Support from Operating Systems
Most email clients contain an "Address book" tool that can access LDAP servers. At present, most server distributions contain an LDAP server (for example, Active Directory in Windows 2000/2003).

Security
Similar to HTTP, LDAP also supports various authentication methods. LDAP over SSL/TLS, called LDAPS, is also common.

User Sector
At present, many users use LDAP, but most of them probably do not even know that their computer uses this protocol.

17.1 Protocol Principle

The LDAP is of the client-server protocol type. The client connects to the server (a well-known port is 389/TCP) and then sends requests in **Protocol Data Units (PDU)** that have ASN.1 syntax and are encoded in BER (Basic Encoding Rules). The server accepts the request, performs the requested operation, and returns results. Communication between the server and the client need not be synchronous, and the client and the server must be able to work in asynchronous mode (for example, the client does not have to wait for a reply for a sent request before sending further requests). The processing of a pending request can be terminated by the abandon command. The LDAP protocol also allows client authentication.

The communication protocols described earlier were communicating in a text form. This is why we have been able to simulate the communication with the help of the Telnet program. In contrast, the LDAP's protocol data units are binary (BER encoded). Hence for LDAP, the appropriate LDAP clients must be used.

17.2 Data Model of LDAP Directory

The **Directory Information Tree (DIT)** is the basic data structure with which the LDAP protocol works. The DIT may be distributed over more than one physical server. Distribution over physical servers is carried out by means of referrals. For example, if we are searching for a record on another server, the record will contain a referral item that contains one or more LDAP URLs with a link to the particular subtree.

A tree is made up of entries. Every entry has an assigned set of named attributes. Such named attributes may be, for example, country (c), organization (o), common/canonical name (cn). An entry in an LDAP tree usually describes an object in the real world (for example, a company, a person, a printer, a computer, or a user group). As an example, we will use an entry for a person:

- Surname (sn): Rasek
- Canonical name (cn): Ludek Rasek
- Telephone (telephoneNumber): 345

Every entry attribute has its own name and value. Some attributes within an entry have a privileged position and their value differentiates the entry from other entries on the same tree level. A group of these *special* attributes forms the **Relative Distinguished Name (RDN)**. By using the RDN, we can choose one entry from all those at the same tree level.

Figure 17.1 shows the tree representing a company's staff. They are at the same tree level, and we can distinguish among them (within the scope of LDAP) by giving everyone attribute(s). The attributes that form the RDN are determined during creation of the entry. The entries shown in Figure 17.1 are of the same type, but they can still have different attributes forming the RDN. The figure shows the entries of the 'person' group, which has mandatory attributes like sn and cn as well as optional attributes like telephoneNumber, description, etc.

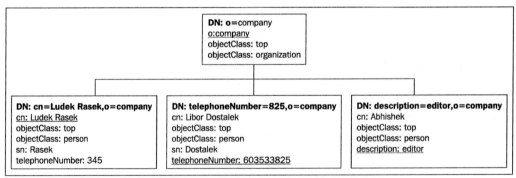

Figure 17.1: Tree structure formed by RDN

In Figure 17.1, the entry for a person named Ludek Rasek contains only one unique attribute, the canonical name (cn), shown as a bold font in the figure. By using this name, we can distinguish this entry from others (i.e., from other colleagues in the same section).

There could also be another person named Ludek Rasek in the company, who works in another department. If so, there are two RDN entries cn=Ludek Rasek within the tree, but these are in different places. In order to distinguish between these entries, every entry is assigned a distinguished name (DN). This name determines the entry's position in the tree, and it is formed by concatenating the RDN entries by which we would get from the tree root to the desired entry. Therefore, our two colleagues, both named "Ludek Rasek" can be distinguished as follows (different parts of DN are highlighted in italics):

- Ludek Rasek (consultant):
  - DN (with full attribute names): canonical name=Ludek Rasek, *organizationalUnit=consulting department*, organization=company
  - DN (shortened names): cn=Ludek Rasek, *ou=consulting department*, o=company
- Ludek Rasek (accountant):
  - DN (with full attribute names): canonical name=Ludek Rasek, *organizationalUnit=accounting department*, organization=company
  - DN (shortened names): cn=Ludek Rasek, *ou=accounting department*, o=company

The following figure shows a part of the tree (only attributes of the RDN are shown):

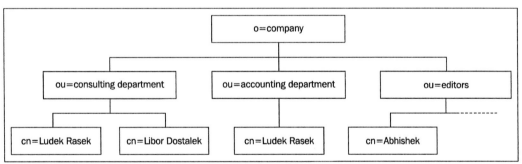

Figure 17.2: Part of the tree

The set of entries within one subtree (with a common root) administered by one or more servers is called as the **naming context**. The root of the whole DIT is formed by the DSE entry (DSE is an abbreviation of DSA Specific Entry, where DSA is an X.500 term for the directory server). There is information within the DSE entry about the LDAP server(s) and the available administered contexts. Figure 17.2 shows a simple example of a data structure administered by an LDAP server. Within a server, there is only one DSE entry.

Figure 17.3 shows another simple example of a data structure administered by an LDAP server. There are three independent trees. A DN within any such tree always has a common suffix. A list of naming contexts administered by the server can be retrieved from the DSE entry (three namingContext attributes are shown inside the DSE box in Figure 17.3).

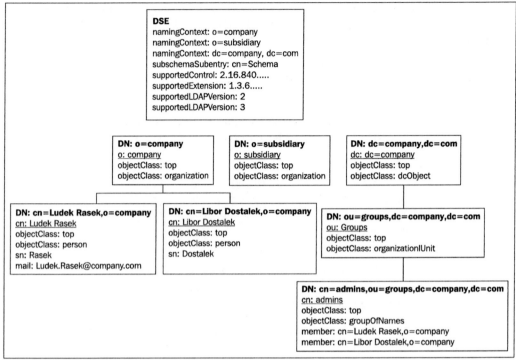

Figure 17.3: An example of a DIT with three contexts including a DSE entry

An entry is formed by a collection of attributes. Every attribute is of a specific type. The type is identified by a short name (for example, mail) and an object identifier (OID). The attribute type is given by:

- The possibility of multiple occurrences of an attribute within one entry
- The possible values of the attribute
- The way of using the attribute value

For example, the mail attribute may include an IA5 string that is not case sensitive. It does not differentiate between font sizes and can occur more than once in one entry.

A DIT contains a schema. A schema is a set of rules that describe which attribute types may be used within a DIT, which entry classes may be used, and which properties the entry classes should have.

Every entry has a class (objectClass) assigned. An entry class determines which attributes may be assigned to an entry. Every entry may have one or more assigned classes. The assignment of classes to entries is carried out with the presence of one or more attributes of the objectClass type. Every entry is assigned at least one attribute of the objectClass type. Entry classes (objectClass) are arranged within a specific hierarchy. If an entry is assigned a specific class, it will automatically obtain the parent's classes as well.

Some of the attributes may be assigned for processing purposes on a particular LDAP server. Such attributes are called as *operational*. Operational attributes may be used, for example, to record access authorizations to an item and its attributes. Operational attributes are not returned as the results of regular search operations unless they are specifically required in the request parameters. The server may create operational attributes automatically and keep information such as the author's name (creatorsName), time of creation (createTimestamp), time of modification (modifyTimestamp), description of entry type (subschemaSubentry), etc.

An LDAP server has to maintain its LDAP schema in such a way as to make it accessible to clients. Every entry in a DIT has an operational subschemaSubentry attribute. This attribute contains the entry's DN—the subentry subschema—wherein it is possible to find all the supported entry classes and all the supported attributes. The subschemaSubentry entry has the following features:

- It contains the cn attribute that is used to form the entry's DN.
- It contains the objectClass attribute with at least two values: top and subschema.
- It contains objectClasses attributes; the values describe the available entry classes.
- It contains attributeClasses attributes; the values describe all the supported attribute types.

There is a specific type of inquiry prescribed for searching items of the subschema entry type (see search examples).

Schemas are described using a special syntax in order to enable their automatic download into LDAP servers and their automatic control. This schema description includes description of entry classes (objectClass), attributes, syntaxes, and comparison rules.

The example below shows the definition of inetOrgPerson class including all higher classes (organisationalPerson, person, etc.). The inetOrgPerson class is defined in RFC 2798.

```
( 2.5.6.6
    NAME 'person'
    SUP top
    STRUCTURAL
    MUST ( sn $ cn )
    MAY (
      userPassword $ telephoneNumber $ seeAlso $ description
    )
)
( 2.5.6.7
    NAME 'organizationalPerson'
    SUP person
    STRUCTURAL
    MAY ( title $ x121Address $ registeredAddress $
      destinationIndicator $
      preferredDeliveryMethod $ telexNumber $ teletexTerminalIdentifier $
      telephoneNumber $ internationaliSDNNumber $
      facsimileTelephoneNumber $
      street $ postOfficeBox $ postalCode $ postalAddress $
      physicalDeliveryOfficeName $ ou $ st $ l
    )
)
( 2.16.840.1.113730.3.2.2
    NAME 'inetOrgPerson'
```

```
SUP organizationalPerson
STRUCTURAL
MAY (
    audio $ businessCategory $ carLicense $ departmentNumber $
    displayName $ employeeNumber $ employeeType $ givenName $
    homePhone $ homePostalAddress $ initials $ jpegPhoto $
    labeledURI $ mail $ manager $ mobile $ o $ pager $
    photo $ roomNumber $ secretary $ uid $ userCertificate $
    x500uniqueIdentifier $ preferredLanguage $
    userSMIMECertificate $ userPKCS12
)
)
```

The class definition contains the following items: class name (NAME), parent class (SUP), structure description (STRUCTURAL), mandatory (MUST), and optional (MAY) attributes.

In the case of attributes, the definition specifies the attribute name (NAME), description of its meaning (DESC), the comparison rule to be used for the equality test (EQUALITY), the rule for the substring equality test (SUB-STR), the uniqueness setting of this attribute (SINGLE VALUE), and specification of the format in which the attribute is transferred in LDAP messages and whether binary transfer is required (SYNTAX):

```
( 2.16.840.1.113730.3.1.3
        NAME 'employeeNumber'
        DESC 'numerically identifies an employee within an organization'
        EQUALITY caseIgnoreMatch
        SUBSTR caseIgnoreSubstringsMatch
        SYNTAX 1.3.6.1.4.1.1466.115.121.1.15
        SINGLE-VALUE
)
```

17.3 LDAP Protocol Data Units

Protocol data units are described using the ASN.1 syntax, and they are transferred using the BER coding subset. LDAP includes the following types of operations (each of them has defined inquiry and reply formats):

- bind: Allows authentication information to be exchanged between a client and a server (i.e., user authentication and establishing the session).

- unbind: Termination of the user's session.

- search: Operation for searching in the DIT. Within a reply, the client receives one of the following types: entry (convenient item), reference to another server, and end of inquiry processing.

- modify: Modification of an entry.

- add: Adds new entry.

- del: Deletes an entry.

- modifyDN: Changes entry's DN (name) enabling *moving* the entry within the DIT.

- compare: Testing whether the entry with a specific DN has the required value of a specific attribute.

- abandon: Termination of a currently running operation.

- **extended**: Enables transfer of various messages between a client and a server. These are encoded into strings; therefore, this is a way of proprietary extension using a standard methodology.

Every protocol unit of a request may be supplemented with additional information called **controls** that may transfer nonstandard extension of the LDAP protocol in a standard methodology. If the server does not understand such extensions, it may ignore them.

We will describe the most frequently used operation, i.e., searching within the LDAP protocol in detail.

17.3.1 The Search Operation

The search operation is the most frequent operation run on the LDAP tree. Searching is the only way of obtaining information from a DIT using the LDAP protocol. The search operation is governed by the following parameters:

- Base: This means the base of the DN entry from which the search begins. The search always runs through the base subclasses with the scope determined by another parameter.
- Scope: This means the scope of a search with respect to the base item. There are three kinds of searches:
  - o Base: This serves for searching the attributes within one entry (see Figure 17.4).
  - o One level: This is used for searching in direct subclasses of the base entry (see Figure 17.5).
  - o Subtree: A search is conducted in the entire subtree of the base entry. If there is a naming context entered as the base entry, then the entire naming context will be searched (see Figure 17.6).
- Handling of referrals (links): How alias objects are to be handled while searching. It may contain the following options:
  - o Do not follow links: The search does not follow the links to other servers automatically.
  - o Follow during search: The links are followed if they are present in the search result (subclass of the base search object).
  - o Always follow: Links will be always followed.
- Time limit: This parameter specifies a time limit for a search period.
- Size limit: The size limit for returned results (number of entries).
- Type only: Whether the result will contain attribute types or values.
- Filter: Specifies the criteria for an entry selection (see Section 17.3.1.1)
- List of attributes: Determines which entry attributes specified by the filter will be contained in the result.

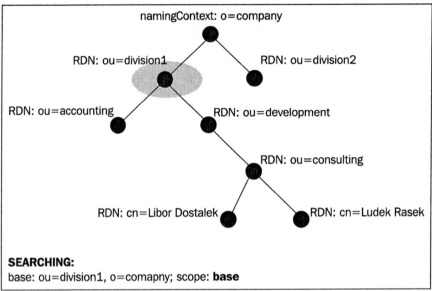

Figure 17.4: Searching within the base scope

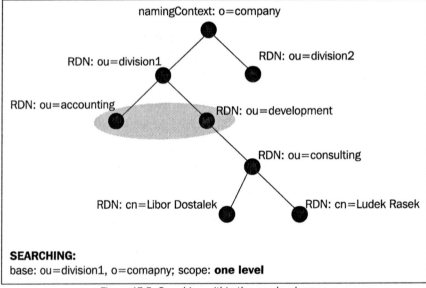

Figure 17.5: Searching within the one-level scope

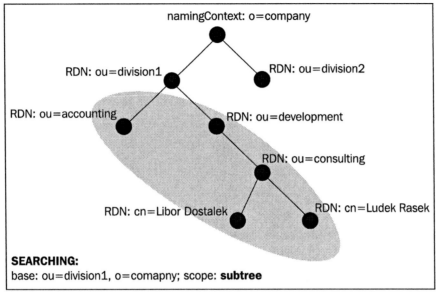

SEARCHING:
base: ou=division1, o=comapny; scope: **subtree**

Figure 17.6: Searching within the subtree scope

The previous figures show various ranges for a search in the LDAP tree. The search shown in the figures originates from the base node with a unique name, DN: ou=division1, o=company. A search within the base scope returns results only in the form of a base node attribute. A search within the one level scope returns only entries that are one level below the search base node. A search within the subtree scope completely searches the whole subtree below the base node.

17.3.1.1 Filters

Filters specify the conditions with which an entry should comply in order to be returned in a search result. A filter is defined using logic operators AND (&), OR (|), NOT (!), the matching rules for equality (=), greater than (>=), lesser than (<=), the presence of an attribute (=*), substring (comparison string contains * as a wildcard), and approximate comparison (=~). The matching rules are extensible, enabling the use of implementation-dependent rules.

Filters have an exactly defined form. Matching rules and logic operators are grouped within parentheses. Parentheses also determine the filter evaluation priorities. The following table shows several examples:

Base	Scope	Filter	Attribute	Description
""	base	(objectClass=*)	namingContext	A special form of query for selection of the DSE and its parameters (in this case, namingContext attribute).
dn:cn=name, dc company, dc=com	base	(objectClass= subschema)		A special form of query for schema referral; describes the entry specified by query base.

Base	Range	Filter	Attribute	Description
o=sales, dc=company, dc=com	subtree	(cn=Alice)	cn,mail	This filter finds an entry with cn=Alice within the entire subtree of a sales department.
o=sales, dc=company, dc=com	one level	(objectClass=*)	dn	A query for retrieving all DN entries on one subtree level, which is typically used in LDAP browsers on expanding the subtree.

Table 17.1: Filters

Some filters describe special types of searches; they are as follows:

- To search with an empty base, the base scope, the `objectClass=*` filter, and a list of attributes in which we are interested, returns the attributes of a DSE entry.
- To search with the base set for a specific entry, the base scope, and the `objectClass=subschema` filter, results in a link to a schema describing that entry.

17.3.2 Further Operations with Entries

Entries in an LDAP tree may be created, deleted, modified, moved (their DN being modified), and compared. All these modifications can be written into an LDIF file (see Section 17.6).

17.3.2.1 The Add Operation

The add operation will create entries in a tree. To create an entry, the user has to enter:

- DN: A unique name of the entry being created
- A list of attributes of the entry being created

A unique name of the created entry is formed by RDNs concatenated in a string so they describe the route through the tree from the root to the parent entry. During the entry creation, the LDAP server will first check whether all DN items comply with the existing entries. After this check, the server is able to determine which part of the DN forms the RDN of the created entry. A pair, namely, the name and the value of the attribute(s), forms this RDN of the created entry.

These attributes that make up the RDN are present in a list of attributes belonging to the created entry. Additionally, the list of attributes must include all the required attributes and also the `objectClass` attribute(s). The list of attributes must not contain the operational attributes that will be added by the server automatically.

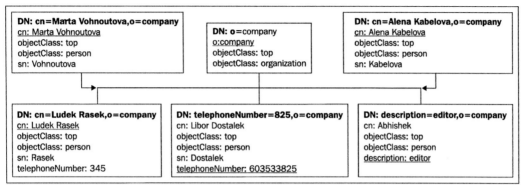

Figure 17.7: Examples of entry creation

17.3.2.2 The Modify Operation

Using this operation, we can modify the set of assigned attributes and their values within an entry. The parameters of this operation are:

- DN: This specifies which entry is to be modified.

- List of modifications: This specifies what should be done with a given entry. The list item always contains a flag of the modification method, the attribute name, and the value set of an attribute.

    The list of modifications is a sequence of particular modifications performed. Either the whole sequence of changes is performed or no changes are performed at all. The list of modifications contains the following types of items:

    - Delete attribute value: This deletes the particular attribute value. If a value is not entered in the request, all attribute values will be deleted (the attribute will disappear from the entry). If all the attribute values are entered—the attribute will also be removed from the entry.
    - Add attribute value: This adds the entered attribute value into the entry if the required attribute is not in the entry yet.
    - Replace attribute value: This replaces all the old values with new ones from the request. If the attribute does not exist, it will be created. If a replacement with an empty value is required, the attribute will be removed from the entry.

The modify operation cannot be used to change attributes forming the RDN.

17.3.2.3 The Delete Operation

Using this operation, we can remove an entry from a tree. The only parameter of this operation is the entry's DN. This operation can only be used to remove branches from a tree (entries without any subclasses). Then removal of a subtree has to be carried out in a client program by a recursive algorithm.

17.3.2.4 The Modify DN Operation

By using this operation, we can change the DN of an entry and move it within a tree. Parameters for this operation are:

- DN: This specifies the entry.
- New RDN: This means the new value of the relative name. This is used for changing the identification among "*siblings*".
- Delete old RDN: This states whether the values of attributes forming the old RDN should remain in the entry or should be deleted.
- New superior: This is an optional parameter which, if present, contains the DN of the new parent of the entry being renamed.

17.3.2.5 The Compare Operation

This operation can be used to compare the value of an attribute from a request with the value of an attribute saved on a server. Its typical utilization is to verify a password, where the server might allow comparison, but not reading of the password attributes.

Parameters of this operation are as follows:

- DN: This specifies the name of the entry to be compared with.
- Attribute name value: This specifies the attribute and the value to compared it with.

17.4 Server Programs

The following is a list of three examples of servers available for testing and utilization of LDAP:

- OpenLDAP (http://www.openldap.org/): An open source project implementing the server as well as the LPADv3 client and client library. OpenLDAP servers can be configured as a distributed network of mutually cooperating LDAP servers administrating one DIT. The OpenLDAP supports replication in a single-master mode and multi-master mode.
- Sun Java System Directory Server (see http://www.sun.com/).
- Windows 2000/2003 Server: As a part of the server, the Active Directory is installed and the AD native interface is LDAP. AD provides a distributed system with servers maintaining the DIT in a multi-master model.

17.5 Client Programs

The following are the examples of a client program.

17.5.1 The LDAP Browser

The LDAP browser is an LDAP client on the Java (J2SE) platform built on Java Naming and Directory Services, and it is portable and usable on a whole range of platforms supporting Java (functions on Linux and Windows with JRE1.3.1). This program works smoothly with an LDAPv3 directory by using anonymous and non-anonymous access and access using SSL. Its functions are carried out by an intuitive user interface that is similar to Windows Explorer (for example, it supports drag-and-drop). It enables easy modification, addition, and deletion of entries. It contains several editors for binary attributes (password, X.509 certificate, etc.).

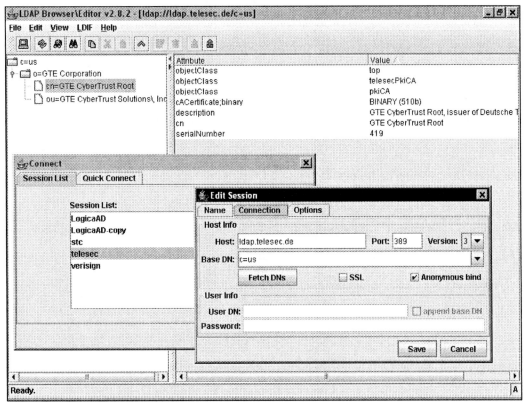

Figure 17.8: A Java LDAP browser

17.5.2 The OpenLDAP Client

An OpenLDPA client is a client part of the OpenLDAP package distributed under the GPL license. It contains a package of utilities to carry out all of the LDAP operations with complete control from the command line. The inputs and outputs of the utilities may be in an LDIF format (see Section 17.6).

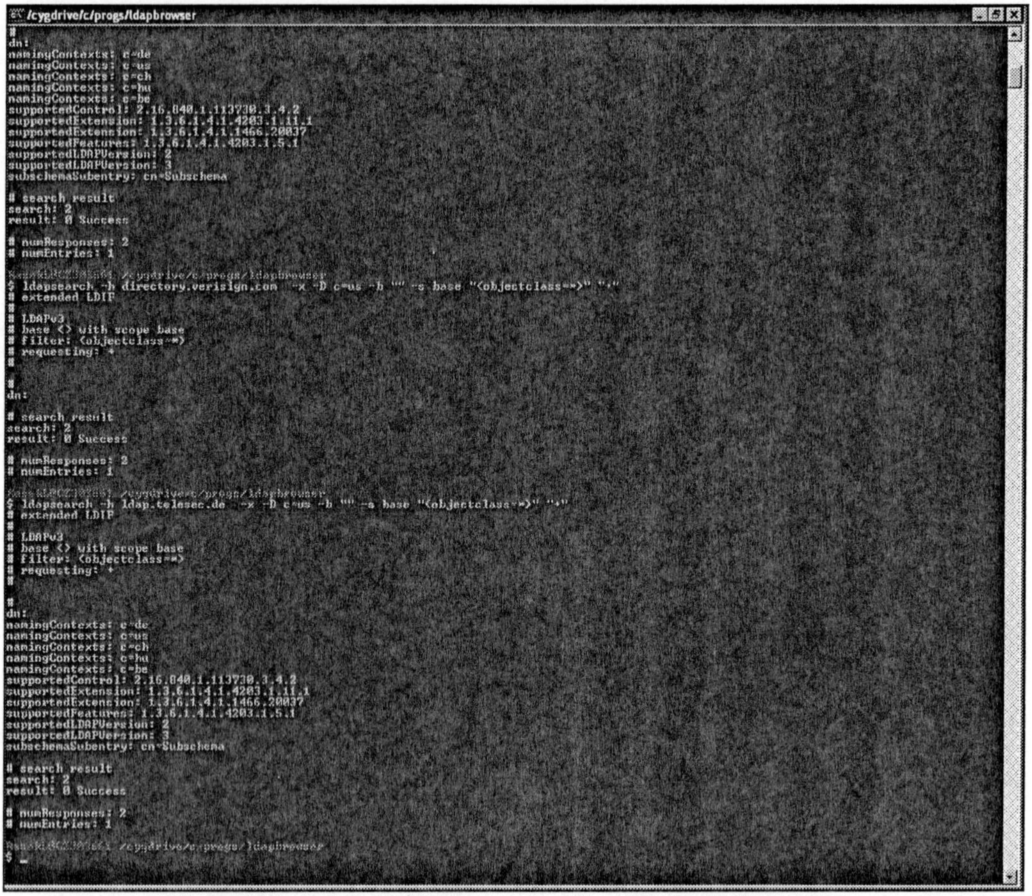

Figure 17.9: An OpenLDAP client command-line utility for LDAP searching

17.5.3 ADSIedit

ADSIedit is available on the installation CD of Microsoft Windows 2003 server. It is a snap-in module for Microsoft Management Console (MMC). ADSIedit is a helpful tool for Active Directory administration because it acts as a low-level editor for Active Diectory using LDAP.

17.5.4 MS Outlook Express and MS Outlook

MS Outlook Express and MS Outlook enable utilization of LDAP as an external source for a directory. Unfortunately, they do not have extensive search ability; they search by only a few attributes.

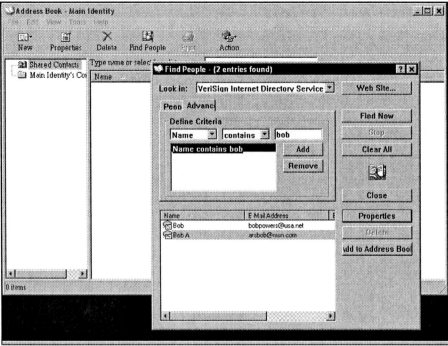

Figure 17.10: The Find People option in the MS Outlook program

17.6 Lightweight Directory Interchange Format

Lightweight Directory Interchange Format (**LDIF**) is a specification of the data format for information exchange between LDAP systems. This format was originally used only for the description of entries in a directory. Now in its current form (defined in RFC 2849), it can also serve for transferring *change-related* information among LDAP servers. There is 1:1 mapping between the operations of the LDAP protocol and types of entries in LDIF files.

An LDIF file is formed by entries specifying particular changes. The file can contain a set of entries to import, or it can contain change-related entries. The basic form of an import entry is as follows:

```
dn: <distinguished name>
   <attrdesc>: <attrvalue>
   <attrdesc>: <attrvalue>
   <attrdesc>:: <base64-encoded-value>
   <attrdesc>:< <URL>
```

The first line of this entry contains the specification of its DN and is followed by attribute values. An attribute value may be entered in three ways:

- Text: The value is a regular text string encoded using UTF-8. The attribute name is separated from the data by a colon (:).

- Data: The value comprises data (binary and text) encoded by Base64. In this case, the attribute name is separated from the data by two colons (::).

- External URL: Data is located in an external source and is specified by a URL. In this case, the attribute name is separated from the URL specification by :<.

Individual entry items are on separate lines. If the data runs on to more than one line, then every consecutive line containing data begins with a space.

All entries are mutually separated with empty lines. Lines beginning with # are ignored (comments).

A
CISCO Routers

It is very important that all network administrators know at least the basics of working with CISCO routers since CISCO is considered the dominant company in this area. Routers of some other manufacturers and also daemon GNU Zebra (http://www.zebra.org/) use similar configuration languages to that which CISCO uses. In this book, we provided examples of not only the configuration of operating systems such as UNIX and Windows, but also of the CISCO configuration language.

CISCO specializes especially in network active elements (boxes) ranging from switches to firewalls. These boxes interest us mostly because of their similar configuration language, and the basics of these boxes are described in this appendix. We will focus exclusively on router configuration. To find out more, visit http://www.cisco.com/ where you can find thousands of pages of complete documentation describing both the hardware and the IOS.

CISCO routers are dedicated boxes that attend to only one thing—routing. They run a specialized operating system called **Internetwork Operating System (IOS)**. So we will actually look at the IOS configuration. Whether the IOS is run on a tiny box or within an expensive appliance will be of little importance.

The IOS is available in many different versions. However, the problem is, which protocols should be supported by the IOS on our router (there are even IOSs with firewalls). The more protocols the chosen IOS release supports, the more memory it will require, which might be a problem, especially for older boxes. From an economic point of view, we will also be interested in the price that, understandably, increases with the increasing number of protocols supported by that particular version. So if we want to use some exotic network protocols, we have to pay a few dollars more not only for the memory, but also for the operating system.

Before buying a router, we should decide on:

1. Buying the hardware box
   o The box should have the appropriate number of network interface types that we need (synchronous interfaces, asynchronous interfaces, Ethernet network interfaces and so on).
   o The box should provide good performance and should have sufficient memory.
   o We have to buy the proper cables.
2. Buying the right version of the IOS operating system

For the purposes of this appendix, I have borrowed a CISCO 801 box and CISCO 1841. Models of the 800 series are low cost CISCO routers embedded in plastic boxes. Other series of CISCO routers (1800 series, 2800 series, 3800 series, etc.) are modular. It is possible to upgrade the router with additional interface cards, memory cards, etc. Just as children have Lego construction kits, network administrators have modular CISCO routers.

The choice of these models is not a coincidence (I could not get a different one), but the choice of the box is not really an issue, since from the point of view of this book, the differences among them are negligible.

Whatever the type of router that falls into your hands, take a careful look at it, especially at the back part with connectors. This is how you find out what type of interface the router has. Other parts of the router are not that important.

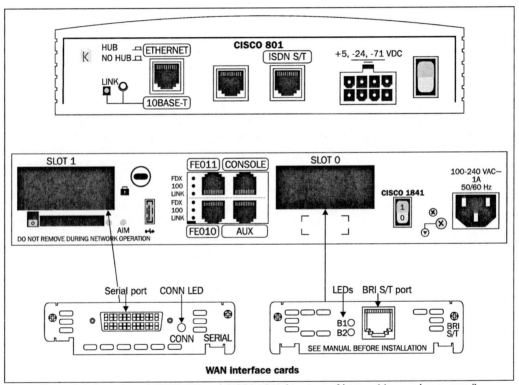

Figure A.1: Rear view of CISCO 801 and CISCO 1841 (courtesy of http://www.cisco.com/)

Not taking into account the power source, all CISCO routers contain similar connectors on their back part. Let's take the CISCO 801 as an example. So going from left to right, the connectors are as follows:

- **An RJ-45 connector** for Ethernet at 10 MHz frequency.
- **An RJ-45 connector for console connection.** This connecter has the V.24 (RS 232) interface. For our purposes, this connector will be the most important of them all.
- **A port for WAN interface cards.** Model CISCO 801 has only one embedded WAN port:
  - **The RJ-45 connector for ISDN Basic Rate (the S/T interface)**: It is important not to forget that the CISCO 802 model is also available, and it has a U interface and an integrated NT-1 appliance. I would like to stress here that it is necessary to talk to your ISDN provider about which interface type they use, so that you save yourself from doing some complicated work later. It is not true that if you connect a router to a U interface, then you are unable to connect other ISDN appliances (for example, an ISDN telephone), since the router of an integrated NT-1 appliance contains an S/T interface enabling it to connect to other ISDN appliances.

Different CISCO router types also use other interfaces such as:

- **An RJ-45 connector for auxiliary port (AUX)**. This is usually used for remote administration. It is a classic asynchronous port allowing hardware data flow control. A modem can be connected to this port as well. A console, by its nature, is a similar port, though it is primarily aimed at the local configuration of the router (not via modem). The main difference between the console and the auxiliary port is that the auxiliary port supports flow control, whereas the console port does not.
- **The WAN ports**: The WAN ports are usually located on changeable CISCO interface cards:
  - Universal serial interface can be found on all modular CISCO routers (Figure A.1 shows an example of a serial interface card). Both synchronous and asynchronous lines can be connected using this port. It is quite likely that it is used for all protocols in serial lines (HDLC, PPP, Frame Relay, etc.) up to 2 Mbps. In the case of CISCO routers, the WAN port uses a specific interface—DB-60—on the physical layer. The choice of a suitable cable then determines a specific protocol on the physical layer that the router will use for communication. So, if we want to communicate by using, for example the V.35 protocol, we have to buy a special cable that has one DB-60 connector on the router side and the V.35 connector on the other side.
  - ISDN card.
  - Interfaces for different types of **Local Area Network (LAN)**, especially interfaces for Fast Ethernet and Gigabit Ethernet.
- **Voice interface cards** and so on.

A.1 Interface Identification

CISCO routers have specific names for individual interface types, for example, **Ethernet** for an Ethernet interface or **Serial** for a serial interface. The same applies to lines. **Console** or simply **con** used for a console (marked sometimes as CTY), **aux** for auxiliary asynchronous interface, **tty** for asynchronous lines, and we should not forget to mention **vty** for network terminals (or pseudo terminals, if you wish to use the UNIX terminology) to which Telnet will be connected via the network.

Since the router has several interfaces, we always have to specify not only an interface's name, but also its number that is set by the hardware configuration. For example, if we have two serial interfaces, then one will be labeled as **Serial 0** and the other as **Serial 1**. Knowing which one is 0 and which one is 1 also depends on the hardware configuration (more information can be found in the hardware manual). We should not forget to include the number even if the box has just one interface of that kind. For this reason, we have to include the number also when specifying a unique console—con 0.

In the case of large routers that are constructed of individual modules, with each of them having a number of ports, the numbering gets more difficult. In this case, the addressing of a particular port consists of two parts: the number of a slot in which the module is inserted and the number of a particular port within the concrete module. These two numbers are separated by a slash. If we include a module with two Ethernet interfaces into Slot 0, then the box will have, among other things, the interfaces Ethernet 0/0 and Ethernet 0/1.

The same applies to network lines labeled as 'vty'. Theoretically, an unlimited number of users can log in via a network using Telnet. They will use the lines in the order they log in, for example, 'vty 0', 'vty 1', and so on. CISCO routers enable you to configure several lines. In other words, theoretically several users can be logged in at the same time. Here the term *logged in* means logged into the IOS system. This number, for example, does not limit the number of people using PPP protocol.

A.2 Cables

It gets a whole lot more complicated when it comes to cables used with CISCO routers. Therefore, when buying a router, it is advisable to discuss with the seller the possibility of changing the supplied cables for different ones, if we find out that we need a different type.

There were no problems while connecting the LAN. I had got the cables from the building administrator who was in charge of structured cabling. I was interested in only two interface types—the WAN and console.

The most often used WAN port is the universal synchronous-asynchronous serial interface with the CISCO DB-60 connector. By choosing an appropriate cable, we will also choose a particular physical layer protocol that will be used by the router for communication. If you intend to use the V.35 protocol, you have to get a cable that has a DB-60 connector on the router side and a V.35 interface on the modem side.

The V.35 interface might be the DTE or the DCE (see Figure 3.3 in Chapter 3). The DTE is usually an end computer, a terminal, or a router and the DCE is usually a modem. Since I will use synchronous transfer, it is important to set the appropriate time source. CISCO routers implicitly require that the DCE be the time source (see Figure 3.2 in Chapter 3).

I found out later that I would also need to try direct communication between two routers and to do this I borrowed another router. When interconnecting both routers via serial lines, I encountered an interesting problem. The routers were lying next to each other without modems. For this reason, I had to directly interconnect the two CISCO routers using the V.35 interface. So I had to create a null modem. Figure 3.5 in Chapter 3 shows how to connect the null modem for the V.24 (RS 232) interface.

Analogously, it is possible to create a null modem for the V.35 interface by crossing the transmitter with the receiver (and the control signal correspondingly). CISCO deals with such interconnection by connecting one router to a V.35 DTE cable and the other to a V.35 DCE. Since one of the cables is male (DTE) and the other female (DCE), it is possible to connect them, thus creating the null modem. It results in synchronized communication, so one party will have to be the time source, while the other will have to follow the first one. (Tip: The `clock` command will have to be added to the DCE configuration.)

A.3 Memory

CISCO routers usually have three types of memory:

1. **RAM**: This is usually used by the operating system (the running operating system is located there). The content of RAM is erased when the router is shut down or there is a power outage. This memory type is usually labeled as `system` in commands.

2. **FLASH**: This memory type is not erased when a power outage occurs. It stores the operating system that is transferred into RAM when the router is switched on.

3. **NVRAM**: This is a smaller rewritable memory that is not erased when a power outage occurs. The router stores copies of the IOS configuration here.

Individual memory types act as file systems. Labeling is similar to the MS-DOS system, although the `A:`, `B:`, `C:` etc drives are replaced by a memory type such as, `flash:`, `nvram:`, `system:` etc. For example, a router's start up configuration is stored in `nvram:startup-config` file. The configuration of a running system is in the `system:running-config` file.

In the newer IOS versions, we can also use the `cd`, `dir`, `pwd`, `delete` commands. By using the `copy` command, it is possible to save the current router's configuration in NVRAM:

`Copy system:running-config nvram:startup-config`

(The same results can be achieved by using the older `write memory` command.)

The `copy` command might also use a URL as a parameter. This will enable us to insert a new version of the operating system into the FLASH memory. You can upgrade your box from the FTP server, i.e., you can copy a new version of the IOS into the FLASH memory by using the following command (you will be asked to supply the data that you have not indicated in the URL specification):

`copy ftp: flash:`

The older IOS versions support only the TFTP protocol and not the FTP protocol. If we run a simple TFTP server on our PC, then we can back up the configuration in its root directory by using the following command:

`copy nvram:startup-config tftp:`

A simple TFTP server for PCs is part of the software that is available at http://www.cisco.com/pcgi-bin/tablebuild.pl/tftp.

A.4 Console

Console is an asynchronous interface. Connect this interface by a cable to the COM port of your PC. Now your PC becomes a console used for configuring the router.

The router is supplied with a cable (a null modem for the V.24 (RS 232) interface) with an RJ-45 connector on the router side. On the router side, you plug the cable into the RJ-45 connector, on the PC side use the 9-pin D-sub connector.

Now let's run the HyperTerminal application on a Windows 2000/XP PC. Set the following properties for the COM port on the PC; speeds of 9,600 bps, 8 data bits, parity none, 1 stop bit and no flow control. Problems could occur only if someone explicitly set different values in the router configuration for managing the terminal.

The HyperTerminal application starts communicating after you switch on the router or when you press the *Enter* key (if the router is already running). The problem, however, is that the router asks you to type a password, which you do not have. The only option is to ignore the preset router start-up configuration (nvram: startup-config) containing the password and begin working with the router as if it were brand new (the original start-up configuration will remain in the NVRAM). So, you have to shut down the router and turn it back on. After turning it on, press the *Ctrl + Break* keys. A ROM Monitor (ROMMON) router firmware command line appears.

I entered the confreg command. Experienced network administrators just enter the hexadecimal value of the configuration register so that the start-up configuration is ignored. I entered the command without those parameters so it got into the interactive mode. I answered all the questions as n (no) until I got to: Ignore system config info? y/n, which I answered as y. I accepted everything without change for the rest of the confreg command and then I entered the boot command, which loaded the IOS operating system.

Here, the password was not required. I refused the first proposed router configuration by answering no and the IOS system command line popped up without the need to enter the password. I entered enable to get into the command mode. Then I copied the original router configuration from NVRAM into the operating memory by using the following command:

Copy startup-config running-config

I changed the passwords and saved the changed configuration in NVRAM with the write memory command. I turned the router off and again turned it on. By pressing *Ctrl + Break*, I got the firmware command line. I used the confreg command to renew the original settings, so the IOS was run from the start-up configuration, i.e., it was loaded from NVRAM.

Nevertheless, the CISCO 801 box was a problem. This box does not support the confreg command. Skipping the configuration at start up depends on the configuration register setting. First, list the BOOTROM variables by the set command:

```
boot# set
set baud          =9600
set data-bits     =8
set parity        =none
set stop-bits     =1
set console-flags =0
set mac-address   =00B0.C28B.76D2
set unit-ip       =0.0.0.0
set serv-ip       =0.0.0.0
set netmask       =0.0.0.0
set gate-ip       =0.0.0.0
set pkt-timeout   =4
set tftp-timeout  =16
set boot-action   =flash
set file-name     ="c800-oy6-mw.122-28a.bin"
set watchdog      =off
set prompt        ="boot"
set ios-conf      =0x2102
```

The configuration register (ios-conf) has the value 0x2102. I wrote this value in my paper notebook as it would be required after the experiment. Now I set configuration register to a new value and rebooted the router:

```
boot# set ios-conf = 142
boot# boot
```

Now, the router skipped the original configuration and I could make the appropriate changes. Next, I rebooted the router, pressed the *Ctrl + Break* keys, and set the original value in the configuration register (0x2102).

A.5 Commands

We can find out which commands we are allowed to be used in the IOS system by using ?.

For example, a question mark entered on the command line in non-privileged mode:

```
Router>?
Exec commands:
  access-enable    Create a temporary Access-List entry
  access-profile   Apply user-profile to interface
  clear            Reset functions
  connect          Open a terminal connection
  disable          Turn off privileged commands
  disconnect       Disconnect an existing network connection
  enable           Turn on privileged commands
  exit             Exit from the EXEC
  help             Description of the interactive help system
  lock             Lock the terminal
  login            Log in as a particular user
  logout           Exit from the EXEC
—More—
```

The question mark command can also be used to obtain a list of commands that begin with a particular character sequence. Just type in those characters followed immediately by the question mark.

For example:

```
Router>p?
*p=ping  pad  ping  ppp
```

Alternatively, we can enter a command followed by a question mark without the parameters and the IOS will give the parameter syntax.

For example:

```
Router>ping   ?
  WORD  Ping destination address or hostname
  ip    IP echo
  tag   Tag encapsulated IP echo
```

The majority of commands referred to hereinafter may be used only in privileged mode, which can be accessed by the enable command. You are requested to enter a password (if one is set) by the system. The privileged mode can be usually recognized by the command prompt not being terminated by the > character, but by the # character.

For example:

```
Router>enable
Password: (not shown)
Router#
```

A.5.1 Non-Privileged Mode

In the non-privileged mode, we can enter some commands that show configuration, but it is impossible to change its functionality in a significant way. Let's have a look at few examples:

telnet, **ping**, **traceroute**: These commands are similar to the commands that we know from the UNIX and Windows systems. What is interesting, however, is that many commands also work with network protocols other than TCP/IP.

terminal: By entering this command, we can set various communication parameters of the terminal. It is important that the same parameters be set on both sides when communicating, i.e., both for the terminal emulating program on the PC and on the router. For example, the terminal type is set to vt100 by entering the following command:

```
terminal terminal-type vt100
```

If the vt100 terminal type is also set on the PC, then the up and down arrow buttons usually work fine for me when going through the command history. I have never managed to set this up in HyperTerminal, therefore I prefer to use the TeraTerm program.

ppp: If I log into a router via a modem using, for example, an asynchronous line, in order to connect to the Internet (or intranet), then I usually authenticate myself as a specific user. As described in Section A.4.1, after authentication, I receive the IOS command line and then I can enter the ppp command to initiate communication in the PPP protocol. The ppp command starts up the PPP protocol. (It is also possible to suppress the usage of the CISCO command line for particular users.)

show: We can obtain various information and statistics by using the show command. The information that will be shown depends on the parameter entered. For example:

- ip shows information about the TCP/IP protocols.
  - show ip route shows the routing table list.
  - show ip arp shows the ARP cache list.

- ○ show ip interface shows information on the individual network interfaces.
- terminal shows the setup of the terminal line configuration parameters.
- users shows information about all logged in users.
- version shows the current version of the hardware and software.

login, logout, exit: I can log in as a particular user by entering the login command. The logout and exit commands terminate the terminal.

enable, disable: I can login in the privileged mode by entering the enable command. The system will ask for a password if it is required. disable is a privileged mode command that returns you to non-privileged mode.

A.5.2 Privileged mode

In privileged mode, it is possible to execute, besides non-privileged commands, the commands used when working with router's configuration and file systems. These are cd, dir, delete, copy, erase (deleting a file), and especially the configure (router configuration) and debug (list packets transferred) commands.

The show command is of much more use here such as:

- show debugging: Shows the current debugging setup.
- show running-config: Shows the configuration of a running system.
- show configuration: Shows startup configuration.
- show logging: Shows a log of events.
- show line: Shows the information about individual lines.
- show <interface>: Shows the current information of a particular interface that is specified as a parameter. For example, the show int serial 0 command will enable you to find out whether the line as well as the protocols are 'up' or 'down' along with a lot of other information.

A.6 Configuration

The router has the following two configurations:

1. **Current (running configuration)**: This is the configuration of the currently running IOS that is displayed by entering show running-config.
2. **Backed up configuration in NVRAM**: The configuration is backed up in the memory that is not erased during a power outage and is used after restarting the router. This configuration is also called the **startup configuration** and can be viewed by entering show configuration. The current configuration is backed up into NVRAM by the write memory command.

As we have mentioned in Section A.3, the startup configuration can be downloaded as a text file via the TFTP or FTP protocols. The text file can be modified in a text editor on our computer, and then recopied back into the router by using, for example, the TFTP protocol.

An example of a simple configuration file is as follows:

```
version 12.2
hostname Router
!
enable password siemens
!
interface Ethernet0
 ip address 192.168.2.100 255.255.255.0
!
interface BRI0
 no ip address
 shutdown
!
ip http server
ip route 0.0.0.0 0.0.0.0 192.168.2.1
!
line con 0
 transport input none
line vty 0 4
 password cisco
 login
!
end
```

Note that the configuration file is composed of individual sections. Sections always start with a command that starts from the first row. In the above example, we have the following sections:

- version specifies the IOS version.
- hostname specifies the router DNS name.
- enable password specifies the password used to access the privileged mode.
- interface Ethernet0 specifies the Ethernet 0 interface configuration.
- The IP address and the network mask are specified by the ip address parameter.
- interface Serial0 specifies the Serial 0 configuration. Note that the interface is shut down by the shutdown parameter.
- line con 0 specifies the console configuration. If the login parameter is not mentioned there, then we log into the non-privileged mode without using a password.
- line vty 0 specifies the first pseudo-terminal configuration for access via network by the Telnet command. Note that even the non-privileged mode requires login (i.e., the login parameter). The password is specified by the password parameter.
- The last section is end.

Let's describe the interactive configuration that is far more common. The most common work of any network administrator begins in the privileged mode by using the configure terminal command.

Here we do not have a full screen text editor that we can use to edit the configuration file, but a very intelligent line editor, which we need to get used to. Interactive configuration begins with the configure terminal command and ends with the exit command.

Each particular section is configured in turn. Configuring a section begins by typing the entire first line of the section after the configure command.

If we were to change the IP address of Interface Ethernet 0 to 195.0.1.196 with the mask 255.255.255.0 in our configuration, then we would execute the following command:

```
Router#configure terminal
Enter configuration commands, one per line.  End with CNTL/Z.
Router(config)#interface Ethernet 0
Router(config-if)#no ip address 192.168.2.100 255.255.255.0
Router(config-if)#ip address 195.0.1.196 255.255.255.0
Router(config-if)#^Z
Router# write memory
Building configuration...
[OK]
```

Note that the initial line was deleted at the beginning by the no command, which contained the entire original line as the parameter.

If we wanted to start up the BRI0 interface in our example (i.e., get rid of the shutdown command), then for the interactive configuration of the BRI0 interface, we would enter no shutdown.

The configuration ends with the exit command or by pressing *Ctrl + Z* (*^Z*).

We should not forget that the configuration file of the currently running system is the one configured by interactive configuration. So after completing the configuration, it is useful to back up the configuration by using the write memory command.

A.6.1 Setting a Password for Privileged Mode

It might have taken you by surprise that the password in the configuration file was shown in plain text form. I chose this possibility only to be more visual. Passwords can be saved in a secured form (altered by a one-way function).

Authentication is also possible by using the **Radius** or **TACACS+** protocols.

If we do not want to use the plain text form for the password in the configuration, then we can alter it by a one-way function and copy it into, for example, the UNIX /etc/passwd file. We cannot enter the password in the regular form, but we should have it prepared in advance via a one-way function.

```
Router#configure terminal
Router(config)#enable password  7  coded_password
```

Another possibility is to enter the password in the regular form and let the configuration command *convert* it by using the one-way function.

```
Router(config)#enable secret  password
```

A.6.2 Web

If we enter ip http server in the configuration file, we start within the router a web server that can be used for the configuration of our router (see Figure A.2). In your PC browser, enter the IP address of the router as a URL.

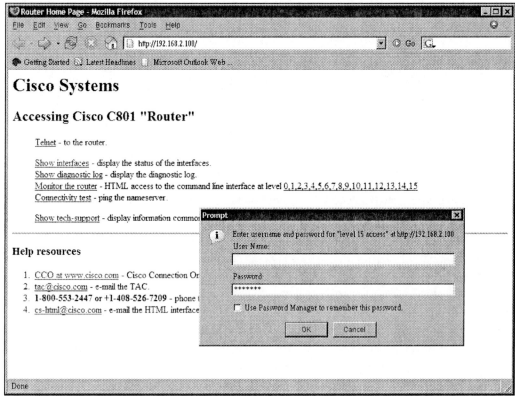

Figure A.2: Web configuration

You will be asked to enter the user name and the password. If the router does not contain a specific list of users, then we do not fill in the User name or Password, but just the password for accessing the privileged mode. Now you can start communicating with the router via the web browser.

A.6.3 ConfigMaker

Another means of router configuration is ConfigMaker for PC that can be downloaded by registered CISCO clients from http://www.cisco.com/go/configmaker. It is a very PC-friendly program (see Figure A.3). By using the Detect function, the program gets the configuration of individual boxes. By using the tools in the left panel, you can design a new network or just adjust the existing one.

You are interactively asked to enter individual parameters. This way a configuration is created for all your boxes and then it is sent back to the boxes by the Deliver function. Among other things, the program is capable of printing configuration pictures. However, the drawback is that if we focus completely on controlling just by using this interface without gaining more information, we would acquire only superficial knowledge. Another drawback is that individual operations take quite some time, but an experienced network administrator will be able to do them faster using the terminal.

On the other hand, when I could not figure out the configuration of individual asynchronous lines, I simply generated it by using the ConfigMaker. I knew at the first glance where I had made a mistake.

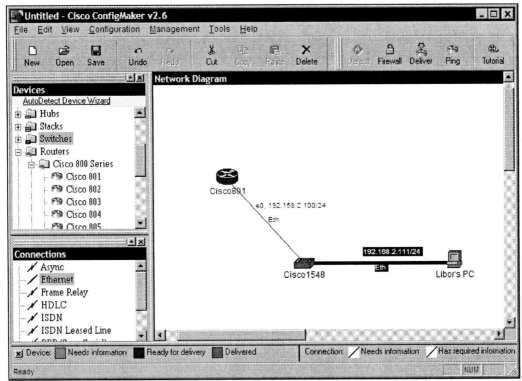

Figure A.3: The ConfigMaker program

A.7 Debugging

The aim is to audit events as they occur. We will be interested in the following two types:

1. Events that occurred during the running of the system. That includes, for example, an interface switched into the *Up* or *Down* mode, whether the router configuration has been changed, etc.

2. Events defined by the administrator. The administrator defines a **trap**, such as writing a report when a protocol data packet has been sent.

First, we have to specify in the configuration where the individual event records will be written. This can be done by entering the logging command in the configuration file:

```
Router# configure terminal
Router(config)# logging console 7
```

This command will print out the output of event records onto the console. The number `7` specifies the most detailed statement. Lower numbers indicate less detailed statements, with `0` being the least detailed. If we also want to have traps recorded, then we add another command (which is important especially for recording events via a network using the SYSLOG protocol):

```
Router(config)# logging trap 7
```

Note that if we do not work directly on the console interface, but on the terminal, then we also have to enable the output of the event records onto the terminal:

```
Router# terminal monitor
```

Since there might be many records and we might want to process them further, there is a practical way of doing this, i.e., by sending the event records to the SYSLOG server over the network using the SYSLOG protocol. The server is usually a part of UNIX.

A simple SYSLOG server for the PC is available at, for example, `http://www.kiwisyslog.com/`.

We run the SYSLOG server on our PC and we enter in the router the following command:

```
Router(config)#logging IP_adress_of_SYSLOG_server
```

By doing this, the event logging to the given IP address is launched. If the SYSLOG server has already been started, then entering the above command will create the first record. If trap records have also been set up, then they will start to appear in the log.

The last thing to be done is set the traps. This can be accomplished by the `debug` command. Its parameters contain the individual protocols in which we are interested, such as:

```
Router#  debug ip icmp
```

ICMP protocol events will be recorded. An example of such a log is shown in the following figure:

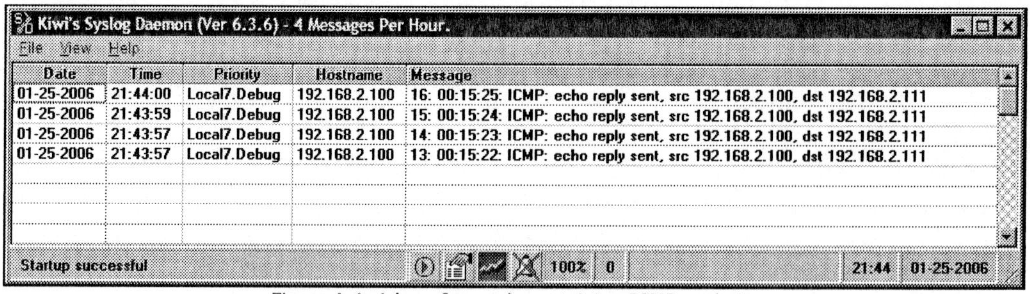
Kiwi's Syslog Daemon (Ver 6.3.6) - 4 Messages Per Hour.
File View Help
Date Time Priority Hostname Message
01-25-2006 21:44:00 Local7.Debug 192.168.2.100 16: 00:15:25: ICMP: echo reply sent, src 192.168.2.100, dst 192.168.2.111
01-25-2006 21:43:59 Local7.Debug 192.168.2.100 15: 00:15:24: ICMP: echo reply sent, src 192.168.2.100, dst 192.168.2.111
01-25-2006 21:43:57 Local7.Debug 192.168.2.100 14: 00:15:23: ICMP: echo reply sent, src 192.168.2.100, dst 192.168.2.111
01-25-2006 21:43:57 Local7.Debug 192.168.2.100 13: 00:15:22: ICMP: echo reply sent, src 192.168.2.100, dst 192.168.2.111
Startup successful
100%
0
21:44
01-25-2006

Figure A.4: A log of records containing ICMP packets

This is not a detailed packet statement from which one could find out things such as passwords, but it is a very comfortable tool for administrators looking for configuration mistakes.

To find out which traps we have set up, enter the `show debug` command. It takes another quite thick manual to actually find out which packets of which protocols can be kept track of in this manner. Quite often, though, a question mark following the `debug` command will work for you just fine.

Index

U

UDP protocol. *See* **User Datagram Protocol**
U-frame, 76
unicast, 235, 236
Uniform Resource Identifier. *See also* **relative URI**
    about, 334
    file scheme, 336
    ftp scheme, 335
    http scheme, 334, 335
    mailto scheme, 336
    nntp scheme, 336
    pop scheme, 337
    telnet scheme, 336
unprivileged port, 248, 249
URI. *See* **Uniform Resource Identifier**
User Datagram Protocol
    about, 14, 269
    broadcasts, 272
    datagram, 270
    datagram, example, 271
    fragmentation, 271
    header, 269
    multicasts, 272
    psuedoheader, 271
    speciality, 272
user protocols, 15

V

V.24 interface, 36, 37
V.35 interface, 36, 37
V.90 recommendation, 49, 50
virtual circuit
    about, 18
    advantage, 18
    datagram transmission, 18

    Frame Relay, 103
    Permanent Virtual Circuit, 19
    Switched Virtual Circuit, 19
Virtual Terminal protocol, 15
voice band, 44, 45

W

WAN, 34
WEP, 125
Wide Area Networks, 34
WIN, 261, 264
window, 261, 264
window scale factor, 266, 267
Windows 2003, 236, 237
WinPcapp, 22
Wired Equivalent Privacy, 125
Wireless Local Area Network
    access point, 123
    antennas, 124
    backbone point-to-point connection, 124
    configuration, 123, 124
    features, 121
    IEEE 802.1X standard, 126
    peer-to-peer network, 123
    roaming, 124
    security, 125
    Service Set ID, 125
    signal transmission, 122
    Wired Equivalent Privacy, 125
Wireless Local Loop, 127
WLAN. *See* **Wireless Local Area Network**

X

X.21 interface, 36, 37

DNS in Action

ISBN: 1904811787   Paperback: 196 pages

Features at a glance:

- Technically detailed with practical solutions

- Comprehensive guide to configuration and administration of DNS servers

- Covers DNS Extensions, delegation, and registration

This book is a detailed guide to the Domain Name System, its implementation, configuration, and administration. It covers the basics as well as the more advanced features and uses of DNS. It describes the basic DNS protocol and its extensions; DNS delegation and registration, including for reverse domains; using DNS servers in networks that are not connected to the internet, and using DNS servers on firewall machines. Many detailed examples are used throughout the book to show perform various configuration and administration tasks.

For more details: http://www.packtpub.com/DNS/book

Please check **www.PacktPub.com** for information on our other titles

Printed in the United States
61668LVS00003B/3